GENERAL
SPEECH

an introduction

McGRAW-HILL SERIES IN SPEECH

Clarence T. Simon, CONSULTING EDITOR

Armstrong and Brandes: The Oral Interpretation of Literature
Baird: American Public Addresses
Baird: Argumentation, Discussion, and Debate
Baird: Discussion: Principles and Types
Baird and Knower: Essentials of General Speech
Baird and Knower: General Speech
Black and Moore: Speech: Code, Meaning, and Communication
Carrell and Tiffany: Phonetics
Hahn, Lomas, Hargis, and Vandraegen: Basic Voice Training for Speech
Kaplan: Anatomy and Physiology of Speech
Kruger: Modern Debate
Loney: Briefing and Conference Techniques
Ogilvie: Speech in the Elementary School
Powers: Fundamentals of Speech
Van Dusen: Training the Voice for Speech

GENERAL
SPEECH
an introduction

A. *Craig Baird* STATE UNIVERSITY OF IOWA

Franklin H. *Knower* THE OHIO STATE UNIVERSITY

THIRD EDITION

McGraw-Hill Book Company
NEW YORK   SAN FRANCISCO   TORONTO   LONDON

GENERAL SPEECH

Library of Congress Catalog Card Number 62–10596

03258

5 6 7 8 9 10 11 12 – MP – 1 0 9 8 7

Preface

THIS THIRD EDITION of *General Speech* has been extensively rewritten. Although the basic philosophy of earlier editions has been retained, the rewriting has made it possible to include many new ideas, new explanations, new examples, and new projects. We have welcomed the suggestions of a number of college teachers who used earlier editions of *General Speech*, and we have incorporated their suggestions into this edition. We believe that these changes have added to the strength of the book.

General Speech is a text for a first course in speech. It is directed to the student who takes such a course in pursuit of a general education. Emphasis is placed upon the objectives in speech education selected as most important for the typical American college student and upon the needs most frequently noted among students. They also are the needs of adults seeking a text which may help them with their speech problems in everyday living.

We consider this a textbook which emphasizes fundamental speech processes and principles. The processes and principles are important for much of our communication. This concept of fundamentals brings within its scope such processes as the speech personality, voice, articulation and pronunciation, visual symbols, ideas, language, and thought—including the organization of thought. It also provides for the study of the principles of procedure in common types of speech activity.

We believe strongly that most students need a new and clearer understanding of what is involved in speaking. They need to understand that the major function of speech is communication. The communication of ideas calls for social skills, purposiveness, selection and arrangement or organization of ideas, and techniques of wording and expression which are appropriate and effective. We have drawn upon many communication disciplines, especially rhetoric and the psychology of communication. We have tried to integrate the thinking of these disciplines to achieve a practical guide for the student.

The stress on practical communication principles is directed to the development of understandings and insights; it is intended to provide a guide for self-evaluation, for practice, and for criticism. These objectives cannot be attained realistically by short-cut tricks or gimmicks. The principles are developed to provide a guide not only for present learning but also for the continued development of effective communication habits by the student even after he has left school.

We continue to emphasize the three points of philosophy expressed in earlier editions. First, we believe that the student must come to see his communication in speech as a form of social behavior. Personality, audience analysis, feedback and listening, standards of articulation and linguistic style, responsibilities, and forms of speech for various purposes and special occasions—all illustrate social expectations and preferences.

Secondly, we believe that, since all speech is learned, the student must regard his tasks as a challenge to his learning. The student's individual needs, his attitudes, his insights, and his observable behavior must be analyzed and evaluated. This can best be done through the collaboration of the student and his teacher as they move along. The principles and exercises in the text have been presented in sufficient number to provide for most individual differences in these respects.

Thirdly, we believe that the selection and organization of ideas is the most important factor in achieving good speech. That is why we present this subject early and keep hammering at it throughout the text. It is our belief that the continued struggle for better speech content will produce not only better speakers but also better-educated men.

The chapters are arranged to give the student what he needs in the order in which we have found he can best learn to improve his speaking. In general the early assignments on speech process are more naturally motivated after the student has come to realize his need for the kind of exercise assigned. It is of course possible that special conditions will warrant the assignment of some chapters in a different order.

Appendix C provides a selection of speeches which may be studied in a number of ways. The speech by Edward R. Murrow has a message which may be of special value to speech students. The teacher is urged to buy or rent the teaching sound films which were made by the McGraw-Hill Book Company, Inc., to accompany *General Speech*. A *Teacher's Manual* with many helpful suggestions for teachers may be obtained from McGraw-Hill by teachers using this text.

"Four Little Foxes" is reprinted from *Slow Smoke* by the late Lew Sarett with the permission of Mrs. Sarett.

A. Craig Baird

Franklin H. Knower

Contents

ix

part three BASIC SPEECH TYPES

part four SPECIAL SPEECH TYPES

APPENDIXES

PART ONE

INTRODUCTION

ONE

Essentials of Effective Speech

IN THE PAST twenty-four hours you have talked more than you realize—in the classroom, on the campus, in the dormitory or fraternity or rooming house, on the streets, in stores, or elsewhere. Certainly you do not consider yourself a voluble talker. Your total number of spoken words, recorded and counted, would no doubt astonish you. The average person of college age has already spoken many million words. Much of your talk has no doubt been casual conversation without real point. But some of it has been brisk utterance aiming at approval of your ideas or proposals.

Communication in the Space Age

You are of this space age. You are also of the age of communication. We Americans have always been active talkers, despite the traditional New England opposition to word baths. In this post-1960 era the word overflow has been an almost unique mark of our national character. We Americans, as never before, have been uninterruptedly vocal in print, face to face, and over the air.

Swift electronic expansion and related technological developments partly explain this multiplication of the number and range of our voices. Despite the current trends toward political conformity our individual platform continues to be, "I will be heard."

3

Our voices, then, echo in thousands of community and service clubs, in social gatherings in homes or elsewhere, in business and labor conventions, on political stumps, in formal and informal lectures, in schools, colleges, universities. The vocal output ramifies ceaselessly through our Congresses, legislative committee investigative rooms, and in educational and other professional assemblies. The talk goes on at the United Nations, at top-echelon political, military, and scientific meetings at Geneva, New York City, Moscow, London, Chicago, Atlanta, Los Angeles. We Americans, with our expanding FM and UHF radio transmitters, have blanketed the nation and beyond with television towers, cables, and sets to bring all things of the hour to focus with teletypes, films, telephotos. Already our rockets have orbited the earth with additional media for quick telephonic exchange. The voices of speakers in New York, Chicago, or Los Angeles can be heard in every byway of our fifty states and in many foreign countries. By means of television the speaker can be not only heard but also seen.

This space-binding revolution has made our individual, national, and international living strikingly communicative.

If talking is so important, then our problem and yours is to learn to communicate more effectively and efficiently.

Why Study Speech?

Why study speech? Certainly you will dismiss the impression that good speakers are born that way and that training is futile. It is granted that if you have no vocal cords or a limited amount of common sense, the discipline of speech study will do little for you. But the evidence all supports the value and effectiveness of systematic concentration on oral communication. Quintilian, the Roman schoolmaster of the second century, was positive that speakers, whatever their native abilities, would profit by training. Demosthenes stuttered, but as Plutarch tells us, he progressed by slow degrees and became Greece's foremost orator.

If you will give several months of energy to the study of speech, you will undoubtedly improve markedly. Your progress, may we add, will not be the result of any short cut to superior skill. Skillful speech is not just a bag of tricks or a set of gimmicks. It can come only as the result of new insights, new ways of feeling, and new forms of behavior. This means hard and steady work, self-criticism, and guidance by instructors. Probably the greatest cause of differences in levels of speech ability among college students is the difference among them in their willingness to work at learning.

Your aim is not to become a Winston Churchill, the greatest British parliamentary orator of our time, or to emulate President John Kennedy, who after his futile summit meeting with Khrushchev at Vienna in June,

1961, televised to millions upon millions with somber but high effectiveness.

Your aim is to talk satisfactorily in your daily contacts with friends and professional associates and to be able, if the occasion calls for it, to organize and present a speech worthy of your ideas, personality, and training. You therefore want to understand and apply systematic methods of speech improvement.

What you are after is ability in communication, not for platform exhibitionism, not for the purpose of exhibiting your good voice and fine platform manners, but so that you may adapt yourself and your ideas to auditors, cooperate with them, and influence them. Your goal is thus a practical one. If you understand and apply systematic methods of speech improvement, what desirable results may you reasonably expect?

1. *Speech skill should contribute to your social and occupational progress and adjustment.* Why is college speech training so often required of prospective engineers, physical education majors, and similar professional groups? Why in recent years have commerce and industry become more and more interested in the values of communication? Why have many industries, for example General Motors and Du Pont, set up training programs in speech making for employees? Why has the National Banking Institute fostered and expanded year by year its program of public address? Why do some corporations give speech tests to applicants for jobs? Why did university alumni, according to a report made by the National Education Association, place speech training near the top of the list of subjects that had been of most value to them in their later careers?

In the home, in factories, on farms and ranches, in some of the 101 organizations in which you are or soon will be involved, your success will to a considerable degree depend upon your speaking effectiveness. As Andrew Weaver of Wisconsin reminded us, "In the United States there are more than twenty thousand different ways of earning a living, and effective speech is essential to every one!" [1]

2. *Speech skill should enable you to be more efficient as a responsible member of your political-economic community.* You will presently (if you are lucky to escape now) pay local, state, and federal taxes. You will pay fines for traffic violations, report for the draft, call the fire department, collect your wages or salary, rent or buy a home, perhaps join a union, deal with stores and discount houses, save blue, green, or other stamps, pay installments, buy insurance, and have a checking or savings account. You will listen to local, state, and national politicians. You will follow news commentators and the continual review of international crises. These

---

[1] Andrew Thomas Weaver, "Toward Understanding through Speech," *Vital Speeches of the Day*, 27:244–247, 1961; Harvey Cromwell, "Effective Speaking: Its Importance," *Vital Speeches of the Day*, 27:217–219, January 15, 1961.

economic and political problems constantly bear down upon you. You are not like the truck driver that Kenneth McFarland described: "He reads no newspapers nor periodicals. He avoids all newscasts and educational programs. . . . He has almost no problems that he recognizes."[2] You recognize your stake in the solution of these problems. If you are neutral or silent, you only help to produce general confusion and deterioration. In this land of secret votes and wide-open conversation, your need is to be individually articulate.

Basic in our American system is the principle that every man has the right and duty to be heard. But acceptance of the principle of free speech does not guarantee effective speech. That skill must be learned. The interchange of ideas through speech and the willingness to accept the responsibilities of effective speech are indispensable for a sound citizenry.

Our American system assumes that the working of our democracy depends upon general unimpeded communication. Ours is a government by talk, as Walter Bagehot remarked of the British system. A further assumption is that those who talk are to be competent. By competency in oral exchange we are not referring to the manner of great political speakers of other days, such as Clay, Webster, and Calhoun, but rather to those methods adapted to our own generations. The principles of speech are the same, but they are obviously adapted to the audience needs, the attitudes, and the behavior of our times.[3]

Aristotle's justification of good speech (rhetoric) as politically necessary still holds. After preliminary definition and analysis of the field of discourse, Aristotle drew these conclusions: (a) Rhetoric or public address is necessary if truth and justice are to prevail over error. (b) Constructive ideas are to be presented so that the rank and file may understand and respond even though scientific proof may be impossible. (c) Both sides of an issue are to be surveyed so that the fallacies may be exposed and truth emerge. (d) Every citizen should orally defend himself against "bad propaganda," again to ensure the furtherance of truth.[4]

3. *You will be judged and known as a man by the quality of your speech.* For right or wrong, for good or evil, people generally put pretty strong faith in the principle "As a man speaketh, so is he." What you know determines to some extent what you say. The way you think is revealed in the way you evaluate and organize ideas. Your use of language generally reflects the education you have had. Your attitudes toward your-

---

[2] Kenneth McFarland, *Eloquence in Public Speaking*, p. 2.

[3] See Karl R. Wallace, "Rhetoric and Politics," *The Southern Speech Journal*, 20:195–203, Spring, 1955.

[4] Aristotle, *Rhetoric*, book I, secs. 1–8. This paraphrase is based on the translation by W. Roberts.

self, your subject, your listeners, and the situation in which you speak are reflected in many ways by tension, bodily response, language, voice, and yes, even in the very substance of your remarks.

Of course you seek no special favors, but you do not want to be misinterpreted. If you want your listeners to give you the benefit of any doubt, you must know how to show yourself worthy of their respect and trust. If you want to reduce the possibilities that you will be misinterpreted, then you need to know something of the ways in which you can give your message the credibility you believe it deserves.

4. *Communication may be a far more complex and difficult task than you have thought.* Perhaps the greatest weakness in communication is th illusion that it is simple and easy. Often communication seems to be successful when it isn't. Now that you think of it, have you not often given directions, explained a point, thought that you had someone persuaded only to learn later that the message the other fellow received wasn't the message you had given him? Something went wrong. There was a barrier to communication; the message was ambiguous; it didn't get through.

Many failures in communication can be avoided if we know enough about communication to talk skillfully. In the study of speech we not only acquire many new ideas about the subject but we learn more about some old ideas we have had. In many cases new skills emerge through latent learning in which we use in a new way ideas and processes we have already learned. We may need to acquire a new image of what it means

Colonel Glenn and family meet President Kennedy.

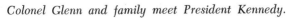

to communicate. When we do we will not make unwarranted assumptions about our speech.

5. *A very basic reason for the study of speech is that it provides a fairly easy way of getting things done.* The infant learns to talk even in his elementary way only when he learns he can get what he needs more easily by this means. Speech is a symbolic activity, and thus by its very nature, it is an economical activity. You have no doubt heard people make the snide remark that talk is cheap. They meant essentially that it is undependable. But it does not differ in this respect from other forms of human activity. What really counts here is that it is an economical way of achieving purposes.

Of course speech which is ambiguous, in error, or inaccurate in some other way may be tremendously expensive. So we see that the better talk is the cheaper it is. Only skillful speech is cheap. We do not mean that it is easy. Effective speech often requires the expenditures of a great deal of energy by the speaker and by the audience alike. Even such energy, however, is as nought compared with the physical exertion and the cost of achieving social purposes by direct physical force. Someone has said that education is a process of learning to do better the things we are going to do anyway. Here is the real challenge of our time of international tension and conflict.

6. *Different communication behaviors require different ways of learning.* Communication activities today are so highly specialized and conventionalized that only some of the rules apply to all communication acts. There is a serious danger in the assumption that when we study some forms of communication behavior we may think that we have learned all there is to know about the subject. In this text we have set ourselves the task of studying oral communication. Some of the rules we shall learn apply to written communication, but some do not. We cannot assume that the good writer necessarily will be a good speaker. The college graduate of our day needs to know how to engage in many types of communication activity.

7. *Your speech can be defended only when it is an expression of ethical principles and influences.* The chief purpose in all speech is to expound and defend those ideas and policies that lead toward a better society. Every word you utter and every response you secure from listeners is to be so tested. Do your listeners respond with attitudes and policies that point toward the "good society"? That is the severe test of your activity as a talker.

As Quintilian, that great Roman teacher of the second century, put it: "Let the orator [speaker] whom I propose to form, be such a one as is characterized by the definition of Marcus Cato, 'a good man skilled in speaking.' My judgment carries me still further; for I not only say that he who would answer my idea of an orator [speaker] must be a good man, but no man unless he be good, can ever be an orator. [speaker]." [5]

Why then study speech? An ability to communicate effectively will certainly undergird your occupational success whatever your job. It will give you social and political integrity. Your speech should represent you as the kind of person you want to be. You may have much to learn about removing the barriers to understanding and acceptance. You should understand communication as an economical way of getting things done. You need to understand the relationships among the various types and forms of communication. And you must know how to give to your speaking genuineness, credibility, and a sense of values. Your communication will thus be morally valid.

What Is Speech?

What is speech? It is communication which, through ideas, language, voice, bodily expression, and speaker's personality, informs one or more other people or influences their attitudes and behavior in harmony with the speaker's purposes. We see that speech is multisymbolic.

The several symbol systems of language, voice, and bodily action operate concurrently to increase the accuracy with which your messages may be interpreted. Speech differs from some other types of communication in that it is an ongoing type of behavior and operates with listeners in a time sequence and an immediate social situation. Your auditors may be in front of you or 1,000 miles away but they hear the message as it is spoken. The contact of speaker with listener, be they near to each other or far apart, is a social as well as a communication experience. This concept of speech has several important implications for the study of speech which we shall return to in later chapters.

Perhaps the following model of speech behavior will point up more clearly the many factors operating in communication. We see that all speech is a part of a particular cultural pattern. This pattern includes the language we use, but it also includes a great many other conventions and customs which influence the message. The specific situation and the occasion provide contexts and climates to be considered. From among the many things available to be said, the speaker selects his ideas. His resources, purposes, and responsibilities shape that message. He makes use of several symbol systems in expressing his ideas. There are many types and patterns of speech such as conversation, interview, lecture, reading, debate, sermon, etc. The skilled speaker will select the appropriate pattern and conform to his audience's expectations for that pattern.

[5] Quintilian, *Institutes of Oratory*, book XII, I, 1. From the translation of J. S. Watson, *Institutes of Oratory*. H. G. Bohn, London, 1956.

The speaker's channels most frequently will be air waves and light waves, but they may include electronic impulses, and even persons as messengers. As a speaker you will be concerned with the stimulation of your listeners. Since there is often resistance to ideas you may have some resistance to overcome. When you are a listener you also have responsibilities for the success of a communication. You must learn to use your own resources to get as much as you can from the message.

As a speaker you will always be concerned with audience effects. As you will see later the dimensions of audience behavior may best be analyzed in terms of speaker purposes and audience effects. You will want to study your listeners constantly as you speak. The messages you get from them in terms of their attentiveness, cooperation, and other responses you can see and hear are called "feedback." The skillful speaker makes use of feedback in adapting his remarks to his audience.

The arrow in the model emphasizes the ongoing nature of speech behavior in time. And finally, you can see that this whole structure is based on learning. It is sincerely hoped that your study of this text will help you learn to be a better speaker. But unless you supply the determination to learn you cannot expect to get far in this direction.

Seven Processes for Speech Improvement

This view of speech as a form of communication behavior suggests seven processes basic to speech improvement. From the speaker's point of

A graphic speech model

view, they are (1) ideas, (2) organization, (3) language, (4) voice, (5) articulation, (6) bodily activity, and (7) speaking personality. Speech improvement depends upon concentration on these basic processes, and you will analyze and apply each of them not as an end in itself, but as it is related to audience demands, needs, and characteristics. Moreover, you will measure your improvement in speech against them not only as discrete and separable items but also as a unit—as a network of interdependent processes.[6]

The following brief explanations of these fundamentals constitute a description of the ideal speaker. Few speakers ever reach such a high level of achievement. With reasonable concentration and application, however, your performance should be adequate in most of these fundamentals and in speech generally, and it may perhaps be exceptional in a few of them.

1. *The effective speaker communicates ideas.* Ideas are probably the most important process of the speech act. Basically we view the speaker as a thinker—as a person dealing with facts and expressing judgments concerning those facts. The comprehension, insight, and convictions of the speaker are thus of great importance if he is to speak to a specific purpose.

Teachers and practitioners of good speech have from the beginning insisted on the primacy of ideas or thoughts. The classical rhetoricians labeled this phase of the speech "invention." According to this principle, content, general concepts, sound thinking, and facts must have first attention in your speech preparation and presentation. To Aristotle and his rhetorical successors, including those who teach and study speech today, thought, logical development, and specific proofs are the heart and soul of any worthwhile speech.

Satisfactory expression of ideas may be judged by the speaker's purposes. He selects and develops his ideas with a view to their impact upon or relationship to his particular audience and his purpose with regard to his audience. He organizes his speech around a central idea, clearly conceived and well worded, with both main and subordinate ideas clearly defined. He is at home with meanings to the extent that he can help his audience avoid semantic pitfalls. His thought reflects sound and informed analysis of his subject and able management of his "forms of support"— the analogies, comparisons, illustrations, and statistics that bolster his ideas.

2. *The effective speaker orders his ideas systematically.* His talk is characterized by unity, coherence (order), and proportion (emphasis, force). Even though his talk may be impromptu, it reflects planning. He resists

---

[6] Loren D. Reid, *First Principles of Public Speaking*, Artcraft Press, Columbia, Mo., 1960, chap. 1, p. 204. W. Norwood Brigance, *Speech*, Appleton-Century-Crofts, Inc., New York, 1952, chap. 8, "Seven Lamps of Planning a Speech," p. 158.

the temptation to indulge in wide and purposeless excursions from his theme. His ideas are logically arranged, and the relation of subordinate topics to his central theme is apparent. He begins purposefully, moves through the main body of his talk, and concludes decisively. He uses summaries, transitions, and introductory statements to link the parts of the pattern together in order to make clear its progression. The result is much more than a mechanical unfolding of an outline; it is a well-organized demonstration of clear thinking.

3. *The satisfactory speaker knows how to use language effectively to formulate, present, and clarify his ideas and their factual basis.* He strives for accuracy in his use of words and their combinations; for clearness, so that his meaning will be understood by his listeners; and for attention-getting and interest-sustaining effects.

He must keep his listeners awake and facilitate their concentration on what he has to say. Thus his language must not be ambiguous; rather, it must be concrete and specific. His grammar is standard; he avoids triteness and undue use of technical and abstract words; he employs colorful, even figurative language. He is not verbose; his words have weight and his style economy. He makes use of interest-getting devices such as periodic sentences, questions, parallel constructions, and emotionally charged language. Thus his style, always idiomatic and conversational, is clear, interesting, mature, and personal. He never adopts the style of a person "delivering" an oral essay.

4. *Effectiveness in speaking requires voice control.* Vocal pitch, intensity, loudness, rate of speech, and voice quality determine the nature of the speaker's voice.

Pitch. Your natural pitch level on the musical scale and your pitch changes should not jar listeners. Your voice should come neither from too near the top of the scale nor from too near the bottom. And you should avoid continually rising inflections and singsong.

Loudness. Adjust your voice to the size of the room or auditorium (or to the microphone or open-air situation). If you are relaxed, you will probably be free from breathiness, loudness, and monotony of delivery. Your volume should be produced without undue strain on your vocal mechanism; clear articulation rather than loudness will help your audience to easy comprehension.

Rate. Speeches should be neither so fast as to baffle comprehension nor so slow as to bore. Avoid "and-uhs" and pauses that make listeners look ceilingward or squirm. Speak at the speed that is normal for you. You will find that a conversational address to your audience will help you to maintain a steady pace.

Voice quality. Your teeth, mouth, tongue, and hard and soft palates are so constructed as to provide voice resonance. If your voice-producing organs are functioning normally, you will not be troubled by nasality, harshness, guttural heaviness, shrillness, stridency, or a metallic or muffled quality. A balance between tension and relaxation will make your voice pleasing to the ear.

Is one of these four components of voice more important than the others? The answer depends upon the individual, the time, the place, the audience, and the speaker's purpose. Speaking is not a mechanical process; it is an art in which the total effect depends upon which elements are emphasized. (For detailed treatment of voice, see Chapter Eleven.)

5. *The effective speaker is efficient in articulation and pronunciation.* A normal, unaffected method of articulating syllables will produce vowels that are pure and unmistakable and consonants that are fully, yet not heavily, sounded. It is unwise to make a fetish of perfection in the shaping of sounds, yet one should avoid being what Edward Bok once called a "lip-lazy American." Substitutions such as "agin" for "again," additions such as "acrost" for "across," omissions such as "reconize" for "recognize," and conspicuous slighting of some sounds should be avoided. It is wise to adhere to the generally accepted standard for the sounds and accents of words.

6. *The effective speaker uses appropriate bodily activity in speaking.* In communication, visual effects are almost as important as auditory effects. Most people are eye-minded and welcome "visual aids"; hence posture, gesture, and movement become key agents of oral expression. Focus your physical energies so as to maintain contact with your audience. Physical activity that is purposeful rather than artificial and meaningless will help to interpret your ideas to your audience and will demonstrate that you are physically spontaneous and alert.

7. *The effective speaker has a well-developed speaking personality.* What you are as a person has great significance for the impression you make as a speaker. Good organization of physical, intellectual, and emotional characteristics is a great asset in winning acceptance for your ideas and attitudes. A well-organized personality will enable you to achieve full use of your intellectual ability, audience adaptation, and ethical responsibility.

Emotional maturity. One of the most significant aspects of emotional maturity is freedom from both undue aggressiveness and undue social dependence, two extremes which are exemplified in most good-sized groups. The tendency to dominate others and to dismiss or ignore opposition is as much to be resisted as the tendency to withdraw into a shell and let others make your decisions and do your talking for you. Smugness, exhibitionism, and the tendency to be domineering, or excessive introversion, shyness, and anxiety at holding a dissenting opinion, are symptoms of immaturity. Your progress in achieving harmonious organization of personality will be reflected in your audiences' reaction to you as a speaker and in the ease with which you are able to accept the responsibilities of speech making.

Intellectual ability. Why are speakers at times confused and flustered? Often it is because they have not carefully thought through their material. Intellectually digesting your material beforehand will prevent possible anxiety during your speech. You must keep uppermost in mind the central idea of your speech; the rational ramifications and the factual underpinning of your idea will then take a logical order in your mind if you have understood your material. Orderly habits of mind and analytic ability depend upon unhampered intellectual functioning, a goal toward which you will constantly strive.

Audience good will. Skillful speaking requires consideration for the audience, tact, humor, and the general ability to get along with others, for the speaker must enter into the concerns, needs, and desires of his listeners. Sympathetic listening is an essential part of effective speaking, and it is based upon genuine respect for the attitudes and ideas of others. Unless you develop the ability to put yourself in the place of others, you may not

The skillful student speaker will have many opportunities to talk to audiences as he pursues his education and his recreation. (Photo from The Ohio State University Department of Photography.)

achieve real contact with them. Audience adaptation requires genuine good will and sincere appreciation of the interests and concerns of your audience. An important step in achieving this skill is the development of techniques of reading the responses of your listeners.

Ethical responsibility. One aspect of the functioning of your personality in the speaking situation is the demonstration of the fact that you are an ethically responsible person, aware that you may do much harm or much good through your remarks. You cannot adopt the philosophy that "talk never hurt anyone"; rather, you must accept the responsibility of discriminating between fact and fiction, between truth and error. As a speaker, you have a secret alliance with moral principles—a commitment which will be reflected in your handling of your ideas and in your attitude toward your audience. (See Chapter Fourteen, "The Speaker's Personality.")

General Effectiveness: An Over-all Criterion

Although these seven criteria constitute an adequate guide to the understanding of your speech performance and provide a definite pattern for improvement in specific aspects of speaking, the ultimate evaluation of your speaking effectiveness may be something more or less than the sum of these seven processes. How is your speaking effectiveness determined? Not simply by judging your ideas, organization, language, voice, articulation, bodily activity, and speaking personality as separable aspects of your speech, but by taking full account of the effects of these *skills in combination.* The total pattern of what happens to you as you become audible and visible to a group is the standard for measuring your effectiveness as a speaker.

Types of Speech Activities

Speeches may be classified as either creative or interpretative, depending upon whether the speaker creates the material of the speech from his own experience or whether he reads aloud (or interprets) the material of others. Speeches may also be classified according to the speaker's purpose with regard to his audience. Speeches are given to interest, entertain, and amuse; to inform and instruct; to convince and to move to action by means of argument and persuasion; and to achieve cooperative consideration and solution of a problem, often by means of discussion.

Furthermore, speeches may be classified according to the situations that call them forth. Some typical speaking occasions are classroom recitations, interviews, campaigns (on campus or elsewhere), school and college debates, discussions, business conferences, sales talks, sermons, radio and television programs, and courtroom procedures.

This course in speech fundamentals is centered around the seven processes described above. The various speaking projects in which you participate in this course should illustrate your improvement in these basic aspects of speech. Thus in this course you will prepare and give speeches that are informative, argumentative, and persuasive, and you will interpret the speeches and writings of others. You will also study debate, discussion, interpretation, voice production, and other forms of communication, although the specialized study of these speech types will be reserved for later, more advanced courses.

Projects and Problems

PROJECT 1: AN INTRODUCTORY TEST OF GENERAL SPEECH ACHIEVEMENT

Purposes of this assignment: (*a*) To make the best four-minute speech you can make at this time; (*b*) to provide a basis for a preliminary analysis of your speech characteristics and abilities; (*c*) to provide a basis for self-analysis of your needs in speech training.

Subject: A speech of self-introduction. Give to the class more than routine information about yourself. Refer to such items as your home town, chief hobbies, travel, summertime and other occupations, athletic, artistic, educational experiences and interests, military service, vocational goals and programs, political, social, and other points of view. You will select from these suggested topics those which have some interest to you and your listeners and those which will enable the audience to become better acquainted with you. Adopt neither an overly modest nor, on the other hand, a proud and assertive attitude in your recounting.

Procedure: Select a topic and organize your thought in outline form. Rehearse with the help of this outline until you can make your speech without notes. If you speak longer than four minutes, the instructor will give you a signal; finish your sentence and take your seat. Your instructor will record his judgment of your speech but will not criticize you in class. After you sit down, make notes on what you feel were the strong points of your speech and on the things that gave you most difficulty in presenting it. Consult the section on "Seven Processes for Speech Improvement" in this chapter for suggestions on the preparation of your speech notes.

PROJECT 2: AN INTRODUCTORY TEST OF ORAL-READING ACHIEVEMENT

Purposes of this assignment: (*a*) To read simple prose material aloud as effectively as you can; (*b*) to facilitate the evaluation of your speech needs by your instructor; (*c*) to help you develop insight into your speech achievement.

Subject: Select a short piece (300 to 500 words) of argumentative or expository prose which expresses an idea you find interesting.

Procedure: Select the material you want to read. Look up meanings and pronunciations of words that are new to you. Read it over until you can present it without hesitating or stumbling. Concentrate on communication of the meaning when you read the selection to the audience. Your instructor will evaluate your speech skill in reading. You also should attempt to make an objective self-evaluation of your skill in using speech processes.

PROJECT 3: AN ANALYSIS OF THE SPEECH AND ORAL READING OF OTHERS

Purposes of this assignment: To develop analytical and critical habits of evaluating speech and oral-reading performances.

Procedure: Use the "Seven Processes for Speech Improvement" discussed in Chapter One for a systematic analysis of the speech and oral-reading perform-ance of at least three of your classmates. Make notes and write a page or two of critical analysis of each performance. Your instructor will judge your paper on the quality of the critical evaluations you have made.

PROJECT 4: AN ANALYSIS OF A TEACHING SOUND FILM, "IS THERE COMMUNICATION WHEN YOU TALK?"

Arrange to show this film made by McGraw-Hill to accompany this text. See the *Teacher's Manual* for suggested questions for discussion of the film.

References

Andersch, Elizabeth G., and Loren C. Staats: *Speech for Everyday Use*, rev. ed., Holt, Rinehart and Winston, Inc., New York, 1960, chaps. 1 and 2.

Baird, A. Craig: "The Educational Philosophy of the Teacher of Speech," *Quarterly Journal of Speech*, 24:546–553, 1938.

Berlo, David K.: *The Process of Communication*, Holt, Rinehart and Winston, Inc., New York, 1960.

Brigance, W. Norwood: *Speech*, Appleton-Century-Crofts, Inc., New York, 1952, chaps. 1 and 2.

Bryant, Donald C., and Karl R. Wallace: *The Fundamentals of Public Speak-ing*, 3d ed., Appleton-Century-Crofts, Inc., New York, 1960, chaps. 1 and 2.

Clevenger, Theodore: "The Speaker and Society," *The Southern Speech Journal*, 26:93–99, Winter, 1960.

Kramer, Magdalene: "The Role of Speech in Education: A Re-evaluation," *Quarterly Journal of Speech*, 34:123–127, 1948.

Lippmann, Walter: *Liberty and the News*, The Macmillan Company, New York, 1927, chaps. 1 and 2.

Micken, Ralph A.: *Speaking for Results*, Houghton Mifflin Company, Boston, 1958, chap. 1.

Mill, John Stuart: "Liberty of Thought and Discussion," in *Unitarianism, Liberty, and Representative Government*, J. M. Dent & Sons, Ltd., London, 1910, pp. 78–113.

Monroe, Alan H.: *Principles and Types of Speech*, 4th ed., Scott, Foresman and Company, Chicago, 1955, chap. 1.

Reid, Loren D.: *First Principles of Public Speaking*, Artcraft Press, Columbia, Mo., 1960, chap. 1.

Wallace, Karl R.: "Rhetoric and Politics," *The Southern Speech Journal*, 20:195–203, Spring, 1955.

White, Eugene E.: *Practical Speech Fundamentals*, The Macmillan Company, New York, 1960, chap. 1.

TWO

Improving Your Speech Habits: Beginner's Problems

How GOOD ARE you as a speaker? The seven processes of effective speech discussed in Chapter One will provide you with a guide by which to review your own case. Have you had considerable experience in debating, oral reading, acting, extempore speaking? Or did you come from a school that offered absolutely nothing that could be labeled as "speech" in the classroom or outside? Did you have so-called "speech training" under a teacher who was interested only in formal grammar or in written composition? Did you have a speech course in which you "got by" with little work and made no real progress? Have you been handicapped by a speech difficulty such as stuttering or by extreme timidity that caused you to avoid oral performances?

A Basis for Your Speech Improvement

Whatever your speech-learning experience, your purpose now is to build up effective speaking habits. If your methods have been bad, you can correct them. If you have been more or less successful in speaking,

19

you can nevertheless get even better results. The suggestions that follow will help you make systematic improvement in speaking skill.

1. *Cultivate a favorable attitude toward speech improvement.* What are the incentives that have stimulated you to definite and continued application in this field? What are the occupational, social, political, and other interests that call for speech competency? The answers to these questions will help you to realize the values that speech training has for you. Your ideals, interests, emotions, and practical ambitions with regard to speech will be continually strengthened if you are convinced that speaking can be learned. You can improve; others with your qualifications have done so.

Everyone wishes to communicate with others. Your motivation for speech making will be reinforced if you will channel this generalized wish to communicate into more formal speech situations. Focus upon specific subjects which are important to you and which you would like to talk about to others. Perhaps you were recently summoned to court for a traffic violation and penalized in a way that you are sure you didn't deserve. Perhaps you would like to seek information and counsel concerning a job. You undoubtedly have many interests about which you would like to converse with others. This impulse to communicate, if you encourage it, will not only sustain your interest in speech but will also carry you far in your training program.

When young Richard Brinsley Sheridan made his first speech in the British Parliament in November, 1780, Woodfall, the reporter, told him, "I don't think this is your line." Sheridan replied with passion, "It is in me, and it shall come out of me!" Chauncey Goodrich, a discerning student of speakers, reported that Sheridan then devoted himself with energy and perseverance to the art of speaking. Goodrich concludes, "He made himself at last a most dexterous and effective debater." During the four days of Sheridan's great debate on the impeachment of Warren Hastings, in June, 1788, the hall was crowded to suffocation; in some instances as much as 50 guineas was paid for a single ticket. Lord Holland called Sheridan's performance "the best oration ever conceived or heard in this country."

A young man of our acquaintance had a major speech difficulty: He stuttered badly. Under careful guidance he persisted in systematic training until he gradually reduced his handicap. Today he is in great demand as a lecturer and has a nationwide reputation as an educator.

Each year speech instructors deal with scores and scores of beginners. Some beginners are excellent at the start; others are immature or are vocally unpredictable. By the end of the course most of them have definitely improved. In hundreds of cases these young men and women, continuing their speech development, demonstrate mature ability in speaking in business, law, teaching, and other areas of community life. Skill comes as a result of training and practice. Speech effectiveness is a matter of systematic learning and improvement.

2. *Learn to understand yourself.* What personality factors account for your being better or worse than others in speaking situations? What past experiences and training explain your personality? Your intellectual, social, moral, and other attitudes undoubtedly affect your speaking methods. They color the subjects you choose, the illustrations you insert, and your way of approaching subjects, developing them, and presenting them to others.

To get a better picture of yourself, it will help to organize information about your background. What of your family and home influences? Your past and present reading habits? Your extracurricular activities other than speech—for example, in journalism, music, athletics? Your hobbies? Your habits and experiences as a listener-observer (do you, for example, often watch television)? Your attitudes toward political parties and issues? Your religious interests and activities? What are your attitudes toward and your experiences in speaking?

Speech improvement is often a matter of the total personality. The way we speak is affected not only by narrowly defined speech skills, but also by what we know, by the way we feel, the way we think, and by our skills in other behavior—in short, the whole man talks. The skilled speaker learns to coordinate and control these human processes to help him achieve his purposes.

Self-examination will not only provide you with subjects for speeches but will also indicate to what areas you will want to give special attention in speech training.

3. *Obtain a knowledge of the basic speech processes and principles.* Prospective speakers need to do more than practice the art. They should have some intellectual comprehension of the bases of the art.

Why is knowledge concerning the seven basic speech processes important? First, although practice is important, an intelligent rather than a trial-and-error method of learning speech is preferable. At the college level, moreover, you are concerned with intellectual insight into facts and principles as well as with the acquisition of skills. Knowledge, in this sense, is not merely something added to skill; it is insight that enables you to develop your personality. Skill without such knowledge is academically hardly worth your while.

Second, intelligent understanding of principles will enable you to adjust more effectively to a greater variety of situations than you could if your education were strictly a matter of developing blind and limited mechanical habits in a specific situation.

Third, many objectives of speech education require more time for attainment than is available in any one course. If you have a reasonable understanding of the facts and principles involved, you will continue to work at these objectives long after the completion of a specific course.

Fourth, a knowledge of the principles and processes of the speech arts is of great value in itself because it involves an understanding of the methods of dealing with ideas, organization, effective use of language, personality factors, attitudes, audience reactions, and the fundamental principles of informational, argumentative, and other types of address.

You will find that knowledge of the history of public address will afford you insight into the basic principles of speech. You may learn much from the record of William J. Bryan, who studied speech at Illinois College; of Albert J. Beveridge at Asbury College (DePauw University) in Indiana; of Daniel Webster at Dartmouth; of John Calhoun at Yale; and of Franklin D. Roosevelt at Groton Academy and at Harvard.

You can likewise discover principles of communication in the study of the theatre, broadcasting, education, administration, business and industrial speech, interviewing, yes, even in conversation. It will help you early in your study of speech to set about clarifying the principles of communication behavior in your thinking. If you do so, you will develop a sound image of what effective speech is like and how it may be developed. Above all you must seek to correct and eliminate any unsound images of speech improvement which you may have, because these sometimes inhibit learning.

Finally, the development of insight into speech principles may enable you to make use of latent learning. Not all your growth as you mature in speech skills will come from a fresh start. You have been speaking as a matter of fact for a long time. Some processes functioned well. Some bits were even skillful. A clear understanding of the principles of speaking should enable you to integrate these achievements into new patterns of behavior.

4. *Analyze your speech needs.* What are your abilities with regard to language, ideas, voice, and the other elements of speech? Objective analysis will help you discover the answers. Review the speech fundamentals outlined in the preceding chapter and get evaluations of your speech from others. Your speech instructor will no doubt guide you in obtaining this information.

For purposes of evaluation, rating charts similar to the one on page 24 are often used. Note that this chart is based upon the seven processes for speech improvement discussed in Chapter One.[1] Although this chart or rating scale includes many items not applicable to you, the items checked

---

[1] The items listed on the chart have been validated as significant variables in speech performance. See Howard Gilkinson and Franklin H. Knower, *Psychological Studies of Individual Differences among Students of Speech,* University of Minnesota, Minneapolis, 1939.

and the accompanying comment should give you considerable understanding of yourself and many clues for your improvement. Obviously,
diagnosis by means of this chart should take place in a normal speaking
situation—a short extempore speech, for example, or perhaps oral reading
from material that you have previously examined.

The judgment of an expert is better than that of a layman. But if a
specialist is not available, the combined judgments of a number of fellow
students will ordinarily produce a reliable evaluation. Student critics may
not always pinpoint your specific abilities and shortcomings, but on the
average, their judgments are a fairly good index of your general effectiveness.

Rating charts do not provide final answers, but if you view them in
relation to the supplementary comments and in relation to your background, the results may be helpful.

5. *Concentrate on speech as social impact.* What is the purpose of
speech? Its aim is to affect the behavior of listeners. Your goal, then, is not
primarily to coin catchy phrases or to perfect your tone, but rather to
make use of vocabulary, voice qualities, and all the other speech processes
toward a worthwhile end. That end is to influence others—to inform
them, to persuade them, to impress them, or to inspire them.

6. *Base your speech aims and methods on intellectual and moral
honesty.* Speaking carries with it responsibilities. Your right to speak is
morally based on your desire to benefit those who listen—and the rest of
the human family. Your responsibility as a speaker is to tell the truth as
you understand it and to avoid distortions of fact and logic.

7. *Get a good background in general knowledge.* Effectiveness in
speaking calls for a broad education. The effective speaker should have
some background in history, economics, natural sciences, literature, and
philosophy. Narrow specialization in one field may have detrimental
effects upon young students as well as upon mature persons. The broad-
caster who has only a knowledge of gadgets and the art of talking over
the air is in a shallow groove. Similarly, speech correctionists, oral readers, or dramatic arts majors who acquire knowledge of their own brands
of speech and side-step the humanities are usually frozen at the lower
levels. In most cases, early and complete specialization limits the area of
possible expansion.

General education will help you to relate one field to another—economics, for example, to literature, history, and philosophy—and will give
you a rich variety of details on which to draw for talks. Furthermore, a
liberal training will help you in the immediate preparation of specific
speeches, since you may tap your storehouse of accumulated learning.
Both theoretically and practically your speech training calls for knowledge
of speech, but this knowledge must be buttressed and transformed by

Speech Performance Scale

Name _____ Date _____ Instructor _____

Project _____ Time _____

Subject _____

Criteria	Rating 1–9*	Comments
1. *General effectiveness:*		
2. *Speech attitudes and adjustments:* Indifferent _____ Loses thought _____ Fidgety _____ Evasive _____ Tense _____ Inappropriate _____		
3. *Voice:* Weak _____ Loud _____ Fast _____ Slow _____ Poor pitch _____ Poor quality _____ Monotonous _____ Poor rhythm _____ Excess vocalization _____		
4. *Articulation:* Substitutions _____ Foreign dialect _____ Additions _____ Regional dialect _____ Slighting _____ Mispronunciation _____		
5. *Physical activity:* Indirect _____ Unresponsive _____ Random _____ Inappropriate _____		
6. *Language:* Ambiguous _____ Wordy _____ Inaccurate _____ Needs force _____ Needs vividness _____ Needs variety _____		
7. *Ideas:* Poor purpose _____ Not clear _____ Poor central idea _____ Dull _____ Weak support _____ Needs originality _____ Undeveloped _____ Insignificant _____ Inaccurate _____		
8. *Organization:* Introduction _____ Sequence _____ Division _____ Conclusion _____ Transitions _____		
Total		

* Rate the speaker in each square by using a scale of 1 to 9 for each of the numbered items. Use 1, 2, or 3 to indicate various degrees of deficiency in the use of the process; use 4, 5, or 6 if he is slightly below average to slightly above average in the process; and use 7, 8, or 9 to indicate relative degrees of skill in his use of the process. Add ratings to get total score.

ample learning in the other representative areas of thought and information.

8. *Practice purposefully.* Knowledge can never substitute for practice, by which we mean preparation for and participation in speech-learning activities, including oral performance in your room or before extraclassroom groups, as well as in the classroom itself. The effectiveness of these practice sessions, however, depends upon the methods by which you conduct them. The following suggestions may help you to practice effectively.

Practice with the intent to learn. Put your heart into what you are trying to do.

Practice for achievement of definite objectives. Know what you are trying to do and do not give up until you have done the best you can do. As your skill in a given direction improves, you will have a better idea of what you want to accomplish. Revise your objectives often.

Practice on projects related to your own level of achievement. If you tackle projects that are too easy, you will soon lose interest. On the other hand, if you attempt projects that are too difficult, you may bog down. For example, do not attempt a thirty-minute talk on "My program for control of the hydrogen bomb" on the basis of twenty-four hours of preparation.

Practice participation in a variety of realistic speaking activities. When you speak, set out to accomplish a specific purpose. Whenever possible, accept opportunities for "real-situation" experiences. Talk before a campus or civic club; interview someone for a well-defined purpose; talk for three minutes over a radio station; participate in a panel with three classmates on some campus or community project. The greater the number of major types of activities in which you participate, the easier it will be for you to adapt to variations in these types of situations.

Space the time of your practice. Cramming on any subject is of questionable value. The development of speech skills seems to require slow maturation through repeated practice; you can hardly expect brilliant results from sudden and sporadic action. The cultivation of good speaking habits is somewhat like the cultivation of trees—growing periods must be alternated with periodic pruning.

Do more than the minimum amount of practice indicated. You may occasionally get by with meager preparation, but it is unwise to curtail your practice in speech. With sufficient practice you can be the well-trained speaker who has something more to depend upon than the good fortune of a happy accident.

9. *Find sources of satisfaction in achievement.* The success of your study will be influenced by the degree to which you can get some reinforcement for your effort. Learning is typically associated with satisfactions, rewards, and sometimes with punishments. Some of these effects

will come from your instructor, your classmates, or your friends. Others can come only from yourself. Can you take pride in your performance? Is it better than it has been? Does it meet the standards you demand? Seek the answers to these questions, but above all seek to find those justified sources of satisfaction in your performance in order that you may really learn.

10. *Evaluate your achievement.* Your study of speech should begin with an analysis of your abilities and needs, and this process of evaluation should be repeated at intervals throughout your training and at the end. You will want to know what you have accomplished, and written examinations (on the principles of speech) and oral testing (by speech performances) should give you accurate information. The evidence of your progress which these evaluations will provide should spur you on to further development.

Preparing a Speech

Most beginners in speech ask, "Shall I plunge ahead with my talks and oral readings and later catch up with the principles expounded in the textbook? Or shall I read and assimilate the fundamentals and techniques before attempting practice? Or shall I work on both principles and practice at the same time?"

The writers of this book emphatically prefer the third of these possibilities. From the beginning you should combine the two aspects of speech activity, because you learn not only by assimilating information but also by doing.

In the following pages you will learn the steps that you should take in preparing and making a speech. When you prepare a less formal communication you will go about it in a similar manner.

Since you cannot at the outset concentrate in detail on all the principles of good speech making, a condensed review of steps to guide you in the first weeks of your training is presented below. These suggestions will be treated in detail in later chapters.

1. *Choose a subject of interest to you and one that will hold the attention of your audience.* Select a topic that you yourself know something about and want to investigate further. If you start with your own first-hand experiences, reactions, and outlooks you will proceed well with your speech planning. Keep in mind also the experiences and attitudes of your listeners. They are presumably college students with scientific, literary, engineering, business, teaching, or other major interests. In addition, they have varied athletic, social, religious, and occupational experiences and outlets.

2. *Limit your subject to a single specific part of the general topic.* Invariably, beginning speakers try to cover the breadth and length of their subject. They talk on the history of baseball, the evolution of domestic science, the rise of labor unions, the development of radio and television. Whittle down your area until you pinpoint a statement that you can profitably present in three, four, or five minutes, such as "The T-formation tactics of our football team this year," "The recent strike at the local packing plant," "Should we establish a book pool on this campus?" or "The character of Dickens's Samuel Weller in *Pickwick Papers.*"

3. *Decide on the purpose of your speech.* You are presumably interested in giving your audience information or in moving them to believe something or to take action as you suggest.

Although you may at the outset not be conscious of a dominant purpose to inform, persuade, inspire, or entertain, you will decide what is to be your main aim and select your ideas and details accordingly. You will frame this aim in a specific sentence. Thus:

Purpose: My purpose is to inform my hearers.

Purpose sentence: I propose to explain to the members of this speech course the main features of the new student union.

Purpose: My purpose is to convince and persuade.

Purpose sentence: I propose to persuade the members of this speech course that they should vote to increase the student activity fee by $5 per year.

Purpose: My purpose is to eulogize.

Purpose sentence: I propose to impress the students in this speech class with the idea that Miss Gilda Grimes, my secondary school instructor in composition and literature, is a superior teacher.

Purpose: To convince and persuade.

Purpose sentence: My aim is to convince the members of this class that they should approve the policy and activities of the Peace Corps.

4. *Gather materials.* Take stock of your knowledge. Do some thinking. Substantiate your information with sources that will give strength to your speech. You will observe processes, interview, read books and periodicals, listen to lectures, including radio and television talks, and otherwise saturate yourself with your subject. You will jot down notes systematically on cards. (See Chapter Three for further study.)

5. *Organize your main ideas under two or three general points.* Beginners often attempt to develop seven or eight main propositions or ideas. You will be wiser. Your first draft of a four-minute speech might begin with four or more main points:

Purpose sentence: Speech should be a three-hour one-semester course for first-year students in my university.

Main points:

   I. It will improve the student's communication skills.
  II. It will improve the student's ability to analyze a topic.
 III. It will improve the student's ability to organize ideas.
  IV. It will improve the student's ability to use oral language.
   V. It will help the student to progress in his occupation or profession.
  VI. It will strengthen the student's social adjustments and relationships.
 VII. It will make the student a better political participant.

There are obviously too many main points in the above outline; furthermore, they overlap. Select about two main points:

Purpose sentence: Speech should be a three-hour one-semester course at my university.

Main points:

   I. Speech training will benefit the prospective lawyer, preacher, businessman, or other professional.
  II. Speech training is important for political participation.

Each of these two points, however, might make a satisfactory speech. A further limitation might be:

   I. Speech training and skills benefit the businessman.
  II. Speech training and skills benefit the engineer.
 III. Speech training and skills benefit the lawyer.

6. *Support each main point with specific and pertinent details.* (See Chapter Six for further study.)

General propositions, as illustrated above, call for detailed supports that prove or illustrate the points. Supporting materials include facts and figures, testimony, specific instances, incidents and anecdotes, analogies and comparisons, quotations.

The following example illustrates the use of details to undergird a general idea:

Main point: Shakespearean plays continue to have wide popularity in the United States in the 1960s.

Illustration: In 1961 the "Emmy award" for the best televised play of the year was awarded the production of Macbeth.

7. *Work out an appropriate introduction and conclusion.*

8. *Outline and compose your speech.* (See Chapter Five for further study.) Develop your speech orally from the outline. Say it aloud to your-

self in order that you may express the substance and details of your topic effectively. Sometimes you should write the speech in full, but throw away or hide your manuscript, for it will become a crutch in your delivery.

9. *Practice the speech aloud until the general pattern and details are well in mind.* Memorize the ideas. Note the sequence and the relationship of supporting materials to each main point. Become familiar with the pattern or order of your thought. Your method is not to memorize your speech as you would a play. You will allow scope for extempore reaction to your materials and to your audience. Good delivery calls for thinking with your audience rather than throwing ideas to them or at them.

Your practice sessions, first with the outline before you and then without reference to it, should later be carried through without backtracking, even though you may hesitate here and there.

10. *You should rehearse the speech from five to ten times on your feet with an imaginary audience before you.*

11. *Prepare so that you can speak extemporaneously to your audience.* This pattern of speaking will give your speech the directness of a conversational style which has a high degree of communicativeness. When you speak extemporaneously you must keep your mind on your subject, with the fullest possible awareness of the meaning of what you are saying. You also will be vividly aware of your listeners and their responses to your speech. This means that you must be direct in manner and in eye contact. Such directness is not only a sign of poise and courtesy, it is also necessary for the feedback which enables you to make effective adjustments in content and in method as you speak.

This extempore style of speaking should enable you to respond vocally and physically to your purpose and ideas. Conversational speech typically is animated and highly inflected. Thus your speaking will reflect your interest, enthusiasm, and confidence.

Of course your extempore speech is well prepared. You have your ideas selected and arranged. You know what you want to emphasize, but you have not anticipated every word you will use. The impromptu speech, in contrast, is one in which you have made no specific preparation and in which your ideas as well as your words are selected as you go along.

The memorized speech lies in the opposite direction from the impromptu speech. Here every word as well as every idea is selected in advance and rehearsed. Although some people can speak well from memory, most of us cannot. We become monotonous, mechanical, and stilted. There is always the chance of forgetting, and this can be a source of real embarrassment.

You should learn to read aloud a manuscript of a speech as if you were talking conversationally. We do not recommend the regular use of a manuscript. There are times, however, when a manuscript is a necessary procedure. When you speak on such an occasion you should know how to read skillfully.

12. *Profit by criticism.* (See Chapters Eight through Fourteen.) Welcome criticism and profit by it. Seek out reactions to your speaking from your instructor and your fellow students. Try to discover both your strong and your weak points.

In following the steps listed above, you will work systematically by beginning your preparation at least two weeks before your talk and by distributing your preparation time so that you may attend to each of these aspects of preparation, including the all-important oral practices.

The stages of your preparation may not always unfold in the exact order indicated here. But the general pattern of surveying your subject and organizing and rehearsing the speech will obviously call for some such sequence. Follow the steps indicated above as long as they help you. Then vary the procedure to meet your needs.

Projects and Problems

PROJECT 1: A SELF-ANALYSIS INTERVIEW

Purposes of this assignment: (a) To develop objective habits of self-analysis in speaking; (b) to formulate effective goals for speech improvement; (c) to carry out an effective personal interview with your instructor; (d) to have your speech evaluated in an interview situation. The self-interview is an analysis of yourself, your speech achievement, and what you can do to improve yourself.

Procedure: Make an appointment with your instructor and carry it out according to schedule. On the basis of the outline for speech criticism presented in this chapter, prepare a systematic and objective résumé of your speech achievement. Describe the goals for improvement or the standards toward which you expect to work in the course. Prepare to control the interview with the instructor by organizing your presentation, asking questions when necessary, and terminating the interview on time. Use your basic speech skills to the best of your ability in the interview.

Facts and principles you should know: Review the speech processes on which you should evaluate yourself and formulate goals. An effective personal interview requires that you (a) prepare carefully for the interview; (b) be honest with yourself and frank with your instructor; (c) make a real effort to get something more than a grade average out of the interview; (d) keep the interview moving, balance attention to various problems, and avoid wasting time.

PROJECT 2: AN EXTEMPORANEOUS TALK

Prepare a brief extemporaneous talk according to the procedure in project 1 at the end of Chapter One. Your talk should be not less than three and not more than four minutes.

Subjects:

My impressions of my early days.

Why I need to be educated.

How I shall earn money next summer.

How I passed the mathematics-skills examination.

Hitchhiking—a lost art.

My boss on my summer job.

A book you should read.

Protocol in the Navy.

Basketball for women.

Basketball versus football.

My jaunt through France (or elsewhere).

My temporary life in Georgia (or wherever you have temporarily lived).

Why I am a good baby sitter.

I skied once.

PROJECT 3: A SELF-ANALYSIS REPORT

Prepare a detailed written statement of your past experience in speaking and social activities and your interests and goals in the study of speech. Your instructor may give you an outline of what to include, or you may use a copy of *A Guidance Questionnaire for Students of Speech,* by Gilkinson and Knower, C. H. Staelting and Company, Chicago.

PROJECT 4: ON FRAMING YOUR PURPOSE

a. Select three ideas to be included in a four-minute speech. Write each as a purpose sentence. Present your report to the class and provide a copy for your instructor.

b. Give the purpose sentence of a speech recently delivered. Be sure to give the author, title, source, date, and place of delivery, and indicate whether it is printed or mimeographed.

PROJECT 5: OUTLINING

Prepare a three-minute speech. See project 2 above or Chapter Three for a suggested subject. Prepare a one-page outline of the speech. Use complete sentences. Include introduction, topic statement, body, and conclusion. Familiarize yourself with this outline. Rehearse it several times but avoid memorization. If the instructor requests it, present the outline to him before you step to the front of the room to speak.

PROJECT 6: USE OF SUPPORTING MATERIALS

Prepare a single-point speech three minutes in length. Use one each of the following forms of support for your main point: instances, figures, comparisons, testimony.

PROJECT 7: PREPARATION AND DELIVERY OF A BRIEF SPEECH

Prepare and deliver a four-minute speech according to the procedures suggested in this chapter. Report at the next meeting of the class your chief problems in preparing and presenting this project. Hand this report to your in-structor, indicating approximately the amount of time you spent in each phase of your preparation for this speech.

References

Andersch, Elizabeth G., and Loren C. Staats: *Speech for Everyday Use*, rev. ed., Holt, Rinehart, and Winston, Inc., New York, 1960, chap. 3.

Braden, Waldo W., and Mary Louise Gehring: *Speech Practices*, Harper & Brothers, New York, 1958, chap. 1.

Brigance, W. Norwood: *Speech*, Appleton-Century-Crofts, Inc., New York, 1952, chaps. 3 and 4.

Bryant, Donald C., and Karl R. Wallace: *The Fundamentals of Public Speaking*, 3d ed., Appleton-Century-Crofts, Inc., New York, 1960, chaps. 1, 5, and 13–14.

Ewbank, H. L., A. Craig Baird, W. N. Brigance, W. M. Parrish, and Andrew T. Weaver: "What Is Speech? A Symposium," *Quarterly Journal of Speech*, 41:145–153, 1955.

Gray, Giles W., and Waldo W. Braden: *Public Speaking: Principles and Practice*, Harper & Brothers, New York, 1951, chap. 2.

McBurney, James H., and Ernest J. Wrage: *The Art of Good Speech*, Prentice-Hall, Inc., Englewood Cliffs, N.J., 1953, chaps. 2–4.

Monroe, Alan H.: *Principles and Types of Speech*, 4th ed., Scott, Foresman and Company, Chicago, 1955, chaps. 2 and 7.

Schramm, Wilbur (ed.): *Communications in Modern Society*, University of Illinois Press, Urbana, Ill., 1948.

PART TWO

DEVELOPING
FUNDAMENTAL
PROCESSES

THREE

Choosing Your Subject

and Purpose

"WHAT SHALL I talk about?" This question disturbs students in speech classes as well as mature speakers who have been asked to "say a few words" before a group. Topics for your first two or three talks in class may cause you little concern. If you are told to "speak for three minutes on an informational or descriptive subject," you will recall your one-day trip from Seattle to Mount Rainier or the way to pitch a curve in baseball.

Later, however, your personal resources appear to fail. You feel as though you have told the world everything you know, except perhaps for some personal experiences that you are loath to talk about. Perhaps your most recent speech fell flat because you could not think of a subject until a few minutes before you rose to speak. Your talk was based on your hurried reading of an article in a pocket-sized monthly digest magazine, and you had little time to digest the main idea or assimilate your material. After this discouraging experience you concluded that success in speaking depends as much upon the subject as upon talking. If you have correctly diagnosed your speech problem, you will recognize that this initial effort of getting a subject is no small part of successful preparation.

Subjects for Speaking

Choosing a good topic—and choosing it early—contributes a great deal to progress through the various stages of preparation, to finding good illustrations, to organization of ideas, and to confident delivery. Conversely, failure to get a subject until the last minute is frequently the cause of meager preparation and eventual frustration.

THE SPEAKER AS A SOURCE OF SUBJECTS

Where can you find ideas to talk about? You as a speaker will be your own best source, although you will have the assistance of many other sources.

Personal experiences. You will constantly draw on your own experiences and observations. For example, if you have lived in Yarmouth, Maine, you are familiar with clam digging and lobster fishing, the use of kelp as fertilizer, and down-East speech. If you grew up in Youngstown, Ohio, cranes, blast furnaces, and rolling mills are vivid in your experiences. These things may seem commonplace to you because they are part of your closely woven daily experience. Other people, nevertheless, will be interested in them.

Your reading and reflection. Autobiographical or semifictional narratives need not, however, constitute the roster of subjects upon which you draw. Your audiences—especially but not exclusively your peers—will be interested in your thinking and reading. If you read the sports page, you have a source of ideas to suit the season. You may interpret the Army or Navy football prospects. The trends of the competitive sports world have appeal even to the unathletic. If you follow the fashions, you can comment on the latest hemline.

Any topic that finds space in the headlines, newsreels, and telecasts will form a likely starting point for your five-minute talk. National and international problems are inexhaustible. The latest trends in such areas as inflation and deflation, strikes, political campaigns and taxes will suggest many possible topics.

Your beliefs. Take an inventory of your beliefs. Everyone has definite convictions on many issues; you have only to realize what these convictions are to capitalize upon them in your speeches. Possibly you have ideas about what should be done in the field of airplane manufacture (military or nonmilitary) in the next decade; about taxes on cigarettes; about English or communications as a required subject; about farm problems or the cost of living; about law, advertising, or personnel work as a profession; or about desegregation in the public schools. You may have had experiences with railroads, farms, mines, or schools that have given you definite beliefs concerning these fields.

Stage, cinema, and television plays. Stage, motion-picture, and television plays furnish abundant topics. Perhaps you have seen *The King and I* or a revival of *Romeo and Juliet*, *Pygmalion* or *The Caine Mutiny*. Such plays are good subjects for short speeches in which you consider the plot, characters, setting, dialogue, tragic or comic effects, performers, and your personal reaction.

Hobbies and special skills. Hobbies are good subjects for speeches because they have the special advantage of being personal and at the same time informational. What is your special interest, either apart from or as part of your schoolwork or job? Mechanical drawing? Meteors and other celestial phenomena? Cryptography? Animal breeding? You can make an interesting speech if you can give some special firsthand information about aerial photography, writing a new story, playing left guard, applying a tourniquet, or dancing certain new steps.

Lectures, radio and television talks, conversations. You have many opportunities to hear well-developed talks. Listen to a lecture and base a speech of your own on one of the ideas. A history professor, for example, stated that most students are grossly ignorant of American history and that our national security depends to a large degree upon a better grounding in that subject. Do you agree? Students have talked well on the topic "The best speaker I have heard in the past twelve months." With radio and television operating during all of your waking and most of your sleeping hours, you have many opportunities to hear commentators, government officials, and panel discussants; these provide an inexhaustible supply of subjects.

Courses of study. Many students think of their courses as distinct and widely separated units of subject matter. Consequently they fail to profit from the merging of these bodies of knowledge. You can make use of your current studies in geography, history, science, English, and other courses for subjects in speaking. You will benefit from synthesizing your knowledge, and your audiences will be interested in, for example, a geographical description of the area in which their community is located, or the complicated personal relations of the English Romantic poets. Writing and then talking about the new information you have absorbed in other courses will help to fix this information in your mind and to integrate the various skills you are acquiring in areas that may otherwise remain widely separated in your educational experience.

Professional and occupational experiences. In every speech class there are students who have held temporary jobs or who have been in the armed services. We have already mentioned the resources of these fields as speech materials. Your work in a dirigible factory, in radio control, at the ticket window of a railroad station, or as a fire warden will be interesting subject matter. In addition many college students who work part time can talk authoritatively concerning their duties as clerks, stenographers, readers, technicians, restaurateurs, or hospital helpers.

Thus repeated canvassing of your personal experiences, convictions and opinions, hobbies and interests, reading and listening experiences, conversations, and occupational record should give you a constantly expanding collection of stimulating subjects.

CONSIDER THE INTERESTS OF THE AUDIENCE

Ask yourself, "What does my audience want to hear about? What are my listeners immediately interested in? What controversial issues confront them?" If they are concerned only with such matters as dating and tomorrow night's basketball game, how can you enlist and hold their attention when you introduce topics representing wider concerns?

In choosing subjects, most students of oral and written communication are self-centered rather than audience-centered. It is harder to answer the question "What are others interested in?" than the question "What am I interested in?" If you have read purposefully the first two chapters of this book, you will be continually alert to the activities, opinions, and reading and the vocational and avocational habits of your audience. Your mental and emotional projection into the minds and personalities of your listeners will provide you with subjects that will appeal to them.

You may begin by passing imaginatively from the role of prospective speechmaker to that of prospective listener. Are the others in the group like you? Put yourself in their places. Ask yourself some questions about them: What are their ages, their weekly earnings, their attitudes toward government, their feelings about meeting strangers, and whom do they admire? Each group has character of its own. Dartmouth students, at least this was true some years ago, can be quickly distinguished from Harvardites. Marines, movie actresses, Wall Streeters, clergymen, Ivy Leaguers, Beatniks and sorority sisters have distinctive characteristics.

CONSIDER OCCASIONS AS SUBJECTS

The occasion of your talk will, in many cases, dictate your subject. Your teacher may specify exactly what your topic is to be. You may be told to talk for six minutes on "Should the Federal government, as a permanent policy, subsidize fully the education of superior students in the college of their choice?" You may have the good fortune to engage in an informal radio discussion with other students on the subject of "The guaranteed annual wage." If you are a high school debater, you may find your proposition already selected for you by the National University Extension Association; if you are a college debater, by a committee of the Speech Association of America. Again, you may be assigned a talk in a college campaign to raise funds for the Red Cross or for the community budget. Or you may be asked to instruct other sorority members on "rushing" or sorority finances.

You will certainly be called upon in a few of the situations listed above, either as keynote speaker or as humble discussant. In your effort to make your speech suitable to the situation, you must be sensitive to the requirements of the hour—the nature of the occasion, the time of day, the audience, the chairman, the specific aim of the group.

When you have thus analyzed sources of subjects, check through a list of subject categories and decide both what you are interested in and what may appeal to your captive or other hearers.

SUGGESTED SUBJECTS

Below is such a list. These topics illustrate the possibilities in several fields. Some of the categories overlap. They may be used for expositional or definitional subjects; for argumentative or persuasive propositions; for eulogistic treatment; or for entertainment purposes. In some cases the topic may be limited more than is indicated here.

Agriculture

Better fertilizers
Hybrid corn
Cultivating a lawn
Making a garden
DDT
Preparing a calf for showing

Animals

What is a cocker spaniel champ?

Art

Abstract art
Aesthetics
Beatniks
Today's poetry
Primitives
Japanese art (or the art of any country)

Books

Will Drury's *Advise and Consent* rank as a superior American novel?
How to speed up your reading

Broadcasting

The public interest, convenience, and necessity
Subscription television
Violence in radio and TV programs
Educational broadcasting
Network control
Blunders on the air
Government-sponsored programs

Censorship

Should "obscene" literature be censored?

Children

Education for the fourth freedom

Conservation

Water resources
Fighting forest fires

Crime

Twelve Good Men
Chicago's underground

Economics

Is automation to be approved?
What is the European Common Market?
Collective bargaining
Reciprocal trade agreements
Unemployment relief
Price controls?
The "Pitchman"

Education

Through college in twenty-four months
Phi Beta Kappa
Mortar Board
The Winston Churchill film
Reading microfilms
Using a slide rule
Grade point system
Honors course
How to pass exams
How to study
Abolishing required ROTC
Physical fitness

Should my university admit only graduate students and those qualified for medicine, law, graduate engineering and agriculture?
Educational TV
The breast stroke
Science education
Should public junior colleges be more fully developed in my state?

Food

How to weigh no more than you should
Synthetic meat
My career as a waiter
Balanced diets

Gambling

Harold's Club at Reno
State lotteries

Health

Polio
How long shall we live?
Barbiturates
Water pollution
Vitamins
Medical care and senior citizens
Cost of drugs
Blood banks
Infantile paralysis
Blue Cross
Salk vaccine
Cigarette smoking
Socialized medicine
Student health center
Too much sun-bathing?

Home Economics

Interior decoration
Setting a table
Designing a dress
Weaving at home
Styles

Humor

Tall tales of a Phi Bet

Insurance

Group insurance

International Politics

Formosa
How may we strengthen the United Nations?
Are we winning against communism in Latin America? (Select a given nation.)
Should and can the United States and Canada establish closer political and
economic ties?

Inventions

Travel tomorrow
The testing of a hydrogen bomb
The space age

Influencing Others

The lost art of keeping friends

Labor

AFL–CIO
International Teamsters Union
Open shop

Literature

Is Robert Frost our leading poet?

Music

Should we condemn the popularity of rock 'n' roll?
Is America going backward in popular music?

Marriage

Why not marriage brokers?
Shall we approve student marriages?

Military Training

Judo in self-defense
Plane jumping

Mind

Ours not to reason why
How to think
Symbolic behavior

Money

Five rules for inflation
Fiat money in America
Shall we coin halfpennies?
Hedging against inflation
Community Chest

Buying a car
Buying a house

Motion Pictures

Walt Disney

Music

"A Bicycle Built for Two"
Marching band
Jazz

National Defense

Has our civil defense program failed?

Occupations

Managing a plant
Road construction
Teaching
Summertime stock company
Ham actor
Radio announcer
Printer's devil
Research chemist
Proofreader
House painter
File clerk
Accountant
Welder
Machinist
Selling
Public relations
Communications research
Administration

Personal Appearance

What is a handsome man?

Personal Power

Winston Churchill as a leader in World War II

Politics

Should we broadcast all proceedings of the United States Senate?
League of Women Voters
Redistricting
Undecided voter
Getting elected

Physical Exercise

Weight lifting

Propaganda

Brain washing

Psychology

Extrasensory perception
Hypnotism
Mental Hygiene
Role playing in industry
Motivation research

Race Relations

Anti-Semitism
What the South Koreans taught the Yankees
Deep South and Deep North

Religion

My favorite television preacher
YMCA
Religion and politics

Science

Space rockets and the moon?
Van Allen bands

Service Clubs

Rotary Club (or Kiwanis, Lions, Optimists, etc.)

Smoking and Drinking

Should cigarettes be permanently rationed?

Social Security

Extension of social security

Speech

Preparing a speech
Delta Sigma Rho
Are most commencement speakers bores?

Sports

Water skiing
National football leagues

Taxes

Should we try to pay off our national debt?
Sales taxes
Withholding tax

Transportation

Should all airports be required to install instrument landing radio beams for each runway?

Travel

Life on an island
Via a cargo ship to the Orient

Vacations

Summer vacationing in the West Indies

Weather

Weather reporting

Limit the Subject

Most speakers, especially amateurs, choose subjects that are too broad. As a result, in addition to wasting a good theme, the speaker treats the subject in general terms and leaves the listener disappointed and wondering why the speaker failed to mention some concrete facts to support his broad statements.

1. *Treat your subject specifically.* Study the specific topics presented in the list of general subject categories on pages 39–45, and note that each topic was arrived at by focusing upon a specific aspect of the general subject in such a way that the scope of the subject was narrowed. To be effective, a speech must treat one specific topic only.

2. *Limit your subject according to the time allotted for your speech.* It is not possible to present in a four-minute speech all the representative arguments for and against a permanent standing army of 2 million and to explain your choice of policy. "The effects of the sun's radiation on the earth" and "The history of athletics in my school or college" are too broad for four-minute speeches. "The development of American foreign policy" can be limited to "America's economic policy toward Brazil in the past year."

3. *Limit your subject according to the intellectual level and interests of your listeners.* The character of your audience is as important in the limiting of your subject as in its selection. Ask yourself whether your listeners want a speech on the theme you have in mind, and if so, what aspect interests them most. The answer will depend upon their educa-

tional level, sex, age, occupational interests, and other factors discussed above.

4. *Limit your subject to meet the needs of the specific occasion.* Sometimes the situation will open a broad avenue for you as a speaker; at other times, it will sharply restrict the scope of your subject.

TEST THE SUBJECT

To test the appropriateness of your subject, ask yourself the following questions before you speak. Then check the success of your topic by a post-mortem examination of your speaking performance.

1. Is the subject suggested by the interests, knowledge, attitudes, and needs of my hearers?
2. Is it appropriate to the occasion?
3. Is it timely?
4. Is it important?
5. Does it add to the listener's knowledge?
6. Does it grow out of my experiences, interests, and observations?
7. Does it grow out of my wish to inform, to entertain, to impress, to convince, to persuade, and to deliberate with an audience?
8. Do I have genuine enthusiasm for the subject?
9. Have I properly limited the subject?

Choose Your Purpose in Speaking

At the beginning of this book we suggested some of the motives that move you to communicate formally as well as casually. Sometimes, for example, you wish to win people over to your view of a political problem. Analysis of the factors that impel you to verbalize your ideas and call them to the attention of listeners reveals that the most important motive involved is your over-all desire to convey to others some part of your experience, interests, needs, hopes, beliefs, faiths, or doubts. You find yourself continually bracketed with the human family, with your immediate family, with your fellow students, townsmen, and other groups. Your daily life is the history of your adjustment to these human beings and their adjustment to you. You cannot easily escape from this world of contact and oral exchange, nor do you normally wish to do so.

Your aim is to get a response from your associates, who are your auditors. The response that indicates they have understood your words may be merely the acknowledgment of a glance or a nod of the head; or their lighted countenances and smiles as you unfold an incident; or their willingness to vote "yes" to your ideas or even to pledge a donation in money, time, or energy. This end, as we have stated, is the true function of speech—to affect the behavior of others.

YOUR CONTROLLING PURPOSES

What concrete responses do you seek? Seven specific purposes probably encompass the things you customarily hope to achieve in speaking: (1) to inform, (2) to analyze a problem, (3) to change or strengthen beliefs and attitudes, (4) to stimulate to action, (5) to impress, (6) to entertain, and (7) to solve a problem through deliberation.

Each of these aims may involve most of the others; a talk that is intended primarily to change or strengthen beliefs will, for example, involve information. However, one purpose should be dominant in each speech, and this dominant purpose will color your selection of ideas, your organization, language, and delivery, and even your speaking personality.

1. *To inform.* You are trying to add to the knowledge of others. Your communicative problem is to present information clearly. You are a reporter. With this aim uppermost you may give a brief statement to subfreshmen on how to register in the college or university. Or you may review what the United States Senate did on a specific day. Or you may explain the layout of the new communications building which you have recently toured.

2. *To analyze a problem.* Sometimes your aim as a speaker will be to present a problem which you do not attempt to solve but which you clarify for your audience. In this role you are both a reporter and an inquirer. The atmosphere you try to create, therefore, is that of inquiry rather than of bold assertion. For example, you may explain the problem of a suggested increase in tuition at your college. You will eliminate from this talk all statements that reveal your own views or tend to shape those of your audience. Organize your material to show (*a*) why the problem is important, (*b*) what the terms involved mean, (*c*) what the chief arguments on both sides are, and (*d*) what questions, impartially stated by you, need to be answered.

3. *To change or strengthen beliefs and attitudes.* When your purpose is to change the beliefs of your audience, you will go one step further than in analyzing a problem. You will not only raise questions but also answer them. Your aim is to influence your hearers to accept your point of view. Shall we have a federal sales tax? Shall we have permanent universal military training? Shall atomic energy be released for commercial uses? Shall we concentrate a larger amount of the Federal budget on "moon" rockets? These are questions on which you may hold a definite view to which you may seek to persuade your audience.

The task of persuading is certainly more difficult than that of informing or analyzing because here you are attempting to strengthen the beliefs of those who see eye to eye with you and to convert those who are indifferent or hostile to your views. Your arguments must be logical and your facts must be handled with particular care. But you may use all the arts of persuasive speaking. (See Chapter Seventeen, "Argumentative Speaking.")

4. *To stimulate to action.* Your argumentative task may be to get not only endorsement of your attitudes, but action as well. If you succeed with your informational talk, the listener will be able to say, "I understand what you have said, and I know more than I did previously." If your analytical speech is effective, he will say, "You have clearly presented the problem." And if your persuasive speech goes over well, his comment will be, "I agree fully with your argument."

The speech that calls for action goes one step further. More than emotional and intellectual agreement is needed if physical activity is to result. In the examples of persuasive speeches cited above, it was enough to gain the hearer's assent to the proposition that we should or should not, for example, have a Federal sales tax. The actuating speech, on the other hand, calls for action according to a program. It not only persuades the listener of what to believe but also of what to do—to pay, read, visit, listen, watch, learn, study, vote, join, buy, give, mark, sign, phone, telegraph.

To deliver a successful talk that evokes action, you will adopt a persuasive aim and mood. In addition to your appeal to intelligence (information, logic, and supporting evidence), you will also motivate your hearers. Your argument will appeal to those drives in your listeners that are based upon their wants, needs, ambitions, self-interest, faith, and hopes.

5. *To impress.* Still another dominant purpose in speech making is to impress or inspire—to bring your hearers to a deeper realization of some attitude or position to which they are already committed. The speech to impress differs from that to convince in that the impressive or stimulative talk assumes that the listeners already believe as you do. You are in effect saying, "May we appreciate more fully this man (or institution, or event)" or "May we condemn more decisively this dangerous man (or institution or event)." Thus campaign speakers pay tribute to the candidates of the Republican party or to those of the Democratic party. You eulogize a person who once taught you, talk about Memorial Day, or condemn leaders of communism.

In some respects speeches of this type are more difficult than others to prepare and present, since it is easy to become mawkishly sentimental, or, on the other hand, to maintain such a matter-of-fact tone that you fail to inspire.

6. *To entertain.* All speeches should have entertainment value in some

measure. Anecdotes, examples, concrete comparisons, and personal experiences help to hold hearers. When your main purpose is to entertain, however, wit will be one of the mainstays of your speech.

But do not resort to extended that-reminds-me stories. Select simple narratives concerning places you have been, books you have read, lively movies you have seen, interesting people you have met.

You may give advice on how to flunk a course; how to get a traffic summons; how to hold a job in a mining camp; how to train a three-week-old colt; how to stop cigarette smoking. You may talk about your chief gripe; your worst movie; why you like Groucho Marx (or Joey Bishop, or George Jessel, or Bob Hope, or Ed Sullivan); when you ran for several campus offices; when you caught a thirty-pound bass; how you dodged a tornado in Texas.

7. *To solve a problem.* You will have many opportunities to cooperate with others in deliberating problems. Problem solving may involve informing, analyzing, arguing, persuading, and impressing. At times it may be facilitated by entertainment. Its principal purpose, however, is to cooperate toward the conception of new ideas concerning a problem. This kind of speaking occurs in the family council and in meetings of the student government, the school board, the department staff, the board of directors, committees in business organizations, labor-management arbitration groups, and in scores of other situations.

Cooperative discussion can succeed only in an atmosphere of genuine desire to arrive at a solution. You can implement discussions of this type by carefully analyzing the problem, stating the issues, and evaluating all the available evidence and the reasoning pertaining to possible solutions.

YOUR PURPOSE SENTENCE

Once you have determined your subject and your controlling purpose, combine them in a single specific sentence—a purpose sentence. To illustrate:

Subject: Voting for eighteen-year-olds.

Purpose: To convince.

Audience: The local Rotary Club.

Purpose sentence: I propose to convince the Rotary Club audience that my state should lower the voting age to eighteen.

Note that the sentence describes both the central idea of the speech (voting for eighteen-year-olds) and the response you hope to get from your audience (conviction or agreement with your ideas). Formulating a purpose sentence will help you in the organization and development of your talk. Writing such a sentence will give you a better idea of what you are trying to do, although you may not state your purpose directly to your audience. In many talks, such as the informal narrative, a formal statement of the theme is unnecessary. In any case, avoid such expressions as "I shall attempt to persuade you."

The selection and limitation of your subject are thus closely related to your communicative purpose. Often the needs and interests of a specific occasion determine your subject. Conversely, your topic will be limited and modified to conform to your speaking aim.

These, then, are the questions you must answer in preparation: What subject shall I select? How shall I limit it? What speaking aim shall I attempt to fulfill? What specific adaptations shall I make in my topic and purpose to obtain maximum response from the listeners-observers?

Projects and Problems

PROJECT 1

Using as a guide the criteria for "testing the subject" suggested in this chapter, test the subject used in one of the talks you made last week in class or elsewhere.

PROJECT 2

Select seven topics properly limited to illustrate each of the following controlling purposes: (*a*) to inform, (*b*) to analyze a problem, (*c*) to change or strengthen beliefs, (*d*) to stimulate to action, (*e*) to impress, (*f*) to entertain, (*g*) to solve a problem. Frame each topic as a purpose sentence. Let your exercise be arranged as follows: (1) subject, (2) controlling purpose, (3) purpose sentence.

PROJECT 3

Listen to a speaker, preferably in a situation in which you are one of the visible audience. Note the subject and title of his talk; determine his general aim and specific purpose; and judge the extent to which he accomplishes his purpose. Write a brief report of your findings and present them to the class.

PROJECT 4

Analyze a printed speech, either a recently delivered speech or one by Webster, Calhoun, Lincoln, Bryan, Wilson, or Franklin D. Roosevelt. Determine the general aim and specific purpose. Decide whether the speaker accomplished his goal. Present your analysis in a brief written report.

For recent speeches, consult *Vital Speeches of the Day* (a fortnightly) or *Representative American Speeches* (an annual collection). For older speeches, see W. M. Parrish and Marie Hochmuth, *American Speeches;* or A. Craig Baird, *American Public Addresses:* 1740-1952. Consult also the speeches in Appendix C.

References

Brigance, W. Norwood: *Speech,* Appleton-Century-Crofts, Inc., New York, 1952, chap. 9.

Bryant, Donald C., and Karl R. Wallace: *The Fundamentals of Public Speaking,* 3d ed., Appleton-Century-Crofts, Inc., New York, 1960, chap. 5.

Gray, Giles W., and Waldo W. Braden: *Public Speaking: Principles and Practice,* Harper & Brothers, New York, 1951, chaps. 5 and 6.

McBurney, James H., and Ernest J. Wrage: *The Art of Good Speech,* Prentice-Hall, Inc., Englewood Cliffs, N.J., 1953, chaps. 5 and 6.

Monroe, Alan H.: *Principles and Types of Speech,* 4th ed., Scott, Foresman and Company, Chicago, 1955, chap. 8.

Reid, Loren D.: *First Principles of Public Speaking,* Artcraft Press, Columbia, Mo., 1960, chap. 2.

Smith, Raymond G.: *The Principles of Speaking,* The Ronald Press Company, New York, 1958, chap. 4.

FOUR

Finding Materials

You HAVE tentatively chosen a subject for your next speech. How will you develop it? Some topics seem to develop themselves; personal experiences and observations provide you with an abundance of relevant materials. Other topics are more difficult to develop because it is not easy to find concrete and original support for them.

What materials do you need for your speech, and how can you go about assembling them? You obviously need an idea or series of ideas as the framework. This aspect of your speech looms large as you begin to develop an outline. The supporting material is the information that amplifies the idea of your speech. It may consist of examples, facts and figures, circumstantial details, illustrations, analogies, and comparisons. It may also include the testimony of those who have reported on related situations or events and the opinions of authorities. (See Chapter Six, "Developing Details.")

Speech materials, in short, are the complex phenomena of our educational, political, social, physical, scientific, philosophical, and religious worlds, of which we make use to our individual purposes. Your problem is to bring to light, select, sift, and fashion the ideas into a direct talk that holds attention.

Techniques for Securing Materials

How can you delve into this vast storehouse and select materials that are appropriate and interesting? In Chapter Three, the sources of speech topics were discussed. When you have selected your topic, you have automatically determined the main idea or ideas of your speech. Your next task is to find material which will expand or explain these ideas. Five principal techniques or skills will help you in finding this material: thinking, listening, personal experiences and observation, talking (including interviewing), and reading (including note taking).

THINKING

Size up your topic mentally before you begin reading. Students often distrust their own ideas; in the presence of faculty experts, the inexperienced student may minimize the value of his own judgments. Speech improvement, like other forms of education, depends partly on the exercise of independent thinking. Emerson's advice to the Harvard students of 1837 is still pertinent. The speaker, according to Emerson, "distrusts at first the fitness of his frank confessions—his want of knowledge of the persons he addresses—until he finds that he is the complement of his hearers—that they drink his words because he fulfills for them their own nature." [1]

Your individual reflection will be a most important element of your speech. Although your informational speech will contain facts from history, for example, or from science, it will be different from any other speech on the same subject. The difference will lie in your individual approach; your own thinking will go into your handiwork. In order to improve the quality of your individual contribution to the subject, you should adopt "modes of reflection" which will enable you to acquire concepts and ideas.

First, inquire concerning the importance of the subject. Ask yourself such questions as: Why did I select this subject? Is it timely, interesting, worth talking about? Do I know much about it? What do the listeners know about it and to what extent will they follow and accept my ideas? Such inquiries arouse your systematic thinking.

Second, ask yourself, What does this subject mean? Consider the clarification of terms and ideas apart from the specific dictionary definitions. An entire speech is often developed from an explanation of "What is a withholding tax?" or "What is time-and-motion study?" Your questioning of definitions and your search for reliable interpretations again demonstrate your mental alertness.

Third, subdivide the subject matter and classify the subdivisions. Cataloguing ideas and data is by no means easy. It invites questions about economic, social, political, physical, and other relationships. It calls for

[1] Ralph Waldo Emerson, "The American Scholar," *Nature Addresses and Lectures,* Houghton Mifflin Company, Boston, 1903, p. 103.

judgment concerning such groupings. Marshaling ideas into categories will sharpen your awareness of methodical division and will stimulate you to further mental exploration. If, for example, your subject is "Qualifications for appointment to the Federson Wholesale and Retail Distribution Company," you will frame questions that invite information. What will the company expect of a job applicant in terms of school training, previous experience, moral integrity, rules and character, industry, initiative, and other factors? As you complete a list of such questions, you will group them into related units, reshuffle your groupings, and achieve a more detailed view of the subject. Experience in analysis and organization (see Chapter Five for more details) will provide a genuinely thoughtful basis for your speech. Talks that explain how to do something or how something works—the expository and informative type of speech—are developed by this method.

Fourth, view your materials in a time order and special continuity. Your topics here are chronological. You, for example, are giving to a forensics group on your campus a brief oral report of the experiences and records of the teams during the college year. Obviously, in your ten minutes you merely follow through the time sequence. But the chronological or historical method usually calls for more than a recitation of date after date. You ask, "Why is this event important?" "What were the results?" This cause-and-effect method would throw light upon the strength and weakness of your university debating team in its platform clash in November against Oxford University.

Fifth, decide what problem is involved and what probable causes and results accompany it. This approach is somewhat like that of the chronological method, but it is more typical of the "problem-and-solution" procedure of persuasive and discussional speaking. You raise questions concerning the sufficiency of alleged causes and ask yourself what course or courses of action will best deal with the problem.

If, for example, your subject concerns juvenile delinquency, medical aid for the aged, highway traffic control, or public ownership of the local bus line, you will attempt to answer such questions as:

I. Problem
   1. What evidence do you have of the existence of this problem?
   2. What are the apparent workings and results of the present event or situation?
   3. What are apparent causes of the problem?
II. Solution
   1. What solutions are proposed by those who have looked into this problem?
   2. What is your own idea of what might be done?

3. What more specific program or method would you offer for corrective action?

4. How practicable, to you at any rate, do your proposals seem to be?

The subject of logical and productive thinking as opposed to crooked thinking is too complicated to be discussed at length in this chapter. However, later sections of this book include discussions of logical thinking as it is related to speaking.[2] For the present, you will find it beneficial to explore your subject by means of these modes of reflection. And you should apply these methods of inquiry in all phases of your subsequent preparation, observation, listening, discussion, interviewing, and reading. Thinking pervades your preparation from start to finish.

LISTENING

Listening as a source of knowledge is a neglected art. In a world which invention has filled with devices to increase hearing capacity and to multiply the opportunities for transmitting the human voice, we allow much of what we hear to go over our heads, or through our heads, without permanent registry. Why? Partly because in many listening situations we steel ourselves against what we hear. It must be admitted that much of what we hear is useless from every point of view. But our immunity—our indifference or apathy—often causes us to miss what is valuable.

If you use the method of listening described below, you can make listening a valuable means of gathering ideas and facts.

1. *Adopt a receptive attitude toward the speaker.* Be charitable concerning his voice, his repetitions, and if he is visible to you, his awkward physical activity or his fumbling with his notes. Whether the speaker is a candidate for public office, your professor of zoology, or one of your classmates, his ideas deserve respectful consideration, although you may later reject them.

2. *Determine to concentrate.* Ignore extraneous noises. Make mental notes on what you hear, and jot things down on paper if the situation permits. Be sure that you get the main ideas, even if you will not be able, like the young Lincoln, to repeat later almost everything the preacher or politician has said.

3. *Give yourself every possible physical advantage to hear well.* Sit near the center and at the front of the room.

4. *Look directly at the speaker in a face-to-face situation.* Focus on his face and his bodily activity; even if his physical movements are awkward, they will sometimes help to clarify his ideas.

[2] See especially Chapters Five, Sixteen, and Eighteen.

5. *Get the speaker's point of view.* This will necessitate keeping an open mind and controlling your biases and enthusiasms.

6. *Help the speaker to establish a feedback response from you.* As he talks, you will silently carry on your part of the dialogue. You will silently raise questions and agree or disagree as if you were indeed speaking in the gaps created by his pauses. The speaker will respond to your close attention and to feedback cues he gets from you, and thus rapport will be established.

7. *Analyze what the speaker is saying and raise questions in your own mind.* Note the way the speaker begins. Why does he use this method? Does he announce his topic? Does he make his terms clear? What is his division of the subject? Do his ideas follow in logical sequence? Is his speech unified? Are his ideas valid? Do his reasoning and his factual materials carry out his evident purpose of giving you information or of impressing you or of persuading you? Answering such questions as these will stimulate you mentally and enable you to listen creatively and evaluate what you hear. (See also Chapter Fifteen, "Informational and Critical Listening.")

PERSONAL EXPERIENCE AND OBSERVATION

For many subjects, you will rely much on your own experiences and observations. A firsthand report of your job, your travels, your recreational or other experiences, or your direct observations of operating a tractor, or selling a Sunray automobile will usually be more attention getting and authoritative than a report on the experiences of others. Ed Murrow's broadcasts from London during World War II, "This Is London," were an unforgettable series not only because of the dramatic situation under which he talked, but because of the details of personal experiences that made up his reports.[3] So Eric Severeid, broadcasting from Paris on "Western European Attitudes, August, 1958," spoke from his extended personal experiences there.[4] Good student speeches have been given on the following subjects: "My experiences as a plane jumper," "My experience in an igloo," "Why I asked to be depledged," "How to invest—and lose."

CONVERSATION AND DISCUSSION

If attentive and thoughtful listening informs and stimulates you, then you will benefit from conversation, informal discussions, and interviews.

[3] See, for example, Murrow's "Farewell to England," March 10, 1946, in A. Craig Baird (ed.), *Representative American Speeches: 1945–46*, The H. W. Wilson Company, New York, pp. 33ff.

[4] See Baird, *Representative American Speeches: 1958–59*, pp. 53ff.

By means of such opportunities for discussion, Charles James Fox, who has been called the world's greatest debater, equipped himself for the stormy combats in the House of Commons in the late eighteenth century. "Fox gained many of the arguments in his speeches by discussing political questions with friends and colleagues." [5] Franklin D. Roosevelt often revised his speeches after discussion with his colleagues, as did Winston Churchill "after hours of discussion."

You can test your thinking and the effectiveness of your presentation in discussion with others. When a speaker has finished his remarks and calls for questions or statements from the floor, you have a valuable opportunity to participate. Discuss, then, with others what you propose to give in a classroom or other speech.

INTERVIEWING

Another method of accumulating additional information is to become an inquiring reporter. Your subject, for example, is "The problem of student car parking." As a student here for two years, you have used your own car or joined a car pool. Your rooming house has been 2 miles away. You have, at times, bicycled or walked to and from the campus. Traffic congestion has had little relief. Well informed though you are, you will nevertheless find it highly desirable to interview the faculty committee which plans to open new lots for student parking, to issue additional stickers for student cars, and to consider the possible prohibition of cars belonging to first- or second-year undergraduate students. In addition, you will interview the editors of the campus daily and other key student leaders. From such sources you will no doubt gather ideas and illustrations to enrich your talk.

Since the interviewee, especially if he is a faculty member, is busy, you will not approach him until you are well grounded in your subject and prepared for a short interview that goes to the point.

READING

If we have had a New Deal in speech making and listening since the advent of radio and television, we have also had a golden age of miscellaneous reading since the invention of the linotype machine and since elementary education has become universal. Lincoln, in his Indiana and Illinois boyhood and youth, had comparatively few books. He studied the *Kentucky Preceptor*, Murray's *English Reader*, Weems's *Life of George*

---

[5] Loren D. Reid, *The Public Speaking of Charles James Fox*, privately published, Iowa City, Iowa, 1932.

Washington, Indiana Statutes, Scott's *Lessons on Elocution,* and a few great classics, including the Bible. We today have access to the ageless volumes, but in addition we can pick and choose from an endless variety of printed matter. Most of us can visit libraries which contain scores and scores of books that bear directly or indirectly upon the subjects that interest us.

Efficiency in reading. When you have found your material, your problem is to assimilate the knowledge contained in the books and articles listed in your bibliography. What are the most efficient methods of reading? Teachers of speech are especially critical of talks based on undigested ideas. Too often, students echo the language of their sources and demonstrate little comprehension of the ideas, with the result that the content of the speech seems foreign to the speaker. How can you read both efficiently and creatively?

Approach every idea or source with an open mind. At the outset, be objective. Do not pass by an article because it appears to contain ideas that you object to or facts that you question. Check your mental approach to guarantee a degree of fairness.

Read with a purpose. Keep clearly in mind what your proposed topic is and what you already think about it. By remembering the over-all purpose of your talk, you will be able to see in perspective the details you are accumulating.

Read first for general ideas. When you are determining or arranging the general ideas of your subject, read your material to get the chief lines of argument contained in it and the conclusions reached in each book or article. In order to discover general principles quickly, read the introductory and summarizing passages and the topic sentences and note the organization and purpose of each paragraph.

Then read for details. When your purpose is to find specific facts and when you already have in mind the general framework of the subject with which you are dealing, read closely in order to accumulate specific facts and details. As you read, ask yourself how these facts fit into your general outline.

Read for definitions and meanings. Give particular attention to the differences in meanings attached to specific words by different authors; this is especially important if you are reading in a field with which you are unfamiliar. In this way you will quickly become familiar with the concepts in the new field.

Assert your personality as you read. Constantly relate the arguments and ideas you encounter in your reading to your own experience and basic concepts. Check the source in the light of your own attitudes. This is what Emerson described as "creative reading." "When the mind is braced by labor and invention, the pages of whatever book we read become luminous with manifold allusion. Every sentence is doubly significant, and the sense of our author is as broad as the world." [6]

Students who are preparing talks should know how to find their way about libraries. They should know the most important books of reference, should be able to find and make use of the appropriate magazines and newspapers, should have some idea of how to get at the immense fund of information in government documents, should be alert to the possibility of using the many pamphlets issued by nongovernmental organizations, and should know where to find bibliographies, how to make convenient lists of references, how to read efficiently, and how to take notes.

The starting point, as you no doubt know, is to get a chart of the library —with its compartments for browsing, its general reading room, its government sections, its card files, its central desk where you will always get full cooperation and help.

With patience you will presently find yourself at home. Often the book you are interested in will be at the bindery or out on call or even lost. But your patience will help you to find substitutes. In using the card file, you will note the Dewey decimal system, or the Library of Congress system, and you will consult a chart to spot the library location of the different categories. If possible you will saunter through stacks and browse among the books of your subject area.

The general steps described below constitute the procedure you should follow in getting library results for your proposed speech.

Consult standard references. In the reference section of the library are encyclopedias, handbooks, and similar books of general and special information. These reference works are on the open shelves and are not to be taken from the room. They will provide an excellent starting point for research on almost any subject.[7]

1. Encyclopedias. First use the standard encyclopedias. Students sometimes search vainly for elementary material on a specific theme, forgetting that there is ample up-to-date information in readily available encyclopedias, such as the *Encyclopedia Britannica.*

2. Special encyclopedias. Special encyclopedias provide information in various fields. You may obtain helpful information from Seligman's *Encyclopedia of the Social Sciences* (fifteen volumes). For religious or philosophical material, you may refer to the *Catholic Encyclopedia,* the *Encyclopedia of Religion and Ethics,* the *Jewish Encyclopedia,* and the *Encyclopedia of Educational Research.*

---

[6] Ralph Waldo Emerson, "The American Scholar," in A. Craig Baird (ed.), *American Public Addresses: 1740–1952,* McGraw-Hill Book Company, Inc., New York, 1956, p. 218.

[7] For additional suggestions for locating books, magazines, and other printed materials, see p. 62, "Prepare a Bibliography or List of References."

3. Yearbooks. You will also find on the open shelves a collection of year-books which will supply up-to-date information on your subject. *The Americana Annual*, for example, gives a dependable survey of current events and biographical items for each year. Similarly useful are the *Britannica Book of the Year* (since 1917), the *New International Year-book* (since 1907), and the *World Book Encyclopedia Annual* (since 1931). The *World Almanac* (since 1868) also has an astonishingly varied fund of information and an excellent index at the front. The *Statesman's Yearbook* (since 1864) and the *American Yearbook* (1910–1919, and since 1925) are likewise fruitful sources.

4. Directories and biographical dictionaries. You will frequently want to identify the authorities in the field in which you are working. Or perhaps you are planning to interview a member of your college faculty. Often you will find such people listed in *Who's Who in America, Who's Who in American Education, Leaders in American Education, American Men of Science, Who's Who in Engineering*, or the *Directory of American Scholars*. For prominent Americans of other years see *Who Was Who in America* or the excellent general biographical source, the *Dictionary of American Biography* (1928–1937) (twenty volumes), edited by John Allen and Dumas Malone, or the *National Cyclopedia of American Biography* (twenty-six volumes, publication begun in 1892). *Current Biography* gives biographies of people featured in the current press. See also *Webster's Biographical Dictionary*.

5. Special references on current problems. An important source for materials on current problems is the Reference Shelf Series, in which about ten issues appear each year. Included in this series is *Representative American Speeches*, an annual collection.

Consult magazines. Periodical literature on every subject is available in quantities. Familiar to most college students are the semiliterary "opinion" magazines, such as *Time, Newsweek, The Atlantic Monthly, Current Events, Current History, Fortune, Harper's Magazine, The Nation, National Geographic Magazine, New Republic, The Saturday Evening Post* (typical of the "quantity" group), *Yale Review, North American Review*, and *United States News*.

A large crop of magazines, largely publishing condensed material from other publications, grew up in the United States in the 1930s. One of the most widely read of this group is *The Reader's Digest*. Others are *Science Digest, Religious Digest, Current Digest, Magazine Digest, Read*, and *Coronet*.

A magazine that is unique in its function is *Vital Speeches of the Day*, a fortnightly that publishes without comment recent American speeches.

In the field of education the *Speech Teacher, American Scholar, School and Society, English Journal,* and many others will prove helpful. In economics and business, the *American Economic Review, Barron's Weekly, Financial World, Monthly Labor Review, Nation's Business,* to mention a few examples, are in most libraries. In sociology, *Survey Graphic, American Journal of Sociology,* and many others are available. In the fields of government, law, and current history there are such magazines as the *American Political Science Review, Annals of the American Academy of Political and Social Science, Current History, Current Events,* and *Foreign Affairs.*

Consult newspapers. Although a considerable number of mediocre newspapers exist in America, there are many papers of high merit and good reputation. Some of these you will consult both for recent news and for background information, which is often contained in feature articles. The *New York Times,* for example, contains a great deal of information, as its indexes show. Other important papers are *Christian Science Monitor, New York Herald Tribune, Washington* (D.C.) *Star, St. Louis Post-Dispatch, Louisville Courier-Journal, Des Moines Register, New Orleans Picayune, Minneapolis Star, Omaha Bee, Denver Post, San Francisco Chronicle,* and *Los Angeles Times.*

Consult government documents. Either through your library or, in some cases, by direct correspondence with the Superintendent of Documents in Washington, you can obtain various kinds of government reports and speeches providing accurate and authoritative materials. For example, the *Statistical Abstract of the United States,* published annually by the U.S. Bureau of Foreign and Domestic Commerce, is a "summary of authoritative statistics showing trends in trade and industry, as well as social progress." It presents figures on area, population, education, finances, wages, and a wide range of other subjects. *The Commerce Yearbook* gives detailed information about business conditions in the United States. *Commerce Reports* and the *Monthly Labor Review* are useful monthly surveys. There are many kinds of congressional documents, including reports of congressional committee hearings, which are useful for many political and current-affairs subjects. You will need the help of your librarian in finding such reports in your library or in ordering them.

The most important government document for speech students is without question the *Congressional Record,* which presents the proceedings of the House and Senate. It is issued daily, with fortnightly indexes.

Consult private organizations. More than twenty-five thousand organizations in the United States publish proceedings, reports, journals, yearbooks, bulletins, monographs, and pamphlets of great value to students. Much of this material can be secured free or at a nominal cost by writing to the organization that publishes it. Much of it can be found in libraries.

(See the latest issue of the *World Almanac* for the addresses of several hundred "Associations and Societies in the United States.") Typical of these organizations are the following:

American Federation of Labor and Congress of Industrial Organizations, Washington, D.C.

American Farm Bureau Federation, Chicago 2, Illinois

American Medical Association, Chicago, Illinois

National Association of Manufacturers, New York, New York

Obtain copies of radio and television broadcasts. Many radio talks are mimeographed and can be obtained upon request. Also, many panel discussions over radio and television—those of "America's Forum of the Air" and the "Northwestern Reviewing Stand," for example—are printed and may be obtained at a nominal cost. Your own tape or wire recordings of radio and television talks can be helpful.

Prepare a Bibliography or List of References

If you intend to spend several hours reading in preparation for a speech of ten or twelve minutes, make use of bibliographical sources, including indexes, in order to avoid hours of partially wasteful rambling through stray books and articles. Using these sources, prepare a working list of references of your own. Your list will not be an elaborate bibliography; but it should be selective, accurately recorded, and thorough within the limits of your subject. Your list should include (1) important bibliographies of the subject, (2) books, (3) magazines, (4) pamphlets and reports, and (5) newspapers.

1. *Start with bibliographies.* Ask your reference librarian for the cumulative *Bibliographic Index,* each cumulative yearly edition of which includes more than four thousand bibliographies on numerous subjects. One or more of the items on your list should be the bibliography or bibliographies already available. Your own list will be more recent and better adapted to your immediate topic.

2. *Use the Cumulative Book Index (successor to the United States Catalog),* which contains a record of almost every book published in the United States. A quick survey of recent numbers will at once suggest pertinent titles. The *Book Review Digest,* with its condensed review of recent books, also offers a convenient source of worthwhile book publications.

3. *Consult the library card files for additional book sources.*

4. *Refer to periodicals.* The special indexes will help you. The *Readers' Guide to Periodical Literature* is well known (or should be) to

every college student. Refer also to special indexes, such as *Agricultural Index, Art Index, Education Index, Index to Legal Periodicals, Index Medicus*, and *Public Affairs Information Service*. These indexes are usually in the appropriate departmental library rather than in the general reference room. Also of value to college students is the *Vertical File Service*, an index of pamphlets and other ephemeral material.

5. *Consult government documents*. Examine the indexes to the *Congressional Record* and perhaps the *Catalogue of Public Documents*. You will probably need the help of the librarian in locating these indexes.

6. *List a few references from recent newspapers.* (*The New York Times Index* will be of help.)

7. *List your bibliographic references systematically.* Use cards or slips of paper so that you can sort your items systematically, placing only one item on each card or slip. Classify the list into sections, such as (*a*) books, (*b*) magazines, (*c*) newspapers, and (*d*) pamphlets. For books and pamphlets, include the author's last name, his first name or initials, the exact title of the book, the volume number or edition number if there has been more than one, the name of the publisher, and the place and date of publication. For example:

Mott, Frank Luther, *A History of American Magazines, 1885–1905*, vol. IV, Harvard University Press, Cambridge, Mass., 1957.

For periodicals and newspapers, list (usually in this order) the author's name, the title of the article, the title of the periodical, the volume and pages, the date:

Brown, Catherine Drinker, "The Lawyers Talk History," *Atlantic Monthly*, 207:31–34, May, 1961.

Note the following sample of bibliographical items on the subject, "Have the Supreme Court decisions on segregation been justified?"

Byrnes, James F., "The South Respects the Written Constitution," *Vital Speeches of the Day*, 23:331–335, March 15, 1957.
Lewis, Anthony, "Integration: Role of the Courts," *The New York Times*, p. E7, June 12, 1960.
Rankin, J. Lee, "An Independent Supreme Court," *Vital Speeches of the Day*, 25:389–392, April 15, 1959.
Salomon, Leon I. (ed.), *The Supreme Court*, The H. W. Wilson Company, New York, 1961.
United States Reports, 347 U.S. 483 (1954), Superintendent of Documents, Washington 25, D.C., 1954.
U.S. Supreme Court decision: *Brown vs. Board of Education of Topeka*, Superintendent of Documents, Washington 25, D.C., 1954.

Taking Notes

Your final step in collecting ideas and details for your speech is to take notes on what you read. Students are often tempted to eschew the whole mechanical process of note taking as a bore and a waste of time; others are ultraconscientious copyists who put down almost everything. Reliance on your memory is unwise if you wish to accumulate and classify many details. Indiscriminate reproduction is also unfortunate because it hinders your grasp of general principles. A sensible procedure is somewhat as follows:

1. Use cards or papers of a uniform size. Notebooks are inconvenient if you intend to shuffle the items into any order.

2. Aim to get the gist of an idea or an article.

3. Place one fact on a card.

4. Tag each card at the top with the topic or division under which the statement or fact falls.

5. Cite at the bottom of the card the exact source. Be accurate and complete in the citation. You will later appreciate your meticulousness here.

6. Quote accurately, but avoid long quotations.

Specimen Note Card

```
                                                    F. D. Roosevelt's
                                                    Speech Training
 F.D.R.'s
    Speech Courses at Harvard

    In his junior year at Harvard "Roosevelt spent two semesters with
 George Pierce Baker . . . in his course entitled, 'Forms of Public Ad-
 dress.'"

 Comperthwaite, LeRoy, "Franklin D. Roosevelt at Harvard," Quarterly
 Journal of Speech, 38:39, Feb., 1952.
```

7. In the main, note facts rather than general opinions.

8. Establish a general scheme for your reading and for the classification of your notes. Begin with a plan which you can modify later.

9. Write legibly.

The purpose of this chapter is to provide you with guides to finding suitable materials for your talks. Only when you have something of significance to tell your audiences can you justly lay claim to their time and attention. Your preparation for purposeful and worthwhile speech making will include reflective thinking, reading, and discussion of your topic.

Projects and Problems

PROJECT 1

The purpose of this project is to test your critical thinking. Select a familiar subject such as "Shall I elect History 113 next year?" Do no reading. Rely on individual reflection. Be prepared to report orally on your subject.

Draw up a brief series of statements (not more than two pages) that answer in turn the following questions: (*a*) What is my problem in selecting the proposed course next year? (*b*) What are the causes of my perplexity or difficulty? (*c*) What other interesting courses are open to me next year? (*d*) Which one of these courses is, on the whole, preferable? What are its advantages over the others? (*e*) What shall I do to act on the conclusion at which I have arrived?

You may substitute any other problem-and-solution subject for the one suggested above.

PROJECT 2

At your next classroom lecture, take notes and concentrate closely on the speaker, according to the suggestions in this chapter. Be prepared to repeat as accurately as you can in a four-minute talk the essentials of that lecture. (You may substitute any public lecture given on the campus.)

PROJECT 3

Interview a faculty member on a special topic chosen by you. Make a five-minute classroom talk in which you give the essence of that interview. Follow the suggestions for interviewing given in this chapter.

PROJECT 4

Read an entire book or an extended article in a recent magazine. Present to the class a brief summary and interpretation of the book or article. In your reading, follow closely the suggestions in this chapter.

PROJECT 5

Prepare a list of references in cooperation with three of your colleagues. Select a controversial subject that calls for recent references. Include at least one reference from a printed bibliography, at least five from recent books, at least five from representative magazines, at least two or three from a representative daily newspaper, at least five from documents. The entire list should comprise some twenty or thirty references and should be prepared according to the suggestions in this chapter. Submit your list to your instructor for criticism and then have it mimeographed for use by the entire class.

PROJECT 6

Select a subject which requires library reading but which is limited in scope. Get your instructor's approval of your topic. You may decide to use the subject of the bibliography you prepared for project 5 above. Take at least twenty systematic notes from several sources, according to the suggestions in this chapter. Be prepared to submit your notes for criticism and inspection by your instructor and by two or three of your classmates appointed for this purpose.

Retain your references and notes; they may be supplemented and used later in your more extended talks.

References

Adler, Mortimer: *How to Read a Book,* Simon and Schuster, Inc., New York, 1940.

Aldrich, Ella V.: *Using Books and Libraries,* rev. ed., Prentice-Hall, Inc., Englewood Cliffs, N.J., 1946.

Barzun, Jacques, and Henry Graffe: *The Modern Researcher,* Harcourt, Brace & World, Inc., New York, 1957, chap. 1.

Brigance, W. Norwood: *Speech,* Appleton-Century-Crofts, Inc., New York, 1952, chap. 10.

Bryant, Donald C., and Karl R. Wallace: *The Fundamentals of Public Speaking,* 3d ed., Appleton-Century-Crofts, Inc., New York, 1960, chap. 6.

McBurney, James H., and Ernest J. Wrage: *The Art of Good Speech,* Prentice-Hall, Inc., Englewood Cliffs, N.J., 1953, chap. 7.

Monroe, Alan H.: *Principles and Types of Speech,* 4th ed., Scott, Foresman and Company, Chicago, 1955, chap. 11.

Nichols, Ralph G., and Thomas R. Lewis: *Listening and Speaking,* William C. Brown, Dubuque, Iowa, 1954, chaps. 1 and 3.

―――― and Leonard A. Stevens: *Are You Listening?* McGraw-Hill Book Company, Inc., New York, 1957.

Reid, Loren D.: *First Principles of Public Speaking,* Artcraft Press, Columbia, Mo., 1960, chap. 3.

FIVE

Organization

and Outlining

Why not simply get all your ideas together on a piece of paper and deliver them to your audience as the spirit moves you? There is a precise answer. Organization of your ideas will help both the audience and you. Systematic structure will give sense, selection, unity, order, and emphasis to your speech.

Consider for a moment what we mean by chaos. It is a lack of order, system, arrangement. The degree to which material is clearly organized or to which disorganized bits are made to fall into place in a system is largely a measure of how much sense can be made out of a message. Sometimes the listener must do this organizing himself, but if the speaker can arrange his materials so that a pattern and sequence are easily grasped by the listener he is more apt to understand, to accept, and to be persuaded to act.

Listeners like unity of idea and mood; they take pleasure in symmetry, for it makes for economy of attention and ease of comprehension. Ideas that are arranged in an orderly sequence carry the listener along with a minimum of distraction. Furthermore, the prominence attached to certain topics and subtopics by means of the time and the status the speaker gives them will help the listener to distinguish the more important ideas of a speech from the less important.

In addition to economy of the audience's attention, a well-established structure will give order to your own thinking as you prepare and deliver your speech. Your very effort to assemble and relate your items will challenge your thinking. Furthermore, a convenient framework for your talk will not only give you a key for easy memorization of the ideas but will also permit greater fluency in speaking.[1]

As we indicated in Chapter Three, your speech, like your written composition, will be more successful if it has a clear-cut purpose. To summarize, the preliminary steps you must take before you are ready to organize the body of your speech are as follows: (1) select and limit your subject; (2) analyze the needs and interests of your audience and the speaking situation; (3) define your purpose; and (4) formulate a topic sentence that incorporates that purpose.

Organization: Introduction, Development, and Conclusion

If you keep your topic sentence and your purpose with regard to your audience clearly before you, you will have little difficulty in organizing your ideas into the main structural divisions of introduction, body or development, and conclusion. This threefold distinction of parts parallels the steps you as a speaker will take to carry your ideas to the group; then you will provide an elaboration of your ideas; finally, you will clinch the speech with a summary or appeal. The purpose of the introduction is to evoke the good will of the audience and to create interest in your subject. The marshaling of the ideas to be imparted constitutes the main body. The final effort to consolidate these impressions makes up the conclusion. These suggestions apply either to a one-point speech or to a longer one.

Are these divisions necessary? Usually they are. Some good speeches have no formal introduction. You will note, however, that the first few sentences of most printed speeches almost invariably constitute an introduction. In some examples a conclusion may seem "tacked on," but ordinarily a final sentence or paragraph by way of summary helps to complete the speaking performance. An abrupt stop may give the impression of a story without an end or of a radio suddenly turned off. It is wise to observe these three general structural features.

If you adhere to these standard divisions of the speech, how much further should you go in dividing and subdividing? It is hard to say. Flexibility of structure is the best rule. Let your decisions depend upon the material, the purpose, and the time limits of each specific speech. In a three- to five-minute classroom speech, for example, you can (1) state

---

[1] See the end of this chapter for examples of simple outlines.

your purpose in a topic sentence, (2) present and illustrate your ideas, and (3) summarize in perhaps one sentence. Thus your speech contains a clearly distinguishable introduction, main body or development, and conclusion. In a longer expository speech you can give more time to integrating these three main divisions.

An argumentative speech will usually require a more formal introduction presenting (1) the importance of the problem, (2) a brief history or background of the subject, (3) an explanation of the terms used, and (4) a statement of issues in the form of questions. The main argument then consists of the development of one or more main points, and the conclusion summarizes and calls for audience endorsement of the speaker's position.[2]

Organization of the Introduction

The length, content, and general effect of your introduction will depend upon your specific speaking aims and the time allotted to you. What do you wish to accomplish? In most cases you hope for at least three results: (1) to establish good will between you and your audience; (2) to give the background of your subject; and (3) to make clear your theme and your purpose.

ENLIST ATTENTION AND GOOD WILL

Your initial job is to enlist the attention and good will of your listeners, whether they are facing you or whether they are radio listeners. At the outset they may be curious about you and your topic; they may be indifferent; or they may be prejudiced against your subject or against you because you are a Scotsman, or a Methodist, or a girl, or a mere youth. Perhaps ten other speakers have preceded you. Perhaps the room is hot or the street traffic is noisy. In any case, you must follow Cicero's advice to the young men of Rome: "Render auditors well disposed, attentive, teachable." [3] Cicero might well give the same advice to you.

1. *You may begin with a personal reference.* President John F. Kennedy, in his State of the Union address to Congress on January 30, 1961, began as follows:

Mr. Vice President, Members of Congress, it is a pleasure to return from whence I came. You are among my oldest friends in Washington and this House is my oldest home.

[2] For more detailed suggestions for the organization of the principal types of speeches, see Chapters Sixteen through Twenty.

[3] Cicero, *De Oratore*, II, chap. 29.

It was here, more than fourteen years ago, that I first took the oath of Federal office. It was here, for fourteen years, that I gained both knowledge and inspiration from members of both parties in both houses—from your wise and generous leaders—and from the pronouncements which I can vividly recall, sitting where you now sit—including the programs of two great Presidents, the undimmed eloquence of Churchill, the soaring idealism of Nehru, the steadfast words of General de Gaulle. To speak from this same historic rostrum is a sobering experience. To be back among so many friends is a happy one I am confident that that friendship will continue.

2. *You may begin with direct narrative.* President Franklin D. Roosevelt, in his address to Congress, December 8, 1941, asking for a declaration of war against Japan, immediately cited the facts:[4]

Yesterday, December 7, 1941,—a date which will live in infamy—the United States was suddenly and deliberately attacked by naval and air forces of the Empire of Japan.

3. *You may begin with a quotation.* Robert Blakely, then vice president of the Fund for Adult Education of the Ford Foundation, opened his address on "Threat to Books" before the American Library Association in New York City on July 4, 1952, in this way:[5]

By permission, my assignment is to speak on "Threat to Books." This, on the Fourth of July, in the dark year of 1952; before the American Library Association; around the corner from where Peter Zenger wrought and fought—seems too good to be true. I invoke the muses to make me more nearly worthy of the occasion—Pericles and Euripides, Milton, and Locke and Mill.

First, I ask, "What is a book?" Milton replies—"A good book is the precious lifeblood of a master spirit, embalmed and treasured up on purpose to a life beyond life."

4. *You may use humor or pleasantries.* Note the directness blended with brief anecdote that President Robert F. Goheen of Princeton University used in opening his address to the freshmen on September 18, 1960.[6]

Gentlemen of the Freshman Class, this service of worship is traditional for the beginning of the academic year at Princeton. It affirms the unity of the University and the high aspiration of mind and spirit which contribute its essential life and endeavor down through the years.

The custom of having the President speak at these Exercises calls to mind the story of the college president who, in a conversation with a young alumnus,

[4] A. Craig Baird (ed.), *American Public Addresses: 1740–1952*, McGraw-Hill Book Company, Inc., New York, 1956, p. 265.

[5] J. R. Kidd (ed.), *Adult Education in a Free Society: Speeches by Robert J. Blakely*, Guardian Bird Publications, Toronto, Canada, 1958, p. 105.

[6] *Vital Speeches of the Day*, 27:6, 1960, by permission.

said: "By the way, did you ever hear me preach?" "Frankly, sir," the young man replied unflinchingly (and borrowing from Charles Lamb), "I never heard you do anything else."

I shall continue to try to avoid that reputation, but I am especially glad to have the opportunity to talk seriously to you as you begin your university careers.

5. *You may begin by referring to the importance of the occasion and the immediate interest of the subject.* Adlai Stevenson, before the Security Council of the United Nations, in New York City, February 15, 1961, began by emphasizing that this was the first occasion for the United States under the new Kennedy administration (and under Ambassador Stevenson) to address the Council. When he was speaking, the United Nations was under severe attack by Nikita Khrushchev and the Communist nations.

President Deane W. Malotte of Cornell University, addressing the Commonwealth Club of California in San Francisco on March 3, 1961, referred to the critical situation in the Latin American countries and the threat of spreading communism under Cuba's Castro. The speaker then developed the problem in detail.

Many speeches on campus issues and situations begin by stressing "the importance of this subject." The occasion may be that of greeting new students, wishing farewell to fellow students, launching a student political campaign, honoring students or faculty members, or appealing for support for a student daily.

6. *You may begin by showing your appreciation of the occasion and of the sponsoring body under whose auspices you speak.* You may thus, at the start of your talk, thank the members of the Lion's Club for their courtesy to you, but do so without too many trite phrases. Your speech, perhaps, will be to the Newman or Canterbury Club, the athletic council, the Young Republicans or Young Democrats, a farmer's cooperative, the Thursday Evening Discussion Club, the local Steel Worker's Committee, or the Civic Music Association.

These suggestions for opening a talk may give you the false impression that introductions must be elaborate and extended, whereas the tendency of the times is to get at once to the point. A word or two about yourself or a reference to your audience will be sufficient. Even these may be omitted, depending upon the time limits and the speaking situation.

Whatever your technique, you will, it is hoped, quickly get on a common footing with the listeners, warm up to them, and feel them do so to you. The six devices suggested above (and various others might be noted) point the way toward fitting your material to your purpose regarding your immediate audience.

EXPLAIN YOUR SUBJECT

Whether or not your introductions are as elaborate as those quoted above, they should include the explanations and facts that may be needed for the unfolding of your subject. You may show the immediate importance of your subject, and you may explain its meaning and something of its background. Often, for example, you will explain a term important to your subject. If your talk is on "The need to expand social security," you will define social security. If it is about a radio transmitter system or the ballistics of military rifles or the handling of infantry mortars or the effects of automation, you will naturally begin with a preliminary explanation of radio transmitters or ballistics or infantry mortars, or automation. If you are making a short talk on what to do about a current problem, you will need to give a brief background as a starting point for the development of your ideas.

STATE YOUR PURPOSE

The third function and third division of the introduction is a statement of your controlling purpose and an enumeration of the points you will prove. Although this is often the last phase of the introduction, it may be placed in the opening sentence. One student speaker began a five-minute talk on the purpose and function of the liberal arts college with the statement: "I wish to talk to you about lend-lease education." He then explained this somewhat enigmatic reference as an international exchange of students and teachers at institutions of higher liberal education. Often the purpose sentence and chief points of development are phrased as questions. President Virgil Hancher of the State University of Iowa opened his address to the graduating class on June 9, 1961, with questions that furnished the chief topics for full treatment. Thus:[7]

Within the hour you have become graduates and alumni of the University of Iowa.

Does it mean anything to you to be a graduate of this university? Is this just another university—one of a hundred or more throughout this broad land of ours? Or is it one that possesses characteristics which have made it unusual, if not unique? I raise this question because from time to time an occasional student, or even an occasional faculty member, fails to discover the nature and quality of the institution.

A speech of some six minutes was introduced as follows:

Ladies and Gentlemen:

On April 17, 18, and 19, 1961, an invading army of some 1,300 anti-Castro Cuban exiles, recruited in the United States was crushed, killed, or captured

[7] Iowa City *Press Citizen*, June 9, 1961.

at the landing region, Bay of Pigs, on Cuba's south coast. Since the Central Intelligence Agency, the Pentagon, and other American government units had directly or covertly supported this invasion, it was a tragedy not only for the exiles but also for the United States. The apparently strong consolidation of the Castro government and its further identification with Communist Russia and Red China have raised the problem of what should be our policy toward Cuba.

EXPLANATION AND DEFINITIONS

Fidel Castro, after two years of rebellion against the Batista government, emerged victorious in 1959. He began taking over and expropriating all Cuban private lands and property. He established the communistic pattern of control and received strong military, political, and economic support from Soviet Russia's Khrushchev and China's Mao Tse-tung.

Division of the subject. The question is, what attitude shall Americans take and what program, if any, shall we follow in grappling with this question? More specifically, is Cuba now a Communist state? If so, to what extent is that nation a military and economic and political threat to the United States and to Latin America? Should the United States and the other American states break off diplomatic relations with Cuba? Should the United States act unilaterally if the other American states refuse to act? Should this nation invade Cuba militarily to end the Communist threat?

Purpose sentence. I propose to show that the Cuban government represents a direct threat to this nation; that unless that country is checked, the threat will increase; and that a concert of American states should establish an economic blockade of that island.

Obviously, the points outlined above called for a much longer speech than was proposed.

Organization of the Body

How shall you develop your speech proper? You may do it in one of several ways or in some combination of these ways. In organizing the body of your speech, you must deal with the problems of selecting your materials, dividing them, and developing the divisions and subdivisions.

METHODS OF DEVELOPMENT

The most common methods of development include (1) chronological, (2) topographical, (3) definitional, (4) classificational, (5) logical, (6) problem solution, (7) indirect or psychological, and (8) journalistic. Adopting any one of these modes or others that fit your material or purposes, you will be able to ascertain the points to be developed in detail and the divisions into which the body of the speech falls.

A short talk would preferably use but one of these methods. A longer speech would obviously combine several. Let us illustrate each of these modes of amplification.

1. *Chronological method* (*time order*). You simply follow the calendar here. The divisions will be those of history or of biography. For example, the body of a speech on "Franklin D. Roosevelt's speech training" can be outlined as follows:

I. Roosevelt's early education was informal. He made frequent trips to England and Europe under private tutors before 1897.

II. He attended Groton preparatory school from 1897 to 1900, enrolling in a classical curriculum and taking systematic training in a debating society.

III. He attended Harvard University from 1900 to 1904 and received his A.B. degree, with chief studies in history, government, economics, and English under Professors Hart, Channing, Kittredge, Copeland, Royce, and in public address under George Pierce Baker. He spoke also in the Political Club and with Presidents of the *Harvard Crimson.*

IV. He was enrolled in the Columbia Law School, 1904–1907.

V. He was admitted to the bar and practiced law, New York, 1907–1910.

VI. He spoke often as New York State Senator, 1911–1913.

The time-sequence treatment is easy to understand and follow. Even when the main points of a talk classify the topics according to some other method, the subdivisions often follow the chronological order.

2. *Topographical or space-order method.* Some material can be arranged according to space relations—from the near to the remote; from East to West (an airplane flight from New York to Los Angeles with landings at Washington, D.C., and Fort Worth, Texas); from bottom to top (a tour of Radio City); or a trip in a space capsule. For example:

Purpose sentence: Navy Comdr. Alan B. Shepard, Jr., was the first American astronaut to demonstrate a successful flight into outer space.

I. On May 5, taking off from Cape Canaveral, propelled by the Redstone rocket booster, in his 2,300-pound Mercury capsule, Shepard traveled at a speed of 4,500 miles per hour to an altitude of 115 miles.

II. He traveled down range more than 300 miles and reentered the earth's atmosphere without a break after fifteen minutes.

III. After this flight, during which he experienced a state of weightlessness, a sense of separation from the earth and the shock of reentering the earth's atmosphere, Shepard was recovered by a helicopter and released on shipboard.

3. *Definitional method.* When the central idea of a talk is represented by a term, the definitional method is appropriate. This method consists of answering the central question of the subject: What is a university? American humor? Communism? Jazz? Religion? Scientific method? High fidelity? Blue Cross? Photoelectric cell? Moonlighting? Featherbedding? Definitions are often necessary in the introduction; they are also often the chief supporting method in the main body. Definitions may be logical or in some other form. If they are logical they will state the general class into which the subject for interpretation falls and then point out the differences between this member and others of the same class. A student speaker, in discussing the problem of arbitration in basic industries, concentrated on an explanation of "basic industries" and a proper concept of the word "arbitration." Arbitration, he explained, is "the investigation and determination of a matter or matters of difference between contending parties, by one or more unofficial persons, chosen by the parties and called arbitrators or referees."

"Arbitration," this speaker explained, "was contrasted with *collective bargaining*—in which negotiation is between the unionists and management for the settlement of their working conditions, wages, and related problems; and with *mediation,* in which situation a neutral representative reports to each group the position of the other and as a result the controversies are dealt with; and with *conciliation,* in which the neutral agent directly attempts to reconcile the differences."

Development by definition may include citing examples of the term. Thus "basic American industries" were those "the paralysis of which would cause the economic unit to quit functioning, the function of which is essential to the national economy and for which there is no substitute." Basic industries would be (a) transportation, (b) sources of fuel and power, (c) steel, (d) iron, (e) alloys, (f) light metals, (g) electronics.

A significant form of definition in modern scientific thinking is called an "operational definition." This is a useful form in much informative speaking. Suppose you are trying to explain "objectivity," "attitude measurement," or "the significance of a statistical difference between two sets of examinations or ratings." You might well define these terms operationally. Objectivity is determined by the independent verification of capable, interested, and experienced persons working independently. An examination is said to be objective when two people following the same set of operations arrive at the same score. Attitude measurement is undertaken by following a set of principles about the selection and evaluation of test items which when properly evaluated form an attitude scale. You determine the significance of a difference between two statistical measures by applying an appropriate formula for the type of data involved and carrying out the computation which will tell you of the probabilities that the difference that you have could have occurred by chance. Of course in your speech you will amplify these parts or steps in the operation.

To make your definition clear-cut and intelligible to your listeners, you will interpret the term in its context. Thus you will relate your term to the usage you have in mind. The dictionary, for example, lists at least fifteen different meanings of "form." Your definitions should be authoritative. The description above of arbitration came from Bouvier's *Law Dictionary* (Vernon Law Book Company, Kansas City, Missouri).

4. *Classification or topical method.* Organization by classification offers numerous possible combinations of material. You are doubtless aware of the thoroughness with which authorities in the fields of zoology, botany, and other sciences classify their data. A similar method of identifying kindred forms and activities can be applied in all other areas of human knowledge. For example, monopolies can be classified as social or natural; public or private; absolute or partial; local or national.

Ideas and aspects of problems may be classified as social, political, educational, physical, economic, military, religious, logical, or philosophical. Many other categories, such as literary, aesthetic, and linguistic, will occur to you. Students interested in a contemporary problem will usually find it convenient to classify representative phases of the subject as economic, social, or political. These divisions, of course, may be concretely illustrated and developed as follows:

Subject: Shall my state adopt a withholding system for the collection of state income taxes?

Purpose sentence: I propose to persuade this audience to support a withholding tax system in our state.

Main points:

I. Such a program would add to the state's revenue (25 per cent of those liable to pay state income taxes do not now pay).
II. The policy would distribute the tax burden more equitably among all citizens liable for income tax payments.

Subject: Drury's *Advise and Consent.*

Purpose sentence: Drury's *Advise and Consent,* high among the best sellers for many months, well deserves to have permanent rank as an outstanding novel.

Main points:

I. Its plot is well handled.
II. Its characters are authentic.
III. Its dialogue is genuine.
IV. It reflects the contemporary Washington, D.C., scene.

Subject: My role as a teacher.
Purpose sentence: My plan is to teach communication skills in a college.

Main points:

I. Communication skills is an important course in the curriculum.
II. I am well prepared to teach such a course.
III. The salary will be satisfactory.
IV. This career will give me the satisfaction of helping learners professionally, socially, and culturally.

5. *Logical (cause-and-effect) method.* To develop a subject by this method, present the causes and results of an event, situation, or condition. Ask yourself what prior factors or events explain or partly explain a given result and what factors or events follow as a consequence of a given event, situation, or condition. These causes or results, in turn, may be classified as economic, political, or otherwise.

Be sure that a cause-effect relationship really exists. Organizing material according to causation or logic is exceedingly difficult, but the method is used in all argumentative, discussional, or persuasive speeches. At times you will be tempted to assume that an event which precedes another event is therefore causally connected to it. Your problem in making such divisions of your materials is to be sure that causal connections do exist and that they have an important or determining effect on the alleged results.

Julian H. Levi, speaking to the Citizen's League of Minneapolis, Minnesota, on November 18, 1959, on "The Crisis of Our Cities," [8] explained that in the mid-century, American cities were in grave trouble. He cited two important causes:

I. The urbanization of our society as a whole is ever increasing. The speaker cited as a major cause of this urbanization the "mechanism of our farms and the consequent increase in the size of the agricultural unit."
II. With large segments of the population moving from our central cities to the satellite suburbs, the physical size of the urban areas is ever increasing.

A speaker in late 1961 argued that the cold war between the Soviets and the West would increase in intensity. His main reasons were listed:

I. The growing competition by the Communists would lead to their underselling the "free" nations in oil, steel, textiles, and other competitive materials.

[8] *Vital Speeches of the Day,* 27:254–256, 1961.

II. China's early possession of atomic production and weapons would increase the military threat.

III. The Communist propaganda threat would be conducted with increased vigor and effectiveness in Latin America, the Middle East, and the Orient.

IV. The methods of infiltration into the "have not" nations would be stepped up.

Richard Cardinal Cushing, speaking at Boston College on October 13, 1960, on "Recognition of Red China," gave several reasons why our recognition of China would be disastrous to the United States and the free nations.[9] We interpret these reasons as follows:

I. Such recognition would "betray American principles and practices."

II. Such recognition would result in "trade benefits to the Red government and not to the free world generally."

III. Such recognition would "deprive us of the means to pursue peace without risk of war." (Systematic exploitation of world tensions is the very essence of the Communist technique.)

IV. Our recognition of Red China would "imply our capitulation, surrender."

V. Recognition would strengthen the alliance between Russia and Red China.

VI. Recognition of Red China would mean the liquidation of free China and the acceptance of Red China by the United Nations. (Red China is not qualified for membership under the terms of the Charter of the United Nations in the view of many people of the free world.)

6. *Problem-solution method.* Problem solving as a method of developing speeches is similar to the problem solving that is part of your daily experience. In your personal life you analyze difficulties, try a variety of solutions, and decide upon the best solution. Problem solving as a way of developing speeches is a more scientific application of the same method. It involves examination and description of a problem; the testing of hypotheses concerning the solution; and the discovery of the solution that fits best with the facts and logic of the situation.

Typically, in discussion speeches, which are customarily developed by this method, such questions as the following are asked and answered:

I. Is the controversial situation (the "felt difficulty") sufficiently disturbing to warrant attempts at a solution?

II. Will the solution I advocate remove the difficulty?

III. Is my solution preferable to other remedies?

IV. Is my solution practicable?

[9] *Vital Speeches of the Day,* 27:242–245, 1961.

This method of development is used for the typical debate case for a proposition of policy, as we shall see in our study of argumentative speaking in Chapter Seventeen. For such a proposition an affirmative debater (or team) would show (*a*) the need for the proposal (identical with I above); (*b*) the inadequacy of other solutions (identical with III above); (*c*) the advantages of this proposal (identical with II above); (*d*) the practicability of this solution (identical with IV above).

The problem-solution method of development is identical with the "motivated-sequence" formula so well advocated by Alan Monroe.[10] It is also the formula customarily used in sales talks. This sequence pattern embodies the (*a*) attention step (see "Organization of the Introduction," above, page 69); (*b*) the need step (identical with I above); (*c*) and (*d*) the satisfaction step and the visualization step (identical with II and III above); and (*e*) the action step (identical with IV above).

You should resort to this structural plan when you prepare talks about controversial matters, whether they are of little concern to the world at large (e.g., "Shall our football coach be replaced?") or whether they are of vast importance (e.g., "Shall we step up the production of hydrogen bombs at the expense of other types of defense weapons?").

7. *An indirect or psychological method.* This method of organization is often used in dealing with a problem toward which the attitude of the audience is unknown or is hostile. When you speak in such situations you spend much of the first part of your speech dealing with the relevant facts and opinions which are noncontroversial or to which your audience can readily give assent. You will want to test the climate and the temper of your listeners so that you may present your thesis in a manner most apt to win their support. The "yes-but" technique has often provided an entering wedge for argument which would be quickly rejected from a speaker who had not demonstrated such good judgment.

Suppose we want to establish the point that the United States should continue to give strong support to the establishment of independent African nations. We must surely admit that the colonial powers exploited and subjugated African natives. African nationals in many cases were not adequately prepared to exercise the responsibilities of sovereign states. But humane considerations and even our own ultimate national security suggest that we support these people even though they have not always followed our own concepts of law and order.

8. *The journalistic pattern.* This method of organizing is quite the opposite of the indirect method. In true journalistic style the headline or your very first remarks will state the gist of your idea. Each main point will be treated briefly in the order of importance. Then the details of each

[10] See Alan H. Monroe, *Principles and Types of Speech*, 4th ed., Scott, Foresman and Company, Chicago, 1955, chap. 16.

main point will be developed as much as your time permits. If you are presenting a radio or television address and a listener tunes out at any time he still will have heard the central idea you want to make. If he tunes in late, he will not have completely missed any aspect of your subject.

SOME PRINCIPLES OF ORGANIZATION

After you have developed the body of your speech according to one of the methods just described, follow these general instructions:

1. *See that the materials are unified.* Ask yourself what two or three main points or aspects of your topic should be stressed in view of your limited time and the interests of your audience.

Lack of unity or general discursiveness sometimes occurs when your talk attempts to explain a process. For example you may explain how to direct a play with details of choosing the play itself, the cast, the patterns of rehearsals, but then you may move into a criticism of contemporary plays or an appeal for the community playhouse.

To ensure unity in the body of your talk, keep your purpose uppermost by featuring and emphasizing the statements that present your division of the subject. In addition, insert enough repetitive, transitional, summarizing, and introductory (topic) phrases and sentences to make the listener experience your talk as a unit rather than as a series of separable items.

2. *Arrange your points in the most appropriate order.* Arrange the divisions of your subject with an eye to audience acceptance as well as to logical sequence. Refer again to the plans of analysis outlined in Chapter Three. See that your method of organization is followed consistently except when departing from it can increase audience acceptance.

3. *Give proper position and space to the important points.* Since one of your purposes is to impress your audience, be sure that you give adequate time to your important points, and be sure that they are advantageously placed (as explained in the preceding section).

Organization of the Conclusion

The conclusion, like the beginning, may have a function other than that of adding to the listener's knowledge of the topic. Usually conclusions include such devices as summaries, series of questions, prophecies, quotations, brief anecdotes, and striking statements. In your conclusion you should summarize what you have said, especially if your remarks have been somewhat complicated. If your speech is to be reproduced, a somewhat longer summary may be in order—a recapitulation or restatement in slightly different language.

The function of the conclusion, however, is often more than that of making clear what has been said. When you have given yourself the assignment of impressing your audience and inspiring them to action, your final words should apply your ideas to the experience and interests of your listeners. You can indicate to your audience ways and means of carrying out your suggestions. You can refer to yourself, either humorously or seriously, and to the occasion. You can perhaps thank the listeners for their courtesy. You can give an impressive quotation or even relate a brief anecdote. These features of your conclusion have persuasive effect.

Make your conclusion short, and make it consistent in style and content with the rest of your speech. Do not allow your talk to end indecisively or abruptly. Spend perhaps one-quarter of your time planning your conclusion, but do not add a peroration. Stop when you are through.

Outlining Your Speech

Why make an outline? Why not think and read diligently and jot down notes from which to speak? How does planning help in speech preparation? An outline enables you to survey your case as a unit, to judge the degree to which your speech makes sense, to note digressions, to size up the major and minor divisions of your analysis, to evaluate the order of your topics, to redetermine the relative prominence of your ideas, to gauge more carefully the length of your speech, to take a second look at your definitions, and to inspect the illustrations, specific facts, and anecdotes (which you should insert in your outline).

An outline is a blueprint which will help you to assimilate more easily the ideas in your talk and to draft your "speaker's notes." In short, properly used, your outline will enable you to make a better speech.

The outline also helps the instructor to judge the kind of speech you intended to make. By comparing your outline with the speech you delivered, he can judge your communicative problem. Did you map out clearly what you wished to say? And did you actually present the speech so as to realize your aim?

HOW TO MAKE A GOOD OUTLINE

For your convenience in constructing an outline, we suggest that you apply standard principles and rules. The suggestions given below can be modified or interpreted to suit your own needs. Some instructors have decided views about methods of outlining; their advice concerning these mechanics will be important. The rules given here are those that speakers have consistently followed; they are based upon the experience of many speechmakers.

1. *Prefix to your outline a clear statement of your title, your subject, and your purpose sentence; sometimes you will want to include a statement of your approach to your speech for a specific audience.* Use as few general terms as possible. Be sure that the statement represents a careful limiting of the general field you have chosen for your talk. If it is an informative subject, word it either as a topic or as a sentence. If it is an argumentative subject, word it as a sentence. Be sure that your statement reveals clearly and concisely the content and direction of your discourse.

Do not confuse the subject with the purpose sentence, which epitomizes the content to be developed and states the speaker's purpose.

Title: Speech for all.

Subject: The need for more speech training in high schools.

Purpose sentence: The purpose of this speech is to convince and persuade this audience of the need for more speech training in high schools.

2. *Organize your outline into three parts: introduction, body, and conclusion.*

3. *Use complete sentences for all main ideas and subpoints.* Details may be indicated at times by a word or phrase. Avoid such phrases as "definition of automation," but give the complete definition in sentence form: "Automation is any mechanization of what was previously accomplished by men's muscles and minds."

If several definitions are grouped under a single heading, the form should be somewhat as follows:

I. The following explanations are desirable for an understanding of democracy:
   A. By democracy I mean that form of government in which both the majority and the minority have equal protection of their economic, political, and personal rights.

4. *Let each sentence contain one idea only; use simple rather than complex structure.*

Not so good:

I. We need better traffic regulation as a means of saving lives, speeding up traffic.

Better:

I. We need better traffic regulation.
   A. Better control of traffic will save lives.
      (Subtopics here)
   B. Better traffic control would speed up traffic.
      (Subtopics here)

Note also that the sentences should be declarative rather than interrogative.

5. *Generally use only impersonal language.* Since the outline is neither a speaker's notes nor the complete composition, it is preferable to omit the continual use of "I" and other words that suggest emotional, attention-getting language.

Not so good:

I. Water pollution is a serious problem in my community.
   A. You and I no doubt understand that it is a hindrance to swimming and other recreation.
   B. Are you not aware that it kills wildlife and fish?

Better:

I. Water pollution is a serious problem in my community.
   A. It has been a hindrance to swimming and other recreation.
     (Subtopics here)
   B. It has killed wildlife and fish.
     (Subtopics here)

6. *Use suitable symbols and indentations.* The customary system of numbering, lettering, and indenting is as follows:

I. (Roman numerals for main heads)
   A. (Capital letters for main subheads)
     1. (Arabic numerals for subordinate heads)
       a. (Small letters for small divisions)
         (1) (Arabic numerals in parentheses for smaller subdivisions)
         (2) (As above)
       b. _____
     2. _____
   B. _____
II. _____

Note that the indentations show the logical relation of main and subideas and forms of support. You do not use symbols opposite such headings as Introduction, Body, and Conclusion.

7. *Ordinarily, each division should have at least two heads.* Logic demands that a division produce at least two parts. But occasionally you may disregard this requirement. If you omit a *B* section after an *A*, the assumption will be that you did not consider it important to your immediate purpose. In such cases you must follow your own judgment, recognizing that some observers may criticize your outline for omissions of this kind.

8. *Use a few main headings.* Check the headings against the purpose

sentence to see that the main points of your outline square with those listed at the outset. Follow the principle of division, and group a number of topics under a few large heads. A listing of ten or twelve points in your outline can usually be regrouped under two or three logical main divisions.

9. *See that each subtopic logically develops the topic under which it is placed.* The entire framework should be a logical unit. If your outline is logical, each head will clarify or support the heading under which you arrange it.

If you are arguing in support of a general proposition you may want to state it as your main idea and then proceed to follow this general proposition with the specific evidence which supports it. Or you may cite evidence and cases first and then proceed to draw your general conclusion. The time sequence here has nothing to do with whether the argument is inductive or deductive. In both procedures cited above the argument is essentially inductive.

We may on the other hand wish to make a specific point as our central idea. Consider the contention that the United States should do whatever it can to depose the Castro government in Cuba. This is a specific contention. We proceed to argue that this contention should be accepted because Castro is apparently a Communist, and a Communist régime so close to the United States is a danger to our country. In sequence here we have proceeded from the specific to the general, but this argument as a whole is deductive in form. The more general proposition follows in rhetoric because it supports the more specific central idea. The time sequence here from the specific to the general does not make this argument inductive. The phrase "proceeds from" in logic means from the accepted evidence to the conclusion to be proved. As we see in speech organization the time sequence in both induction and deduction may be either from a specific statement to a general one or from a general statement to a specific one.

The following outline is an example of lack of coordination, poor subordination, and bad phrasing:

I. Freedom of speech.
   A. Being able to express your thoughts freely.
   B. Being able to take part in the governing of your country.
   C. Our government based on the individual.
   D. Our country's success depends on the individual's expressing his thought.

Better:

I. Freedom of speech is extremely important both personally and politically.

A. Free expression of thoughts results in self-confidence and increase in practical success.
B. Free expression permits more effective participation in the operations of government.
   1. Effective government depends upon participation by each citizen.
   2. This participation includes the exercise of free speech.

Words may be included to test the proper relationship of main ideas and substatements. Expository outlining, for example, may be tested by using "in that" to indicate the relationship of main and more detailed explanations. Argumentative outlining usually inserts "for" as the link between a main proposition and the supporting proof. In an outline for an indirect approach to the subject you may use the connection "therefore."

Expository outlining

I. Our new addition to the student union comprises three main divisions (in that)
   A. The first is a general recreation room.
   B. The second is a cafeteria.
   C. The third is an auditorium.

Argumentative outlining

I. Our new student union fills an important need on our campus, for
   A. It provides general recreation facilities, for (evidence to support this topic)
   B. It provides a cafeteria, for (evidence to support this topic)
   C. It provides an auditorium, for (subtopics to show the benefits)

10. *Include in your introduction the steps necessary to the effective unfolding of your subject.* Usually include (*a*) the situation that calls up the speech, or other remarks designed to integrate you and your topic with the audience and the occasion; (*b*) an explanation of terms; (*c*) a statement of the purpose sentence (often in the form of a question); (*d*) a statement of the partition or division which you propose to develop. (See pages 69–73.)

11. *In your conclusion, include a summary or make use of some other device to reinforce or apply the ideas previously developed.*

12. *In the main body of the outline include the details of amplification —the examples, illustrations, comparisons, facts and figures, authorities, and similar details.* Note the details included in the informational outline at the end of this chapter.

After the conclusion of your outline insert the exact source of any material quoted or cited from printed sources.

THE OUTLINE AND THE SPEAKER'S NOTES

Once you have prepared a satisfactory outline, what is the best way to use it? Should you carry it with you to the platform and speak directly from it? Certainly not; it would cramp your speaking style. Should you memorize it? Probably not. Should you write a full speech from it and recite the results verbatim? You may write your speech, but you will not have time to memorize the composition, nor would it be wise to do so. The best procedure is to draft a few "speaker's notes" from your material —catch phrases that will guide you in making the speech (if you feel you need such support). These notes are for you alone, and their form depends upon your requirements. Your aim is to develop skill as an extemporaneous speaker; hence you will make both an outline and speaker's notes, and you will regard the latter as an abbreviated, informal, and private version of the former.

INFORMATIVE SPEECH OUTLINE

Introduction

I. *Title:* Consumers' Research
II. *Subject:* An organization which provides consumers with information which may aid in making intelligent choices.
III. *Purpose sentence:* The purpose of my remarks is to inform the audience about Consumers' Research.
IV. *Approach:* If you had to buy a television set or a suit of clothes or even a fountain pen, would you know the best buy for the amount of money you had to spend? Faced with a bewildering variety of products and the conflicting claims of advertisers, the consumer is often at a loss to know which product to buy. Fortunately, there is an organization which helps the consumer—you—to make up his mind.

Discussion

I. Consumers' Research is a nonprofit organization which gives consumers reliable information on the relative value of merchandise.
   A. It was founded about twenty years ago by a group of public-spirited citizens.
   B. It operates as a scientific, technical, and educational organization.
   C. It tests and reports on well-known brand-name products. Transition: More specifically, it operates in the following manner:
II. Consumers' Research uses various methods to arrive at its findings.
   A. It has its own testing laboratories.

1. Some products are subjected to performance tests.
   a. Shoes are put on mechanical feet which simulate walking.
   b. Fountain pens write endlessly on rolls of tape.
2. Some products are subjected to chemical analysis.
   a. Cosmetics are analyzed for their component parts.
   b. Drugs and patent medicines are broken down to reveal their ingredients.
   B. Consumers' Research uses impartial outside reports to obtain information.
   1. It uses reports from the American Medical Association.
   2. It uses reports from various government agencies such as the Bureau of Standards.
   C. In the case of household appliances and automobiles, it makes wide use of surveys of repair shops.
   1. It asks which items appear most frequently for repairs.
   2. It seeks the most frequent causes for breakdowns. Transition: It would not be enough if these tests were made but not publicized.
III. Consumers' Research makes its information available to everyone.
   A. It issues monthly bulletins for subscribers at $3 per year.
   1. The bulletins report on a product from the standpoint of quality and economy.
      a. A $69.50 suit from Company A. was rated as being of no higher quality than a $45 suit from Company B.
      b. A 25-cent jar of one brand of facial cream was rated as being as high in quality as brands costing $3 to $5.
   B. It issues an annual cumulative index on a wide variety of products.
   C. The bulletin and the index are available in all public libraries.

Conclusion

I. Consumers' Research helps the purchaser to decide wisely on his purchase.
   A. It is nonprofit—has no business associations.
   B. It uses scientific methods to discover the quality of products.
   C. It reports its findings on a comparative basis in monthly bulletins and annual reports.

Sources:

1. J. F. Kennedy, "President's Message on Consumer Protection," *Consumers' Report*, 27:56–57, May, 1962.
2. *Consumers' Research Bulletin*, November, 1961; September, 1962.

Projects and Problems

PROJECT 1: PREPARATION AND PRESENTATION OF A SPEECH, FOLLOWING ONE OF THE METHODS OF DEVELOPMENT

Prepare an extemporaneous talk on some subject suggested in the list in Chapter Three. Make an outline of your talk according to the suggestions of this chapter. Prefix to the outline: (*a*) your topic, (*b*) your controlling purpose, (*c*) your purpose sentence, and (*d*) your main headings with a statement of the method by which the subtopics are to be developed, such as the method of (*a*) chronology, (*b*) topography, (*c*) definition, (*d*) classification, (*e*) logic, or (*f*) problem solution. Hand the outline to the instructor before you deliver the talk. Invite the class to make comments on your methods of preparation and presentation.

PROJECT 2: METHODS OF DEVELOPMENT IN A REPRESENTATIVE SPEECH

Find in one of the volumes of Baird's *Representative American Speeches,* (or other collections of speeches, or the speeches of the Appendix) an example of development by (*a*) classification, (*b*) definition, (*c*) logic, and (*d*) problem solution.

PROJECT 3: METHODS OF DEVELOPMENT OF A GIVEN PROPOSITION

Indicate a method of development under each of the following topic sentences (include in each case at least three statements representing three tentative subtopics): (*a*) College education sometimes stifles intellectual independence. (*b*) A powerful enemy of the American public is the American newspaper that distorts the news. (*c*) Literature is often taught badly in colleges. (*d*) The best novels of Somerset Maugham (or some other contemporary novelist) are classics.

PROJECT 4: DEVELOPMENT OF AN ARGUMENTATIVE TALK

State in ten or twelve sentences the main points you would make in a five-minute argumentative talk on the topic, "The Federal government should provide for the tuition, board, room, and books for four years of college (in the college of their choice) for all high school graduates who pass satisfactory college-entrance examinations and who demonstrate their limited financial ability," or on a similar topic.

References

Baird, A. Craig: *Argumentation, Discussion, and Debate,* McGraw-Hill Book Company, Inc., New York, 1950, chaps. 6 and 7.

Braden, Waldo W., and Mary Louise Gehring: *Speech Practices,* Harper & Brothers, New York, 1958, chap. 3.

Brigance, W. Norwood: *Speech,* Appleton-Century-Crofts, Inc., New York, 1952, chaps. 11, 12, and 14.

Bryant, Donald C., and Karl R. Wallace: *The Fundamentals of Public Speaking,* 3d ed., Appleton-Century-Crofts, Inc., New York, 1960, chaps. 9 and 10.

Crowell, Laura: "Building the 'Four Freedoms' Speech," *Speech Monographs,* 22:266–283, 1955.

Dickens, Milton: *Speech: Dynamic Communication,* Harcourt, Brace & World, Inc., New York, 1954, chap. 15.

Gray, Giles W., and Waldo W. Braden: *Public Speaking: Principles and Practice,* Harper & Brothers, New York, 1951, chaps. 13–15.

McBurney, James H., and Ernest J. Wrage: *The Art of Good Speech,* Prentice-Hall, Inc., New York, 1953, chap. 12.

Monroe, Alan H.: *Principles and Types of Speech,* 4th ed., Scott, Foresman and Company, Chicago, 1955, chaps. 14 and 17.

Quintilian: *Institutes of Oratory,* trans. and ed. by J. S. Watson, H. G. Bohn, London, 1856, books III and VII.

Sandford, William P., and W. Hayes Yeager: *Principles of Effective Speaking,* The Ronald Press Company, New York, 1950, chaps. 10 and 11.

Smith, Raymond G.: *Principles of Public Speaking,* The Ronald Press Company, New York, 1958, chap. 14.

White, Eugene E., and Clair R. Henderlider: *Practical Public Speaking,* The Macmillan Company, New York, 1954, chap. 7.

SIX

Developing Details

To DECIDE on the major ideas to be presented in a speech is one thing. To amplify those ideas with interesting and logical details is another. Certainly we agree that in speaking, as in writing, conciseness is a virtue. But this is not to say that brevity is always a virtue. Even a proverb, spoken to those who are familiar with it, must sometimes be repeated and amplified. Your ideas are as important as the amount of support you give them and the significance of that support.

The purpose of your speech—to inform, to impress, to entertain, to convince, to analyze, to move to action—will determine the character and the quantity of your supporting materials. Amplification is no mere exercise in diluting your ideas; each enforcing item serves its purpose in producing the total effect.

What kind of material can you use to support your ideas? Representative types include definitions and explanations, particulars, instances, figures and statistics, comparisons and contrasts, cause-and-effect sequences, testimony of authorities, quotations, incidents or anecdotes, and questions.

These types of materials can best be illustrated with reference to one major proposition or assertion, as follows:

America has produced important speakers.

Definition: Important speakers are those who have strongly influenced audiences through integrity of ideas, speech structure, persuasive language, and effectiveness of personality and delivery.

Particulars: It has produced platform orators who, in the courtroom, in legislative assemblies, in the pulpit, in industrial situations, and on occasions for tribute and commemoration have demonstrated their influence.

Instances: It has produced such speakers as Webster, Clay, Calhoun, Douglas, Lincoln, Ingersoll, Beecher, Bryan, Wilson, and F. D. Roosevelt.

Figures: Brigance's *History and Criticism of American Public Address* includes the studies of twenty-eight major speakers.

Comparison: It has produced Webster, Wendell Phillips, Ingersoll, Douglas, Wilson, and others who compare favorably in ideas, language and delivery with Burke, the younger Pitt, Erskine, Bright, and David Lloyd George of Britain.

Cause and effect: It has produced great orators because great issues to be settled, the American atmosphere of freedom, and general national intelligence encouraged the development of public address.

Testimony of authorities: Charles Richardson, professor of American literature at Dartmouth College, stated, "Thinking men might ignore the American traveler, theologian, poet, but the American political orator spoke so that his words resounded across the Atlantic . . . and it became necessary to listen to what he was saying."

Quotation: "Literature in times of crisis becomes the words of the men of action, of men who understand the power of words as weapons of warfare. The poets come afterward. We are here concerned with men who have used words to direct the course of American history." W. N. Brigance (ed.), *A History and Criticism of American Public Address,* McGraw-Hill Book Company, Inc., New York, 1943, vol. I, p. vii.

Incident and anecdote: William Jennings Bryan, speaking before the Democratic Nominating Convention in Chicago in 1896, defended "free silver" and replied to those delegates who favored the gold standard. "Bryan's penetrating voice carried to the far corners of the hall. . . . The tired delegates were aroused. . . . As he concluded, the twenty thousand people before him rose as a unit in applause. . . . Bryan continued to speak until he reached the memorable conclusion: 'You shall not press down upon the brow of labor this crown of thorns; you shall not crucify mankind upon a cross of gold.' . . . No description of the scene at the conclusion of Bryan's speech can be adequate. There was a 'delirium of excitement,' 'hysterical frenzy.' The silver platform was adopted, and he was nominated the next day." Here was an example of one of America's great orators in action. (Adapted from Brigance, *op. cit.,* pp. 902–903.)

Questions: Has not America produced speakers of the first water? Orators who in Congress argued intelligently on critical issues? Jurists who expounded with clarity and logic the fundamentals of American constitutional law? Political speakers who voiced the deepest hopes of Americans as well as their practical needs? Preachers whose eloquence fostered the religious idealism central to American civilization?

We can now proceed to comment in detail on each of these methods of developing ideas.

Development by Definition and Explanation

Your over-all purpose in communication is to make your meaning absolutely clear. In order to be accurate, you will select the words that best describe your idea or object. What are some of the barriers to accurate communication of your ideas?

1. Many words take on special meanings for individuals—meanings remote from those the speaker had in mind.

2. Meanings are constantly changing.

3. A single word or term often carries several meanings.

4. Some terms are abstract and elude our efforts to give equivalent tangible definitions.

5. Association can give words quite unexpected connotations.

6. The context in which a word is used influences its meaning and sometimes contributes to ambiguity.

7. Lack of uniformity in the audience's attitudes, experiences, and general education makes prediction of their reactions difficult.

8. Technical, new, and erudite terms that are commonplace to one group may be new and strange to another. Before a group familiar with the fields of psychology and sociology, for example, you may use such terms as "group dynamics" and "interpersonal relations," terms which might be meaningless to another group. (For further discussion of language, see Chapter Ten.)

Development by definition and explanation can help promote maximum clarity. If you are discussing communication, single out the type of communication you are concerned with. Do you refer to the act of communication, as, for example, the communication of smallpox or of a secret? Exchanges of meanings by way of language? Popular media such as newspapers and radio? A new type of language course?

Dictionary definitions alone are not usually sufficient. Besides, you will usually have to expound not one word but a combination, such as "the free nations," "the cold war," "Ivy League." Therefore, in addition to the help you can get from a dictionary, you must interpret your terms by enumerating details; describing the operation involved, if your term is an object, agency, or institution; explaining its purpose; reviewing its origin and history, including the etymology of the term; comparing and contrasting it with other closely related concepts. Of course you will not use all these patterns for defining any single word or term; but one or several of them will be helpful in each of your speeches.

Note how Walter Lippmann defined "Western culture" in his address, "Education without Culture," before the American Association for the Advancement of Science at its meeting in Philadelphia on December 29, 1940:[1]

> It is necessary today in a discussion of this sort to define and identify what we mean when we speak of Western culture. This is in itself ominous evidence of what the official historian of Harvard University has called the "greatest educational crime of the century against American youth—depriving him of his classical heritage." For there will be many, the victims of this educational crime, who will deny that there is such a thing as Western culture.
>
> Yet the historic fact is that the institutions we cherish—and now know we must defend against the most determined and efficient attack ever organized against them—are the products of a culture which, as Gibson put it, "is essentially the culture of Greece, inherited from the Greeks by the Romans, transfused by the Fathers of the Church with the religious teachings of Christianity, and progressively enlarged by countless numbers of artists, writers, and philosophers from the beginning of the Middle Ages up to the first third of the nineteenth century."

Development by Instances or Examples

Instances, or examples, are probably the most frequently used form of development. How do instances and examples differ from particulars? The latter more typically describe or enumerate parts that make up the whole as in many expositional or informative speeches. Instances, on the other hand, usually constitute the evidence to justify a conclusion or generalization. Instances are usually identified with argumentative or persuasive discourse, although such supports also explain an expositional concept.

Suppose you assert that youth often demonstrates mature accomplishment. What cases (evidence) can be cited? Rollo W. Brown gave as examples: (1) Lindbergh flew to Paris when he was twenty-five; (2) Keats was dead at twenty-five; (3) Pitt was prime minister at twenty-four; (4) Mendelssohn composed his music for "A Midsummer Night's Dream" at sixteen; (5) Chatterton died at eighteen; (6) Jane Austen wrote perhaps her best novel at twenty-one; (7) Hamilton was prominent at seventeen; (8) Kipling was at his zenith at thirty.

Instances, then, enrich and validate your ideas. Ask yourself the following questions: (1) Have I used enough instances? (2) Are they representative of the field as a whole? (3) Are they easily understood by the listeners? (4) Are they so numerous as to lose their interest or value? (5)

---

[1] A. Craig Baird (ed.), *Representative American Speeches, 1940–41*, The H. W. Wilson Company, New York, 1941, p. 296.

If they are hypothetical, are they concretely and interestingly stated? (6) Are the facts which they represent verified?

Development by Figures and Statistics

In developing your topic you may often cite figures to illustrate or prove your point. In an argument that "higher education is worthwhile financially," the following figures were presented:[2]

The actual cash value of a college education was recently presented on the General Electric Bowl. On this TV program reference was made to figures recently released by the United States Census Bureau which compared the total life earnings of persons with differing amounts of education. The person completing the elementary school receives an average income of $182,000. The high school graduate receives $258,000. The college graduate increases his total life earnings $177,000 over the high school graduate to a life total of $435,000.

Note the following accumulative figures and the source of the data, as given in a speech by Prof. J. E. Hawkins before the Florida Academy of Sciences at Gainesville on February 17, 1961:[3]

To illustrate the high degree of ignorance of our high school graduates the following results of a random test to 154 freshmen at Colorado State University were presented in the December 16, 1960, issue of *The American Statesman.*

When asked to name any five planets of our solar system, 27 percent could not name any. Ten percent named either the sun or the moon as planets. Nine students listed a planet called "plato." The ancient Greek socialist would have been happy to learn that he had gone into planetary orbit.

Almost half of the students who were quizzed could not name Newton as the formulator of the law of gravity. Over one out of three could not name any of the Great Lakes. Ten percent could name only one. Some listed the following as Great Lakes, Lake Wisconsin, Salt Lake, Lake Tahoe, Lake Champlain, and Lake Mead.

Thirty-six percent did not know what continent the Andes Mountains are on. Answers such as "East Continent," "West Continent," and "Italy" suggest that some of the students don't even know what a continent is.

When asked "Where is the Eiffel Tower located?" 19 percent (almost one in five) had no idea. More important, a number of students listed "Pizzo, Italy." Apparently these students had Paris, Pisa, the Leaning Tower, and the Eiffel Tower all mixed up in their minds in one indescribable mush, with pizza pie floating on top.

[2] Facts as presented by the Citizens' Committee for the Universities Bond Issue, Springfield, Ill., 1961.
[3] *Vital Speeches of the Day,* 27:415, 1961.

Eighty-one percent of the students questioned did not know what the word "Hellenic" means. Many who had apparently vaguely heard of the "Pan-Hellenic," thought that Hellenic had something to do with "togetherness" or with "fraternity."

Ninety percent had never heard of Jean Sibelius.

Professor R. H. Zoellner, who gave the test, summed it up as follows: "They [the students questioned] are in my opinion, the most dangerous sort of political tinder. A clever demagogue, given the right kind of propaganda machine, could convert many of them to an 'American' brand of totalitarianism in six months flat. They simply would not be equipped to resist his idea."

What are statistics? They are figures so grouped as to bring out their comparative significance. They are groups of facts systematically collected and classified so that one group may be compared with another and an inference or interpretation made. In using statistics, however, make certain, for the sake of accuracy and honesty, that the compilers are unprejudiced authorities. In your talk, quote the source of your statistics and be ready, if one of your listeners should request it, to cite the author or official organization, volume, page, date, and other means of identification. Inquire whether the sampling was systematic. When you refer to an "average student" or an "average college," be sure you know the basis for that classification. Is the college classed as average on the basis of its enrollment, the sex of its students, its endowment, its athletic teams, its age? Was the study based on freshmen only, or seniors only, or even on a limited number of athletes and scholars?

To give vividness to your figures, translate or interpret them for the audience's understanding and interest. Without distorting them, use approximate figures—when appropriate—in round numbers only: In 1960 John F. Kennedy was elected President of the United States over Richard Nixon by 112,000 popular votes.

Development by Comparisons and Contrasts (Analogies)

Comparison and contrast are ways of showing likenesses and differences. We match one situation, person, or event about which we know a good deal with another about which we would like to know more, in order to throw light on the less well known. The method proceeds from the known to the unknown, from the well known to the strange, from the like to the unlike, from the literal toward the figurative.

The comparison may be direct and literal. "Baseball is a great game in this country. Why should it not also become the national sport of Great Britain?" "Our college has a good record in intercollegiate debate. Why should we not do as well in athletics?" Note that the subjects under comparison belong to the same class: sports, college activities.

Often the similarities are comparatively remote: We may compare a forceful public speaker and a dive bomber (in their devastating results); a huge air armada and a dike (each protects the country). Churchill used comparison subtly in his address of September 11, 1940, suggesting that Germany might invade England: "The next week or so will be a very important period in our history. It ranks with the days when the Spanish Armada was approaching the Channel." All Englishmen knew of the Spanish Armada. No one of them could foresee the shape of events in the immediate future. But Churchill, by implication, would have them expect a fortunate duplication of this earlier event.

Often the comparisons are historical. Note Senator J. William Fulbright's method (both historical and figurative), August 21, 1958:[4]

> A frightening historical parallel has occurred to me with increasing frequency in recent weeks. Fifteen or sixteen centuries ago the Roman empire was all-powerful, rich, successful—and complacent. Neither the Roman emperors nor the Roman Senate could bring themselves to be overly concerned with the crude and boorish people to the north. Emperors were judged by the public entertainment they arranged, and the wealth and substance of the empire was dissipated in lavish consumption. When anyone was so inconsiderate as to call attention to the gathering clouds on the horizon, he was denounced as a prophet of gloom and purged of un-Roman activity. In 1958 the critic is charged with "selling America short."
>
> This picture is admittedly oversimplified. But in broad outline it is pertinent and valid. The fall of great empires follows a well-defined course. On the outside the civilization is a hard, shining surface, full of glitter and superficial accomplishment. But inside the outer shell, invisible decay does its work. And the hard shell collapses on the empty center when that civilization collides with a challenge it no longer has the power to meet, because it was indifferent to the challenge too long.

Comparisons and analogies will make your exposition much clearer and more interesting. When properly interpreted and backed by other types of argument, analogies serve the same purpose as proof. In using comparisons, ask yourself: (1) Is the comparison clearly and interestingly stated? (2) Is the comparison logical? That is, do listeners accept it as plausible and pertinent? (3) Are the facts which you state or imply in your comparisons true? (4) Is your comparison trite and therefore boring ("ship of state," for example)?

Contrast is merely comparison in reverse: Opposites are contrasted to point up their differences. Any object or quality becomes more vivid and dramatic when seen in juxtaposition with others: white and red; novels

---

[4] A. Craig Baird (ed.), *Representative American Speeches: 1958–59*, p. 129.

and plays; democracy and dictatorship; Korean battlefields and Iowa countrysides; free enterprise and socialism; Frenchmen and Spaniards. Use contrasts that are genuine and logical as well as vivid. Be sure that the two things discussed belong to the same class.

Development by Cause-and-effect Sequences

Explaining the factors that produce a given situation or condition is a logical procedure. Familiar examples of such reasoning are the following: "If you want to be well educated (effect), I advise you to read many books (cause)." "Unless we continue to resist the Chinese People's Republic (cause), the entire Orient will succumb to communism (effect)." "He'll surely get there (effect) after he gets his diploma (cause)."

"Should Red China be admitted to the United Nations?" The issue was dramatically revived in the political campaign of 1960 and came to a climax in 1962. The argument in the United States against such admission centered in these causes: (1) The Red Chinese have expressed open contempt for the purposes and principles of the United Nations. (2) They continue to stand convicted as aggressors in Korea. (3) They continue to support aggression in Indo-China. (4) They occupied defenseless Tibet and Laos. (5) They have supported guerrilla and subversive movements in Malaya and throughout the rest of Southeast Asia. (6) They have executed millions of captive subjects and forced other millions into slave labor. (7) They have extorted millions of dollars from overseas Chinese who try to buy safety and protection for relatives at home. (8) They have extended their subversive activities to Cuba and Latin America.

What were the effects of the Soviet sputnik on October 4, 1957, and the later Soviet launchings?

Stated, for example, Andrew R. Cecil, in his speech "Search for World Leadership," at Florida Southern College, Lakeland, March 10, 1961:[5]

The appearance of Soviet sputniks was a great blow to our national pride. We were catapulted from a state of blind confidence into depths of inferiority complex when we awoke suddenly to the fact that our mortal rival took the lead in an area in which we like to think we excelled—sciences and technology. Our image of Russia altered radically. Once we pictured Russians as bearded, backward peasants, and the Russian armed forces as grenade-throwing dullards; now the revelation of Soviet advances caused a dangerous swing in the pendulum of public opinion to the opposite extreme—just short of admiration for the efficiency of a Communist dictatorship.

Development by cause-and-effect sequences implies that a specific relationship exists between the events involved. Ask yourself these questions as you use the cause-and-effect method:

[5] *Vital Speeches of the Day,* 27:410, 1961.

1. Have I described clearly and accurately each event which I have attempted to arrange in a causal sequence?
2. Is my assumption that a cause-and-effect relationship exists in this case justified?
3. Have I overestimated the influence of a given cause over a given effect? [6]

Development by Authority

Audiences often silently refuse to accept our word but react favorably if we quote an authority or cite a source of our facts. If we assert that the national debt as of June 30, 1960, was 286,331,000 billion dollars we should also refer to the *Statistical Abstract of the United States* of that year as our source or to the *Britannica Book of the Year 1961*, page 122.

Note the use of authorities in the argument of whether higher education is worthwhile as presented by the Citizens Committee for Universities Bond Issue of 1960–61:

> Before continuing with this discussion, the thinking voter should ask himself this question: "Is higher education really worthwhile?" Benjamin Franklin said, "An investment in knowledge pays the best interest." William Jennings Bryan said, "The boy who drops out of school under the delusion that the money he can earn will be worth more than an education makes a fatal mistake. Just as the wood chopper can afford to take time off to sharpen his ax, so can the young person afford to defer money earning until he has completed his education."

Senator Robert C. Byrd, of West Virginia, speaking at Ravenswood, West Virginia, on January 26, 1961, on "Russia's New War against Free Nations," argued that the aim of Russia was to destroy the economy of the United States.[7] To prove his case he cited Nikita Khrushchev himself.

> Of course, the real economic target on which the Kremlin has its aim is the United States. Nikita Khrushchev let the cat out of the bag in a speech he made in Moscow on May 6, 1959.

> "The main bulwark of the contemporary capitalist world," Khrushchev said, "is constituted by the United States, which has a more highly developed production and a higher standard of living. In order to achieve victory in the competition between the two systems (capitalism versus communism), we must catch up with and overtake those barriers to competition with capitalism—not with ballistic missiles, not with atomic or hydrogen bombs, but with our organization and unity. With a higher level of production."

[6] For further comment on causal reasoning, see Chapter Seventeen, "Argumentative Speaking."

[7] *Vital Speeches of the Day*, 27:297, 1961.

The Soviet boss then went on to say, "Having achieved the level of production of the most highly developed state [the United States], we will not stop at that, but will advance with ever greater drive. We Communists say: 'Capitalism will fail as everything obsolete fails and dies away.'"

In order that the testimony you cite may be accepted without question by your hearers, ask yourself the following questions concerning the authority you quote:

1. Does he have special training in the field in which he is alleged to have authority?

2. Is he free from prejudice?

3. Is his testimony accurately reported, and is it specific? Be sure that you have not unintentionally misquoted your source. Do not make vague references to authorities: "A prominent member of a college faculty recently denounced the 'one hundred best books' type of higher education"; or "One of the student speakers contended that movies are a menace to higher education."

4. Is the authority or source well known and acceptable to the audience?

5. Have you cited too many sources? Quote sparingly. Two or three apt references in a five- or ten-minute talk should be adequate.

Development by Quotation

In addition to quoting authorities and witnesses to confirm your points, you can also insert quotations from poetry or prose for added interest. Professor William G. Carleton, of the University of Florida, in addressing a student assembly at the Mississippi State College for Women on April 26, 1955, quoted from many sources, including Senator Depew and George Bernard Shaw:[8]

Others of us Americans are too active physically. We make a fetish of energy and of strenuous physical exercise. Surely you have heard the remark of the late Senator Depew who at the age of eighty said: "The only exercise I get is acting as pallbearer to my golf-playing friends." George Bernard Shaw once said: "When I feel the urge to violent exercise, I lie down, keep quiet, settle my nerves, and then the urge passes." Many Americans would be wise to follow the example of Depew and Shaw.

Although such illuminating quotations may occur at any point, they usually give the opening and closing of the speech added impressiveness.

Bower Aly began his address, "The Danger of Education," at the Oregon Press Conference, Eugene, Oregon, on February 17, 1961, with a quotation:[9]

[8] *Vital Speeches of the Day*, 21:1364, 1955.
[9] *Vital Speeches of the Day*, 27:367, 1961.

As some of you know, my favorite indoor recreation is the reading of history. And one of my favorite histories is Bradford's *Of Plymouth Plantation*. In his fourth chapter Bradford described the reasoning that led the Pilgrims to leave the city of Leyden and embark on a voyage to a new world:

> After they had lived in this city some eleven or twelve years . . . those prudent governors with sundry of their sagest members began both deeply to apprehend their present dangers and wisely to foresee the future and think of timely remedy.

Charles Nutter, before the Oklahoma Press Association, Oklahoma City, January 27, 1961, ended his address thus:[10]

> In conclusion, I am reminded of the philosophical heritage which Theodore Roosevelt left us nearly a half century ago.
>
> Americanism, he said, means the virtues of courage, honor, justice, truth, sincerity, and hardihood—the virtues that made America. The things that will destroy America are prosperity at any price, peace at any price, safety first instead of duty first, the love of soft living, and the get rich theory of life.

In order to have a ready source of quotations, keep a notebook or card file with systematic headings and place in it brief excerpts from your reading.

Development by Incident and Anecdote

Incidents and anecdotes have distinct value for injecting life and movement into your talk. No speech should proceed far without at least one short narrative, which may be highly personal or biographical and which may or may not be humorous. Brief stories such as those used in after-dinner speeches are pertinent in almost any kind of speaking and on almost any occasion. Wendell Phillips, William Jennings Bryan, and our contemporary platform leaders have produced telling results by this form of support. Stories and personal narratives illumine, clarify, and convince.

President Louis Norris of Albion College, whose speech "We Know in Part" was given at Michigan State University, East Lansing, on March 20, 1961, inserted a brief incident for attention-getting purposes:[11]

> We talk of "new frontiers" but by what bench mark is this promised land to be surveyed?
>
> Perhaps you will find it in a man. David Garrick was noticed one evening in Drury Lane Theater suddenly to transform his acting from listlessness to brilliance. Samuel Johnson, who was present, observed this magic change coincided

[10] *Vital Speeches of the Day,* 27:297, 1961.
[11] *Vital Speeches of the Day,* 27:410, 1961.

with the entrance of Edmund Burke. Greatness and stability call for greatness and stability. Find your man, if you would find your greatness, and then find the bench mark by which he organizes his life.

Edmund Pitz, speaking on "The Real Danger of Communism" at New Brunswick, New Jersey, on February 28, 1961, referred to Lenin, chiefly for direct argumentative appeal:[12]

In the early years of the 20th century a self-unemployed lawyer and political exile was living in a run-down boarding house. He lived on handouts. He wrote angry tracts, made rabble rousing speeches, and plotted the Revolution. As World War I drew to a close he seized control of a great country and set brush fires on every continent. The man's name was Lenin. He had no physical power at the outset, but he lived for an idea. It was an evil idea to which he devoted his life, but the Marxist ideology which consumed him forged ahead until it clothed itself with today's Soviet military machine. But the power was in the idea; once this idea took hold of men's minds, military weapons gravitated toward it. If the idea should lose its hold on men's minds, the weapons would start to fall away.

Where will you get these short incidents? Collections of speeches contain them. *Modern Eloquence, Representative American Speeches, Vital Speeches*, Sarett and Foster's *Modern Speeches on Basic Issues*, Harold F. Harding's *Age of Danger*, and similar publications contain a considerable number. Your own experiences should be your chief source. From the speeches you hear, jot down the stories that seem to succeed and keep them in a card file or notebook. Most effective speechmakers follow some such systematic method of accumulating materials for quick reference.

Development by Questions

Occasionally paragraphs or smaller sections may be developed by casting the material in question form. Since your sentence pattern in speaking is usually declarative, the substitution of the interrogative mood introduces variety and suspense and subtly invites the audience to share more closely in your diagnosis of the thesis.

The interrogative sentence is essential in framing issues. As we observed in Chapter Five, issues are statements in question form of the arguments that differentiate the affirmative from the negative on any proposition. They are the questions to which the affirmative will answer "yes" and the negative "no." For example, the discussion leader announces that his group is to reflect on the question (or issue), "Shall eighteen-year-olds vote in the United States?" The main issues are the following: (1) Are they sufficiently experienced in economic matters? (2) Are they educa-

[12] *Vital Speeches of the Day*, 17:365, 1961.

tionally prepared? (3) Are they as well equipped politically as they will be at twenty-one? Such questions make up the agenda of an informal round table, suggest the outline of a series of public talks, or provide the blueprint for an individual argumentative talk. In analytical speeches, the question technique is quite useful.

Closely related to the "issue" form of question is the rhetorical question. The wording of the rhetorical question, however, unlike that of the issue, is slanted to achieve a given response. The analytical speaker will ask: "Shall we repeal the poll tax?" The rhetorical question is really a vigorous assertion disguised as a question. It should not be used too often.

Dean W. C. Lang, dean of instruction at Iowa State College, Cedar Falls, as commencement speaker at the State University of Iowa, February 4, 1961, concluded with questions:[13]

> Can we as a people begin to think steadily about national priorities which will place sacrifices upon us and revise our value system? Will we re-examine our attitude toward freedom and avoid the all too frequent error of equating support of cherished ideas with the proper exercise of this privilege? Will we begin to examine and implement the assumption that the "good life" is not to be measured primarily and surely not solely in terms of entertainment and indiscriminate indulgence of the senses? Do you understand and will you interpret to the community the significant role of a really liberal education in the survival of free men? Will you have the courage to tell your state representatives you are willing to tax yourselves more, to sacrifice some sensory pleasure so your university may be properly supported? Will you implement the liberation of the mind by the support of what may be unpopular causes if these causes reflect your convictions? If not, all will be lost. For "if the salt has lost its savor, wherewith shall it be salted?" Will we arouse ourselves to a sense of shame when we observe that we expend as much, if not more, on each of these categories—tobacco products and alcoholic beverages, new and used cars, and recreation—as we do on education and then declare we cannot spend more for our schools? While more money is no complete answer, can't we at least stop being hypocrites? . . .
>
> Can we lead our people to think seriously about the role of their schools? That the goal of each student and teacher must be excellence according to his ability and that mediocrity or "getting by" is not enough? . . .
>
> Can we develop in ourselves and in others a real sense of urgency without becoming hysterical? Can we seek new political directions in world law, limited national sovereignty, and expanded political loyalties without being overwhelmed by screams of "subversion?" The threat before us is such that it will require a sustained, organized effort in all these areas.

[13] *Vital Speeches of the Day*, 17:335, 1961.

Projects and Problems

PROJECT 1

Explain in simple language, using a diagram if necessary, one of the following technical terms: (*a*) fuselage, (*b*) fluorescence, (*c*) protoplasm, (*d*) galaxy, (*e*) fourth dimension, (*f*) corona, (*g*) hail.

PROJECT 2

Explain in a two-minute speech one of the following slang terms: (*a*) ballyhoo, (*b*) hokum, (*c*) nerve, (*d*) whoopee. (For other representative slang terms, see Lester V. Berry and Melvin Den Bark, *The American Thesaurus of Slang.*)

PROJECT 3

Give a speech in which you develop by the use of examples one of the following topics: (*a*) The period before 1860 was the golden age of oratory in the United States. (*b*) I have heard several pleasant radio voices recently. (*c*) Debaters should argue only what they believe. (*d*) Aptitude tests should be substituted for achievement tests for admission to American colleges. (*e*) Our higher education system still retains much that is medieval. (*f*) Modern civilization in America tends to produce general ugliness in the landscape. (*g*) Contemporary painting in America is very promising. (*h*) Most college students know little about the Bible. (*i*) The United States is a leading nation in the world today.

PROJECT 4

Give a short talk in which you make use of statistics. Explain clearly the meaning of the figures you quote. For examples of the use of statistical material, consult the bulletins of learned societies (for example, *Speech Monographs*), congressional publications (the current issues of the daily edition of the *Congressional Record*), or current speeches published in *Vital Speeches of the Day.* Suggested topics: (*a*) The trend of the stock market will probably be upward (or downward). (*b*) We are in for a period of inflation (or deflation). (*c*) The enrollment of college students has been steadily increasing and will continue to do so. (*d*) The United States Navy is larger than that of any other nation. (*e*) The national health of the United States should be improved.

PROJECT 5

Give a short speech in which you do one of the following: (*a*) make use of analogy and comparison. (Use one of the topics listed above.) (*b*) Support your idea by means of contrasts. (For example, show what discussion is by contrasting it with debate, persuasive speaking, and propaganda.) (*c*) Trace causes and results. (Suggested topics: The causes of World War II. Why the United States abandoned isolation. Why the American people will vote mainly the Democratic, or the Republican, ticket in the next national election. The prospects for educational use of television. Results of the American occupation of Germany. Why the Korean armistice came in 1953.) (*d*) Include one short quotation and one incident. (Suggested topics: Why I am patriotic. My experience in a mine.)

References

Brigance, W. Norwood: *Speech*, Appleton-Century-Crofts, Inc., New York, 1952, chap. 13.

Gray, Giles W., and Waldo W. Braden: *Public Speaking: Principles and Practice*, Harper & Brothers, New York, 1951, chap. 11.

McBurney, James H., and Ernest J. Wrage: *The Art of Good Speech*, Prentice-Hall, Inc., Englewood Cliffs, N.J., 1953, chap. 9.

Monroe, Alan H.: *Principles and Types of Speech*, 4th ed., Scott, Foresman and Company, Chicago, 1955, chaps. 11 and 13.

SEVEN

Adapting to the Audience and the Occasion

ORAL COMMUNICATION, as we explained in Chapter One, is always an aspect of adjustment to a specific situation that includes a listener. In the preceding chapters of this book we have referred to your speech in its relation to your audience in discussing selection of subject, ideas, organization, supporting details, language, and delivery.

The various types of speech are the tools, and human nature is the substance on which we work. We do not cut diamonds with glass, chisel stone with wood, or etch on bronze with lead. The tools of speech are among the most varied and complex of man's inventions for relating himself to others. To use the tools of speech effectively we must know not only which ones we have at our command but also something about the human nature on which we work.

What Is Audience Adaptation?

Aristotle, for example, observed that a speech grows out of the interaction of the speaker, his subject, and the people addressed. Of these three

105

agencies, Aristotle concluded, the audience determines the purpose and over-all effect of the speech.[1]

Your audience, then, is highly important. Your effectiveness will depend not only on what you say, but the extent to which your listeners can identify themselves with you and your message. Your speaking problem is *adaptation*—your adjustment to the human beings you are trying to inform, entertain, inspire, or move to action.

This requirement of adapting to your audience does not mean that you are to throw away your ideas or remake your personality to conform to what you think the audience would want in you. If you are practical, however, you will take account of the ideas, the prejudices, the comprehension, and all other known facts about those who are to face you. Your job is to understand those people.

How do you find the key to their minds? Do you try to predict how others will react to a subject on the basis of your own experiences and inclinations? Do you assume the existence of the statistically "average" man and direct your words to him? Do you attempt to reach your auditors by being logical and objective?

Analyzing the Audience

If communication is to be more than target practice in the dark, we must analyze our audience and adapt the methods and materials according to our findings. How do we do this?

George Campbell, in his Philosophy of Rhetoric,[2] states that the hearers are to be considered from a "twofold point of view, as men in general and as these men in particular."

THE STUDY OF AUDIENCE IN GENERAL

Our audience may be composed of one person or many. What are the universal characteristics of human beings? We will do well to give consideration to what the sciences of psychology and sociology tell us about human nature. When we do this we might end up with a description somewhat as follows:

We inherit certain physiological characteristics and abilities. These characteristics identify us with the animal kingdom. We have biological needs or drives. We learn more or less conventional ways of satisfying

[1] Aristotle, *Rhetoric*, book II.
[2] George Campbell, *Philosophy of Rhetoric*, Harper & Brothers, New York, 1851, pp. 93–94.

those needs. We have many sensations, feelings, emotions, and cognitive reactions. We acquire habits, some good, some bad. We develop complicated mental processes, memory, thought, language, curiosity, imagination, judgment, knowledge, and if we are fortunate perhaps a bit of wisdom. We develop tastes, preferences, interests, find preferred foods, friends, work, and relaxation. We mature, accept responsibilities, cooperate, and exercise some freedoms. We develop self-awareness, pride, a sense of values, a realization of the dignity of man—all of which helps us rise above our animal nature. We experience insights and relations and create art and beauty for our enjoyment. We seek to survive but also to contribute to the common good and the betterment of our world. Our world is orderly and as human machines we like this because it enables us to carry on our lives with an economy of energy. We resist changes or any stimulus which creates discord in our lives, yet we seek variety within this unity. Everything doesn't happen at once, but piecemeal. Now we are concerned with this aspect of our lives, now with that. While all men are doing most of these things each is an individual. In our culture we value both commonality and individuality. Differences and conflict create tension and struggle within ourselves or between ourselves and others. Dissonance is unpleasant and we seek ways of achieving or returning to a state of harmony.

This is man in general, man to whom we speak in the person of our families or friends, and strangers as well, persons to whom we talk individually and in groups. How are we to systematize our approach to the problem of adaptation to such an audience? It may be well to consider as a first step what we mean by audience.

The word "audience" generally refers to people gathered to hear a message. If the message is also pictorial they may see it in part. But people aren't necessarily an audience. Audience in short is a kind of human behavior peculiar to people who receive ongoing communication. The word is misused when applied to persons who read a newspaper, because many characteristics of this type of communication activity are different. An audience is not just an assembly of people. We do not have a true audience situation unless the receivers of the communication want to hear a message, are capable of receiving it, and cooperate to interpret it with maximum accuracy and to feed back their responses in some way to the communicator.

THE STUDY OF THE SPECIFIC AUDIENCE

Since we identify audience as a kind of human communication behavior, our system of audience analysis ought to focus primarily on vari-

What differences do you see in the way the audience is responding to student speakers in these two pictures? (Photos from one of the educational films produced by McGraw-Hill to accompany this text.)

ables in communication, not just variables in the human animal. Perhaps the most important variable in communication is the variable in purposes of the communication and its actual effects upon the listeners. This is important because the communication is used to produce changes in these dimensions of behavior. We propose to call these dimensions the primary dimensions of audience response or behavior. Audiences and people within audiences will behave differently along these dimensions.[3]

[3] See Wilbur Schramm, *The Process and Effects of Mass Communication*, University of Illinois, 1934, for a somewhat similar pattern of audience analysis.

PRIMARY DIMENSIONS

1. *The size of the audience.* The size of the audience is an important dimension because the magnitude of the response will depend in some ways on the number of people involved. If you know something not known to your audience and you share it with them, you do not have less of the idea. Perhaps expressing it will clarify your own thinking and therefore extend your grasp of the subject. But whether this is true or not you will have multiplied in a way the total amount of this information to achieve a product equal to the size of your audience. The significance of this concept in advertising should be self-evident. It explains why consumer research organizations are so concerned with the measurement of the size of the audience. Your audiences in class will be of a fixed size, but you do have a responsibility to stimulate as many members of your audience as possible to get your message. If you ever campaign for election or for some other cause you will want to attract as large an audience as possible.

2. *The interests of the audience.* The first step in adaptation to audience interests is to get the listeners' attention. People attend to what interests them. Unless we can get attention, not just for the sake of attention, but attention to some important aspect of our message, the communication doesn't get to first base.

The interests of people in general and of any one person from time to time vary greatly. Yet many people maintain fairly stable interests over long periods of time. We are all interested in meeting our biological needs, yet we also possess strong interests in meeting these needs in conformity with the provisions, mores, and conventions of our culture. When we participate in any kind of ongoing activity we are interested in carrying this activity through to completion or closure. We are interested in conserving energy, retaining the *status quo*, or maintaining a pace and order which we enjoy. But if we do not approve the *status quo*, if we experience dissonance or anxiety or intense motivation, we are interested in carrying on some activity which will reduce this unpleasant state of affairs. Because we can be forward-looking creatures, we are interested in ideas that facilitate our plans for the future and in counteracting any influence which might frustrate or disturb those plans. We are interested in exercising those habits which bring us satisfaction. We are interested in our own rights and privileges in our society, but we are also interested in gaining social acceptance and social approval. Such interests as these are common. Any communication in which we engage must be shaped in light of such interests in an audience.[4]

[4] See Chapter Eighteen for a discussion of attention and interests relative to persuasion.

3. *The knowledge of the audience.* Knowledge is not always an all-or-none matter. You are aware of the fact that people differ in the amount of knowledge they possess. Certainly they will differ in what they know or understand about your subject. If you wish to extend their knowledge you will need to make some educated guesses about how much they know. And of course you will need to relate the new and unknown to the known. Any communication in depth will of necessity cover a wide range of knowledge, and some listeners will learn more than others. You will want most of all to save time and maintain interest by not dwelling at length upon those aspects of your subject already well known to your audience.

You may well ask, What experience has my audience had with this subject? Will they be alert to new information? How can I select material that will extend the range of understanding of many of my listeners?

4. *The belief of the audience.* What is the attitude of the listeners toward your subject? What political, religious, economic, aesthetic, and other prejudices are they likely to have? Their group affiliations, needs, wants, and desires will determine their prejudices.

Often audiences may be classified in relation to your subject in one of the following ways: (*a*) They may be interested in knowing more about it and, if the topic is controversial, they may welcome your additional support to their convictions. (*b*) They may be indifferent to the subject or neutral if the proposal calls for their decision. (*c*) They may be opposed to your subject if it is boring to them or if it is objectionable or contrary to their beliefs.

These attitudes you can measure, for example, in the classroom. Before you begin your talk, place your topic on the blackboard and invite each listener to record on paper his reaction to it, as favorable, neutral, or opposed. After your talk, each member will again record his attitude. We agree that little change usually occurs in a group of twenty-five listening to a four- or five-minute speech. But the method of measuring audience shifts of attitude is sound, and properly applied to larger audiences, it may reveal your influence as a speaker.

To influence your listeners favorably, you will decide why their preliminary attitudes are thus and so. Have they read widely and discussed this subject? Have they had firsthand experience with it?

As you proceed, are your listeners cordial, receptive? Do they seem to be attentive and responsive? And are you using illustrations and other elements of good communication to carry these auditors with you?

Your job is harder if the listeners are visibly bored. You will attempt to begin with ideas and details that may shake them out of their lethargy and create curiosity and expectation.

What if most of them at the start are opposed to your topic? You will need to unfold your ideas by beginning with ideas they will accept and lead them on by successive steps from preliminaries to the final and more critical conclusions.[5]

5. *The activity level of your audience.* Since you will sometimes speak to persuade people to action, you need to know something about the way they have behaved or are able to behave about your subject. Have they performed similar acts in the past? Do they have the resources, including knowledge and skill, to do what you are asking? Do you know of any reservations or doubts which must be dispelled before you can get the desired response? Can you give them adequate reasons for action? Perhaps all these matters are involved in your proposal? Can you dwell upon these motives to create and release the energies necessary for action? [6]

SECONDARY DIMENSIONS

The secondary dimensions of an audience are those characteristics of listeners which influence their attendance, interests, knowledge, attitudes, and other behavior (primary dimensions) and which are subject to modification by communication although they are not its primary objectives. There are several of these secondary dimensions.

6. *The social and cultural orientation of the audience.* Are these people accustomed to audience behavior? Do they feel at ease as listeners? Are they aware of their purpose and function? Do they have a sense of responsibility as auditors? Do they know how to do the kind of listening expected of them? Are they a captive audience or are they present from choice? If present from choice, do they have an active interest in listening to learn? Is this a homogeneous group of listeners? What is the basis of their unity? To what kind of social group do they belong? To what social pressures do they react? Are they already motivated by a single dominating purpose? Is their motivation deep-seated and of long standing or only incidental and temporary?

A significant aspect of this dimension involves the ways in which the audience thinks of you as a speaker. Have the listeners doubts concerning your special knowledge of the subject? People like swimming, but you have been a lifeguard. People are interested in television, but you have participated in the "Steel Hour" (or some other important show). People have been interested in stuttering, but for one whole day among strangers, you pretended to stutter in order to understand better the attitude of the genuine stutterers. Your talk should quickly make clear your ability to handle your subject.

[5] See Chapter Seventeen, "Argumentative Speaking," for further discussion of communication for the development and change of attitudes.

[6] See Chapter Eighteen, "Persuasive Speaking," for further discussion of speech to move to action.

What kind of reputation do you have with your listeners? Are you a stranger to them? Or are you of only lukewarm interest to them? If they know anything favorable about you, can you then not without braggadocio refer to your firsthand experience as a firewarden and plane jumper in Oregon? Or your two years in the air force? Or your two years of successful coaching in high school basketball? Or your successful selling of air conditioning?

What impression has your audience of your social attitudes, your humor, and good will? What impression has it of your moral qualities—your honesty, integrity, and sense of responsibility; of your personality—your mannerisms, language, style of speaking? Honest self-analysis will help you to answer these questions. Any of these identifying traits can be turned to good account if you select your ideas, illustrations, humor, language, and methods of delivery with an understanding of what the audience thinks and expects of you. Audience adaptation is a powerful element in your success as a speaker. The ancient rhetoricians called this effort by a speaker to make himself credible "ethical proof." In modern psychology of persuasion it is called "credibility of a speaker."

7. *The talents and capacities of your audience.* Since the success of your talk depends upon your audience as well as upon yourself you will need to know something of the kind of people to whom you are talking. What of their intelligence? Are they adept at any particular type of reasoning? Are they sensitive, temperamental people? What kind of work do they do? What are their tastes, skills, appreciations, achievements? Do certain personality types predominate? What are their resources in experience and accomplishments?

8. *Adaptation to the audience expectations of the occasion and the situation.* Review the exact audience conditions under which you are to speak. What is the purpose of the gathering? Is it a college debate? A meeting of a campus club? Church club? Radio talk? An assembly of high school speech students, businessmen, housewives, a speech class in which you are enrolled?

More specifically, what is the purpose of the gathering? Is it to increase information about a specific fact or situation interesting to the group? Is it to seek general education and entertainment, as in a popular lecture? Is it to pay tribute to a person or event, as on Founders Day? Or Washington's birthday? Is it an occasion to line up party votes? To assign certain ones to canvass for funds? To take specific action on some resolution? To sell a product?

What physical conditions exist? How many people are present? How big is the room? Is it too hot? Too cold? Badly lighted? Badly ventilated? Is it an open-air situation? With much passing traffic? Are you to talk via a loudspeaker? Can the listeners hear you easily? Can they see you without intervening pillars? Is your lectern too high? Too low? Absent? Are your visual aids ready? What is the proposed procedure for the occasion? Is your talk to be one of a series in the classroom? Are you one of a panel? What is the order of speaking? How long is each speech to be? Is your clock (or somebody else's) working?

TERTIARY DIMENSIONS

The tertiary dimensions of your audience are those characteristics of your listeners which may indicate some of the primary or secondary dimensions but which are not subject to modification by communication. They are often some of the first questions to be asked about an audience.

9. *Age*
10. *Sex and marital status*
11. *Cultural origin, nationality*
12. *Place of residence*

The value of these audience dimensions is that they provide a quick index of knowledge, interest, attitudes, and perhaps of resources. But our communication does not change these dimensions. There are probably better ways of learning what we want to know about the other dimensions, but because the tertiary dimensions do provide some cues we include them here.

Preliminary alertness to some of these facts about your audience will forewarn you and forearm you in the selection of ideas, illustrations, and appeals and so may go far in making or breaking your talk.

Develop Your Talk in View of Your Adaptation to Your Audience, the Occasion, Your Subject, and Your Speaking Purposes and Personality

Learn to study your audiences as you speak as well as during your preparation. When you learn to do this you will find that they give you many cues about the way they are thinking. The development of skill in the interpretation of feedback is one of the most important skills of speaking. It is frightening to many speakers, and they evade it by indirectness. A little experience, however, some poise, and skill in eye directness will enable you to read these cues while you talk to a large audience just as you probably do at other times. If you extemporize as you are directed to do, you will learn to adjust your talk in many ways to the signals your audience sends you.

Part of your job of adapting to audiences is to create a climate for their favorable hearing of your message. As a speaker you are in a sense a leader. If you are to lead you must take responsibilities. When you take the responsibility nothing is too unimportant for you to consider in shaping the context for your message.

Your subject, its organization, illustrations, details, language, and delivery will depend upon the results of your analysis of the audience. Adapt your material to appeal to the listeners' needs and desires. In your choice of ideas, supporting details, language, and delivery, appeal to the concern for security, freedom, material comfort, social approval, popularity, pride, fair play, sympathy, adventure, escape from boredom, intellectual and aesthetic satisfactions, reverence, duty, and self-sacrifice. (For a detailed discussion of motives and motivation, see Chapter Eighteen, "Persuasive Speaking.")

Appeal to your audience's interest in you as a person. Identify yourself as a person by means of anecdotes and reference to your own experiences.

Be considerate of the convictions and loyalties of your audience. Make it clear in your speech that you respect your listeners as a group or, at any rate, as individuals. If you are trying to make them change their minds, show your respect for them by giving them good reasons for accepting your proposals.

Beware of "high-pressure" techniques. Self-respecting persons shy away from overaggressive, blunt, and domineering speakers. Little permanent satisfaction derives from "telling off" your audience. Avoid scolding, insulting, and sarcastic remarks. Shock and ridicule strike deep and are not easily forgiven. Those who use such techniques often have a mistaken sense of their own efficiency and importance. On the other hand, adjustment to your audience does not mean giving in concerning your convictions. It means trying to gain your ends as a speaker without sacrificing your integrity to do so.

The more you expect from your audience, the more slowly you must move. If necessary, take your trip by stages. Do not expect to accomplish everything at once. Above all, cultivate your ability to sense the appropriate time to stop.

Each communicative act is unique, and every aspect of it contributes to its difference from every other act of communication. We have sketched these aspects only briefly here with the hope of clarifying and pointing up the significance of each of the parts.

Note in the projects and problems below how these suggestions for audience adaptation may be concretely applied.

Projects and Problems

PROJECT 1: ADAPTING THE SPEECH TO THE SITUATION

You are familiar with Lincoln's Gettysburg Address. The ideas contained in it might have been expressed in a great many different ways if they had been developed and presented in other situations. It might have been prepared (*a*) as a legal document, (*b*) as a luncheon-club speech, (*c*) by a movie press agent, (*d*) with the help of a committee, and (*e*) as part of a typical textbook. Read the following examples of parts of this address prepared (in the spirit of exaggeration) to illustrate such adaptations.[7] In the blank space following the number of each illustration, write the appropriate number from the list, above, of purposes for which the ideas might have been presented.

(1) _____Fellows, you all know back in 1776 the British Colonies in America revolted and set up a new government organized along popular lines. Well, now we're in a great civil war, to see whether or not a government like ours is practical enough to last. We are holding a meeting on one of the big battle-fields of the war, to dedicate it as a cemetery for the men who were killed here. I think all you fellows will agree we're doing the right thing. But when you come right down to it, fellows, we might as well save our breath.

(2) _____Eighty-seven years ago certain of the British colonies in America revolted and set up an independent democratic government. This form of government was experimental, and the present Civil War is being fought to determine whether or not it is practical. A great battle of that war was fought on this spot. The men who died here are buried here, and the present assemblage is for the laudable purpose of dedicating the cemetery. In reality, however, nothing of importance will be accomplished by the ceremony.

(3) _____A stupendous conflict . . . for Liberty!
And then . . . an amazing new nation!
New battle!
Fought by armies famous throughout the world as
The Blue . . . and The Gray!
And now . . . A Super-cemetery!

(4) _____WHEREAS, In the year 1776 founders of this republic set up and instituted a new government, based on equalitarian principles and practices; and WHEREAS, A civil war is now in process of prosecution to determine the expediency of said government and said principles; and WHEREAS, We are assembled at the locale of one of the major combats of said war, to dedicate said locale, in accordance with the propriety of such an action, as a place of interment of the defunct of said internecine encounter; there be it *Resolved,* That, to preclude the possibility of the decease of said defunct having been negatory, null, or void, we hereby frame and provide a solemn resolution, i.e., that is, and to wit—that this government in particular and equalitarian principles in general shall not under any circumstances undergo, suffer, or experience the extremity of termination.

(5) _____Fourscore and seven years ago (better say "eighty-seven") our fathers brought forth ("founded" would be a better word) on this continent a new nation (Let's put the name in there, too) conceived in liberty (that sounds awkward: say "with the idea of freedom") and dedicated to the proposition that all men (we ought to include women too. We have a big field) are created equal.

Now we are engaged in a great civil war (make this the first paragraph—

---

[7] Adapted from H. A. Batten, Marcus Goodrich, and Granville Toogood, *The Written Word,* Greenberg: Publisher, Inc., New York, 1922.

we take too long to get into the story) testing whether that nation or any nation so dedicated and so conceived (see above) can long endure. (Endure what? Make it "last.") We are met (say "have met") on a great battlefield of that war (name it).

("We're sorry, Mr. Lincoln, but it simply won't do. You don't seem to be able to get your idea across in plain, forceful language. Take it and think it over, and see if you can't give us a good, hard-hitting, straight-from-the-shoulder speech.")

PROJECT 2: ADAPTING THE SPEECH TO AUDIENCES WITH DIFFERENT DEGREES OF UNDERSTANDING

For an informative speech, select a subject on which you may justly claim to be something of an expert or about which you at least know more than many members of your audience. Prepare two short speeches on this subject. One speech should be to persons who know little or nothing about the subject. The other should be to those who know quite a bit about it. First, you will be called on to present the speech for the relatively uninformed audience. At the next class meeting, you will be called upon to present the speech for those who are better informed. After you finish the second speech, report on the differences you attempted to make.

PROJECT 3: ADAPTING ARGUMENT TO THE ATTITUDES OF AN AUDIENCE

Prepare two short argumentative speeches on the same subject. In the first, try to convince an indifferent audience of the truth of your proposition. In the second, try to convince an antagonistic audience of the soundness of your belief. You will present these speeches at successive class meetings. After the second speech, discuss the differences in your speeches with your classmates.

PROJECT 4: ADAPTING THE SPEECH TO AUDIENCES OF MEN AND WOMEN

Select an interesting subject and discuss with the class the differences you would make in speeches on this subject to an audience of men and to an audience of women.

PROJECT 5: ADAPTING THE SPEECH TO PERSONS OF DIFFERENT AGES

Prepare an informative speech to be presented to a group of adults. Then consider how you would explain the same subject to an eight-year-old boy. You will be asked to make the speech to the class and then report the changes you would make in explaining the subject to a child.

PROJECT 6: ADAPTING THE SPEECH TO THE FORMALITY OF THE SITUATION

Write out two versions of a talk. One should be in informal and conversational style as you would present it in a "bull session" to a group of friends. The other should be written as a radio script in more formal style.

PROJECT 7: ADAPTING THE EMOTIVE APPEALS TO THE AUDIENCE

Select a subject for a persuasive appeal to action. Then select audiences of two different types. Prepare both speeches.

PROJECT 8: IDENTIFYING DIMENSIONS OF AN AUDIENCE

Collect a set of pictures of audiences from newspapers, magazines, at your local newspaper photographic file. Using a projection machine, show the pictures to your class. See how many important dimensions of each audience you can identify in the pictures.

PROJECT 9: ADJUSTING TO AUDIENCE FEEDBACK

Hold an extemporaneous speech exercise in which each speaker is given a topic and excused from the room for two or three minutes of preparation. In the meantime you are to cue members of the class to make certain responses to the speech. When the speaker returns to make his speech, he is to see if he can interpret these responses and make an appropriate adjustment to them. As soon as he has made his adjustment, discuss his way of handling the problem.

References

Andersch, Elizabeth G., and Loren C. Staats: *Speech for Everyday Use,* rev. ed., Holt, Rinehart and Winston, Inc., New York, 1950, chaps. 4 and 5.

Brigance, W. Norwood: *Speech,* Appleton-Century-Crofts, Inc., New York, 1952, chaps. 6–8.

Bryant, Donald C., and Karl R. Wallace: *The Fundamentals of Public Speaking,* 3d ed., Appleton-Century-Crofts, Inc., New York, 1960, chaps. 3, 18, and 19.

Crocker, Lionel: *Public Speaking for College Students,* American Book Company, New York, 1956, chap. 21.

Gilman, Wilbur E., Bower Aly, and Loren D. Reid: *The Fundamentals of Speaking,* The Macmillan Company, New York, 1951, chap. 19.

Gray, Giles W., and Waldo W. Braden: *Public Speaking: Principles and Practice,* Harper & Brothers, New York, 1951, chap. 5.

Micken, Ralph A.: *Speaking for Results,* Houghton Mifflin Company, Boston, 1958, chap. 4.

Sandford, William P., and W. Hayes Yeager: *Principles of Effective Speaking,* 5th ed., The Ronald Press Company, New York, 1950, chap. 10.

EIGHT

Developing Confidence

IF YOU FEEL some tension and apprehension about making a speech you may be assured that you are not unique in this respect. Perhaps your major reason for taking this course is that you lack confidence and you hope to acquire some sure-fire formula for overcoming nervousness. The fact is that there are no quick and ready cures for stage fright. Nevertheless there is hope. We have learned a great deal about stage fright in recent years, and we know that many students can go a long way toward controlling and eliminating this disturbing condition. The best procedure is to study your particular problem along with the facts and principles of adjustment set forth in this chapter and to work patiently to apply them. Learning to make new adjustments may take time, but there is little doubt that you will benefit from intelligent, patient, and persistent effort.

In this chapter we will explore what is known about stage fright and examine its causes and symptoms. Then we will study some methods by which you can work to develop confidence in the speaking situation.

Some Facts about Stage Fright

There are several fairly distinct components of this type of human behavior. We shall refer to them as the "affective," the "physiological," the "behavioral," and the "cognitive" reactions of the phenomenon. First there is an unpleasant feeling with overtones of fear. Then there are certain apparently uncontrollable physiological reactions which seem inappropri-

118

ate and disturbing. There are also overt behavioral manifestations which may or may not be observed by others. And finally there is the cognitive awareness of dissonance or confusion. These four aspects of stage fright have a certain inherent relationship, although we cannot measure the unique effect of any one of them separately. The person experiencing stage fright cannot judge its intensity because he has never experienced the feelings and reactions of another person. The experience, however, is real, and there is always the urge to control and eliminate such dissonant states. It has been demonstrated that stimuli which influence one of the variables in a dissonant state tend to spread their influence to other elements of the state. Fortunately, in stage fright there are ways of working on each of these four components. Perhaps this accounts for the fact that most students who work intelligently at stage-fright control achieve a reasonable measure of progress.

A survey of a variety of groups of college students revealed that from 60 to 75 per cent of the students questioned admitted that nervousness disturbed them in speaking and that over 30 per cent considered it their most serious problem.[1] These figures are based on attitudes students are willing to report; and it is probable that the students questioned minimized rather than exaggerated their fears. Some persons are nervous about a great many things they do; others are nervous only about speaking, and then only in certain situations. It is generally impossible to predict on the basis of a person's reaction to one situation what his reaction to another will be. Yet there is a general consistency in the way a person responds to such stimuli.

Some students become so intensely worried that they cannot eat or sleep before they are scheduled to speak. You may feel that you will die or wish you could. Fortunately you probably won't be able to escape your misery in this manner. Excessive anxiety not only causes acute distress but reduces mental efficiency. Degrees of nervousness can be plotted along a continuum from indifference through positive stimulation to a state of highly charged disintegration. Students at either end of this continuum have serious problems as speakers. The Speech Attitude Scale and Speech Experience Inventory[2] both show scores having a marked correlation with felt and observed degrees of confidence.

Newcomers to speech making as well as professionals, the young and the old, experience stage fright. It can occur at unexpected times. Although thorough preparation may reduce nervousness, it is not a sure preventive. Long experience in speaking in some situations will not assure

[1] Howard Gilkinson and Franklin H. Knower, *Psychological Studies of Individual Differences among Students of Speech,* University of Minnesota, Minneapolis, 1939.
[2] See Franklin H. Knower, "A Study of Speech Attitudes and Adjustments," *Speech Monographs,* 5:130–203, 1938.

a person of confidence in speaking under other circumstances. Although it is impossible to predict feelings in one situation from feelings in another, it is possible to predict from an adequate sample of a person's feelings what his feelings will be on the average in another adequate sample of his behavior. Several studies have indicated that nervousness is likely to be more acute among college women than among college men. This would suggest that the problem is to some extent a matter of development, for Knower's study indicated that men of high school age tend to be more nervous than women.[3]

Experiments indicate that students tend to rate themselves as a little more nervous than they believe is average, whereas they rate one another as a little less nervous than average. Students who have stage fright can take comfort from the fact that most of us look less nervous than we feel. As people get older they tend to be less subject to stage fright, but age is no immunization. It can happen to anybody at any age.

Nervousness is not related to differences in measured intelligence among college students. It is a condition which may afflict the capable and the less capable alike. Perhaps it is even negatively correlated with intelligence, for those who are markedly deficient do not know enough to worry. What is important for you as a student of speech is to realize that nervousness can be reduced. Although there are no dependable methods of eliminating it entirely, most people can reduce the strain of stage fright through persistent efforts, as you will see in this chapter.

You need to understand that not all nervousness can be classified as stage fright. Since a speech situation is one in which the speaker as well as the speech is to be judged, it is quite normal for the speaker to have a deep concern about the outcome. As a speaker you also feel a sense of responsibility for your cause and for your listeners, which may give rise to some anxiety. This anxiety is normal and may well serve to motivate you to your best effort. This kind of anxiety state is typical of, but ordinarily much less intense than, true stage fright. A stage fright response is an expression of unreasonable fear, producing a dissonant condition which is very unpleasant and disintegrative.

Causes of Stage Fright

The causes of stage fright are complex and varied in most persons. To say flatly that it results from inadequate preparation, emotionality, sensitivity, conditioning, conflict, habit, or egotism is an unwarranted over-

[3] Franklin H. Knower, "A Study of Speech Attitudes and Adjustments," *Speech Monographs*, 5:130–203, 1938; Theodore Clevenger, Jr., and Gregg Phifer, "What Do Beginning College Speech Texts Say about Stage Fright?" *The Speech Teacher*, 8:1–8, 1959; Theodore Clevenger, Jr., "A Synthesis of Experimental Research on Stage Fright," *Quarterly Journal of Speech*, 45:134–145, 1959.

simplification of the facts. Neither is there any evidence that it is an unlearned or inherited response to the speech situation.

To understand the manner in which speech fears may develop, it is necessary to know something about the nature of individual differences in emotional behavior. Many types of experiences cause the individual to develop tendencies to respond with uncontrolled emotion. Such tendencies can result from leading a "sheltered" life in which the individual is shielded from stimulation by even mild crisis situations. They can result from being brought up on the theory that "children should be seen and not heard"; from being reminded of real or imagined physical or social differences so that excessive timidity and a feeling of inferiority result; from not being allowed to forget a mistake; and from being repeatedly bullied in unpleasant situations. Intense emotional reactions forcing the release of pent-up emotion are characteristic of persons who have grown up under these circumstances. Persons with high emotional potentials who have not formed the habit of making clear-cut decisions and acting upon them with satisfaction develop psychological conflicts. Any stimulus which upsets a person's equilibrium and creates a state of dissonance creates a climate for stage fright. Purely incidental experiences may cause the individual to become deeply aroused emotionally and to remain in a prolonged state of uneasiness. This condition may be likened to a smoldering fire; in calm weather it is relatively harmless, but in a lively breeze it can quickly blaze into flames that cause widespread destruction.

A situation which makes us feel nervous need operate only once to condition us to fear reactions in similar circumstances. Some persons are disturbed by one element in the situation, some by another. In speech making, some of these disturbing factors are a mistaken image of what is expected of us and of the role we are to play as a speaker, inadequate preparation, the appearance of an unexpected person, an unexpected occurrence, the reactions of members of the audience, the sudden awareness of a mistake or deficiency, and the failure or imagined failure to meet a standard. In most of these situations the emotional response originally appears when we feel a sense of insecurity in the situation. When our security appears to be threatened and we do not know how to respond, our defenses are shattered. Although our emotional responses are useful for protection from physical danger, we become confused when, in a social situation in which we do not see or refuse to admit the existence of danger, we make the instinctive responses appropriate to physical danger.

Symptoms of Stage Fright

Withdrawal. The symptoms of emotional behavior in stage fright are all subject to reasonably precise explanations. Many speakers show a tendency to withdraw in such habits as looking at the floor or ceiling, looking out of the window or over the heads of the audience, putting their hands in their pockets or behind their backs, or retreating behind a table or speaker's stand. All these habits represent incipient retreat or flight from an unpleasant situation. Avoiding the eyes of the audience indicates that the speaker feels he needs all his powers of concentration to recollect and utter what he has to say. He feels that if he looks at the audience, their reactions will distract him.

Physiological reactions. Pounding of the heart, increase in the rate of heartbeat, gasping for breath, dry mouth, perspiration, and blushing are the results of changes in physiological processes associated with fear reactions. Fear reactions have biological survival value only when they release sufficient energy for struggle or flight. To provide such energy, a reflex reaction of the organism in fear is to release glycogen (a form of food reserve) from the liver into the blood stream. The use of this energy involves metabolism or a form of combustion. Metabolic action is in turn dependent upon oxygen supplied to the blood by the lungs. We gasp for breath when we are afraid, not because we have any less air in our lungs than under normal conditions, but because we need more.

In order to be used by the body, glycogen must be pumped by the heart into the peripheral muscles—legs, arms, hands, back, and so forth—and waste materials must be carried away. The charge of emotion speeds up heart action in order that blood may circulate more rapidly. Tension in the muscles of blood-vessel walls is relaxed, and blood rushes to the surface of the body to rid itself of waste matter through the pores of the skin by means of perspiration. Whether we blush or blanch depends upon whether the blood is allowed to circulate rapidly close to the surface of the body through relaxation of capillary muscle walls, or whether an excessive amount of blood is drawn from the surface of the body to fulfill physiological functions primarily in the trunk. The sinking feeling which speakers sometimes feel in the pit of the stomach is probably associated with the indigestion accompanying emotional response.

Tension and muscular conflict. When the organism is energized in conflict and then fails to use this energy in the biological responses of struggle or flight, it tends to use the energy in tension (the straining of antagonistic muscle groups against each other), in trembling (the intermittent relaxation and tension of the muscles of antagonistic groups), and in fidgeting and random behavior (the attempt of the organism to return to normal from an unpleasant state of tension). Trembling occurs in those regions most responsive to the conflicts of antagonistic muscle pairs—the vocal folds, the finer muscles of the face, the arms and hands, and the knees. Tension and trembling in the body are analogous to vibration in a motor.

The feeling of awkwardness that some speakers experience results from the fact that the abnormally tense muscles do not respond so readily and flexibly as they do in their normal state. The mouth becomes dry as a result of neural and chemical influences on the glands, together with tension in the muscles of the gland ducts and the muscle walls of the mouth through which these ducts lead in secreting saliva into the mouth, and as a result of the neural link of the salivary glands with digestive processes which are stopped during intense emotion.

Conflict of intellectual and emotional behavior. To understand other symptoms of stage fright it will be helpful to learn something of the physiology of man's nervous system. Man's capacity for emotional response is biological; as an infant he does not differ much in this respect from the lower animals. Intellectual behavior, however, is something man learns. The use of language, the retention of ideas in memory, the ability to reason, and other complex cultural and social skills are possible because they are learned.

A common aspect of the cultural training of children is the encouragement of the inhibition of emotional responses. The ability to inhibit emotional responses, then, is also a form of intellectual behavior. Achievement in the inhibition of emotional behavior is probably dependent upon both the intensity of the emotional reaction and the strength of cortical or intellectual resistance to the emotion. The two types of behavior in a sense compete for control of the organism. If intellectual reactions are to function at their best, it would seem necessary to inhibit intense emotional reactions. When it is impossible to inhibit emotional reactions, some of the person's intellectual behavior is also seriously interfered with or destroyed. The unpleasantness of dissonance arises from the experience of conflict and uncertainty. Thus the inability "to think on one's feet," forgetting what one had intended to say, slips of the tongue, going blank mentally, and the inability to control muscular action are traceable directly to the fact that for the time being emotional reactions have taken control. We might say that when the charges of emotional reaction become too great, the cortex blows a fuse and the lights of the intellect go out or at least become badly short-circuited. This situation leads to what we may call the Law of Stage-fright Control: *Anything which increases the efficiency of intellectual activity or reduces the intensity of conflicting emotions will help in developing confidence in the speech situation.* Later we shall discuss in more detail the procedures for reducing stage fright.

Voice reactions. Nervous reactions in speaking affect voice control in many ways. One of the most common effects is a rise in pitch. Since tension in the vocal folds is one of the factors determining the pitch of the voice, it is easy to see how emotional stress produces an unusually high pitch. Monotony and harshness of voice result from the difficulty of controlling muscles under tension.

In a state of emotion, the body makes heavy demands upon the breath stream. The vocal folds must adjust themselves to allow air to pass, and the result is weakness or inaudibility of voice or the inability to "speak above a whisper." When it occurs in conjunction with increased tempo, voice weakness may be explained as withdrawal behavior. The nervous speaker tries to make himself inconspicuous and to get through his speech as quickly as possible.

Psychological reactions. The speaker in a state of stage fright reacts psychologically to his physiological condition. In some cases the individual has the characteristic physical symptoms but is not disturbed by his psychological reactions. Such cases no doubt result either from intense emotional response to speaking accompanied by strong intellectual control or from intense stage-fright reactions now partially overcome. A clear picture of the symptoms of nervousness, together with some insight into their bases, is useful in applying the principles for developing control over the condition.

Learning to Develop Confidence

There is no simple way to develop confidence which will work for all persons. Some reeducational techniques work directly toward the elimination of stage fright, some attack the problem indirectly to reduce the probability and severity of the reaction, and others help the speaker live with the reaction and make the most of his abilities in spite of this distraction and discomfort. Each individual must discover the method that is best for him.

The principal suggestions we have to offer can be classified under the two parts of the Law of Stage-fright Control already mentioned: reducing the intensity of emotional reaction and increasing the efficiency of intellectual activity. It should be understood, however, that in many cases these two factors overlap: Some techniques which reduce the intensity of emotion also build up cortical or intellectual control. We shall consider first the ways of reducing the intensity of the fear reaction.

REDUCING THE INTENSITY OF EMOTIONAL REACTION

Study the psychology of emotion. It is a well-known fact that "we are afraid of what we don't understand." When we acquire insight into the nature of our emotional responses and learn that what was considered a mystifying, embarrassing peculiarity is a commonplace experience subject to natural law and reasonably precise explanations, the panicky feeling which aggravates fear gives way to hope and determination to develop new habits of response. William James long ago pointed out that when we become curious about emotional responses and "abstract the mind stuff" from them, that is, think about them as they are experienced in order to analyze and report on their nature, the full force of the emotional reaction is greatly reduced. In effect, when we do this we substitute intellectual behavior for emotional behavior. Cognitive activity can exercise a beneficial effect on emotional activity. Thinking about our emotions also involves accepting them and enables us to develop an objective attitude toward them. Discovering the original causes of our fears is a helpful step in relieving their pressure.

Think and talk about your emotions as an objective fact. "Confession is good for the soul." When you are troubled about an emotional response, it is helpful to find someone to listen to your story. In psychiatry the effects of such a confession are called "mental catharsis." In the worst days of the London blitz during World War II, a listening squad was organized to send persons to listen to the stories of those who had been bombed out of house and home. The feeling that someone was interested in hearing a personal account of the experience relieved the emotional distress of the victims. Sharing the feeling with others not only releases emotional tension, but also raises the emotional response to a conscious level where one deals with it intellectually.

Some advisers may suggest to you that you ignore your condition. For the person undergoing the agony of this struggle with himself this cannot be done. In fact, your behavior is already evasive. You cannot forestall this evasion with further evasive tactics. Far better to face it. Accept it as a part of you and seek to understand it. Then you have already begun by using techniques for controlling it. As you develop skill with these techniques you become less concerned about it.

This advice to talk about your emotions does not mean that you should thrust them upon others at every opportunity. The classroom, however, is an ideal place for carrying on this kind of emotional reeducation.

Resolve personal conflicts. Inferiority complexes appear as frequently in persons who merely imagine or accept irresponsible suggestions of inferiority as they do in persons who may really be inferior to others in some aspect of their functioning. A boy of Norwegian background who grew up in a predominantly Swedish community had been told so frequently that Norwegians never amounted to anything that he was unable to take himself seriously. Red hair, freckles, fatness, bowlegs, a facial scar or birthmark, shortness in boys and tallness in girls, living in the country or on the "wrong side of the tracks," belonging to a minority group, failure in competitions or examinations, unfriendly acts of others, and hundreds of other minor differences and experiences are often magnified out of all proportion to the significance of the facts. Mental conflicts and anxiety over such matters may be relieved by learning the facts about them and taking a constructive course toward solution. Ask yourself such questions as these: Do the differences actually exist in a noticeable degree? If so, are they really as important as some persons think they are? Can any significant handicaps I have be overcome by a program of development which eliminates them or even turns them into assets? Are there not intelligent methods of compensation available which eliminate the difficulty?

Conflicts sometimes develop when we have opposing desires or ambitions. Examples are conflicts between the admitted need for expression of self-confidence and the abhorrence of egotism; the enjoyment of doing our best and the dislike of pretension; the enjoyment of recognition from our associates and the fear of being so outstanding that we are left conspicuously alone; the wish to render useful service, and the objection to butting in; the desire to talk about ourselves and the fear of being considered a braggart; the desire to maintain reputable moral standards and the fear of being considered a prig; and the recognized need for persistence in attaining social objectives and the aversion to becoming a bore. Such conflicts usually remain on the unconscious level until we recognize them or until someone points them out to us. Usually with a little friendly help, we can formulate intelligent plans of action which will in time resolve them.

Counter unpleasant and disorganizing emotions. Most persons are incapable of experiencing opposite emotional reactions at the same time. If the speaker becomes intensely interested in what he is to accomplish by his speaking, if he can find some humor in the situation or feel righteous indignation over a cause he expounds, if he feels a wholesome sense of rivalry, if he appears to be confident even when he is not, if he enjoys participating in group activities where success is enjoyed with others or where it accompanies work well done, the disorganizing and unpleasant effects of fear may be effectively banished.

Substituting a pleasant for an unpleasant emotion in adjustment is a form of compensation. Common experience and common sense both attest to the success of the method when properly controlled. Examples of it are whistling to keep up one's courage, assuming indifference to ward off anticipated disappointment, or losing oneself in feverish activity as a distraction from grief. The sergeant who leaped out of his foxhole to the attack with the charge to his comrades, "Come on, you so and so's, do you want to live forever?" was substituting one emotion for another.

Develop habits of voluntary relaxation and control of activity. When you have been keyed up and must relax in order to get vitally needed rest, what is the natural method of achieving this objective? You yawn. When you yawn, you stretch, tense your muscles, take a deep breath, let the air out slowly, and then let your muscles relax. General relaxation may be attained in some degree by taking several deep breaths in fairly rapid succession. Grasping the speaker's stand is a device often used to induce tension as a step toward relaxation. Some speakers report that they can speak more easily sitting down than standing up. The psychological principles by which the intensity of emotional responses is reduced through controlled relaxation are not thoroughly understood, but if the speaker discovers that they work for him, he may derive some value from using them.

Do not submit to unnecessary mental and physical strain. If you can expect to do your best as a speaker only when you are rested and well, see to it that you get the necessary rest and health care. For a great many people, speaking is hard work. What you can do as "all in the day's work" under optimal conditions may be too much for the maintenance of poise and self-control when you are tired or affected by loss of energy. Although artificial stimulants are temporarily effective, they are not a substitute for natural vigor and pep.

INCREASING THE EFFICIENCY OF INTELLECTUAL ACTIVITY

Know what is reasonably to be expected of a speaker. You as a speaker must judge when you have satisfied reasonable requirements. You are overly optimistic if you hope to please everyone. You may realize that you are not doing your best upon a particular occasion; but you will understand that this, too, is a normal variation in human functioning. If you are aware of what your audience may reasonably expect and if you have attained sufficient objectivity in speech analysis to know that you have no real cause for dissatisfaction, then you can concentrate on the job at hand. If you do not have a reasonably clear understanding of speech standards and methods of self-analysis, then these are the first goals you should set for yourself. Until you have developed skill in judgment on such matters you should look to your instructor or some other experienced speech critic for evaluation of your performance. Remember that one of your aims is to get rid of any mistaken images you may have of what is expected of a speaker.

One way to gain an understanding of what is expected of you is to look upon your speaking activities as if you were playing a role. You change the roles you play in life at least several times a day, so this is no new experience. You may not have thought of yourself as a speaker. Or perhaps you haven't considered speech an important part of the roles you want to play. Beginning with what you know about speech, try now to play the role of a person using these principles. It may give you a new feeling, a new understanding, and, yes, some new or latent skills may be brought into play. Together these learning behaviors will bolster your courage and skill as a speaker.

Prepare as thoroughly as possible. Although thorough preparation offers no assurance that you will not be emotionally disturbed on a particular speaking occasion, lack of preparation only invites inefficiency and mental panic. Students sometimes report that they have performed poorly in spite of careful preparation or have performed relatively well when they selected a subject at the last moment. Appearances are deceiving in such cases for two reasons. Preparation for a speech on a subject selected at the last moment is not poor if the topic has grown out of the speaker's experience and if he has already done considerable thinking and developed positive feelings about it. In the opposite case, the well-prepared speech that failed was not really well prepared, for thorough preparation involves careful study of the subject, organization of the material into a pattern which facilitates memory, rehearsal aloud and under conditions similar to those under which the speech will be presented, and spaced learning rather than cramming. In order to adapt to any situation, it is wise to assimilate more material than you will need for the speech you have planned.

Use mnemonic devices. As we have seen, organized material is easier to remember than unorganized material. Stories are easier to remember

Much of the talking you'll do will be done under difficult circumstances! You need to know how to do it efficiently and cheerfully. (Photo courtesy Cincinnati and Suburban Bell Telephone Company.)

than the points in the analysis of an abstract or technical proposition because the sequence of events in the story has an inherent order or organization. If your speech concerns abstract ideas, arrange the points for ready retention. Use anecdotes and examples wherever possible, since they are more concrete and are easier to remember than other types of material. Personal experiences and startling facts are easy to retain because of their intensity and vividness. Refresh your memory of your material immediately before you speak and prepare the beginning of your speech with special care. You will recognize these techniques as applications of the principles of learning discussed in Chapter Two. Use notes to refresh your memory if you must, but learn not to read directly from them or depend entirely upon them.

Use directed movement to keep your mind active. Some directed movements commonly used by speakers to help them collect and organize their thinking are deliberate pauses; moving from one side of a table or stand to the other; picking up and putting down a book, paper, or pointer; taking a drink of water; restating a previously stated idea; and making a general statement about the subject. Occasional movements of this type are accepted by the audience as a matter of course. Too frequent use of them, however, is distracting.

Develop an effective philosophy of speaking. It has been pointed out by James that "confidence equals success over ambition." [4] In a situation where one's ambition is indicated by the figure 2 and his success by 1, it follows that his confidence is indicated by the fraction ½. It should be apparent that confidence can be changed by modifying either of the values of the fraction.

If you hope for more than you have a right to expect, you will probably be disappointed and unduly worried. Few speeches are important enough to be chiseled in marble, cast in bronze, or even set in type. Practice with one person or a small group at first, and gradually increase the size of your audience. Speak often. When you as a beginning speaker learn that your best efforts, even though they fall short of perfection, are probably fair expressions of yourself and that there is no justification for deceiving others even in speech, you will be on the road to the development of goals that are within the realm of possibility. The numerator in the fraction can be modified if you see to it that your best efforts do not fall below a minimum standard of achievement. If you are conscientious, if you make an honest effort to know your subject, to organize it well, to forget yourself, to render a real service, and to interpret results in the light of reason, you may achieve results which are far more permanent than you can possibly realize at the time. Sound but unpretentious

[4] See William James, *Psychology, Briefer Course,* Holt, Rinehart and Winston, Inc., New York, 1900, p. 187.

achievement in a difficult project is of greater value than a chorus of approval for achievement in an easy project. Although the success of a speech is to be judged on the basis of the results attained, remember that as a beginner you cannot afford to make success so difficult that all enjoyment of achievement is lost.

Projects and Problems

PROJECT 1: GETTING YOURSELF ACROSS

Arrange to show the sound film, *Getting Yourself Across*, developed by McGraw-Hill Book Company, Inc., New York, to accompany this text. See the *Teacher's Manual* for suggestions about the use of this film and questions for classroom discussion on the film.

PROJECT 2: NARRATION OF A PERSONAL EXPERIENCE

Purposes of this assignment: (a) To increase objectivity, directness, relaxation, and enthusiasm; (b) to improve ability to extemporize in a conversational manner; (c) to develop skill in projection to the audience.

Suggested content: (a) An experience which gave you a thrill. (b) A good intention which went wrong by accident. (c) A practical joke which was enjoyed by all. (d) An embarrassing experience. (e) An experience with hobbies. (f) Your first job. (g) Experiences with teachers. (h) A travel experience.

Procedure: Select as a subject an experience which will be interesting to others. Arrange the main points of the story for continuity and interest. Prepare an introduction which explains the background and characters of the story. Rehearse from your outline and prepare to speak without notes. Be ready to observe and react to the responses of your audience.

Facts and principles you should know to carry out this assignment:

I. Interest in a story is influenced by:
   A. The story. It should have:
     1. A theme which arouses human interest.
     2. An introduction which presents necessary background.
     3. Main points clearly developed without unnecessary details.
     4. Rapid movement up to the climax.
   B. The method by which it is presented. The speaker should:
     1. Have sufficient vocal force to be easily heard.
     2. Be able to dramatize by use of voice and action.
     3. Show that he really enjoys telling the story.
     4. Adapt his narrative to the responses of his audience.
II. Personal adjustments required of the speaker include:
   A. Ability to laugh at himself, but sufficient poise to avoid laughing at his own jokes.

B. Physical and vocal responsiveness to materials.

C. Vocal force and fluency necessary for projection and movement in the story.

D. Ability to talk about himself without appearing egotistical.

PROJECT 3: A SPEECH OF STRONG CONVICTION

Purposes of this assignment: (*a*) To develop skill in defending convictions; (*b*) to develop confidence in speaking; (*c*) to improve fluency, projection, directness, and expressive action.

Subjects: (*a*) A firm conviction which you believe your audience should share. (*b*) A cause which you believe to be misunderstood. (*c*) A principle for which you feel a deep and moving loyalty.

Consider such specific subjects as:

The hypocrite	The doublecrosser
The coward	Critics of the younger generation
The "yes" man	The meanest man I ever knew
The schemer	The Fifth Amendment
If I had a million dollars	The Red Cross
The future of chemical engineering	Why I believe in America
A pal I once had	Some common annoyances
Cuba under Castro	Communism and the dignity of man

Procedure: Select a specific subject and outline your ideas about it. Arrange an introduction which (*a*) predisposes the audience toward a favorable response and (*b*) justifies your attempt to speak upon this subject.

Rehearse your material with (*a*) full concentration upon the importance of your topic; (*b*) use of language which expresses your feeling; (*c*) spontaneous and motivated expressive action.

Prepare to study the responses of your audience.

Facts and principles you should know to succeed in this assignment: The most effective speaking is done by persons motivated by a great conviction. Important controversial ideas are seldom accepted by an audience if the speaker expresses them halfheartedly.

The effective expression of strong conviction requires (*a*) vocal force and fluency, (*b*) vigorous and well-integrated expressive activity, (*c*) language not only realistic but also forceful, and (*d*) reasons which are not only sound but also acceptable.

The material for this speech should be relatively simple and strong in interest value. Although the speech should be carefully prepared, it should be delivered with abandon to the immediate motivation.

PROJECT 4: READING OR TELLING FUNNY STORIES

Purposes of this assignment: (*a*) To develop techniques of using humor to reduce nervousness; (*b*) to acquire skill in voice control for the purposes of telling a funny story; (*c*) to develop your sense of humor.

Subjects: (*a*) A funny story from *The New Yorker*. (*b*) Some anecdotes which illustrate a point. (*c*) A short story by Irvin S. Cobb, Stephen Leacock, Ring Lardner, or Mark Twain. (*d*) Poetry by Don Marquis, Ogden Nash, William Kirk, or Tom Daly. (*e*) Types of humor.

Procedure: Decide upon the material you will present. It may be a reading, a story, or a speech using anecdotes or some other type of humor. It should be something which you think is funny and which represents a type of humor you would enjoy sharing with others. Prepare the material carefully and present it to your classmates with the intention of getting the maximum response from them.

Facts and principles you should know to succeed in this assignment: You must get into the proper frame of mind for telling stories. Humor is infectious if listeners are in the right frame of mind. The subject and situation, therefore, must be appropriate. Good fun is wholesome; it is not biting or sarcastic. Characterization must be realistic, and suggestive action, voice variation, and articulation must be carefully controlled. Details should be vivid. Punch lines need careful timing. Use pauses to obtain emphasis. You need to know how to control tensions and how to relax. Build toward the climax, and avoid obvious elaboration of the moral or point; listeners like to get that for themselves. Although you as the speaker may show your appreciation of the humor, you should not lead the laughter.

PROJECT 5: SPEECH WITH VISUAL AIDS OR DEMONSTRATIVE ACTION

Purposes of this assignment: (*a*) To help overcome the feeling of awkwardness and tension in the speech situation; (*b*) to develop some facility in using the symbolism of bodily action in speech.

Subjects:

Fencing
Shadow boxing
The grip and swing of a golf club
First-aid practice
Playing a musical instrument
Adjusting the sights on a rifle

Handling a fly rod
Cartooning or sketching
Pantomime of a character
Diagram of the organization of a company

Procedure: Decide what you would like to do and carefully plan your demonstration and use of action. Practice or rehearse the presentation several times. Get as much action as you can into the performance. Try to maintain an effective balance between tension and complete relaxation. Concentrate on putting over the idea you are trying to explain. Be sure your audience can see your action or diagram at all times. Be sure to explain clearly as well as to demonstrate the action.

PROJECT 6: A PERSONAL-PROBLEM SPEECH

Purposes of this assignment: (*a*) To develop directness and audience adjustment in conversational style; (*b*) to talk about a personal problem with objectivity; (*c*) to practice thinking on your feet in responding to, and synthesizing, audience suggestions.

Subjects: (*a*) A choice of vocation. (*b*) The adjustment to be made to a particular person or situation. (*c*) How to overcome an objectionable habit, attitude, or sensitivity. (*d*) Making the most of an opportunity. (*e*) A prejudice I should like to overcome. (*f*) Getting along with persons who annoy me. (*g*) Achieving goals against handicaps.

Procedure: Prepare an outline stating the issues clearly. Reveal your inclinations and your judgments of them. Anticipate and prepare answers for expected suggestions. Summarize and evaluate suggestions before taking your seat.

Facts and principles useful in preparing this project: Most audiences will respond well to sincerity and frankness. Although to laugh at oneself is wholesome, as a speaker you should not be profusely apologetic or falsely humble, and you should not laugh too much. Introduce your topic in a way which will orient your audience to the problem, but omit nonessential details and get quickly to your main point. You should not defend yourself too sharply against criticism. If you are too severe, the audience will sense it. Show that you can take criticism courageously. Work to show discriminative judgment in approving useful and rejecting impractical suggestions. Learn to look directly at the audience and the individuals in it with poise and reserve as they talk to you. Keep suggestions in mind for summarizing the performance.

PROJECT 7: SPEECH ATTITUDE SCALE

Purposes of this assignment: (*a*) To gain a better insight into your speech attitudes and adjustments; (*b*) to help plan a program for developing better speech attitudes and adjustments.

Procedure: Fill out a copy of Knower's *Speech Attitude Scale* (to be provided by your instructor) and hold a conference with your instructor about your score on it.

References

Brown, Charles T.: *Introduction to Speech,* Houghton Mifflin Company, Boston, 1955, chaps. 18–21.

Bryant, Donald C., and Karl R. Wallace: *The Fundamentals of Public Speaking,* 3d ed., Appleton-Century-Crofts, Inc., New York, 1960, chap. 4.

Dickens, Milton: *Speech: Dynamic Communication,* Harcourt, Brace & World, Inc., New York, 1954, chap. 13.

Festinger, Leon: *A Theory of Cognitive Dissonance,* Row, Peterson & Company, Evanston, Ill., 1957.

Irvin, John V., and Marjorie Rosenberger: *Modern Speech,* Holt, Rinehart and Winston, Inc., New York, 1961.

Oliver, Robert T., and Rupert L. Cortright: *Effective Speech,* Holt, Rinehart and Winston, Inc., New York, 1961, chap. 3.

Sandford, William P., and W. Hayes Yeager: *Principles of Effective Speaking,* 5th ed., The Ronald Press Company, New York, 1950, chap. 2.

Thonssen, Lester T., and Howard Gilkinson: *Basic Training in Speech,* D. C. Heath and Company, Boston, 1953, chap. 4.

Young, Paul Thomas: *Motivation and Emotion,* John Wiley & Sons, Inc., New York, 1961.

NINE

Using Effective Language

Words are much more than so many nouns, verbs, and adjectives to be used in your speech without much concern for subtlety of meaning or exact effect.

If you have seriously tried to communicate to others the nebulous workings of your mind—the complicated emotion and imagination, the reasoning helping to shape a decision—you are aware of some of the language pitfalls of communication.

Your limited vocabulary, for example, may be largely unintelligible to your audience. Your terms may be accurate but technical. Or your words may be simple but not an accurate transfer of your meaning. Or this reflection of meaning may be blocked by involved sentence structure, misplaced reference words, or misuse of tenses and number.

At the same time you may have observed that your first impulse in reacting to a stimulating experience is to utter your feelings. It is as though you were not aware of what had happened to you until you had found words which expressed your feelings. Language, effectively used, clarifies and translates for others your ideas; unfolds the ideas with sequence, relevancy, and impressiveness; illuminates the thinking with interesting and persuasive elements; furnishes the word symbols by which the delivery itself—voice, articulation, gestures—is helped.

Effectiveness in the language of the speech will thus lead your audiences to understand your message, remember it, respond favorably, follow your suggestions and appeals in their later behavior.

134

Effective "style" depends upon the speaker's having (1) an idea worthwhile, (2) a motive and desire to communicate it, (3) a clear conception of that idea, (4) a sensitivity to the audience's attitudes and capability of responding to the speech, (5) the speaker's ability to adapt the speech to the immediate time, place, and audience, (6) and "a command of language adequate to express the idea in words." [1]

Effective language, or style, will have the qualities of (1) adaptation to the audience, occasion, subject, and speaker, (2) accuracy, (3) clearness, and (4) impressiveness and interest.

These four qualities of language usage are essentially those of classical rhetoricians.[2] They, with later variants, are a convenient approach to the study and application of efficient language. These four approaches suggest the main problems and techniques underlying language efficiency. The speaker's over-all obligation is to adjust his vocabulary to his subject, audience, occasion, and self. More specifically, his duty in language is to attempt an accurate representation of his ideas; then, with another look at his audience, he must be sure that his language is clear; and finally, he must so enforce his materials as to make them interesting and impressive or persuasive.

These four qualities of language obviously merge into one another. It is convenient, however, to discuss and apply them separately. The minimum requirements are that the language will be both clear and impressive.[3]

Rhetorical Guideposts to Effective Use of Language

How may these qualities of language usage be specifically applied? Although you are not chiefly interested in perfecting style, you are much concerned that your words should contribute to the total pattern of your ideas, organization, language, and delivery. For you, style is not a decoration, but a technique of composition that helps you to verbalize, clarify, and transmit your ideas persuasively and impressively.

Note the elements of style as concerned with both words and their composition. Language usage deals both with the selection of individual words and their combination into phrases, clauses, and sentences, and into the larger elements of the composition, involving the introduction, main body, and conclusion. The suggestions below concerning the four qualities of language will refer both to words and to their arrangement.

---

[1] Lester Thonssen and A. Craig Baird, *Speech Criticism*, The Ronald Press Company, New York, 1948, p. 430.

[2] Cicero, *De Oratore*, book III.

[3] Thonssen and Baird, *op. cit.*, p. 431.

ADAPT YOUR LANGUAGE

Adapt your language to your audience, the occasion, your speaking purpose, and your own personality. Just as such adaptation is necessary for efficient organization and delivery, so adjustment of language obviously helps in communicating and obtaining the response you want. How will you make these language adjustments?

Identify yourself with your audience. Try to visualize the individual and collective personality of your listeners, their probable attitudes toward you and your ideas, their interests, experience, knowledge and thinking habits. You can probably make an accurate guess about the general traits of your audience; and experience will no doubt lead you to make more satisfactory adaptations. According to your analysis of your audience, you can use language that is learned or idiomatic, formal or informal, standard or colloquial—or even slangy—national or regional, humorous or solemn, technical or popular.

Audience adaptation means that you will use a conversational style. The language of speech is different from the language of reading. When you compose a speech, you should hear the sounds and orally test the words for their effect.

The language of your speeches should be that of good idiomatic conversation. It should not be like the language of a textbook or essay. Conversational speech is elliptical; you say "phone" instead of "telephone," "coed" instead of "woman student in a college which both sexes attend," and "movie" instead of "motion picture." You use contractions such as "isn't," "didn't," and "can't." Short words are preferable to polysyllabic synonyms. Words of many syllables may be impressive, but they are ordinarily not so well understood or so vigorous as their shorter counterparts. Sometimes the requirement of exactness leaves you no choice. But if a short and simple word can carry your meaning, use it. In most speeches it is appropriate to describe a man as "husky" rather than "robust," as "grouchy" rather than "irritable."

We are not here endorsing slang as the best medium for effective language adaptation. Within limits, according to the specific audience habits and preferences, the drunk person may be labeled as "balmy" or "addled" or "batty" or "pickled." Despite its color and familiarity, slang is usually quickly coined and as soon forgotten, like much of the Beatnik jargon of 1960. It also sounds foreign to sophisticated audiences to whom the particular vein of slang is not familiar. The speaker who lapses into slangy informality too often misjudges his audience.

The conversational mood will lead to a free use of personal pronouns— "I," "you," and "we." Even here you will need caution to avoid the impression that you are highly self-centered.

Your style should be oral rather than written. Repetition and the insertion of introductory, transitional, and summarizing phrases, clauses, and sentences are more characteristic of speeches than of written material. Provide your listener with assistance in binding your ideas together and in following their progress. Readers of the printed page obviously do not need so much help in following the thread of thought from paragraph to paragraph.

The language of the speaker should be simpler than that of the writer. Avoid pretentiousness or indirectness. Winston Churchill, probably the greatest orator of this generation, uses simple Anglo-Saxon and Biblical words. Note these illustrations:

> The day will come when the joybells will ring again throughout Europe, and when victorious nations, masters not only of their foes but of themselves, will plan and build in justice, in tradition, and in freedom a house of many mansions where there will be room for all. (January 20, 1940)
>
> Let us therefore brace ourselves to our duties and so bear ourselves that, if the British Empire and its Commonwealth last for a thousand years, men will say, "This was their finest hour!" (June 18, 1940)

Adapt your language to the immediate occasion. Usually your understanding of your audience will solve the problem of adjustment to the specific occasion. Different occasions obviously affect your language; college debates, memorial services, farewell dinners, greetings to freshmen, Red Cross drives, founder's day banquets, and other gatherings have their own language requirements.

Adapt your language to your purpose. If your aim is to inform and if your student audience is reasonably interested in your topic as announced, you can concentrate on clarity and accuracy—denotation. If, however, your aim is to convert or to stimulate, you will be at pains to introduce more connotation. The extent to which your purpose is informative or, on the other hand, persuasive, like the demands of audience and occasion, should partly explain the character of your oral style.

Adapt your language to your personality. The audience wants contact with you as an individual rather than with an unknown person masquerading in the style of a Webster or Roosevelt or Churchill. If, then, you are naturally formal or informal, you will remain so, except that you will modify your style to eliminate the words that call undue attention to themselves. Capitalize to the best of your ability on your own personality. There is point to Buffon's statement that "the style is [or should be] the man." Your language, then, should be the expression of your own experiences, attitudes, interests, intellectual and emotional activity, and of similar factors that account for your individuality.

BE ACCURATE IN YOUR USE OF LANGUAGE

Words should accurately mirror the reality they are intended to symbolize. You must achieve a high degree of correspondence between the symbol and the referent ("thing itself," object, or event). If necessary, pause to define vague words to the satisfaction of your listeners. Although overpreciseness may strip your speaking style of agreeable spontaneity, cold accuracy is preferable to verbal looseness.

What are the several types of language inaccuracy to be avoided?

Avoid ambiguity and inconsistency of meaning. As this paragraph was written, the political leaders of this country were talking about "sacrificing our sovereignty" in proposed international commitments. Almost every speaker used "sovereignty" in a different sense. Sometimes a single speaker even had in mind first one meaning and then another: (1) "Sovereignty is the supreme political power that determines and administers the government of a state in the final analysis." (2) "Sovereignty is the dominion of one state over another state without the latter's consent." (3) "Sovereignty is that feature of our traditional government which is identical with the greatness, independence, and achievement of the United States." One word, as your dictionary will remind you, may easily have five or ten well-recognized meanings, as well as several slang and regional meanings.

Avoid exaggerated or all-inclusive language. Loose use of language is illustrated by such statements as: "Englishmen have no sense of humor." "College education serves no useful purpose." "Middle Westerners are isolationists." "The churches have sold out to the capitalists." "Latin Americans hate the Yankees." "Practically all Americans are morons." What we really mean is that some Middle Westerners are isolationists, some preachers have been unduly influenced by the wealthy members of their congregations, some Latin Americans dislike certain traits of the citizens of the United States. When we use exaggerated language, we sacrifice accuracy in the interest of making a striking statement. We startle audiences, probably without expecting them to take our reckless verbiage too seriously.

To correct immaturity of thinking and expression, examine your own attitudes and prejudices; check your assertions against the facts; treat all statements as relative rather than absolute. Although you need not bore others by protesting every generalization they offer or by making a show of your own precision, you should develop an awareness of verbal looseness.

Avoid emotional distortions. Your language in speech making should be both accurate and objective. Objective language is that which points directly to the facts without emotional distortion. The objective speaker assumes a detached attitude toward his materials and reports as any bystander would. Oral style, to be sure, should often have emotional coloring for interest and impressiveness; but it should not gain this quality at the expense of factual accuracy or truth. When your over-all purpose is persuasion and argument, you will state this purpose openly and still retain a well-balanced attitude toward speech materials.

Name calling, the device of destroying an argument by attacking a person or institution, is perhaps as popular today as in Greek and Roman legal and popular-assembly speaking. "Communist," "red," "pink," "imperialist," "capitalist," "atheist," "crook," and their equivalents have been hurled back and forth as a substitute for analysis and appraisal of the ideas for which those so labeled may stand.

The reverse of this technique, the glorification of oneself, one's colleagues, and one's cause, is also a tool of the propagandists, especially preelection campaigners. Those on one's own side are devoted to "fair play," the "square deal," and "evenhanded justice." They are "upright" and "honest." They have "generosity" and "magnanimity," and their institutions are "illustrious," "democratic," and "enduring." This technique is legitimate, but lofty words are no substitute for facts and logic.

Heightened language, then, is not inconsistent with accuracy and objectivity. Although your vocabulary should not be stripped of emotional language, you should weed out those terms that carry obvious bias.

MAKE CLEAR STATEMENTS

Speaking is more than a matter of reporting accurately what you have in mind. Equally important is clearness. Said Aristotle, "Let excellence of style be defined . . . in its being clear." Unless you are understood, you do not communicate. The distinction between accuracy and clearness is not always distinct. The four qualities of style obviously interact. But clearness is essential.

What are the chief barriers to clearness? Lack of clearness may result from faulty arrangement of words in your sentences. Or you may use the same word in different senses in a given speech. The ambiguity mentioned above as violating accuracy also blurs clarity.

Words may be used unidiomatically or as wrong parts of speech. Say, for example: I agree to (not "with") the proposal. This is different from (not "than") the other proposition. I differ with (not "from") you concerning the merits of Daniel Webster. He proved to be superior to (not "than") the other speakers. He lives quite a way (not "ways") from New York. He doesn't talk as (not "like") you do. In a little college such as ours you have (not "get to have") more social life than you have in a university. You should (not "had ought to") do a better job with this talk. Jones and I (not "myself") demanded an answer. Fewer (not "less") people came into the London streets after the bombing. He's doing well (not "good"). What kind of (not "kind of a") show is this? Almost (not "most") everybody knows the right answer. There are not (not "nowheres near") so many as there were last year. We could (not "couldn't") hardly say that he was right. Where did you say he lived (not "lived at")? I don't know that (not "as") I understand you. He ran behind (not "in back of") the auto. He is younger than I (not "me").

Define your terms. Since clarity depends to some extent on frequent explanation of words, the role of words in such service is obvious. In Chapter Six, "Supporting Details," you learned something about methods of definition. In Chapter Ten, "Language and Semantics," you will gain further insight into the definitional process. Here you will note that your term or word can be clarified not simply by a dictionary definition but by an explanation of how it works. Ruth Krauss, in her delightful collection of childhood definitions, illustrates the advantage of such operational definitions as "hands are to make things"; "a door is to open"; "the world is so you can have something to stand on"; "toes are to wiggle." [4]

The definition may be a history of the term, a contrast, or a comparison: "A bat is a mouse with wings." It may be a description of the results of the agent or events: "A masterpiece is a creative work that stirs the imagination and gives permanent pleasure."

Use concrete language to promote clearness as well as accuracy. Many abstract words have emotional appeal, but their connotations for different individuals may be so varied as to produce no reaction. The expression "life, liberty, and the pursuit of happiness" vaguely suggests an American ideal, but the words evoke little specific uniform meaning in the minds of listeners. For abstract terms, substitute concrete ones that readily call up in the minds of your listeners common pictures, associations, and experiences. For example, instead of referring to a young man as "a soldier home from the Far East," you might better refer to him as "Corp. Tom Johnson, home from Pusan and Panmunjom on a thirty-day furlough."

Herbert Spencer, in his essay on style, illustrates the greater effectiveness of the concrete by means of two examples. *Abstract:* "In proportion as the manners, customs, and amusements of a nation are cruel and barbarous, the regulations of their penal code will be severe." *Concrete:* "In proportion as men delight in battles, bullfights and combats of gladiators, will they punish by hanging, burning, and the rack." [5]

[4] *A Hole Is to Dig*, Harper & Brothers, New York, 1952.
[5] Herbert Spencer, "The Philosophy of Style," in William T. Brewster (ed.), *Representative Essays on the Theory of Style*, The Macmillan Company, New York, 1905, pp. 173–174.

Contrast the following pair of abstract and concrete statements and consider the difference in their effects on an audience: "In the Korean conflict we suffered heavy casualties." "Based on figures from official and United Nations sources, the United States in the Korean conflict lost in dead 25,600; in wounded 106,000; missing and presumed dead, almost 8,000; captured and returned, about 4,600."

For concreteness, substitute individual names for general classes of people; use specific dates, days, and hours; give figures and statistics (usually in round numbers); include instances, illustrations, dialogue, figurative and literal analogies, direct quotations from authorities, brief anecdotes. Try to test every word for its precise associations.

Complicated sentence structure also impedes clearness. A characteristic fault of young speakers is that they construct long compound sentences in which statements of equal value are strung together by means of "and" and "but," with the result that several ideas are vaguely combined in one sentence. Check your speeches for long, straggling compound sentences, and deliberately cultivate simple structure. Review a standard text on English grammar for instruction in sentence formation.

By these approaches to good English usage and by definitions and concreteness, you can no doubt minimize vagueness and confusion in speaking and render language a more effective medium for communication.

Weirton Steel Company executive talks to some students of steelmaking from abroad. (Photo courtesy of Weirton Steel Company of Weirton, West Virginia.)

BE INTERESTING AND IMPRESSIVE

Communication is a problem not only of securing understanding through clearness but of holding attention and arousing interest. These qualities, far from being merely decorative or ornamental, are indispensable. They and they alone will ensure adequate response to the effort to convince, persuade, entertain, impress, and actuate.

Attention and interest, according to James Winans,[6] who quotes William James, are practically identical: "What we attend to and what interests us are synonymous terms."[7]

The speaker must, whatever else he has in mind, create and hold attention. Interest and attention relate to the speaker's poise, his ability to appeal to the fundamental interests and motives of his listeners,[8] their interest in novelty, curiosity, humor, conflict.

What qualities of speech can you cultivate or what devices can you employ to improve your ability to create and sustain interest? They include (1) concreteness, (2) conciseness, (3) illustrations, (4) parallelism, (5) rhythm, (6) figures of speech, (7) variety, (8) originality.

Concreteness, a mark of clearness, also sustains interest.

Use concise language. Wordiness is an unfortunate habit of most amateurs and many others who should know better. The temptation often is to pile up words about words. Such speakers remind us of an instance:

"Did you hear Mr. Pilaster last night?"
"Yes, he talked for about an hour."
"What did he talk about?"
"He didn't say."

Lincoln's Gettysburg Address contains about 275 words. The late Elmer Davis, Director of War Information during World War II, achieved wide popularity through broadcasts usually only five minutes long. Governor Hatfield, of Oregon, at the Republican Convention in Chicago in July, 1960, achieved fame partly because his speech nominating Richard Nixon for the presidency was limited to about five minutes.

The influence of radio and television and the temper of the atomic-scientific age help to explain why more and more we demand short speeches.

Conciseness does not, of course, mean telegraphic brevity. Rather it means the avoidance of superfluous words. Express your idea in the fewest possible words without sacrificing the essential thought and with-

---

[6] James Winans, *Public Speaking*, Appleton-Century-Crofts, Inc., New York, 1915, p. 53.
[7] William James, *Psychology, Briefer Course*, p. 448.
[8] See Chapter Eighteen on "Persuasive Speaking."

out ignoring the rhetorical principles of clearness and audience interest. A statement of 300 words may be concise. A sentence of twenty words may be annoyingly diffuse.

The wordy speaker proceeds somewhat as follows. "Perhaps not one quarter of the people who listen to a superior speaker give an address worthy of the highest approval have a clear understanding of the representative elements of an effective speech." A more concise talker might say: "Perhaps not one-quarter of the listeners have a clear understanding of the chief elements of a superior speech."

Use varied language. Probably the greatest vice of inexperienced speechmakers is repetition. Although repetition is more permissible in speaking than in writing, student speakers in particular should avoid useless repetition of the same words. "Very," for example, is overworked. The constant repetition of one word in a single speech is evidence of a barren vocabulary. Synonyms and antonyms add variety and freshness to oral style. Roget's *Thesaurus of English Words and Phrases,* Webster's *Dictionary of Synonyms,* and Fernald's *English Synonyms* are helpful tools.

Vary also the sentence structure. Most of your sentences consist in order of a subject and a predicate. But the simple construction used to effect maximum comprehension may also produce maximum dullness. Occasionally, for increased suspense and accelerated movement, reverse this order; or use the periodic structure. For example: "To assure the continuation of progress in the United States, to move toward the greater freedom and greater opportunity for our citizens, to fight for peace in the world, there is a broad and proven path." [9]

Balanced structure gives emphasis through contrast. For example: "We must hope for the best; we must look for the worst." "He talks isolation; he votes intervention." "If we win this war, we shall liberate many nations; if we lose, we shall enslave ourselves." The dangers of overusing this construction are apparent.

Questions help to keep listeners alert. Every speaker knows the value of asking questions—even if he allows no one except himself to answer them. Questions may be used to create suspense, stimulate the audience, and introduce a new aspect of the subject.

Imperative sentences, too, are useful: "Go to South America! What do you find?" "Consider the program of democracy." "Tell me what this government is trying to do through its labor policy!"

Study syntax as well as word selection in striving for rhetorical effects. Weld your ideas together by means of sentences that grammatically and

[9] Adlai Stevenson, *Major Campaign Speeches, 1952,* Random House, Inc., New York, 1953, p. 124. Reprinted by permission.

rhetorically do more than merely follow on the heels of one another in an uninterrupted series of subjects and predicates.

Avoid hackneyed language. Originality in speaking is achieved by expressing your ideas in a combination of words slightly different from those used by a million other speakers in a million other speeches. Why do we use hackneyed expressions? One speaker coins a phrase that catches on like a popular song, and subsequent speechmakers and conversationalists appropriate it. Eventually listeners refuse to react to this too familiar phrase, although originally it may have been excellent. The statement "America is a land of opportunity," made originally by Thomas Paine, is now shopworn.

Debaters, who model their language after that of the courtroom, use excessively such phrases as "honorable opponents," "I have proven," "Therefore we still maintain," and "I wish to prove three points." Similarly, public speakers in general, especially campaign orators and the speakers who introduce them, use such hackneyed words and phrases as "It gives me great pleasure," "We are assembled," "It is an honor for me to address you," "My friends," "Last but not least," "In conclusion, let me say," "This is a new day," "The immortal Shakespeare," and "The Good Book."

To hold attention and to sustain interest, your language must be accurate, clear, and impressive and vivid. You will need words that suggest as well as denote. If your listeners are to accept your beliefs, to take action, and to feel deeply concerning your subject, you will adopt the language of emotion and imagination.

Words with strong emotional overtones are called "loaded words." These words stimulate vigorous reaction, favorable or unfavorable, to the ideas with which you the speaker identify the word or words. "Tightwad," for example, evokes an unfavorable response, as do "radical," "miser," "traitor," "jailbird," "anarchist," "communist," "wishy-washy," and "quitter." The word "atrocities" has in the past few years called up associations with the treatment of American prisoners in the Korean conflict. Other words evoke a highly favorable emotional response: "sacred trust," "square deal," "broadmindedness," "smile," "uprightness," "heroic." Woodrow Wilson, asking Congress to declare war on Germany in 1917, and Franklin D. Roosevelt, asking for a declaration of war against Japan in 1941, made speeches with strong emotional overtones.

Use figurative language. To hold attention and to sustain interest, you will use the language of vividness, or "connotative language," which suggests much in addition to literal meanings. If you wish your listeners to accept your belief, or to take action, or to feel deeply concerning a subject, you will adopt this language of emotion and imagination.

Figurative language, by no means the exclusive property of poets and orators, is a justifiable means of accomplishing practical speaking ends. Appropriate figures of speech are almost indispensable elements in lively oral composition. The simile (comparison of one object or idea with another object or idea of different kind or quality), metaphor (direct identification of the objects, ideas, or relationships being compared), personification (attributing the qualities of a person to an object), and analogy (extended comparisons between objects or relationships) make ideas clear and emphatic and, in addition, sometimes furnish convincing evidence. The comparison or contrast must be clearly expressed. The purpose in using connotative language is to illustrate the unknown by the known; the comparisons you use, therefore, must be appropriate and the illustrations familiar.

Avoid trite figures of speech. The following expressions are too shopworn to carry meaning: "ship of state," "school of life," "gilt-edged securities," "the last straw," "light as a feather." But note the following vital figures of speech used in recent years:

Ralph Bunche, a representative of the United Nations in the Republic of the Congo during the antiforeign uprising in July, 1960, said:

The United Nations, as it is doing, may scurry about valiantly with its fire-fighting machinery and put out a war-fire in Indonesia today, in Palestine tomorrow, and in Korea and Kashmir or Greece the next day. But new war-fires will continue to flare up and one day one of them, fanned by a furious wind storm of human conflict, may very well get out of hand.

Henry Cabot Lodge, Jr., the United States representative at the United Nations when the Soviet government in vain asked the Security Council to condemn the United States for its alleged aggression in sending a RB–47 plane over Russian arctic waters (a Russian claim that Lodge refuted with detailed evidence), said in an earlier speech:

Human affairs cannot be conducted on a basis of ignoring evil, of sweeping things under the rug.

President-nominee Senator John Kennedy, in his acceptance speech at the Democratic National Convention in Los Angeles, California, July 15, 1960, resorted to figurative language. For example:

The times are too grave . . . to permit the customary passions of political debate. We are not here to curse the darkness, but to light the candle that can guide us through that darkness to a safe and sane future. . . .
There has been a change—a slippage—in our intellectual and moral strength. Seven lean years of drouth and famine have withered the field of ideas. Blight has descended on our regulatory agencies—and a dry rot, beginning in Washington, is seeping into every corner of America—in payola mentality, the expense account way of life, the confusion between what is legal and what is

right. Too many Americans have lost their way, their will and their sense of historic purpose.

Use parallel structure and contrast. The recurrent use of a grammatical construction in phrases or sentences that are parallel in meaning is effective if not overdone. Winston Churchill used such phrasing in his expression of the determination of the English people when threatened with invasion in 1940:

> We shall fight on the beaches.
> We shall fight on the landing field.
> We shall fight in the fields and in the streets.
> We shall fight in the hills.
> We shall never surrender.

Similarity of structure and ideas adds tremendously to the force of utterance. The effectiveness of the device, however, depends on whether it grows out of the speaker's feeling and whether it is spontaneous rather than labored. Do not try to imitate these stylistic effects, but do examine the outstanding speeches of the day, or of previous times, to see how often superior speakers express themselves in colorful phrases.

Language effectiveness, then, is skill in acceptable choice of words, those that are best adjusted to a given audience, to the speaker's personality, to the occasion, and to the subject—words that are current, intelligible, and varied. You will use definitions to clarify your ideas, an adequate vocabulary, a sentence structure varied in length, complexity, and arrangement of words. You will avoid involved elaborations. You will effect impressiveness of language by parallel structure, climax, and figurative terms. Suitable introductory, transitional, and summarizing terms and sentences will aid in clarifying and impressing your ideas.

Suggestions for Improvement

What specifically can you do to increase your command of language and make your speeches semantically and rhetorically more effective? Your problem is, first, to become more familiar with some of the thousands of dictionary words, and, second, to assimilate enough of them to give you readiness in extempore speech. Groping for words in a speech cripples your effectiveness before a group. You can improve your command of language by reading, studying model speeches, studying logic and semantics, listening, studying the words you encounter every day, and writing your speeches.

Reading. Almost all speakers of importance, including Edmund Burke, Daniel Webster, Theodore Parker, Wendell Phillips, Charles Sumner, Woodrow Wilson, and Winston Churchill, have read widely and have been students of language.[10] If you are to develop an extensive vocabulary, you cannot stop with the minimum textbook assignments in your courses. Find time for the systematic reading of biography, important fiction, history, and argument. Read silently and aloud, both for content and for appreciation of language distinctions.

Studying model speeches. Read the speeches of Woodrow Wilson, Winston Churchill, Franklin D. Roosevelt, Clarence Randall, and other important contemporary speakers.[11] Outline the speeches; note methods of illustration; make a précis (short summary) of each speech; and examine the vocabulary.

Logic and semantics. Elect courses in semantics, logic, and argumentation. Learn to test both facts and inferences by means of specific instance, authority, analogy, causal relations, and deduction. Testing fallacies will sharpen your awareness of word meanings.

Listening. Listen to outstanding radio speakers and campus lecturers. Note their choice of words.

Word study. Develop the habit of definition. Elect discussion courses and join discussion groups in which you may gain experience in the exact definition of controversial terms. Look up words with which you are only vaguely familiar; keep a record of them and practice their application.

Study synonyms, antonyms, and word history. Roget's *Thesaurus of English Words and Phrases,* Crabbe's *English Synonyms, Antonyms, and Prepositions,* Smith's *Synonyms Discriminated,* and Soule's *Dictionary of English Synonyms* have long been recognized as important sources. Above all, get a good dictionary and use it faithfully. You will see the results in your speaking skill.

Writing, revision, oral practice. Case histories of important speakers indicate that they have written and rewritten their speeches for presentation, both in school and subsequently, and have habitually put their ideas on paper and subjected themselves to the discipline of repeated revisions. Such experiences will undoubtedly give you a better grasp of words in extempore speaking. Contrary to popular belief, extempore speaking involves thorough preparation, including writing and rewriting; enough oral rehearsals to rid you of a mechanical English style; the memorization of

[10] Concerning reading habits of prominent American speakers, see W. N. Brigance (ed.), *History and Criticism of American Public Address,* McGraw-Hill Book Company, Inc., New York, 1943; Marie Hochmuth, W. N. Brigance, and Donald Bryant, *History and Criticism of American Public Address,* Longmans, Green & Co., Inc., New York, 1955, vol. III.

[11] See A. Craig Baird (ed.), *Representative American Speeches,* The H. W. Wilson Company, New York, published annually, 1937–1959. See also *Vital Speeches of the Day,* City News Publishing Company, New York, published fortnightly. See also A. Craig Baird (ed.), *American Public Addresses: 1740–1952,* McGraw-Hill Book Company, Inc., New York, 1956.

ideas rather than words; and continued oral practice to add extempore ease.

Study some of the modern scientific investigations of language. Students of the reading process have carried on a more or less continuous investigation of the characteristics of language which make for clarity and effectiveness in writing. These characteristics also contribute to the clarity of language in speaking. The work of Flesch[12] has come to stand for at least one group of these scholars. A widely used test for intelligibility of language has been developed by the Dole-Chall [13] team. Flesch suggests that you beware of long involved sentences. Although there must be some variety in length, use a liberal proportion of short sentences. If you find yourself becoming involved in a long sentence, try to make two short sentences instead. Beware of big words. When a shorter, simpler word will do the job, use it. Use personal words and pronouns to maintain interest. You might find it revealing to write out one of your speeches, then look up the Flesch formula for readability and apply it. You might be surprised at how difficult your language level is.

Osgood, Succi, and Tamenbaum[14] have shown that you can measure the meaning words carry. Words have different dimensions of meaning, occupying as it were a certain semantic space. Words have only more or less commonality of meaning. Even though two conversationalists use the same word as they talk with each other, they may not be associating the same meaning with the word. These scholars use the term "semantic differential" to label the technique they have developed to measure the commonality of the meaning space a word occupies for different people. You will come to a clearer understanding of the problem of using words meaningfully if you study the process by which the semantic differential measures meaning.

Projects and Problems

PROJECT 1

Discuss with the class briefly your special experiences in the use of language in your recent speeches.

PROJECT 2

Arrange to show the sound film *Say What You Mean* developed by McGraw-Hill Book Company, Inc., to accompany this text. See the *Teacher's Manual* for

[12] Rudolph Flesch, *How to Test Readability*, Harper & Brothers, New York, 1951.

[13] See Jeanne S. Chall, *Readability*, Bureau of Educational Research and Services, The Ohio State University Press, Columbus, Ohio, 1958.

[14] Charles E. Osgood et al., *The Measurement of Meaning*, University of Illinois Press, Urbana, Ill., 1958.

suggestions about the use of this film and questions for classroom discussion on the film.

PROJECT 3

Discuss with the class the question, "What four or five outstanding speakers do I recommend for the study of their language?"

PROJECT 4

Listen to a visiting speaker on the campus or a political, religious, or business speaker over radio or television. Report orally from your notes his chief usages of language.

PROJECT 5

Discuss: To what extent shall we endorse the practice of writing speeches before their delivery?

PROJECT 6

Write in full a four-minute speech which you will deliver before the class without the manuscript or notes. After class comment, state the extent to which you memorized the manuscript, your experience in its composition, your oral rehearsals of it.

PROJECT 7

From important speeches identify each of the following. Refer to the context of the quotation in each case: (*a*) "I know not what course others may take, but as for me, give me liberty, or give me death." (*b*) "Liberty and Union, now and forever, one and inseparable." (*c*) "I am loath to close. We are not enemies but friends." (*d*) "Life is a narrow vale between the cold and barren peaks of two eternities." (*e*) "The only thing we have to fear is fear itself."

PROJECT 8

Discuss each of the following words by comparing it with its representative synonyms: (*a*) time, (*b*) testimony, (*c*) synonym, (*d*) socialism, (*e*) slang, (*f*) reason, (*g*) progress, (*h*) extemporaneous, (*i*) education, (*j*) diction, (*k*) circumlocution, (*l*) word, (*m*) evidence, (*n*) narrow (adjective).

In addition to any standard dictionary, see above, under "Word Study," references to books on synonyms.

PROJECT 9

Copy from the Appendix and present to the instructor an example of each of the following: (*a*) oral as distinct from written style, (*b*) concreteness, (*c*) conciseness, (*d*) figurative language.

PROJECT 10

List from any speech you have recently listened to, or read, several examples of trite phrases.

PROJECT 11

Rewrite each of the following sentences to improve the construction. (In parentheses after each of your revisions, suggest what was allegedly open to question.) (*a*) Governor Hatfield of Oregon only spoke two minutes in nominating Vice President Nixon for the presidency. (*b*) The distinguished member from Rhode Island cannot help but agree to the statement. (*c*) It tastes good like a cigarette should. (*d*) He is shorter than me. (*e*) Let's you and me do it. (*f*) I cannot hardly help but think so. (*g*) Who are you looking for? (*h*) These kind of politicians should be denounced. (*i*) We most always stand for justice. (*j*) Somebody left their book on this table. (*k*) So you see that this administration has failed, due to their ignorance. (*l*) My data is accurate and complete. (*m*) Refer back to your notes on the lecture.

PROJECT 12

Check the meaning of the following words, often misused, and frame a sentence in each case with correct usage: (*a*) likely, liable; (*b*) fewer, less; (*c*) accept, except; (*d*) affect, effect, (*e*) between, among; (*f*) credible, credulous.

PROJECT 13

Comment on the following idioms: (*a*) at about, (*b*) all the further, (*c*) anywheres, (*d*) can't seem, (*e*) I didn't get to go, (*f*) hadn't ought, (*g*) seldom or ever, (*h*) out loud, (*i*) identical to.

PROJECT 14

Prepare and deliver a four-minute speech of explanation or information on some laboratory experiment or other scientific topic, in which your main language purpose with words is to be clear.

PROJECT 15

Prepare and deliver a four-minute speech in which you attempt to persuade your listeners to agree with your point of view. Pay special attention to language factors of interest in addition to those of clarity and accuracy.

References

Baird, A. Craig: *Argumentation, Discussion, and Debate,* McGraw-Hill Book Company, Inc., New York, 1950, pp. 203–213.

Black, John W., and Wilbur E. Moore: *Speech: Code, Meaning, and Communication,* McGraw-Hill Book Company, Inc., New York, 1955, chaps. 5–7 and 10.

Black, Max: *Critical Thinking,* 2d ed., Prentice-Hall, Inc., Englewood Cliffs, N.J., 1952, pp. 147–166.

Brigance, W. Norwood: *Speech,* Appleton-Century-Crofts, Inc., New York, 1952, chap. 15.

————: *Speech Composition,* Appleton-Century-Crofts, Inc., New York, 1945, pp. 120–275.

Bryant, Donald C., and Karl R. Wallace: *The Fundamentals of Public Speaking,* 3d ed., Appleton-Century-Crofts, Inc., New York, 1960, chap. 16.

Chall, Jeanne S.: *Readability,* Bureau of Educational Research and Services, The Ohio State University, Columbus, Ohio, 1958.

Chase, Stuart: *The Power of Words,* Harcourt, Brace & World, Inc., New York, 1954.

Dickens, Milton: *Speech: Dynamic Communication,* Harcourt, Brace & World, Inc., New York, 1954, chap. 9.

Evans, Bergen, and Cornelia Evans: *A Dictionary of Contemporary American Usage,* Random House, Inc., New York, 1957.

Flesch, Rudolph: *How to Test Readability,* Harper & Brothers, New York, 1951.

Follett, Wilson: "Grammar Is Obsolete," *Atlantic Monthly,* Feb., 205:73–77, 1960.

Gray, Giles W., and Waldo W. Braden: *Public Speaking: Principles and Practice,* Harper & Brothers, New York, 1951, chaps. 16–18.

———— and Claude M. Wise: *The Base of Speech,* Harper & Brothers, New York, 1946, chaps. 8 and 9.

McBurney, James H., and Ernest J. Wrage: *The Art of Good Speech,* rev. ed., Prentice-Hall, Inc., Englewood Cliffs, N.J., 1960, chap. 17.

Osgood, Charles E., et al.: *The Measurement of Meaning,* University of Illinois Press, Urbana, Ill., 1958.

Reid, Loren D.: *First Principles of Public Speaking,* Artcraft Press, Columbia, Mo., 1960, chap. 13.

Richards, I. A.: *The Philosophy of Rhetoric,* Oxford University Press, New York, 1936, lecture V.

Soper, Paul: *Basic Public Speaking,* Oxford University Press, New York, 1949.

Spencer, Herbert: *The Philosophy of Style,* John B. Alden, New York, 1888.

Strunk, William, Jr., and E. B. White: *The Elements of Style,* The Macmillan Company, New York, 1959.

Thonssen, Lester, and A. Craig Baird: *Speech Criticism,* The Ronald Press Company, New York, 1948, chap. 15.

TEN

Language and Semantics

DURING RECENT YEARS students of speech have given increasing attention to the questions, Do the speaker's words mean what he intends them to mean? Does the language reflect closely the ideas that the speaker hopes to put across?

More specifically the questions concern (1) words and terms in their setting and context as contributing to meaning, (2) the methods of definition that help to clarify and explain, and (3) the relation of words to the referents or experiences from which they spring.

You will be able to communicate more effectively if you are aware of some of the principles of semantics, the science of meaning. It is impossible to present here a full summary or analysis of general semantics, but it is important for you to understand certain principles of language usage that semanticists have emphasized and that students and teachers of speech have long recognized. The application of these principles may not be immediately obvious to you, but you are urged to keep them in mind so that you may refer to them from time to time.

1. *Words are to be distinguished from the referents—objects, experiences, "things"—which they symbolize.* Words are the symbols and the things are the referents. "The word is not the thing." [1] We live in two worlds, the verbal world and the world of our experience (sometimes called the "extensional world"). The verbal area is related to the expe-

---

[1] S. I. Hayakawa, *Language in Thought and Action,* Harcourt, Brace & World, Inc., New York, 1939–1940, p. 29.

rienced world as the map is related to the territory. The map, the semanticists remind us, is not the territory itself.

This "book" is not identical with the collection of printed pages you are now reading. Words are merely the sounds and signs by which we echo or represent in the mind of the listener the event or experience about which we wish to talk (or write).

2. *Words are to be distinguished from the mental processes or "thought" from which they spring.* The referent or equivalent source (substitute stimulus), as the psychologist reminds us, stimulates the cortical areas. This mental-emotional activity or thought in turn translates itself into the audible symbol—the word, an attempt to name the experience. As "words" stem from objects, events, experiences, so do they also channel outwardly from this mysterious "thinking" activity.[2]

3. *Verbalization should correspond to the thinking.* "Her mind never knew what her mouth would say next" is a description of what may prevail in many a conversation and sometimes in more formal speaking. "I hate you for arriving so late," smiles the lovely girl to her boy friend. Her intonation, gestures, and attitude constitute a nonverbal communication that belies the misleading words. When, however, the political speaker proclaims, "I believe in the equality of races," a sentiment sometimes contrary to his real thinking and feeling, the situation is ominous for the cause of accurate communication of ideas.

The problem is obviously how to select the words that will transfer honestly and fully the mental "speech." The problem is both to say what you mean and to do so with the most appropriate and intelligible language.

4. *Words are an important agency in producing perception.* (Perception, as used here, is the process by which words—substitute stimuli—cause us to respond to the objects, situation, or experiences symbolized by these stimuli.) The speaker provides the verbal symbols to which the listener responds. This response is often "subvocal talking"; it may or may not correspond to the kind of "talking" to which the auditor attends. Every speaker hopes, nevertheless, that his thinking and speaking will find perfect duplication in the thinking and "subspeaking" of the listener.

5. *Word symbols enable the listener to construct his own thinking pattern.* Language helps to establish a connection between the words that are addressed to the listener, the thinking of the speaker that produced the language, and the referents themselves that presumably moved the speaker to his thinking and expression of the idea. "Speakers do not give meaning. When we speak with the purpose of 'conveying information'

[2] For a diagrammatic explanation of this experience of the speaker through the stages from stimulus to the communicative act itself, see Wendell Johnson, "The Spoken Word and the Great Unsaid," *Quarterly Journal of Speech*, 37:419–429, 1951.

we are engaged in the attempt to stimulate some other person into developing certain ideas which, when fully assembled, will constitute for him the meaning which we wish him to have."

The speaker does not automatically transfer his meaning to the listener. When we attempt to communicate in formation or to persuade, we are stimulating the listener to respond in such a way that these receptive patterns (perceptions) "when fully assembled, will constitute for him the meaning which we wish him to have." [3]

6. *Successful "reconstruction" of ideas by the auditor will depend upon his experience, his interest, his intelligence, his command of language skills, and upon the "vigor, persistence, and efficiency of methods of work."* The reconstruction will never be perfect. Although the speaker often attains reasonable success in his communicative aim, the listener's many blocks may distort or nullify the speaker's attempt in a given situation. The listener may be comparatively ignorant; he may be prejudiced toward the speaker or toward others of the audience. He may mildly or strongly oppose the question as supported. His age, nationality, religion, occupation, cultural interests, economic status, representative needs, wants, and desires may all work against the success of the speaker.

7. *Words have both denotative and connotative elements.* The denotation of a word is its literal, descriptive meaning. Denotation is identified with the idea of the referent (the object itself, the original experience). It represents traits that may be directly verified or confirmed by the listeners, since they are matters of scientific description or dictionary definition. Connotation, on the other hand, is that significance of the word added by the emotional and imaginative insight or personal attitudes of the speaker or listener. Denotation represents extensional reporting, literally the projection of the thing in time-space relationships. Connotation, by contrast, reflects the "intensional" description, that which conveys the intention, purpose, or personal interpretation.

Nikita Khrushchev, visiting the United States in 1959, denoted a stocky, physically vigorous man who smiled, frowned, gesticulated. To his foes and critics outside the Iron Curtain in that year his name connoted dictatorship, duplicity, cruelty, possible world destruction. To loyal Soviet Communists his name embodied political, military, and ideological leadership and the fulfillment of the Marxist philosophy of world supremacy.

"A low-pitched voice of moderate intensity" is a largely denotative description. "A voice soft as the glow of altar candles" is highly connotative.

Every word and every group of words have both denotative and connotative meanings. The symbol arouses suggestions (connotation) that cluster about the idea itself (denotation). Some words and combinations

[3] Andrew Weaver, *Speech*, Longmans, Green & Co., Inc., New York, 1923, p. 28.

of words—for example, the language of poetry—are obviously more suggestive than others. The word "think" arouses associations different from those evoked by the synonymous terms "reflect," "cogitate," "consult," "deliberate," "ponder," "muse," "ruminate," "brood over," "mull over," "con over," "rack one's brains over."

Both denotation and connotation are important in communication. The aim of denotation is to call up literal meanings. Denotative language is typically informational and objective and comparatively unemotional. The aim of connotation is affective and emotional.

To illustrate, the sentence, "The American Explorer went into orbit on January 31, 1958, as the result of a three-stage firing," is a simple statement that can be quickly verified.

But note the alternative report: "The United States Explorer roared upward with its fiery white legs, a flaming monster that surged free from the dance of flame that fired it, climbing faster and faster until it exultingly pushed itself into orbit, a majestic earth satellite."

The bare facts thus become saturated with emotional and imaginative suggestion. Denotative speaking and writing obviously serve logical and factual purposes. The connotative meanings of the advocate, poet, fiction writer, and orator also play an essential role in communication. No basic contradiction exists in these two kinds of meaning. Connotation communicates the emotional significance which we attach to the factual reality of denotation.

8. *Words must be understood in their contexts.* Words, phrases, and ideas take their significance from the contexts in which they are used. The pattern of thinking and communication in which individual words and ideas occur must be viewed as an organized whole. A unit of thinking should be analyzed in relation to the whole of which it is a part, the entire architectural unit of which it is a single stone.

One political speaker said, "Some discredited campaigners have implied that I have misappropriated the public funds." His opponents played up merely the statement, "I have misappropriated public funds."

Psalm 53 states, "The fool hath said in his heart, There is no God." Critics have been known to argue that the Bible itself contains the declaration, "There is no God."

A reviewer of films may be quoted in an advertisement as having said that a motion picture was "brilliant," whereas what he really said with tongue in cheek was that it was "a brilliant flop."

The Associated Press reported that Senator John Kennedy, on the eve of his acceptance of the Democratic nomination at the Los Angeles Convention in 1960, "telegraphed a request for support by Gov. Orval E. Faubus in the forthcoming presidential campaign. The Massachusetts senator also invited Faubus to be on the platform when he [Kennedy] formally accepts the presidential nomination tonight." In view of Faubus's strong stand in support of segregation in Arkansas, Kennedy was roundly criticized for singling out Faubus for such marked attention. The printed report quoted above, however, omitted the full Associated release which stated that Kennedy had sent identical invitations to "every governor." This isolated item ignored or suppressed the context of the full statement, a report of which appeared in later press editions on the same day.

9. *Explanation or definition of a word or "object" is a process of selection or abstraction of certain aspects of the referent or "thing itself."* Obviously it is impossible to explain in limited time or space and with limited power of "abstracting" what in detail is a typewriter or a democrat or a gentleman. We cannot catalogue and expound every detail of the phenomenon before us. We single out the representative or characteristic features that suit our purpose and point of view. Dickens describes one of his characters by announcing, "In came Mrs. Chuzzlewit—one vast substantial smile." It is impossible to achieve "allness" in such descriptions. Description depends on skill and judgment in selectivity. Mrs. Chuzzlewit was apparently identified best by her joviality. Frank recognition of the limitations of such selectivity or partial description will provide a protection against the language confusion that might otherwise follow. The semanticists, to make us aware of the unexplored section of a subject under observation, of the endless details which we omit as observers, suggest the addition of "etc." to our definitions. Thus, "debate is a form of persuasive speaking in which the speakers are arranged on opposite sides of a subject and are given limited time for reply to each other, etc."

This process of selecting or abstracting is an experience in starting with the thing we perceive, not with the word but with the object of our experience—"that which our nervous system selects from the totality of the situation." In selecting, we move from a concrete level of direct observation to a second, more general stage in which we give a name to the object of perception. The name thus is not the object, but stands for it. To illustrate, we first observe (experience, perceive) a figure before us. He is sandal-footed, girded with a simple cloth, ugly of feature, physically mature, and rugged. At a second stage we name him Socrates. This name is not the figure itself, but stands for it. Moving up the ladder of selection to a third level or stage, and leaving out certain concrete features of Socrates as a specific person, we put him in the group of Athenians. He had much in common with the Athenians of his day. But in grouping him, we omit many features, such as his ugliness. Moving further upward on the ladder of selection, we include him among the Greeks. He is now generalized among the Peloponnesians, Spartans, and other groups making up the Greeks. Still further selecting or generalizing, we exclude traits peculiar to the Greeks and include them and our original Socrates among the Europeans. As a final step in moving up the ladder from the concrete to the abstract, we identify Europeans with mankind in general. We have thus omitted practically all reference to the special characteristics of Socrates of the Athenians, Greeks, and Europeans. This process the semanticist describes as "moving up the abstraction or selection ladder" from the sensory level of perception, where we focus upon the individual case by means of our eyes and ears, to the area where practically all the definite elements are absent. We may illustrate this ladder diagrammatically, to be read upward from the bottom.[4]

VI. "Mankind"

VI. Mankind is at a high level of abstraction.

V. "European"

V. Socrates as part of the Europeans has more of his characteristics omitted, in order to be enclosed in this larger body.

IV. "Greek"

IV. When he is referred to as a Greek only his characteristics in common with those of the entire region are included.

III. "Athenian"

III. When we place Socrates in company with all Athenians we have included only those characteristics in common of Athenian 1, Athenian 2, Athenian 3, and so on. The characteristics peculiar to individual Athenians are necessarily omitted.

II. "Socrates"

II. The word "Socrates" is not the word, but the name we give to this object of our observation. The name is not the object, but is merely a label to stand for the object. It omits many of the details that make up this particular person.

I. "Thing itself"

I. This is the individual we perceive, the object of our experience in this case; that which our sensory organs react to and that which our nervous system selects from the totality before us. Many of the characteristics of this object are omitted in our perception.

Why select or abstract? We cannot carry over all the details of the specific object of observation when we identify it with others. We need to use some sort of abbreviation. Out of our need to describe these relationships comes a "shorthand." [5] Hence we speak of mankind (versus Freddie), typewriters (versus Corona), animals (versus English setter),

[4] We are indebted to Hayakawa, *op. cit.*, p. 169, for suggestions concerning the abstraction ladder.

[5] *Ibid.*, p. 170.

democrats (versus J. V. Yesman, a voter), and hundreds of other abstractions, including God, universe, love, freedom, aesthetics, art, transportation, knowledge, idealism, entertainment.

The abstract terms, according to the semanticists, should often be enclosed in quotation marks to indicate their remoteness from any concrete base.

10. *Repeated definition or explanation of words is necessary if we are to have communication.* Confusion of meanings goes on constantly. To check this confusion, we must acquire the habit of definition. In the process of communicating ideas and of receiving them, we must continually question our own meanings and those of others. Speeches need not be punctuated at every point with definitional insertions, but a careful scrutiny of meanings, as we prepare and present speeches or as we listen to them, will anticipate and minimize many verbal difficulties.

11. *More effective language will result if terms are defined by relationships of concepts.* The classification that emphasizes hard and fast uniqueness and separation needs qualification. The dictionary method of indicating (*a*) genus and (*b*) differentia sometimes implies that the thing described has a peculiar character of its own. In reality, sharp distinctions and the dichotomy (separation into at least two categories) are hardly a genuine division. Things are seldom "either . . . or." Classificational definitions, then, should be qualified. Sanity and insanity, beauty and ugliness, strength and weakness, stuttering and nonstuttering, poetry and prose, discussion and debate, and all other concepts are relative to each other. Poetry and prose, for example, shade into each other as do the colors of the spectrum. Our aim, then, is to stress not simply the dictionary differences, but also the likenesses or relationships.

12. *A word or term has multiple meanings according to the experiences of those who use it.* The assumption is that there is not one and only one meaning, but rather that there are multiple meanings. Dictionaries exist not to give the one final definition, but to provide a history of word meanings and to array these so that the speaker can select the one that best expresses his purpose. Thus, "form" is (*a*) an image; (*b*) the shape of anything; (*c*) a body, especially a human being; (*d*) one of the different modes or aspects of existence; (*e*) one of the different aspects of a word; (*f*) a manner or method as regulative or prescriptive; (*g*) conduct regulated by custom; (*h*) manner or conduct testified by a prescribed standard; (*i*) manner of performing something; (*j*) physical and mental condition; (*k*) ideal or intrinsic character of anything; (*l*) order, as in presenting ideas; (*m*) the seat, bed, or lair of a hare; (*n*) a long seat, bench; (*o*) the rank of students in school; (*p*) that by which shape is given or determined; (*q*) printed matter, as type, secured by a frame so that an impression may be taken therefrom.

Consider also the synonyms, "form," "figure," "shape," "conformation," "configuration," "outline," "contour," "profile." It is impossible to know which definition is preferable or which synonym to select until we know the special referent the speaker has in mind and what his specific communicative aim is.

13. *Definitions should point toward the extensional (experience and observation) level by specific examples and operational description.* Definitions often pass from one vague level to another equally vague. "Liberty" may be defined as "freedom"; and "freedom," "liberty." And thus we move in a meaningless circle. These definitional distortions occur when a speaker discusses "principles" and refuses to refer to "particulars."

Such confusion can be avoided if the communicator will illustrate concretely the meaning he has in mind. Often a vague term can be translated into something meaningful if the speaker will say, "This is how it works," and will outline the operation of his term.

14. *Constant changes in word meanings make definitions and explanations necessary.* The world is "in process." Because we use a limited number of words to describe an immense number of things and because fresh experiences and reactions lead us to modify our symbols, our vocabulary is never static. Some words, to be sure, become obsolete. Many others, however, refuse to die; they continue to change their garb and take on new connotations.[6] The word "villain" today denotes a sinister person quite different from the simple peasant it originally denoted. Korsybski suggests that we "date" terms to make clear their changing and tentative significance; thus "the United States, 1936," was different from "the United States, 1962." Similarly the meanings of "Russia," "food," "democracy," "technicolor," "weapons," "private enterprise," "romance," and every other word in general use are shifting, and mental dating is necessary, especially in our reading.

15. *Classification by two values only is to be avoided.* Speakers and writers often see things in terms of two values only, such as hot and cold, good and bad, right and wrong, virtue and vice, affirmative and negative. Most events and problems, however, range along a continuum in which items and positions shade into each other. We thus have a broad area of relationships and choices rather than two sharply separated classifications. Political theorists may be erroneously labeled as either democratic or totalitarian in their thinking. In reality their position may range from advocacy of complete anarchy through democracy, socialism, republicanism, oligarchy, monarchy, fascism, nazism, communism, to unlimited dictatorship. The ancient Greek ideal of "the golden mean," although not in itself always the best-grounded position, was at least a

[6] Hayakawa, *ibid.*, pp. 293ff.; Stuart Chase, *The Power of Words*, Harcourt, Brace & World, Inc., New York, 1954, chap. 13.

protest against calling all things either black or white, and did suggest the logical gradations that are to be considered in any choices.

Projects and Problems

PROJECT 1

Define (compare and contrast) the definitions given in Webster's *New International Dictionary*, the *Standard Dictionary*, *The Century Dictionary and Cyclopedia*, and Murray's *New English Dictionary* for each of the following: (*a*) semantics, (*b*) language, (*c*) referent, (*d*) perception, (*e*) style, (*f*) rhetoric, (*g*) syllogism.

PROJECT 2

"Verbalization should correspond to thinking." Give examples of sections of speeches or conversation that apparently depart from this principle.

PROJECT 3

"Word symbols enable the listener to construct his thinking pattern." Analyze your thinking as you attended a recent lecture. To what extent was the meaning of what you heard obscure to you? What are the probable reasons for the obscurity? (This is a project for informal classroom discussion.)

PROJECT 4

"Language meanings are constantly changing." Illustrate by tracing the history of five representative words, such as (*a*) radio, (*b*) style, (*c*) cynosure, (*d*) pedagogue, (*e*) salary.

PROJECT 5

Discuss each of the following words, by comparing it with its representative synonyms: (*a*) time, (*b*) testimony, (*c*) synonym, (*d*) socialism, (*e*) slang, (*f*) reason, (*g*) progress, (*h*) extemporaneous, (*i*) education, (*j*) diction, (*k*) circumlocution.

PROJECT 6

To illustrate the principles of rhetorical and semantic adaptation to your audience, prepare and hand to the instructor two written speeches (300 words each) on the same subject, based on the same outline. The subject should involve special information. One speech should be for an audience familiar with your material and topic; the other, for a group largely uninformed on this subject but otherwise fairly well educated. Deliver one of these speeches to the class.

PROJECT 7

Select a paragraph from a speech. Rewrite the paragraph, substituting more accurate words and phrases.

PROJECT 8

Criticize the following definitions from student speeches: (*a*) Belief is conviction about anything. (*b*) By "an American" we mean a citizen of the United States. (*c*) By a closed shop we mean a shop where only union men work. (*d*) We shall define an international police force as an army recruited from all nations and placed under an international organization. (*e*) By price control we mean "actions which are deliberately undertaken to affect, limit the movements of, or settle prices." (*f*) What do we mean by government controls? In the first place, we do not mean to continue the present emergency controls. What we do propose are such rules and regulations and policies as will, in effect, allow our Federal government to direct and control all aspects of our economy. (*g*) The vocal cords are the two folds of mucous membrane which project into the larynx.

References

Chase, Stuart: *The Power of Words,* Harcourt, Brace & World, Inc., New York, 1954.

Hayakawa, S. I.: *Language in Thought and Action,* Harcourt, Brace & World, Inc., New York, 1939–1940.

Johnson, Wendell: *People in Quandaries,* Harper & Brothers, New York, 1946, chaps. 8–10 and 12.

Lee, Irving J.: *Language Habits in Human Affairs,* Harper & Brothers, New York, 1941, chaps. 6–9.

Ogden, C. K., and I. A. Richards: *The Meaning of Meaning,* Harcourt, Brace & World, Inc., New York, 1923.

Richards, I. A.: *The Philosophy of Rhetoric,* Oxford University Press, New York, 1936.

ELEVEN

The Speaking Voice

To COMMUNICATE effectively calls for a good speaking voice as well as for skill in other aspects of speech. Of course there are some people who get by sometimes with almost any kind of voice, but we should not be satisfied with "getting by sometimes." We want to do the job of communication creditably and with all the skill we can command—not just because speech is more pleasant that way, although that is important too, but because the times we do not get by may be the most important times in our lives. Voice has some important functions in speech, which we shall discuss in a moment.

You in Your Voice

Besides its function in speech, voice also serves several supplementary functions. Among your friends your voice is your name in the dark or even over a telephone. Among friends and strangers alike your voice tells many things about you: your emotional state at the moment; something of the attitude and purpose with which you speak—an important part of context; and some characteristics of your personality. Are you lazy, careless, insensitive to delicate situations or even typical social expectations? Rightly or wrongly people will interpret your voice as an indication of such tendencies. You become so accustomed to your own voice that you are not aware of what it tells others about you.

The chief purpose of voice study is to help you achieve professional

162

competence in its use. And there are many jobs which require a professional voice. Consider the importance of a good speaking voice for teachers, preachers, broadcasters, actors, personnel workers, airport traffic control operators, military officers, salesmen.

You must realize that you do not hear yourself as others do. You hear yourself by both air-borne and bone and muscle channels of vibration. Others hear you only through air-borne vibrations. This makes a difference in what is heard.

The voice, like writing and the telegraph, is a projector of communication. By means of articulated sounds, it transmits language symbols. Through the failure to transmit an individual word successfully, poor voice production can cause the loss of the meaning of a whole sentence.

You will remember that we defined speech as a multisymbolic activity. One of the symbol systems or codes is the voice itself. The voice carries meaning not only through the sounds of words but also by means of tones, loudness, rate, and inflectional patterns which reveal the attitudes, moods, and personality of the speaker.[1] This code is sometimes referred to as a prelinguistic code as if it terminated with the development of language in the child and in the race. A little observation will verify the fact that it is used along with the other codes by the most intelligent and mature of men. Such commonplace statements as "I didn't like his tone" and "It wasn't what he said, it was the way he said it" remind us forcefully that meaning in speech is communicated by many qualities of the voice. It has been shown that skill in the use of the voice is correlated with ratings of general effectiveness in speech.[2] The voice expresses the age, sex, degree of emotional tension, and personality of the speaker.[3] Although voice control alone cannot assure effective speech, speech may fail hopelessly without it.

How Effective Is Your Voice

According to Harry Barnes, who analyzed the voices of 1,661 beginning students in a required speech course at the State University of Iowa, ". . . sixty per cent of the group were not classed as effective in the control of their voices during their speaking performance. Forty-seven

[1] See Delwin Dusenbury and Franklin H. Knower, "Studies in the Symbolism of Voice and Action," *Quarterly Journal of Speech*, 24:424–436, 1938, and 25:67–75, 1939; Franklin H. Knower, "Analysis of Some Experimental Variations of Simulated Expressions of the Emotions," *Journal of Social Psychology*, 14:369–372, 1941.

[2] Franklin H. Knower, "The Use of Behavioral and Tonal Symbols as Tests of Speaking Achievement," *Journal of Applied Psychology*, 29:229–235, 1945.

[3] Melba Hurd Duncan, "An Experimental Study of Some of the Relationships between Voice and Personality among Students of Speech," *Speech Monographs*, 12:47–60, 1945.

per cent were marked poor or below in their voice and voice control." [4]

In a study of air traffic control operators recently carried out for the Federal Aviation Agency a critical incident analysis was made of malfunction and inefficiency caused by voice characteristics.[5] The following faults are cited in order of their frequency of occurrence in this investigation:

Too fast	Anger or irritation in the voice
Weak	Poor voice quality
Hesitant	Too slow
Too loud	Trailing off
Poor phrasing	Monotone
Pitch too high	Vocalized pauses

The frequency of these faults may fall into a different order for other jobs. But our point is that many of the people in this study were not aware of their faults. Such matters are critical.

Many beginners in speech have weak, indistinct voices. Others artificially declaim or "orate." Many are unable to project and seem to ignore their audience. Some are breathy, speak too fast, or have a monotonous delivery. A few have organic difficulties, such as cleft palate, poor teeth, and vocal paralysis. No attempt is made in this book to analyze or treat these defects, but many of them are remediable. The student who finds that he needs to correct a defect of this type should consult a speech pathologist for guidance in overcoming his problem.

Some speech deficiencies are caused by personality problems involving nervousness, irritability, and lack of confidence. Inadequate preparation also causes poor voice control, uncertainty, and lack of confidence. Quite apart, then, from organic handicaps, most speech students need to give serious attention to voice production both in conversation and in more formal speaking.

What Constitutes a Good Voice?

Audibility. When you speak you must be heard without strain upon yourself or upon your listeners. Many persons who are accustomed only to the soft and moderate tones of informal speech do not make themselves clearly heard even in a small room. On the other hand, a voice which is too loud is also objectionable, for it not only hammers the eardrums but also shocks the social sensitivities. More beginners in speech

---

[4] Harry G. Barnes, "A Diagnosis of Speech Needs and Abilities of Students in a Required Course in Speech Training at the State University of Iowa," unpublished doctoral dissertation, State University of Iowa, Iowa City, 1932, p. 231.

[5] Henry M. Moser, *A Voice Training Manual,* Federal Aviation Agency, Washington, D.C., 1962.

have weak voices than loud. The degree of loudness you need depends, of course, upon the size of the group and the acoustics of the room as well as upon the audience situation. In the presence of noise, the voice must be louder than in a relatively quiet place. The skilled speaker has sufficient control of loudness to project his voice adequately in all ordinary speech situations. Loudness is related to all the physical attributes of speech, as we shall see later.

Fluency. A second standard of a good voice is fluency. The ideas of your speech should be presented as rapidly as the audience can grasp them. Fluency is essentially a problem of rate, and rate should vary with the types of material you present, your mood and personality, and other factors in the speech situation. Most beginners tend to speak too rapidly. If you fill your pauses with a vocalized "ah," "er," or "uh," the rate is slowed down and the listener is distracted. Excess vocalization represents an unconscious attempt to keep the attention of your listeners while you are searching for a word or an idea. The severe stutterer provides an extreme example of lack of fluency.

Pleasantness. Your voice must not only be clearly audible, but it must also be reasonably pleasant. Of course, voices which are so loud that they irritate or so weak that the listeners must strain to hear are unpleasant. But unpleasantness is more commonly associated with vocal resonance than with loudness. Voices that are harsh, guttural, or raspy; metallic, shrill, or nasal; wheezy or breathy; too soft and formless—all are unpleasant for listeners. Abnormally high pitch and tempo that is too fast or too slow are also unpleasant. If your voice can be clearly heard, if you speak at a rate that is easy to follow, if your tone is resonant and flexible enough to be used meaningfully, then your voice will achieve an acceptable standard of pleasantness.

Meaningfulness. Your voice should reveal good will, purpose, and interest in that purpose on behalf of your listeners. It should reveal poise, human quality, friendliness, and the degree of confidence you have in your subject. We have suggested earlier that the voice carries many meanings other than the meanings suggested by the words. These meanings are contained in the voice code. The kind of voice you have and the way you use it are this code. It is the meanings revealed by the symbols of this code that we call to your attention here.

This means that your voice will be steady, authoritative, and credible. It will have clarity, simplicity, and character. A message which is confusing and causes an incorrect response lacks meaningfulness; a message which is ambiguous and requires a repeat is inefficient and costly.

Flexibility. The opposite of flexibility is monotony or lack of variety. Ordinarily, effective speech is conversational in pattern. Ideas are expressed in a variety of tones and at a variety of rates; these vocal variations do not occur in a regular stereotyped pattern, as in the chant and in singsong speech; they are not arbitrary and mechanical variations, but depend upon your thought and should reflect your attempt to adjust your communication to your particular listeners.

Improving Your Voice and Voice Control

At least four steps are involved in voice improvement. First, a clear understanding of the elements of voice improvement, including breathing, phonation, resonance, articulation, loudness, rate, pitch, and quality. Second, a clear understanding of your own vocal skills and limitations. Third, systematic practice in voice improvement. Fourth, systematic evaluation of your progress. In this chapter we shall analyze these four steps and set forth principles to guide you in your program for a better voice.

It is common for students hearing the playback of the first record of their voices to exclaim, "Do I sound like that?" We do not hear ourselves as others hear us. Our associates, too, become accustomed to our voices and frequently overlook qualities that would be distracting to someone meeting us for the first time.

An important factor in voice improvement is the development of an ear for effective voice production. You must learn to distinguish your habits in the use of your voice from the standard of usage set forth here as a goal in learning. Physiological limitations in hearing may interfere with the process of setting up such goals. If you have a severe hearing defect, you may not only suffer from poor vocal habits, but you cannot expect to improve your voice as readily as a person without a hearing defect. If you have normal hearing, you can acquire a better ear by noting the characteristics of good voices.

Listening to the recorded voices of persons whose speech meets the standard is a good way of becoming acquainted with desirable vocal characteristics. Recording your own speech will be helpful in comparing your habitual voice with the standard. Get the feeling or sensations involved in producing standard tones. A competent critic who can listen and advise and point out differences will be a great help in guiding you to the development of new voice standards.

When you have clearly distinguished between old vocal habits and those you must work to develop, the next step is systematic and persistent practice. Practice at first on material planned to make the new forms of expression easy. Drill materials are commonly of this type. (See, for example, the projects at the end of this chapter.) As soon as possible, you should practice with materials and in situations in which the new habits are expected to function. You cannot expect the speech-laboratory voice drills alone to be sufficient to fix the new habits of voice in daily speech.

Practice in oral reading and in rehearsing extempore speeches is helpful in voice improvement. These procedures are open to you: (1) You may work mechanically to produce the voice changes you seek in the new habit; (2) you may focus your attention on the variation of meaning to be conveyed; or (3) you may combine the "mechanical" and the "naturalistic" methods of improving your vocal habits. Although mechanically formed habits may at first seem artificial, they should function quite naturally when the skill is thoroughly developed.[6]

Some vocal habits have a close relationship to characteristic moods and to general traits of personality. A weak, timid voice may not be readily improved as long as its possessor shyly avoids social situations. In such cases, voice exercises must be combined with gradual changes in habits and personality. You will need to adjust to your individual case the textbook theories of why and how sounds are produced. At this point your instructor will be of help. Each of the exercises suggested below can be applied to your own needs and carried out under the constructive guidance of your speech instructor.

Finally, gauge your progress, reminding yourself that improvement in almost any direction does not take place overnight, but comes only through successive stages of development that are sometimes not very clearly marked. Even in driving an automobile, real skill comes only after repeated trips through traffic and over highways.

1. *Cultivate proper breathing.* Adequate use of the power mechanism is the first requirement in developing a good voice.

Proper breathing in speech depends upon three factors. First, the lungs must retain enough air to make it unnecessary to pause within a phrase to breathe. Second, the muscles which regulate expiration must be sufficiently controlled to exert strong and steady pressure upon the breath stream. And third, this pressure must be exerted without causing undue tension in other muscles involved in voice production, particularly in the muscles of the larynx. The chest (or thoracic) cavity may be expanded in three directions—upward, outward, and downward. Breathing patterns involving upward expansion of the chest are called "clavicular"; those involving outward expansion are called "thoracic" or "medial"; and those involving downward expansion are called "diaphragmatic." Individual patterns of breathing often involve combinations of these elementary types. The clavicular pattern is least likely to produce effective speech because it provides least expansion of the lungs, it is the most difficult to control, and it is more commonly associated with laryngeal

[6] Charles H. Woolbert, "The Effects of Various Modes of Public Reading," *Journal of Applied Psychology,* 4:162–185, 1920.

tensions. Diaphragmatic breathing provides greatest lung expansion; it is the most easily controlled pattern of breathing, and it is least likely to cause undesirable tension in the vocal musculature.

Normal breathing is rhythmical; that is, the time taken for inspiration equals the time taken for expiration. During speech, the time taken for expiration greatly exceeds the time for inspiration. Although most persons acquire their breathing habits quite accidentally, the extent of control can be improved with conscious effort. The development of good breathing habits for speech is a process of modifying reflexive and accidentally acquired habit patterns of muscular action so as to achieve the necessary supply of controlled air pressure with the least exertion and superfluous tension. The fact that adults employ different patterns of muscular action for breathing is sufficient evidence to indicate that breathing habits are acquired. And evidence that many speakers have improved their breath control indicates that the early, accidentally acquired habits can be profitably modified.

2. *Cultivate proper phonation.* The second process of voice production is phonation. When the vocal folds of your larynx (vocal bands) are brought closely together and set in vibration by the force of the breath stream, a vocal tone is initiated. The pitch and some other characteristics of your tone are the result of the nature and operation of the vocal folds and other muscles of the larynx. Whispered speech and unvoiced or voiceless sounds, as we shall see later, are produced without the vibration of the vocal folds. The fundamental pitch of the voice is determined by the rate of vibration of the vocal folds as a whole. The overtones are produced by the segmented vibration of the folds, and the rate at which the folds vibrate is dependent upon their length, thickness, and tension. The quality of your voice is influenced by the capacity of the folds to set up vibrations of the frequency that can best be reinforced by your vocal resonators (air chambers in the head and throat). Many persons have not learned to speak at the pitch level which will produce their best possible voice. Your study of voice should include an evaluation of your most satisfactory pitch. We will deal with this problem further under the heading, "Develop Satisfactory Pitch Control."

3. *Work for satisfactory resonance.* The third fundamental vocal process is resonance. Resonance, or the lack of it, is responsible for the relative pleasantness and strength of the voice. Voices that are hoarse, raspy, metallic, nasal, or cramped and mouthy are the result of the poor functioning of resonators. The main vocal resonators are the pharynx, the mouth, and the nasal cavities.

Changes in resonance also produce changes in the meaning communicated by the voice. Qualities of voice which suggest personality traits, moods, and emotional conditions are often determined by the ways in which tones are resonated. You may at times want to cover up your true feelings for a useful social purpose. When this occurs it is most important to maintain control over resonance. The vowel sounds of speech are strongly influenced by resonance.

4. *Articulate properly.* Articulation, the fourth of the physiological processes of voice, will be discussed in greater detail in Chapter Twelve. We shall content ourselves here with the statement that the major articulators include the lips, tongue, jaw, and the hard and soft palates.

5. *Cultivate control of loudness.* What constitutes adequate vocal intensity? The voice should be sufficiently loud to be heard easily. Listeners who must strain to hear are likely to stop listening. Variation in vocal intensity, however, is necessary to emphasize and subordinate ideas, to give words acceptable pronunciation by stressing certain syllables, and to make speech interesting. Listeners easily tire of uniform loudness.

You need not shout to achieve force in speaking. But your voice must be firm, vigorous, and well controlled. You will need more force to be heard by a large group of listeners than by a small group. Speaking outdoors or in the presence of competing noises and other distractions requires more force than speaking indoors and in places where there are no distractions. Physically energetic people like a more vigorous speaker than do people who lead sedentary lives. Forceful ideas uttered in an indifferent manner lose some of their vigor. A speaker who cannot suit the vigor of his voice to the vigor of his ideas seems insincere.

A weak voice may be due to such factors as personality, imitation of a poor model, fatigue, or a hearing loss. A voice which is too loud may be due to a hearing loss, a poor model, excessive drive or anxiety, or personality.

Achieving better control of loudness sometimes requires a new attitude toward the value of intensity in speaking. Some victims of stage fright rationalize weak voices by claiming that they do not want to be loud. Such reasoning sometimes represents the avoidance of responsibility. However, using a vigorous tone for useful purposes will result in satisfaction rather than embarrassment.

A vigorous voice is dependent upon breath control—upon breathing deeply and using waist and chest muscles energetically to force air from the lungs. Loudness can also be increased by raising the pitch of your voice. Experiment with modification of vocal intensity both by variation of pitch and by variations of breath pressure. Find the best pattern of resonance for giving your tone body and volume. A cramped throat and mouth, with muscles tensed, may make the voice more piercing, but ordinarily they do not make the voice more pleasantly vigorous. If your speech is too fast, slow it down, for it is difficult to achieve forceful tones if you speak at a very rapid rate. Avoid letting your voice trail off at the end of a sentence. Practice intensity control in exercises and every-day speaking activities until it becomes a habit. (See project 2 at the end of this chapter for exercises in loudness control.)

6. *Control your speech rate.* Your speech should be fluent but neither too hesitant nor too gushy. Say your words slowly enough to be understood and fast enough to sustain the audience's interest. In speaking, this is ordinarily between 130 and 150 words per minute, and in oral reading it is between 150 and 175 words per minute.[7] The discussion of light subjects and the presentation of simple narrative material and exciting ideas can be carried on at a faster rate than the presentation of complicated instructional material in unfamiliar subject-matter areas. When a number of listeners are included in the discussion (other things being equal), the rate should be slower than when there are only one or two persons. Situations involving distraction require a slower rate than situations which are free from distraction. Sight reading is ordinarily slower than the reading of familiar material.

Rate variation is an effective way of suggesting the nature of the thought being expressed and the relative emphasis to be given it. The timing of the punch line, for example, is very important. Practice to determine your most effective rate in speaking and oral reading. Your speaking rate should vary with the relative importance of the ideas, and it should never be so fast that your phrasing or emphasis suffer.

Poor phrasing may be caused by a voice which is too fast or too slow and hesitant. The vocalized pause tends to reduce the rate and confuse and irritate your listeners.

Speech that is too fast is characterized by the shortening of vowel sounds and of pauses. Nervous speakers frequently give the impression of trying to express what they have to say before they forget. Mumbling sometimes gives the erroneous impression of a rapid rate, whereas drawling of continuant sounds, long pauses, vocal stumbling, repetition of words, and intrusion of "ah," "uh," and "and ah" result in a slowed rate. Rates that are too fast or too slow do not permit normal variation in speeding up or slowing down for expression. The absence of variation in rate produces monotony; and an arbitrary pattern of rate variation that does not accurately suggest or reflect the ideas discussed confuses listeners.

Monotone is influenced by all the attributes of voice, but rate is certainly one of the more frequent types of monotone. Gestures with the hands and other appropriate bodily movements may help you to overcome monotone. It is almost impossible to be active and monotonous at the same time.

[7] Ernest Fossum, "An Analysis of the Dynamic Vocabulary of Junior College Students," *Speech Monographs*, 11:88–96, 1944.

Rate problems are sometimes associated with personality factors, fatigue, or excitement. A speaker who knows too little about his subject may speak more slowly than one who is thoroughly familiar with it. Fatigue, characteristic reserve, or a depressing mood also slow down speech. The hyperkinetic or excitable person, on the contrary, is too fluent and needs to slow down his rate to the mood and speed of comprehension of his listeners.

The task of controlling speech rate appears to be relatively simple, but it may require considerable practice. First, learn to vary the length of time required to articulate vowel and other continuant sounds. Second, learn to vary the duration of interphrasal and intersentence pauses. Third, eliminate nonpurposive or useless sounds, stumbling, and repetition. If your speech is too fast, slow it down by increasing the duration of sounds and by the frequency and length of pauses. If it is too slow, speed it up by reversing these techniques and eliminating intrusive excess vocalizations.

Mechanical practices in developing rate control should be considered only a step in habit formation. The student should always remember that his essential purpose is to improve communication. It is relatively useless to expect work on mechanics to overcome deep-seated personality difficulties that cause problems in rate of speech. Such problems should be approached through the treatment of the personality.

If you are dependent on such excess vocalizations as "er" and "ah," have a friend listen to your speech and signal you whenever you use one of these sounds. This will be distracting at first, but it will help you break your dependence on this habit.

For exercises in rate control, see project 3 at the end of the chapter.

7. *Develop satisfactory pitch control.* The pitch of your voice is an important signal of your intentions. It communicates to the listener as much as rate and loudness do, and it should suggest the mood of what you want to say.

Your pitch should not be too high or too low. A pitch that is habitually too high produces a piercing, metallic quality, suggesting strain and discomfort; a pitch that is too low produces hollow, hoarse tones that are often inappropriate and unpleasant. The best pitch level for your normal speech is determined by the structure of your larynx, or voice box, and by your resonators. It may not be the pitch which you have developed by habit; you can unconsciously acquire habits that interfere with effective voice production. Test your voice at various levels to determine whether or not you habitually speak at your best pitch level. If you do not, find the pitch level your resonators reinforce most effectively. It should be high enough to permit lowering and low enough to permit raising for contrast. Inflectional slides, steps, and patterns are useful in communication. Remember, however, that regular pitch changes that disregard meaning and produce singsong effects are confusing and distracting.

In order to develop effective control over pitch you should learn to hear pitch patterns. Become aware of pitch in ordinary communication, and practice exercises such as those suggested in project 4 at the end of this chapter.

8. *Cultivate a pleasing and responsive voice quality.* Quality is that characteristic which makes one voice differ from another in harshness, huskiness, guttural sounds, nasality, and richness of tone. Quality is one of the most complex of the physical attributes of the speaking voice. It is influenced by, and influences, each of the other elements. Even more than other characteristics of your voice, it reveals your personality and your frame of mind. A pleasing voice equips the speaker with a considerable vocabulary of tonal qualities to reveal emotional variations.

It is equally important that your voice quality reflect you as a person and the meaning of the message you wish to communicate. Work to create a voice that is warm, steady, respectful, and interesting.

Improvement in voice quality requires analysis of personal problems and practice in the new pattern of resonance until it becomes a skill. Work to sharpen your ear for changes in quality of voice. Free your neck, throat, and mouth muscles of interfering tensions. If you speak too fast, slow down by giving duration to speech sounds. Practice to develop a wide vocabulary of tones.

For exercises in cultivating a pleasing voice, see project 5 at the end of this chapter. Remember, however, that personality development can do more to eliminate faults in voice quality than can mechanical drills. Alertness as opposed to tension or complete relaxation is conducive to good voice quality. Concentrating on the thoughts to be expressed will help you overcome your inhibitions about responding to ideas and feelings that you and your audience can share.

The skills you acquire by drill or in isolated projects must be exercised in the pattern of speech activity as a whole if they are to be of much value to you. Only perpetual attention to voice development in the normal social uses of speech over a long period of time will produce lasting results. If you develop vocal skills in isolated situations, however, you may with effort transfer these skills to your everyday speech.

Projects and Problems

PROJECT 1: ANALYSIS OF SKILLS IN USING THE VOICE

Purposes of this assignment: (*a*) To obtain a systematic evaluation of your vocal skills; (*b*) to obtain guidance in the development of vocal skills.

Procedure: Find a part of an article, a book, or a speech which you think might be interesting to your listeners. It should take at least three and not more than five minutes to read. Then prepare a three-minute speech about the subject. Present your speech to the class, and then read the selection to the class. Your instructor and your classmates will rate you on the use of your voice.

PROJECT 2: DEVELOPMENT OF LOUDNESS CONTROL

Do the following exercises as directed:

a. Do you know how to inhale by active use of the diaphragm and exhale by active use of the waist muscles when speaking? This is the first step in developing tone control. Stand erect with shoulders back, open your mouth, and pant like a dog. Place your hand across your diaphragm and note the action of the diaphragm during this exercise.

b. Simulate a yawn by standing erect, taking a deep breath, throwing your arms up, and stretching. Then relax and expel the air from your lungs as vigorously as possible. Note the feeling of vigorous contractive action of the waist muscles in this process.

c. Stand erect in a place where you can push against a wall with one hand. Count to ten in a normal voice, taking a separate breath for each count. Then repeat the exercise while pushing vigorously against the wall with one hand, allowing the waist muscles to contract vigorously on each count. Can you get a stronger tone by exerting pressure as you push?

d. Read the following sentences, using a single breath for each sentence. Do not lower vocal intensity at the end of the longer sentences.

I don't want to go.

The engineer cautioned us to drive slowly.

Deep, well-controlled breathing is required to read a long sentence on one expiration.

Scarlett O'Hara, the heroine in *Gone with the Wind,* was a Southern beauty of great personal pride, ambition, and will power, who would make any ordinary sacrifice to achieve her ends.

e. Try to read the first part of the following sentences normally, and the last part forcefully without raising the pitch.

You must not come in here; please move along.

If we win that victory, what a celebration we shall have.

I believe in a program for the preservation of peace, but certainly not peace at any price.

f. Read the sentences in exercise *e* again, and this time raise the pitch of the last phrase to increase intensity of the voice.

g. Note that the following passages[8] are separated by broken lines. Read the first part in a confidential undertone, the second part in a normal voice for a small room, the third part with the intensity necessary for a small auditorium, and the fourth part with the intensity necessary for a large auditorium.

[8] From the State of the Union speech by President Franklin D. Roosevelt, January 6, 1942, *Vital Speeches,* 8:195, 1942.

Plans have been laid here and in the other capitals for coordinated and cooperative action by all the United Nations—military action and economic action. Already we have established, as you know, unified command of land, sea, and air forces in the Southwestern Pacific theater of war.

. . . .

For the first time since the Japanese and the Fascists and the Nazis started along that bloodstained course of conquest, they now face the fact that superior forces are assembling against them. Gone forever are the days when the aggressors could attack and destroy their victims one by one, destroy them without unity of resistance. We of the United Nations will so dispose our forces that we can strike at a common enemy wherever the greatest damage can be done.

. . . .

The militarists of Berlin and Tokyo started this war, but the massed, angered forces of common humanity will finish it.

Destruction of the material and spiritual centers of civilization—this has been and still is the purpose of Hitler and his Italian and Japanese chessmen. They would wreck the power of the British Commonwealth and of Russia and of China and of the Netherlands and then combine their forces to achieve their ultimate goal, the conquest of the United States.

. . . .

They know that victory for us means victory for freedom. They know that victory for us means victory for the institution of democracy, the ideal of the family, the simple principles of common decency and humanity.

They know that victory for us means victory for religion. And they could not tolerate that. . . .

Our own objectives are clear; the objective of smashing the militarism imposed by war lords upon their enslaved peoples; the objective of establishing and securing freedom of speech, freedom of religion, freedom from want, and freedom from fear everywhere in the world.

h. Read the following paragraphs[9] in a forceful voice and at a rapid rate. Then read them slowly. Listen to the difference in general effectiveness and intensity at the two rates of speed.

No man can speak for the South. No one man can—by himself alone—define the beliefs of the people of this great region. But all of us and each of us must assume and exercise some degree of responsibility for persuading this nation to heed what we have to say.

We must make clear what we believe.

We must set the record straight.

We must, finally, stand together in unity and pursue with determination a course to victory.

That is our outline of duty.

[9] From Alan P. Shivers, "The South Must Be Admitted to Full Partnership," *Vital Speeches,* 21:972, 1955.

At the outset, let us establish one fact firmly.

Gathered here tonight, we are Texans, we are Louisianans, we are Southerners. Of these allegiances we are proud. We are honored by the heritage with which we are endowed.

But, in our hearts, we are—first and last—Americans. When we speak of duty, we speak of duty to our country. We acknowledge no loyalty greater than our loyalty to America. By that standard, we regard no principle as worthy, and we accept no cause as just unless it will contribute to the lasting strength of America, our America. It is our love for our country—not our pride in our region—which impels us to undertake this fight for principle.

i. Read the following paragraphs[10] with different degrees of variation of force. Read the first part with monoforce—without variation in the amount of force—the second part with a moderate degree of conversational variation of force, and the third part with a wide variation of vocal force.

Our task as I see it is really three-fold:
First, we must vigorously develop our freedoms at home.

Secondly, we must extend such help as we appropriately can to those countries abroad which are the next likely targets of Communist penetration. We must help awaken in those countries a clearer realization of what will happen to them if international communism takes over. And when I say "we" I do not mean just the government of the United States. The great private American organizations have their role on this world stage, and working with similar groups in the free nations can do much to improve social conditions and strengthen the barriers that stand in the way of Communist success.

And, finally, we must make the most of the latent but nonetheless real force of freedom that has not been killed behind the Iron Curtain, even in Russia itself.

There is the plain evidence that the urge to escape to freedom is still a live and potent force. This applies to both Russia and the satellites. As you know, it is far from easy to satisfy this urge. This is particularly true of the people in the countries behind barbed wire where the obstacles are so great that only a percentage of those who attempt it make good their escape to freedom.

j. Read the following sentences, giving considerable force to the underlined phrases and normal force to the phrases not underlined.

I know not what others may think, but as for me, give me liberty or give me death.

This is the last time I shall request that those in the back row keep quiet.

We shall make our preparation; then we shall bomb, and blast, and burn them into surrender.

The mills of the gods grind slowly, and they grind exceeding small.

[10] From a speech by Allen Dulles, "Progress of Freedom Abroad," *Vital Speeches,* 21:870, 1954.

k. Read the following sentences without, then with, vigorous stress on the underlined words.

He who laughs last laughs loudest.

It's a marvel to me that she stays with it.

"Mister," he said, "you dropped something."

The boys in North Africa certainly didn't agree with him.

Sarcasm is a woman's weapon.

If I were in his place, I wouldn't stand for it.

"The only thing we have to fear is fear itself."

PROJECT 3: RATE CONTROL

Practice the following exercises:

a. Read the following sentences rapidly or slowly as the meaning suggests:

Watch out! It's hot.

Please let me do it.

They trudged wearily up the trail.

Come as quickly as you can.

The fried pheasant is delicious.

What a beautiful view you have from this window.

b. Read the following selections rapidly or slowly as the meaning suggests:

"Bowed by the weight of centuries,
He leans upon his hoe."—MARKHAM

"The day is cold, and dark, and dreary."—LONGFELLOW

"And slowly answered Arthur from the barge,
The old order changeth, yielding place to new."—TENNYSON

"And next comes the soldier,
Sudden and quick in quarrel."—SHAKESPEARE

c. Read the following selection as rapidly as you can without mumbling or falling into a staccato pattern of articulation.

Speak the speech I pray you, as I pronounced it to you,—trippingly on the tongue; but if you mouth it, as many of our players do, I had as lief the town-crier spake my lines. Nor do not saw the air too much with your hand thus, but use all gently, for in the very torrent, tempest, and as I may say, whirlwind of your passion, you must acquire and begat a temperance, that may give it smoothness. Oh! It offends me to the soul to hear a robustious periwig-pated fellow tear a passion to tatters,—to very rags,— to split the ears of the groundlings; who, for the most part, are capable of nothing but inexplicable dumb show and noise. I would have such a fellow whipped for o'erdoing Termagant; it out-Herods Herod. Pray you, avoid it.—SHAKESPEARE *d.* Read the following paragraph as slowly as you can without drawling.[11]

During the whole of a dull, dark, and soundless day in the autumn of the year, when the clouds hung oppressively low in the heavens, I had been passing alone, on horseback, through a singularly dreary tract of country, and at length found myself, as the shades of the evening drew on, within view of the melancholy House of Usher. I know not how it was,—but, with the first glimpse of the building, a sense of insufferable gloom pervaded my spirit. I say insufferable; for the feeling was unrelieved by any of that half-pleasurable, because poetic, sentiment with which the mind usually receives even the sternest natural images of the desolate or terrible. I looked upon the scene before me—upon the mere house, and the simple landscape features of the domain—upon the bleak walls—upon the vacant eye-like windows—upon a few rank hedges—and upon a few white trunks of decayed trees—with an utter depression of soul which I can compare to no earthly sensation more properly than to the after-dream of the reveller upon opium—the bitter lapse into everyday life—the hideous dropping off of the veil.

e. Try reading the selection in exercise *c* slowly, and the one in exercise *d* very rapidly. Report on the differences in effect of rate of reading on the moods of these selections.

f. Read the following sentences using a short pause at the places marked with a single dash, a moderate pause at the places marked with two dashes, and a long pause at the places marked with three dashes:[12]

I beg your pardon. — That was a mistake. — — I was wrong. — — — I beg your pardon. — But you have tried me very sorely. — — You have intruded upon a private trouble — that you ought to know must be very painful to me. — — — But I believe you meant well. — — I know you to be a gentleman, — and I am willing to think you acted on impulse, — and that you will see tomorrow what a mistake you have made. — — It is not a thing I talk about; — — I do not speak of it to my friends, — and they are far too considerate to speak of it to me. — But you have put me on the defensive: — — you have made me out more or less of a brute, — — and I don't intend to be so far misunderstood. — — — There are two sides to every story, — — and there is something to be said about this, — even for me. — — When I married, — I did so against the wishes of my people — and the advice of all my friends. — — You know all about that. — — God help us! who doesn't? — — — It was very rich, rare reading for you, — and for every one else who saw the daily papers, — — and we gave them all they wanted of it. — — — I took her out of that life — — and married her — because I believed she was as good a woman — as any of those who

[11] Edgar Allan Poe, "The Fall of the House of Usher," *The Works of Edgar Allan Poe*, P. F. Collier & Son Corporation, New York, 1903, vol. II, p. 145.
[12] Richard Harding Davis, *Van Bibber and Others*, Harper & Brothers, New York, pp. 317–318.

had never had to work for their living, — — and I was bound that my friends — and your friends — should recognize her — and respect her — as my wife had a right to be respected; — — and I took her abroad — that I might give all you sensitive, fine people — a chance to get used to the idea of being polite to a woman who had once been a burlesque actress. — — It began over there in Paris. — — She had every chance when she married me — that a woman ever had — — — — all that a man's whole thought and love and money could bring to her. — — And you know what she did. — And after the divorce — — and she was free to go where she pleased, — and to live as she pleased, — and with whom she pleased, — — — — I swore to my God that I would never see her nor her child again. — I loved the mother, and she deceived me, — and disgraced me — and broke my heart — and I only wish she had killed me.

g. Read the following selection, using duration of vowel sounds to slow down the rate.[13]

This brave and tender man in every storm of life was oak and rock, but in the sunshine he was vine and flower. He was the friend of all heroic souls. He climbed the heights and left all superstitions far below, while on his forehead fell the golden dawning of the grander day.

He loved the beautiful, and was with color, form, and music touched to tears. He sided with the weak, and with a willing hand gave alms; with loyal heart and with purest hands he faithfully discharged all public trusts.

He was a worshipper of liberty, a friend of the oppressed. A thousand times I have heard him quote these words: "For justice all places a temple, and all seasons summer." He believed that happiness was the only good, reason the only torch, justice the only worship, humanity the only religion, and love the only priest. He added to the sum of human joy; and were every one to whom he did some loving service to bring a blossom to his grave, he would sleep tonight beneath a wilderness of flowers.

Life is a narrow vale between the cold and barren peaks of two eternities. We strive in vain to look beyond the heights. We cry aloud, and the only answer is the echo of our wailing cry. From the voiceless lips of the un-replying dead there comes no word; but in the night of death hope sees a star, and listening love can hear the rustle of a wing.

h. Read the first paragraph of the following selection in a monotone, and the second with conversational variety.[14]

When I had made an end of these labors it was four o'clock—still dark as midnight. As the bell sounded the hour, there came a knocking at the street door. I went down to open it with a light heart—for what had I now to fear? Then entered three men, who introduced themselves, with perfect suavity, as officers of the police. A shriek had been heard by a neighbor during the night; suspicion of foul play had been aroused; information had

[13] Robert Ingersoll, *The Works of Robert G. Ingersoll,* vol. XIII, pp. 389–391.
[14] Edgar Allan Poe, "The Tell-tale Heart."

been lodged at the police office, and they (the officers) had been deputed to search the premises.

I smiled—for what had I to fear? I bade the gentlemen welcome. The shriek, I said, was my own in a dream. The old man, I mentioned, was absent in the country. I took my visitors all over the house. I bade them search —search well. I led them at length to his chamber. I showed them his treasures, secure, undisturbed. In the enthusiasm of my confidence I brought chairs into the room and desired them here to rest from their fatigues, while I myself, in the wild audacity of my perfect triumph, placed my own seat upon the very spot beneath which reposed the corpse of the victim.

i. Time yourself in reading the following passage.[15] A good reading rate is 150 to 175 words per minute. Does your rate approximate this speed?

No thoughtful person can doubt that freedom of speech, freedom of press and freedom of assembly are vital to democracy itself—they are part of its very blood stream.

Only by free public discussion and free public criticism can the people be steadily sure that the will of the majority still prevails. Anyone who is inclined to feel that in times of national danger criticism of the government must be ruthlessly suppressed, should remember that two years ago it was the rising wave of popular criticism in Great Britain which overwhelmed the shuffling and indecisive leadership of Neville Chamberlain, and placed Winston Churchill in power. But while our constitutional democracy thus protects and, to maintain its integrity must protect, the civil liberties of the people, we must keep in mind that these civil liberties, freedom of speech, press, and assembly are not absolute. They are limited by the rights of others, and by the demands of national security. The rights of minorities do not rise above those of the majority. An outvoted minority may demand the right of orderly public criticism of public officers and public policy, but it enjoys no right of obstruction, no privilege of undermining the accepted policy of the government by conspiracy, sabotage, incitement to resistance or disobedience to law. Submission by the minority to majority decisions is as vital a part of the democratic process as is the protection accorded by the majority to the civil liberties of those who have been outvoted.

This delicate balance of majority and minority rights in a democratic nation calls for constant and thoughtful compromise and adjustment. In time of national danger it becomes increasingly difficult to maintain a decent respect for freedom of speech, freedom of press, and freedom of assembly. We face today, and we shall probably face in greater measure tomorrow, two serious dangers to these fundamental civil liberties. One of these dangers arises from the fact that the national security in a crisis like this makes necessary a curbing of freedom of speech, press, and assembly which would be indefensible in times of peace. The framing of these restrictions and the enforcement of them must be confided to our national public officials, and

[15] From a speech by Robert E. Cushman, "Civil Liberty in Time of National Defense," *Vital Speeches,* 8:143, 1941.

there is constant danger that they may go too far. The second danger is that popular hysteria will demand of the government unreasonable restrictions of civil liberty. There is much less danger that arrogant public officers will tyrannically override the liberties of a protesting people, than that an intolerant public opinion will not only permit but demand the complete suppression of minority rights.

PROJECT 4: DEVELOPMENT OF PITCH CONTROL

a. Sound the vowel "a" or "ah" at your habitual pitch level. Vary the pitch upward, then downward, a half step at a time until you have gone as far as you can toward either extreme. Try to find the pitch level at which you get the strongest resonance for your fundamental pitch. Is it higher or lower than your habitual pitch? Repeat the sound five times at the level at which you get the best tone.

b. Read the first third of the following paragraph[16] in a monopitch, the second part with moderate pitch variation, and the third part with marked pitch variation. Listen to the effect of the differences.

On Robert Burns

"I think Burns," said Robertson, the historian, "was one of the most extraordinary men I ever met with. His poetry surprised me very much; his prose surprised me still more; and his conversation surprised me more than both his poetry and prose." "His address," says Robert Riddle, "was pleasing; he was neither forward nor embarrassed in his manner; his spirits were generally high; and his conversation animated. His language was fluent, frequently fine; his enunciation always rapid; his ideas clear and vigorous, and he had the rare power of modulating his peculiarly fine voice, so as to harmonize with whatever subject he touched upon. I have heard him talk with astonishing rapidity, nor miss the articulation of a single syllable; elevate and depress his voice as the topic seemed to require; and sometimes, when the subject was pathetic, he would prolong the words in the most impressive and affecting manner, indicative of the deep sensibility which inspired him. He often lamented to me that fortune had not placed him at the bar, or the senate; he had great ambition, and the feeling that he could not gratify it, preyed on him severely."—ANONYMOUS

c. Read the following stanza from Wordsworth's "Daffodils" twice. Read it once with marked emphasis on the mechanical rhythm of the verse. Read it a second time with changes of inflection to bring out the meaning of the verse, but with subordination of the pitch changes to the pattern of rhythm.

> I wandered lonely as a cloud
> That floats on high o'er vales and hills

[16] From James O'Neill and Andrew Weaver, *The Elements of Speech*, Longmans, Green & Co., Inc., New York, 1933, p. 151.

When all at once I saw a crowd,
A host of golden daffodils;
Beside the lake, beneath the trees,
Fluttering and dancing in the breeze.

d. Read the following sentences with an upward or downward step in pitch as indicated.

Come ↑ here.

How ↑ much?

It's ↓ nonsense.

Strike ↓ hard.

You may pick it up, ↑ but handle it with care.

I loved the excitement, ↓ but I am very tired.

The plan of the attack, ↓ because of the presence of mines, ↑ was changed at the last moment.

If any of you are doubtful, ↑ and I suspect some of you are, ↓ here is the proof.

e. Read the following sentences with an upward or downward slide as indicated.

Isn't that a beautiful sight? ↓

He doesn't know the meaning of ethics. ↓

I have tried everything. ↑

Is that what you mean? ↑

I've never doubted it for a moment. ↓

Now, what do you say to that? ↑

Now, what do you say to that? ↓

How do you do this? ↑

How do you do this? ↓

Drive to the end of Summit. ↓

He won't believe it. ↑

I simply will not permit it. ↓

f. Read the following sentences in a pitch pattern which conveys the suggested emotional meaning.

I am tired, and discouraged, and very blue.

I am so excited. It seems almost too good to be true.

You fiend! You'll suffer for this.

Watch out! There's a rattler.

Jim? Now, there's a good sport.

The poor little tyke seems to be in great pain.

Well! I never expected to see you here.

The sense of loss seems more than I can bear.

I wonder if I shouldn't go, after all.

I have never been so sure of anything in all my life.

The inspiration of the service in the cathedral was an experience I shall long remember.

g. Bring to class a poem or piece of emotional prose of our own choosing, and demonstrate the use of pitch variation in communicating the meaning of the passage. Listen to the reading of others to develop an awareness of pitch changes.

PROJECT 5: DEVELOPMENT OF VOCAL QUALITY

a. Loosen up any tension in the muscles interfering with effective resonance by the following exercises:

(1) Drop the head forward as if you had fallen asleep sitting up. Relax the neck muscles until the head seems to bounce. Try letting it drop backward in the same way.

(2) Let the jaw muscles relax and drop the jaw in a relaxed manner, opening the mouth as far as possible. Start slowly and then increase the rapidity with which you say the word "bob." Relax and let the air push the lips out from the teeth as far as possible in this exercise.

(3) Relax the cheek muscles and blow out the cheeks as far as possible. Start slowly and then increase the rapidity with which you say the word "bob."

(4) Repeat the word "who" three times: (*a*) with high pharyngeal resonance as when you yawn and say "ho hum," (*b*) with relaxed pharyngeal resonance, (*c*) with a definite attempt to get resonance from the oral cavities.

(5) Repeat the sentence, "It's a very fine thing," twice: (*a*) Tense the muscles of the soft palate. (*b*) Relax the muscles of the soft palate.

(6) Sound the vowel in "ah" beginning with a whisper and gradually phonating the tone until you get a full resonant tone; then gradually aspirate the tone until the sound is whispered.

(7) Push against the wall and practice relaxing the muscles of the neck and mouth until you can say with a clear tone, "I am working to control relaxation of my speech muscles."

b. Develop resonance in your vocal attack by use of the following exercises:

(1) Count to ten: as if counting out pennies on a table; as if giving telephone numbers to a receiver with difficult telephone connections; as if counting with difficulty the number of persons in a party barely visible in the distance; as if "counting off" in doing setting-up exercises; as if "counting out" a man in the ring.

(2) Utter each of the following statements in a fully resonated positive tone:
"We came, we saw, we conquered."
"We have met the enemy and they are ours."
"We have just begun to fight."
"Ship ahoy! Ship ahoy!"
"Open—'Tis I, the King."
"Stand, the ground's your own, my braves!"
"Roll on, Thou deep and dark blue ocean—roll!"

Read a passage of ordinary prose carrying the pattern of sharp vocal attack necessary for these sentences into ordinary reading.

c. Try saying the sentence, "How does this gadget work?" in the following ways: with a tense throaty whisper; with a nasalized whisper; with an open mouth resonance; with aspirated tone; with high metallic tones; with highly nasalized tones; with raspy, harsh, throaty tones; with relaxed muscles and open mouth.

d. Read the following paragraph twice, at first as rapidly as you can with intelligibility for a small group, then slowly, as you would if addressing a large audience. Note the greater ease with which tones can be resonated at a slower rate. Listen for quality differences in the reading of others.

It is for us, the living, rather to be dedicated here to the unfinished work they have thus far so nobly carried on. It is rather for us to be here dedicated to the great task remaining before us, that from these honored dead we take increased devotion to the cause for which they gave the last full measure of devotion; that we here highly resolve that these dead shall not have died in vain, that the nation shall, under God, have a new birth of freedom, and that the government of the people, by the people, and for the people, shall not perish from the earth.—ABRAHAM LINCOLN

e. Work on the following exercises for the development of a tonal vocabulary.
(1) Pronounce the word "well" to indicate the following meanings:
I never would have thought it possible!
What do you want? I am very busy.
That's a small matter.
Now, let me think a minute.
So you thought you could get away with it!
I am very pleased to see you.
(2) Read the question "What are you doing?" as it would be expressed by the following characters: a burly policeman; an old man or woman; a half-frightened child; an ignorant, shiftless tramp; a fond young husband.
(3) Read each of the following sentences twice, first in a monotone, and then with a tonal quality suggested by the emotional mood of the sentence.
It's a beautiful night.
I wish I could remember where I have seen that face.
Say that again, and smile when you say it.
My! You think you're smart, don't you?
I never thought you would sink low enough to do a trick like that.
We'll have dinner at the Ritz, see a show, and dance all night.
So sorry. There are no more tickets for tonight. Next! What can I do for you?
I never want to see your face again. Now get out.
Isn't he a cute little thing! And he's only five.
I have never known anyone who seemed to be such a thoroughly good man.
There doesn't seem to be any use trying. I'm thoroughly beaten.
Watch out! You'll hit that car!
I am so full, I feel as if I'd burst; and it was all so good.
We're so proud of Steve. He takes his honors like a man.

f. Select a poem which expresses a mood with which you sympathize, and read it for the class in a vocal tone which expresses the mood. Listen critically to the vocal quality of your classmates.

References

Anderson, Virgil A.: *Training the Speaking Voice,* Oxford University Press, New York, 1942, chaps. 1–8.

Black, John W., and Wilbur E. Moore: *Speech: Code, Meaning, and Communication,* McGraw-Hill Book Company, Inc., New York, 1955, chaps. 2 and 3.

Brigance, W. Norwood: *Speech,* Appleton-Century-Crofts, Inc., New York, 1952, chap. 17.

Gilman, Wilbur E., Bower Aly, and Loren D. Reid: *The Fundamentals of Speaking,* The Macmillan Company, New York, 1951, chap. 10.

Gray, Giles W., and Waldo W. Braden: *Public Speaking: Principles and Practice,* Harper & Brothers, New York, 1951, chap. 21.

Hahn, Elise, C. W. Lomas, Donald Hargis, and Daniel Vandraegen: *Basic Voice Training for Speech,* 2d ed., McGraw-Hill Book Company, Inc., New York, 1957.

Holmes, F. L. D.: *Handbook of Voice and Diction,* Appleton-Century-Crofts, Inc., New York, 1940.

McBurney, James H., and Ernest J. Wrage: *The Art of Good Speech,* Prentice-Hall, Inc., Englewood Cliffs, N.J., 1940, chaps. 18 and 19.

Monroe, Alan H.: *Principles and Types of Speech,* 4th ed., Scott, Foresman and Company, Chicago, 1955, chaps. 4 and 5.

Powers, D. G.: *Fundamentals of Speech,* McGraw-Hill Book Company, Inc., New York, 1951, chaps. 7–10.

Van Dusen, C. R.: *Training the Voice for Speech,* McGraw-Hill Book Company, Inc., New York, 1953.

TWELVE

Articulation and

Pronunciation

ARTICULATION AND pronunciation both concern the formation of the sounds of spoken language, although pronunciation involves also some additional sound-formation features. Articulation refers to the systematic modification of vocal tones to form the vowel and consonant sounds used in speech. A sound is misarticulated when it is formed in a way that is not acceptable to the auditors. Pronunciation, like articulation, refers to the acceptable utterance of language sounds—specifically to the production of the sounds contained in individual words without substitutions, additions, omissions, inversions, or misplaced accents. Since certain differences in procedure are appropriate for the study and improvement of articulation and pronunciation, we will return to pronunciation later in this chapter. Pronunciation, we have suggested above, is the broader term, but the principles of articulation apply in the pronunciation of individual words.

Why Study Articulation?

Obviously articulation is important to satisfactory communication. Even though your pitch, rate, loudness, and quality may be well controlled, oral communication may fail if you run words and syllables together; if you mangle your medial or final consonants; if you fail to distinguish between similar but different sounds, as in "tin" and "ten," "fife" and "five," "wet" and "whet," "fussy" and "fuzzy." Americans are described as "lip-lazy" because they are in general poor articulators. Good articulation depends upon proper use of the jaw, teeth, tongue, lips, soft and hard palates, and breathing mechanisms.

Two criteria of satisfactory articulation. The most significant criterion of satisfactory articulation is that sounds must be so articulated that speech is intelligible. Many words in our language differ from others only in the articulation of a single sound; failure to articulate the distinguishing sound properly can cause confusion between two words. (Note the words compared above.) The confusion of the numbers "seven" and "eleven" in military orders has caused loss of life. Although listeners may eventually discover the right word and thus the meaning from the context, poor articulation slows down communication and renders it inefficient.

A second criterion of satisfactory articulation is social acceptability. Articulation can be compared to diction with regard to levels of social acceptability; there are substandard, informal, and formal levels of articulation. There is no authority in our country to prescribe the exact manner in which sounds are to be made. A degree of exactness completely acceptable to some persons is considered crude and unpleasant by others. Standards which would not be questioned in lively informal speech would be wholly inappropriate for formal occasions. We must be prepared to achieve a level of skill in articulation which meets the demands of the most exacting listener.

Methods of Improving Articulation

1. *Study the organs of articulation.* Persons who acquire a clear understanding of the function of the organs of articulation find that it helps make sense out of the principles of articulation and accelerates the process of improvement. These organs are the jaw, lips, teeth, tongue, hard palate, soft palate, and breathing mechanisms. The muscles of the inner surfaces of the resonance cavities of the mouth and the pharynx also operate to determine the shape of the oral cavities, which modify tones to cause the distinctive quality of the vowel sounds. Chronic inflammation of these surfaces or deformities in them may seriously affect articulation. The muscles of the larynx, moreover, are responsible for distinctions between the voiced and the voiceless sounds.

In a sense, the ear also serves as an organ of articulation. Unless we hear clearly the sounds we make, we may articulate poorly. Our purpose here is not to study the structure and function of the articulatory organs in detail.[1] An explanation of the organic basis of articulation, however, will help us to understand the classification of the sounds of English speech.

2. *Study the sounds of English speech.* The sounds of speech vary considerably as different persons make them. The purpose of the study of articulation is not to obtain perfect uniformity among all persons; sounds exist in families called phonemes and the student should learn to make each sound in such a way that it is clearly acceptable as a member of the phoneme to which it belongs.

Students usually associate sounds with the letters of the alphabet. It is helpful to think of the sounds themselves as the units of articulated speech: The sounds of the word "hurt," for example, are h-r-t rather than "aich-you-are-tee." Specialists in the study of language sounds have developed the science of phonetics, with a systematic set of phonetic symbols in which each sound family, or phoneme, has one symbol. These symbols are presented in Appendix A. A student who plans to become a professional in the field of communication should study these symbols and make them his own. The diacritical marks used in the dictionary, on the other hand, are an attempt to provide symbols for sounds by using marks over the letters of the alphabet. For the purposes of the average student, diacritical marks will be sufficient. The marks employed in the vowel classification presented in the next section are derived from Webster's *New International Dictionary*.

3. *Distinguish among vowels, diphthongs, and consonants.* The three main types of speech sounds are vowels, diphthongs, and consonants. Vowels consist of relatively unmodified voice (that is, voice in which there is little interference with the outgoing air), whereas consonants consist of voice modified by the same type of friction or stoppage which,

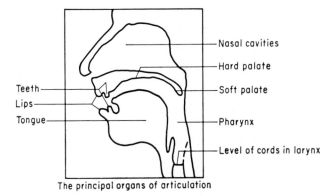

The principal organs of articulation

[1] Students who wish to study articulatory processes in greater detail will find the works cited at the end of this chapter helpful.

in part, produces the sound. One or more of the organs of articulation (the vocal folds, tongue, soft palate, hard palate, lips, teeth, jaw) modify or interfere with the free exhalation of air to produce consonants. Diphthongs are combinations of vowel sounds produced as one sound, such as *i* in "ice," a combination of *a* and *i*.

The differentiation of vowel sounds is initiated by the vibrations of vocal cords and is influenced by the resonators. These areas may be located on a vowel parallelogram or triangle as it is sometimes called, as indicated by the accompanying chart. Front vowels, in which the highest part of the tongue is toward the top of the mouth and ranging downward, are the *e* of "be," the *i* of "bit," the *e* of "bet," and the *a* of "tan." The *u* of "but" is a midvowel, as is the *a* of "ask," with the highest part of the tongue drawn back somewhat in the mouth.

The back vowels range upward from the *a* in "father" to the *oo* in "fool," with the highest part of the tongue toward the back of the mouth.

Vowel Parallelogram

Front vowels		Back vowels
ē (i) be		ōo (u) boot
ĭ (I) bit	Å (ə) about	ŏo (u) foot
ĕ (ε) bed	ŭ (ʌ) but	ô (ɔ) low
ă (æ) hat		ä (a) far

The principal diphthongs are the *u* of "use," the *o* of "hole," the *ou* of "ouch," the *a* of "day," the *i* of "light," the *e* of "feet," and the *oi* of "oil." Although some of these are considered single sounds, careful study will reveal them to be combinations of sounds.

Consonants, as we have seen, are produced by interference with the free expiration of breath. All consonants may be classified as either voiced or voiceless. Voiced consonants are accompanied by a vibration of the vocal cords (bands or folds). Many consonants are matched or paired; the muscular adjustments that produce voiced and voiceless "twins" are alike except that the cords are vibrated to produce the voiced sound. Examples are *g* and *k*, *d* and *t*, *b* and *p*, and *v* and *f*.

Nasal consonants are resonated chiefly through the nasal passages: *m*, *n*, and *ng*. The stop plosives, as the term implies, are formed by blocking the air stream and then releasing the sounds explosively. Voiced stop plosives are *b*, *d*, and *g*. Voiceless stop plosives are *p*, *t*, and *k*. Moser[2] has recently completed some studies which give us a number of interesting ideas about our speech sounds. The relative frequency of vowel sounds and diphthongs is listed as follows:

[2] Henry M. Moser, *One Syllable Words*, Air Force Command and Control Development Division. Technical Note 60–58, Bedford, Mass., 1960. See also Moser, *A Voice Training Manual*, Federal Aviation Agency, Washington, D.C., 1962.

1. ǐ as in hit
2. ǎ as in hat
3. ǔ as in hut
4. ä as in hot
5. ě as in heck
6. ā as in hay
7. ô as in hawk
8. ō as in hoe

9. ē as in he
10. ī as in high
11. ōō as in who
12. å as in her
13. ou as in how
14. ū as in hue
15. ŏŏ as in hook
16. oi as in hoist

The sounds most frequently confused are those which are immediately across from each other on the parallelogram or those immediately above or below each other. The back vowels tend to be more frequently confused than the front vowels.

Confusion among the consonants arises among those sounds articulated in the same manner. These include:

p t ch k
b d j g
m n ng
o r
f th s ch sh h wh
v th z j zh wh
w y wh

4. *Identify the sounds with which you have difficulty.* Test yourself systematically to determine which sounds cause you difficulty. (Note the test in project 1 at the end of this chapter.) You are not likely to be aware of your own shortcomings. When people tell you to slow down or to talk louder they may merely mean that you should articulate more clearly. Vowels that are frequently misarticulated are *a* as in "bad," *e* as in "get," *i* as in "fish," and *u* as in "just." The diphthong *ou* as in "down" is frequently perverted to an *au* sound. Consonants that commonly cause difficulty are the aspirate and fricative sounds, characterized by a rustling friction of the breath, such as *s, z, ch, dz, sh, zh, f, th, v,* and *wh*. The *n* sound is often substituted for *ng*, and *t* is often erroneously produced by a glottal stop rather than an explosion between the tongue and hard palate. The *t, d, p, b, k,* and *g* sounds are sometimes exploded when they should merely be stopped by the articulators. The *w* sound is sometimes substituted for *r*, in such words as "bright." These are some of the most common misarticulations. Make a systematic analysis of your articulatory habits in order to discover and correct your personal variations.

5. *Apply sufficient breath pressure as you sound consonants.* Be sure you sound with sufficient accuracy and fullness such plosives as *p* in "pour," *b* in "ban," *d* in "dote," *g* in "gill," *t* in "talk," *k* in "cap," and *h* in "hill." Be sure to articulate fully medial and final consonants, such as the *l* in "asleep," the *t* in "cut," and the *s* sound in "trace."

6. *Mouth, jaw, lips, and tongue should be active in articulation.* Make a tape recording of your voice and note your articulatory weaknesses and your progress. Read passages, including those listed at the end of this chapter, before a mirror and observe your vocal activity or lack of activity in articulation. Practice (see again the projects at the end of this chapter) such words as "kept" versus "kep," "ask" versus "ass," and "exactly" versus "exackly."

7. *Avoid lip-laziness.* Perhaps the most common difficulty in articulation is what is called "lip-laziness." The difficulty, however, does not concern the lips alone; other articulatory organs are also involved. The result is mumbling or general oral inaccuracy. To overcome such a habit you will need a sufficiently clear and vigorous tone to carry sound differences to your listeners and sufficient control of all the articulatory organs to use each of them as needed to modify the basic tone. Some persons, on the other hand, go to extremes in activating the articulatory organs and thus produce a kind of affected niceness of enunciation, particularly of certain words about which the speaker is self-conscious. This fault, however, is not so common as underarticulation.

8. *Analyze for articulatory excellence any of the speech recordings now available.* For example, listen to the RCA Victor *Hamlet,* as read by Laurence Olivier. (Note especially Act III, scene ii. See project 3, Chapter Ten, for this passage from *Hamlet.*)

9. *Learn the International Civil Aviation Organization Alphabet.* It may be helpful for you to know the latest word-alphabet vocabulary. In the ICAO alphabet, a particular word or sound is used to designate—in a manner free from confusion—each letter of the standard alphabet. Moser[3] has studied dozens of words and their sound confusions as spoken by the nationals of many different countries to produce this alphabet, which is shown below.

ICAO Alphabet

A	ALFA	N	NOVEMBER
B	BRAVO	O	OSCAR
C	CHARLIE	P	PAPA
D	DELTA	Q	QUEBEC
E	ECHO	R	ROMEO
F	FOXTROT	S	SIERRA
G	GOLF	T	TANGO
H	HOTEL	U	UNIFORM
I	INDIA	V	VICTOR
J	JULIETT	W	WHISKEY
K	KILO	X	X-RAY
L	LIMA	Y	YANKEE
M	MIKE	Z	ZULU

[3] Moser, *ibid.*

Methods of Improving Pronunciation

Improving pronunciation is a matter of selecting the proper sounds, putting them together into syllables and words, and uttering these combinations distinctly, giving each syllable the proper stress. Articulation, as we observed earlier, forms the basis of pronunciation.

1. *Use the pronunciation acceptable to the more careful speakers of this country.* You are familiar with Standard American or with Eastern, Western, or Southern standards of articulation and pronunciation. Good articulation and pronunciation for one region is not considered substandard in any other. There are, of course, a great many variations within each region. Extremes of regionalism in articulation and pronunciation are atypical and subject to criticism by persons of exacting standards even within the region. Your personal standards should conform to the standards of the better-educated citizens of the region in which you expect to spend your life. However, it is wise to develop the skill necessary to adapt your articulation to the standard preferred by the country as a whole.

Foreign accents and dialects present a problem closely associated with regionalism in articulation and pronunciation. Some foreign languages do not employ all the sounds of English. Other languages contain sounds which differ considerably from similar English sounds. It is these sounds which cause the most difficulty in learning a new language. Differences in the inflectional patterns and intonations of languages also cause difficulty. Although it is no disgrace for your speech to reveal the country of your origin, dialectal characteristics are a source of distraction and confusion in communication. The use of dialect is especially to be deplored when the speaker trades upon it as a sort of affectation in speech to which he attaches false cultural values.

2. *Reproduce speech sounds accurately.* There are five common classes of pronunciation errors: substitution, addition, omission, inversion, and misplaced accent. Although it is not always possible to place a mispronounced word in one of these classes exclusively, the classification serves a practical purpose in understanding and improving pronunciation. Some examples of each class are listed below:

SUBSTITUTIONS: agin for again
fer for for
bak for bag
wuz for was
suite for sweet
ADDITIONS: ca(l)m for calm
fore(h)ead for forehead
rem(i)nent for remnant

pang(g) for pang
across(t) for across

OMISSIONS: col for cold
reconize for recognize
dimond for diamond
eights for eighths
battry for battery

INVERSIONS: occifer for officer
calvery for cavalry
casual for causal
interduce for introduce
pervide for provide

MISPLACED ACCENT: adúlt for ádult
résearch for reséarch
superflúous for supérfluous
impótent for ímpotent
futíle for fútile

What are the causes of these pronunciation errors? Words are mispronounced for a number of reasons. One is spelling. Words are not always pronounced as their spelling suggests; moreover, spelling provides no clue to accent. Some errors are caused by failure to note changes of pronunciation for words serving different linguistic functions. Words are sometimes mispronounced because they are confused with similar words. Other words are mispronounced because of misarticulation of sounds contained in them.

Probably most mispronunciations occur because the words were first heard mispronounced or because the first pronunciation was a bad guess which initiated the habit of mispronouncing. It is better to make a good guess at a new word than to mumble it, for mumbling always produces mispronunciation. But there is no substitute for the habit of checking pronunciations in a good up-to-date American dictionary. Moreover, pronunciations, like other language forms, change with time. If most well-educated people "mispronounce" a word in a certain way, this pronunciation is almost certain to be accepted in a short time. The dictionaries attempt to follow rather than dictate acceptable pronunciation.

3. *Pronounce each word according to its proper syllabication.* Avoid omitting syllables. Children say "A'rab" for "Ar-ab," and some people use "ho-mog'-o-nous" for "hom-o-ge'-ne-ous."

4. *Let the requirements of the speaking situation govern your pronunciation.* When you are speaking in a large auditorium or when you are competing with noises, retard your pronunciation to ensure the listener's comprehension. Slow pronunciation is also a means of stressing important ideas.

5. *Obtain a good dictionary and check your pronunciation constantly.*

Remember that even the best dictionary is not an absolute authority. It may be out of date for a particular word. It will not guide you on comparative stress or accent on various syllables. This can come only from a good ear. But it is nevertheless a very significant source of information about word sounds.

Projects and Problems

PROJECT 1: A TEST OF ARTICULATION

The following exercise in speech sounds should help you to identify any sounds with which you have difficulty. The sound to be identified and tested is indicated after each number by means of the markings used in Webster's. The first word contains the sound in a prominent position. Some of the other words in the list contain the sound, and some do not. Pronounce the words aloud and underline those which contain the sound you are testing. Check the line to the left of the number for all sounds on which you need further work. Listen to the reading of others to note how they produce these sounds. For a short form of the test, do only the items marked by an asterisk.

_____	1.	ē	feet, fit, date, eat, me, egg, fill, seen
_____	*2.	ĭ	dill, deal, it, pit, peat, pet, duck, dick
_____	*3.	ĕ	get, git, dale, end, shall, yet, enter, out
_____	*4.	ă	pat, pet, as, den, leg, rock, rack, dad
_____	5.	å	ago, up, lute, policy, fallen, bath, tuba, toot
_____	*6.	ŭ	cud, cod, utter, just, shot, tuck, dude, put
_____	7.	ä	far, fur, on, want, had, luck, caught, ah
_____	8.	ô	caught, cut, doll, gun, tuck, owl, nod, coat
_____	9.	ŏŏ	took, tuck, tune, could, crux, group, drew, wolf
_____	10.	ōō	spoon, spewn, ooze, whom, luck, shoe, beauty, put
_____	11.	ū	you, rue, hue, food, fuel, feel, pew, full, fool
_____	12.	ō	coal, cull, oboe, slow, mutton, brow, cod, opus
_____	*13.	ou	cowed, kayoed, bough, ton, gun, rot, crayola, out
_____	14.	ā	pain, pen, pun, eight, tell, flay, Iowa, hail
_____	15.	ī	like, lick, aisle, race, won, tiger, spy
_____	16.	oi	loin, line, bird, fine, toy, murder, voice, tall
_____	17.	m	mere, beer, ear, home, bill, robe, mop, summer
_____	18.	n	new, drew, under, dole, pew, pan, pants, singing
_____	*19.	ng	singing, sinning, rank, ran, rag, rang, ram, tinkle
_____	*20.	p	pour, more, whip, paper, cap, bees, robin, slap
_____	21.	b	ban, man, pan, robe, sober, baby, cob, rim
_____	*22.	t	Ted, dead, cad, madder, cut, feed, biting, three
_____	*23.	d	dote, tote, gad, mat, radio, fated, bat, tin
_____	24.	k	cap, gap, bagging, tackle, brig, kill, crew
_____	25.	g	gill, kill, rag, bucky, raking, core, fling, age
_____	*26.	r	roar, wore, hear, weep, deride, very, bar, weed

———— 27. l lay, pray, wake, little, camel, seal, sole, asleep
———— 28. f fly, ply, safe, differs, divers, have, thigh, wife
———— 29. v vain, bane, fat, proof, leave, unveiling, wail, live
————*30. th thank, tank, they, zinc, swath, sin, anything, bass
————*31. th thy, vie, thigh, loathe, fat, sigh, mother, cloth
————*32. s saw, thaw, miss, shaw, trace, recent, clash, graze
————*33. z zoo, Sioux, boys, vice, lazy, noose, aphasia, place
————*34. sh ship, sip, cheap, mash, explosion, suit, fishing, shoot
———— 35. zh garage, garish, entourage, rajah, vision, mirage, ocean, cortege
————*36. wh where, wear, vile, while, winter, wheat, witch, bewhiskered, white
————*37. h hill, gill, hinge, unhang, hurrah, who, rehash, wheel
————*38. w way, whey, swine, whet, chair, fight, wise, quiet
———— 39. y yam, lamb, jello, yellow, onion, jeer, set, young
————*40. ch cherry, sherry, Jerry, etching, leech, lush, ridge, chum
———— 41. dz gin, chin, just, badge, richer, soldier, magic, pitching

PROJECT 2: ARTICULATING DIFFICULT SOUND BLENDS AND COMBINATIONS

a. The following exercises for relaxing tension and "tuning" the articulators are to be done by the entire class in unison: (1) Count to twenty-five using a vigorous vocal tone. (2) Count to twenty-five using the adjectival form of the numerals. (3) Repeat the last exercise in a strong whisper. (4) Write out combinations of numbers and practice calling them out rapidly.

b. Practice the following exercises on sound combinations and prepare to do them individually when called upon.

(1) Peter Prangle, the prickly, prangly pear picker, picked three pecks of prickly, prangly pears from the prickly, prangly pear trees on the pleasant prairies.

(2) Big black bugs brought buckets of black bear's blood.

(3) Pillercatter, tappekiller, kitterpaller, patterkiller, caterpillar.

(4) A big black bug bit a big black bear.

(5) Better buy the bigger rubber baby buggy bumpers.

(6) A tutor who tooted the flute,
Tried to tutor two tooters to toot.
Said the two to the tutor, "Is it harder to toot, or
To tutor two tooters to toot?"

(7) Betty Botta bought a bit of butter,
"But," said she, "This butter is bitter
If I put it in my batter
It will make my batter bitter;
But a bit of better butter
Will make my bitter batter better."
So she bought a bit of butter,
Better than the bitter butter,
And it made her bitter batter better.
So 'twas better Betty Botta
Bought a bit of better butter.

(8) Thomas a Tattamus took two T's,
To tie two pups to two tall trees,
To frighten the terrible Thomas a Tattamus!
Now do tell me how many T's that is.

(9) He was a three-toed tree toad, but a two-toed toad was she. The three-toed tree toad tried to climb the two-toed tree toad's tree.

(10) How much wood would a woodchuck chuck if a woodchuck could chuck wood?

(11) Sister Susie went to sea to see the sea you see.
So the sea she saw you see was a saucy sea.
The sea she saw was a saucy sea.
A sort of saucy sea saw she.

(12) Seven shell-shocked soldiers sawing six slick, slender, slippery, silver saplings.

(13) A skunk sat on a stump. The stump said the skunk stunk, and the skunk said the stump stunk.

(14) A biscuit, a box of biscuits, a box of mixed biscuits, and a biscuit mixed.

(15) Theophilas Thistle the successful thistle sifter in sifting a sieve full of unsifted thistles sifted three thousand thistles through the thick of his thumb. See that thou, oh thou unsuccessful thistle sifter, sift not three thousand thistles through the thick of thy thumb.

(16) Amidst the mists and coldest frosts
He thrusts his fists against the posts
And still insists he sees the ghosts.

(17) Let the little lean camel lead the lame lamb to the lake.

(18) Nine nimble noblemen nibbling nonpareils.

(19) Esau Wood sawed wood. Esau Wood would saw wood. All the wood Esau Wood saw Esau Wood would saw. In other words, all the wood Esau saw to saw Esau sought to saw. Oh, the wood Wood would saw! And oh, the wood-saw with which Wood would saw wood. But one day Wood's wood-saw would saw no wood, and thus the wood Wood sawed was not the wood Wood would saw if Wood's wood-saw would saw wood. Now, Wood would saw if Wood's wood-saw would saw wood. Now, Wood would saw wood with a wood-saw that would saw wood, so Esau sought a saw that would saw wood. One day Esau saw a saw saw wood as no other wood-saw Wood saw would saw wood. In fact, of all the wood-saws Wood ever saw saw wood Wood never saw a wood-saw that would saw wood as the wood-saw Wood saw saw wood would saw wood, and I never saw a wood-saw that would saw as the wood-saw Wood saw would saw until I saw Esau saw wood with the wood-saw Wood saw saw wood. Now Wood saws wood with the wood-saw Wood saw saw wood.

PROJECT 3: ARTICULATING DIFFICULT SOUNDS

Find two to three pages of prose which develop an idea of interest to you. Go over the passage and underline all sounds with which you have difficulty. Practice reading until you can articulate all sounds clearly and acceptably.

Read another similar passage to see if you can articulate all sounds effectively without further study of them. Listen to the typically difficult sounds as produced by others in doing this exercise.

PROJECT 4: UNDERSTANDING THE PHONETIC SYMBOLS

Turn to Appendix A and study the phonetic symbols until you know them. Your speech will be criticized at times with phonetic symbols, and you should have a clear understanding of the sounds for which they stand.

PROJECT 5: ARTICULATING COMMON WORDS

In the following passage, entitled "Advice to Speech Students," you will find about 50 per cent of all words in the speech of a group of American college freshmen and many other common words with which some students have difficulty. If you can acceptably articulate the sounds of this passage, it is probable that you will have little difficulty with common words. Practice reading this passage until you can articulate all sounds effectively.

Advice to Speech Students

Both men and women college students need some speech education. It is natural that not all our friends can help us. The first reason for this is that a person doesn't find it easy to be tactful. Secondly, a friend will now and then hesitate because he really does no better. Next, who can say just how another person's faults must be changed? Only about ten out of a thousand have a clear picture of any one fault, although they must have a number of goals. Again, some faults are not so very bad. And, last but not least, many of the habits we have today may change in a few months. Yet what your life has been while you were trying to carry on cannot finally escape you in an instant or even before the year is over. It is a fact that this was what a man once went to Europe for.

My advice here is that you must be kept doing your school lessons in speech. I say this merely so that, in time, as you go up the ladder of success, you will be better able to do what you want.

Although you may think that such new habits of saying things aren't ways by which other people climb out of their despair, they are; and if you would escape from trouble, there is still time. When asked by any individual around town where you learned about this subject, you had better beg to answer by going into the case and putting the several explanations together. You could also tell something of why you now fill a far larger room with listeners. Whether or not you wonder at what we mean is less important at the moment than your being moved toward the skill in speech for which you came to get help.

References

Anderson, Virgil A.: *Training the Speaking Voice*, Oxford University Press, New York, 1942, chap. 8.

Black, John W., and Wilbur E. Moore: *Speech: Code, Meaning, and Communication,* McGraw-Hill Book Company, Inc., New York, 1955, chap. 4.

Brigance, W. Norwood: *Speech,* Appleton-Century-Crofts, Inc., New York, 1952, chap. 18.

Fairbanks, Grant: *Voice and Articulation Drillbook,* Harper & Brothers, New York, 1940.

Fields, Victor A., and James F. Bender: *Voice and Diction,* The Macmillan Company, New York, 1949.

Gilman, Wilbur A., Bower Aly, and Loren D. Reid: *The Fundamentals of Speaking,* The Macmillan Company, New York, 1951, chap. 11.

Hahn, Elise, Charles W. Lomas, Donald Hargis, and Daniel Vandraegen: *Basic Voice Training for Speech,* 2d ed., McGraw-Hill Book Company, Inc., New York, 1957.

McBurney, James H., and Ernest J. Wrage: *The Art of Good Speech,* Prentice-Hall, Inc., Englewood Cliffs, N.J., 1953, chap. 20.

Monroe, Alan H.: *Principles and Types of Speech,* 4th ed., Scott, Foresman and Company, Chicago, 1955, chap. 6.

Powers, D. G.: *Fundamentals of Speech,* McGraw-Hill Book Company, Inc., New York, 1951, chaps. 11–14.

THIRTEEN

Physical Activity and

Visual Aids

ALTHOUGH THE VISIBLE actions of the speaker are not in themselves language, they do have symbolic meaning. The visual code, or action, is the third symbol system of speech in the order in which we have discussed them in this book. The two symbol systems previously discussed are the codes of language and voice. Visible symbols are often used as a substitute for oral or written language, as in the gestural language of the deaf and dumb, the reading of lips by sight and touch, the arm signals of combat forces, smoke signals, and semaphore or blinker codes. The use of these symbols involves many of the problems of speaking. Physical action in speaking, however, is not a substitute for but a supplement to speech. The speaker's action—his position, movements, appearance, manner, and habits of physical adjustment—and visual aids, such as charts or models, create their communicative effects quite apart from linguistic or vocal symbols. For the sake of effective study, we must consider this aspect of speech as we have other processes of speaking—in isolation from, as well as in conjunction with, the total speech act. This code is to be considered neither a primitive nor an immature part of speech. It does much to facilitate or hamper normal communication.

The Values of Action

The first impressions we get of a speaker are derived from his observable behavior. Most of us have learned from experience that first impressions may be misleading, but we also know that in speaking they are important in orienting the audience to what follows. Experienced speakers are sometimes greatly surprised at the impressions they have created in others. In order to know ourselves better, we should make a careful study of our own behavior. We might discover traits—both good and bad—of which we were wholly unaware.

The visible symbols of a speaker may be specific and denotative or general and highly connotative. We do not describe a series of specific gestures or expressions for practice in this book. The student will no doubt have adequate latent skill for the exercise of most of the gestures he will use. The biggest barrier to the use of action is that some speakers do not feel right about expressing themselves physically. One of the chief aims of this chapter is to help the student realize that action is a proper and acceptable mode of communication.

Gestures and other physical expressions serve a major function in orienting the listener to the linguistic expression of the idea. They provide a setting, a climate for the language which expresses a feeling or attitude. When the context is consistent the spoken idea receives more emphasis and impact.

Dale[1] has shown that learning is directly related to a cone of experience. Our direct personal experiences have most meaning for us. Contrived experiences—dramatizations, demonstrations, exhibits, broadcasts, motion pictures, and tape recordings—give a high degree of reality and credibility to a message which verbal symbols alone do not give. We need to do all we can in communication to give our listeners the full feeling of reality even in the verbal messages we send. Careful consideration of the tonal and visual codes can do much to accomplish this. Since "seeing is believing" we should give our listeners a chance to see as well as hear.

1. *Personality cues.* Let us consider the speaker's bearing or poise, energy level, facial characteristics, social attitudes, and neatness or orderliness. A speaker who can carry himself relatively straight without being tense, who can stand quietly without swaying, rocking, squirming, or fidgeting, and who can respond alertly to the stimuli in his surroundings gives the impression of being confident and efficient. The antics of the clown or the old-time revivalist suggest that the speaker is overanxious or

[1] Edgar Dale, *Audio-Visual Methods in Teaching,* The Dryden Press, Inc., New York, 1954.

exhibitionistic. A speaker who is so energetic that he appears to be addressing a pep rally or who is so lacking in energy that he appears to be incompetent, indifferent, or afraid of consequences cannot inspire confidence as a person who makes efficient use of his energies. Affected nonchalance is inappropriate in most speaking situations.

If the demands of the situation require the speaker to keep his personal reactions in the background, a blank expression or a poker face will be tolerated. Otherwise, listeners will react most favorably to responsive facial expressions. A pugnaciously set jaw, a set smile, or an evasive, faraway look of boredom will probably be interpreted by an audience as signs of emotional immaturity or maladjustment. The speaker who habitually wears one of these expressions is often unaware of the fact that he formed the habit in an earlier stage of his personality development. Such habits can be modified with relative ease once they have been pointed out.

Characteristics of this kind need not occur in extreme form to be perceived. An audience can even infer the tastes and social sensitivities of a speaker from his clothing and personal appearance. The listener who is not persistent enough to analyze the situation may not be aware of the causes of his reaction. But stereotyped judgments are often made on the basis of fleeting suggestions of this type. Love at first sight, like spontaneous personality clashes, may be explained on the basis of reactions to unconscious indications of personality.

2. *Signals of your intentions.* Effective speaking demands sufficient control of the visual and tonal as well as of the linguistic parts of speech to make them all suggest the same thing at the same time. Audiences can readily interpret visible expressions of the speaker's attitude.[2] In this respect the eye appears truly to be quicker, or at least surer, than the ear. When there is a conflict between what is said in language and what is said by action, the action is more readily believed than the words. Consider the expression, "When you say that, smile."

The speaker who is unduly emotional in response does not obtain from his audience adequate consideration of the intellectual content of what he has to say. If his emotional reactions are not appropriate to the situation, he must learn to keep them under control. Physical expressions of distrust and dislike are likely to evoke a negative response from an audience or a vindictive response from a top sergeant or a shop foreman.

On the other hand, an audience will respond positively to your expressions of emotional reaction to the materials of your speech.[3] In addi-

[2] Delwin Dusenbury and Franklin H. Knower, "Studies in the Symbolism of Voice and Action," *Quarterly Journal of Speech,* 24:424–436, 1938.

[3] Franklin H. Knower, "The Use of Behavioral and Tonal Symbols as Tests of Speaking Achievement," *Journal of Applied Psychology,* 29:229–235, 1945.

tion to objective facts and intellectual processes, speech materials involve such attitudes as great conviction, righteous indignation, admiration, affection, doubt and hesitation, surprise, grief, disappointment, and hope. If you as a speaker reveal your feelings about your materials, you will find most audiences ready to respond positively.

3. *Emphasizing your meaning.* Recent experiments in immediate and delayed memory for facts and principles presented with and without visual aids indicate the superiority of instruction with visual aids.[4] Maps, charts, diagrams, and laboratory demonstrations have long been considered sound educational supplements to the informative lecture. It is not always practical or possible for the speaker to carry about actual pictures of the objects and events about which he speaks, but descriptive and suggestive action can be a good substitute. Such action is especially helpful in suggesting size, shape, texture, distance, direction, location, movement, speed, weight, and force.

The manager of a crew of vacuum-cleaner salesmen who canvassed from door to door found that the sales of his group had begun to fall off. In their sales approach, these men offered to inspect the household vacuum cleaner for needed repairs. Their opening line was "Do you know that if the base of the brushes on your cleaner is more than a quarter of an inch from the floor, it can't clean your rugs effectively?" The following week, the salesmen were instructed to supplement the words with action; as they asked the question they were to demonstrate by raising a hand, holding the forefinger and thumb close together. The twenty salesmen gained access to ninety-seven more houses than during the previous week, and the manager attributed this to the persuasive effect of the simple visible action.

The effectiveness of words is enhanced by vigor of expression and by the force of the action which accompanies them. Skill in the use of visible action provides the speaker with a variety of means of holding interest. Many types of action and gesture have specific suggestive value. They are often used in informal speech but may be used in the most formal of situations as well. Examples are the upward movement of the hand of the clergyman as a signal for the audience to rise, the open hand held aloft as a means of quieting a restless audience, and the bow which serves as an acknowledgment of applause. More informal actions are nodding the head, shrugging the shoulders, crossing the lips with the fingers for silence, beckoning, holding the nose, and scores of others. A code of such gestures is used by the staffs of radio and television studios to communicate silently during broadcasts. Verbal communication can often be enriched by such action.

[4] Franklin H. Knower, David Phillips, and Fern Koeppel, "Studies in Listening to Informative Speaking," *Journal of Abnormal and Social Psychology,* 40:82–88, 1945.

This kind of behavior provides the audience with visual sensations of the idea. A supplement and sometimes a substitute for such visual stimulation is a vivid description which can create in the response of the listener an image of the idea under consideration. Great emphasis in some quarters of our society is placed upon the activity of the "image makers."

4. *Getting attention.* A significant characteristic of attention is that it does not remain focused on one subject for a very long time. The average person's span of attention is short, although it may be increased. The speaker who makes adroit use of action enables his auditors to shift their attention and still follow his discourse. An extreme example of the use of action for controlling attention is provided by the magician. He directs our attention by the use of action in such a manner that other action necessary for performing his tricks goes unnoticed. More common examples of the use of action to direct attention are the salesman's use of paper and pencil, the habit of looking at an object to which we want to attract attention, and movement from one part of the platform to another to mark a transition in ideas. A speaker who looks at his watch while he is speaking will be surprised to see how many members of his audience do likewise.

Your visible action as a speaker will provide empathic release of the muscle tensions of your audience. The chairs in most halls where formal speeches are made are not designed for the comfort of the audience. For this reason the members of a seated audience will become restless if you set a pattern of quiet and inactivity. If, on the other hand, you accompany your speech with appropriate visible action—especially if you deliver an energetic speech—you provide your audiences with a release of tension through their suggestibility to action and you facilitate their comfort in listening. The same principle applies in some degree, as we have seen, to the speaker. If you accompany your speech with appropriate action, you release tensions which may otherwise find an outlet in distractive action. To keep your audience's attention, then, you should consciously develop habits of action which help you in speaking; in this way you can eliminate other habits of action which may handicap you.

Characteristics of Effective Action

Let your action show that you are interested in communicating with your audience. Do not look at the ceiling, at the floor, or over the heads of your listeners. If you use a manuscript, read *to* the audience—not *from* your pages. Make your bodily action purposeful; avoid random activity such as squirming, fidgeting, pacing, fingering your ring, rolling your handkerchief, and tossing chalk. Concentrate on your communicative goal, and let your total bodily activity be controlled by this purpose. Deliver your speech with the physical liveliness that your theme demands.

Are you successful in using bodily activity in speech? Through study, you can improve. But do not expect your action to be completely effective in the learning stages.

The principal agencies of expression are the head and face, shoulders, arms, hands and fingers, body, legs, and feet. Most expressive action involves a high degree of integration of parts of the body acting as a whole to produce suggestive positions, facial expressions, and patterns of movement.

Every character actor knows that the manner of standing or walking, the position of the shoulders, the placement and movements of the hands, the tilt of the head, and the expressive lines of the mouth and eyes suggest variations in physical conditions, moods, character, and personality types. Position and facial expressions are not so uniformly interpreted as are patterns of physical movement. This fact appears to indicate that *the most effective form of physical expression is a pattern of action in which location, form, line, and movement are well coordinated in at least a brief, continuing series of actions.*

To formulate specific rules about such matters as distribution of weight, the position of the feet, the posture of the body, and the placement or movement of the hands would result merely in the stereotyping and cramping of expressive action. Such rules might be appropriate for acting a specific role, but since the typical speaker in normal speaking activities plays many roles from hour to hour, it seems more important to develop adaptive patterns of physical expression than to limit and freeze expressions.

1. *Timing.* An important aspect of adaptive action is timing. Effective action should precede by an instant the accompanying words and tone of voice expressing the idea. If the action either occurs at the same time or follows the verbal expression of the idea, the effect is ludicrous.

2. *Audience adaptation.* Consider the composition of your audience in connection with your visible action. If your listeners are primarily white-collar workers who lead a sedentary life, they will not be sympathetic to an overactive speaker. If they are persons who enjoy physical work, the speech that is not accompanied by energetic expression will not challenge them. Action in reading is less important than action in speaking; it should be suggestive only, and not impersonative. Action appropriate to informal speaking is more varied, more highly personalized, and less reserved than that appropriate to formal occasions. Action for large groups is ordinarily more formal than that for small groups; it should also be simple and slow but energetic.

3. *Posture.* Good posture allows the speaker to use his arms, hands,

eyes, and other organs and muscles freely. In addition, posture itself conveys meaning.

What posture is best? It is better not to formulate precise rules. Your posture should express self-control, energy, and friendliness toward your audience. Effective bodily action and physical poise are the result of experience in speaking more than of special exercises or movements carefully rehearsed for a given speech. You will need the advice of your instructor and your classmates on your individual case.

Your posture should be easy and natural, and your body should be relaxed. Your posture will reflect your attitude toward your audience and your speech. Remember that it is better to err on the side of dignified bearing. Avoid standing at military attention, planting your weight almost entirely on one foot, rocking on your toes and heels, leaning over the footlights (or platform) toward your hearers, clutching your arms, or keeping your arms continually behind your back.

4. *Purposefulness of movement.* When you go to the front of a room or to a platform to address a group, walk with decision but without militancy. When you turn to face the group, do not make an awkward sweep; if you have a speaker's stand before you, do not fall upon it, entwining your legs wearily behind it. If, after you have talked for a few minutes, you wish to change your position, you may do so with such spontaneity that your listeners will not consciously observe it.

Immobility kills speech as surely as excessive movement. No set rules can be made concerning the amount and kind of movement, for both must be determined by the temperament and cultural habits of the speaker, by the character, size, and physical surroundings of the audience, and by the subject and the occasion.

5. *Appropriateness of gesture.* Gesture usually refers to movements of hands, arms, shoulders, head, and eyes, as opposed to general bodily movements. The effective speaker keeps his arms relaxed and available to interpret his ideas. When the impulse comes, he will gesture appropriately. (See projects 1, 2, and 3 at the end of this chapter.)

6. *Directness of eye contact.* Many speakers find it difficult to look their audiences directly in the eye. Aside from the psychological value to your audience of direct eye contact, its principal value is that it enables you to observe the responses of your listeners and to adjust to them. Speaking involves reciprocal social stimulation. If you are to be an effective speaker, you must keep in touch with your audience.

Learning to Be Active

Developing effective habits of physical action is first of all a matter of recognizing the need for and the values of this aspect of speech making.

Study the performances of other speakers and observe when their visible action is effective and when it is weak. Then follow this procedure:

1. *Analyze your own performance to discover your problems.* Study the principles and criteria of effective action.

2. *Develop goals for your own achievement.* With the help of your instructor and your classmates, decide what you should do to improve your physical activity in speech making. Give particular attention to this aspect of speech in your preparation.

3. *Develop control over specific patterns of tension and relaxation in the muscles of the face, neck, hands, back, and legs.* Learn to control and vary the release of energy. Practice characterization and the simulated expression of feelings and emotions.

4. *Concentrate on putting your full meaning across.* Use all the agencies at your command to do this. Develop conscious actions in study and practice so that action becomes a habit, which you exercise unconsciously when you speak.

5. *Practice action, particularly in the types of speech activity where action is easy to use.* These include demonstration or visual-aids speeches with sample objects, drawings, maps, and routine patterns of action involved in the performance of some activity; story telling; and speeches expressing strong conviction. Work on the kinds of action with which you as a person have most difficulty, as well as on those which you find relatively easy. Finally, be patient.

Visual Aids

Our general remarks on the importance of visible action in speech making apply with equal force to visual aids. Here we shall discuss some of the major types of audio-visual aids and major principles of their use in speaking.

1. *Types of visuals.* Demonstration models, scale models, mock-ups, cutaways, or other three-dimensional devices will help your listeners come close to reality. In some cases, you can use the real object, such as a new can opener, a golf club, a camera, in the speech. This is good if it does not distract in some way from the idea. Cutaways are used where the inner working of a part is normally covered. Big objects which cannot be carried about can be represented in scale models or stereographs. Scale models are built for such subjects as new car and airplane designs, buildings, museum exhibits, housing developments, statues, and public works. The globe is an example of such a model which is fascinating to all. Nonessential features are removed to avoid distraction. Important features are emphasized. Sometimes parts are movable in order to make changes and comparisons. You may want to build your own model to be

used in a speech or perhaps you can borrow a suitable one. They abound in most large educational institutions or in metropolitan centers. Many companies will gladly loan an exhibit to a responsible person for the advertising they get from its use.

Flat graphic visualizations may provide a visual demonstration of features that are hard to describe, such as space, size, numbers or statistics, comparisons and trends, relationships of parts, emphasis and impression. Sometimes they can be made to suggest properties such as motion which they do not have. They often tell a story very vividly. Posters and cartoons can simplify and dramatize. A comic strip with a known cast of characters can tell a story in sequence. Charts such as the key-facts chart illustrated by our speech-behavior chart in Chapter 1 can condense and bring within the span of attention a complex set of variables. An organizational chart can show lines of responsibility through heads and subheads. Maps can show space, direction, and dominant features, such as cities, rivers, coast lines, mountains, etc. They are useful for emphasizing specific detail in a certain background needed for understanding.

Graphs present numerical or statistical data. Bar graphs serve for quantitative comparisons and can be prepared to illustrate a number of points in your speech. If there are few comparisons, place the bars vertically; if there are many comparisons, place them horizontally. Scale the comparisons accurately, and use the same scale throughout. It is not

A model of a manufacturing process is explained by a production engineer. (Central Soya Company.)

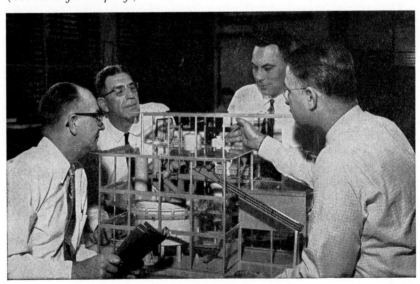

This is how it is done. (*e*) A circus barker or an auctioneer. (*f*) Formal and informal action adjustments.

Procedure: Select a subject and outline what you are to say. Anticipate and plan the general pattern of action you will use. Put yourself into the spirit of your ideas and respond as you concentrate on their expression.

Facts and principles useful in preparing this speech: A speaker's physical presence (even when he is absolutely motionless) always expresses something. Learn to make your presence and action contribute to the impression you want to create. Different moods and styles of speech require different patterns of expressive action. Suit the action to the word and thought.

Effective action ordinarily requires alertness without tension, responsiveness without exaggeration, poise and avoidance of fidgeting without stiffness, directness of eye contact without staring, use of energy with reserve, timing, and coordination.

The principal forms of expressive action are descriptive, suggestive, and emphatic. A speaker will ordinarily feel awkward during the development of new habits expressive of action. When new patterns of action become habits, they seem as natural as old habits. Skillful action requires elimination of self-consciousness; although you will be wise to practice physical activity, it should be so habitual that it is unconscious when you deliver your speech.

PROJECT 4: THE USE OF VISUAL AIDS

Purposes of this assignment: (*a*) To learn to use visual aids in speaking; (*b*) to develop freedom of bodily action and responsiveness to material; (*c*) to improve confidence in speaking.

Subjects: (*a*) The tracing of relationships of the parts of a system. (*b*) The performance of a play, game, or other act of skill. (*c*) The construction of an object. (*d*) The operation of a tool, instrument, or machine.

Procedure: Select a topic and organize your information. Pay particular attention to order of presenting material for clarity. If you are to draw a diagram, plan the essential features of the drawing. Complex and difficult diagrams should be prepared in advance. Rehearse your speech, using the object or diagram, until you can present your speech without notes.

Facts and principles useful in this assignment: In using visual aids, be sure your material can easily be seen by the audience. Beware of complicated, elaborate, or involved diagrams, yet avoid oversimplification. Arrange material so that the main points stand out. Label important materials so that the audience will become quickly oriented. Face the audience for as much of the time as possible. Make sure that you do not stand between auditors and points of a diagram as you discuss it. For emphasis, direct your attention at intervals where you want your audience to look. Avoid distracting activity. Do not ordinarily circulate an object in the audience unless all can study a sample as you talk. Learn to use the diagram as a suggestive outline of your speech. Never make the unwarranted assumption that your audience will see all that you see in your diagram without emphasis and explanation.

References

Ball, John, and Francis C. Byrnes (eds.): *Visual Communication,* Michigan State University, East Lansing, Mich., 1960.

Black, John W., and Wilbur E. Moore: *Speech: Code, Meaning, and Communication,* McGraw-Hill Book Company, Inc., New York, 1955, chap. 11.

Brigance, W. Norwood: *Speech,* Appleton-Century-Crofts, Inc., New York, 1952, chap. 16.

Dale, Edgar: *Audio-Visual Methods in Teaching,* The Dryden Press, Inc., New York, 1954.

Irwin, John V., and Marjorie Rosenberger: *Modern Speech,* Holt, Rinehart and Winston, Inc., New York, 1961, chap. 14.

McBurney, James H., and Ernest J. Wrage: *The Art of Good Speech,* Prentice-Hall, Inc., Englewood Cliffs, N.J., 1953, chap. 21.

Monroe, Alan H.: *Principles and Types of Speech,* 4th ed., Scott, Foresman and Company, Chicago, 1955, chap. 3.

Oliver, Robert T., and Rupert L. Cortright: *Effective Speech,* The Dryden Press, Inc., New York, 1951, chap. 15.

———, Dallas C. Dickey, and Harold P. Zelko: *Communicative Speech,* The Dryden Press, Inc., New York, 1955, chap. 10.

Wittich, Amo W., and Charles F. Schuller: *Audio-Visual Materials,* Harper & Brothers, New York, 1953.

FOURTEEN

The Speaker's Personality

RALPH WALDO EMERSON once said, "What you are thunders so I cannot hear what you say." He reminds us realistically and pointedly of the great importance of the speaker's personality. Again in his *Journals,* he put it, "Eloquence [or public address] is the art of speaking what you mean and are."

Your speech is a part of you as a person. For this reason you must consider your personality as a factor in speech making, as well as your ideas, language, organization, and expression. Few if any of the many skills necessary to effective speech making are more influential in determining your final results than the kind of man or woman you are.[1] "The whole man speaks" means that speech depends upon both physiological and psychological processes—upon your aptitudes, abilities, experiences, feelings, loyalties, emotions, interests, ambitions, adjustments, and personality traits.

What Is Personality?

Personality concerns you as an individual as you relate yourself to other individuals and groups. Gardner Murphy describes it as "the social

[1] Dayton Heckman, Franklin H. Knower, and Paul Wagner, in *The Man behind the Message,* The Ohio State University, report that 200 professional communicators considered the personal attributes of the communicator one of the most significant determinants of the success of his communication.

force of the individual." [2] The word "person" is related to the Latin word for "mask." Greek and Roman actors used masks to portray characters in their plays; they spoke their lines *per sonna*—through masks or personalities. Your personality, like these masks, determines in part the impression you as a speaker make on others. As you associate and communicate with your fellows, they react to your voice, words, and gestures, but also to your less obvious qualities. Your listeners may rate you as insincere, tactless, unduly assertive, pugnacious, uncertain, indifferent, arrogant, or perhaps as friendly, direct, sympathetic, pleasant, and intellectually and morally honest.

It is worth your while to find out what impression you make on others and to strengthen the traits that impress them favorably. Moreover, you do not merely want to act an acceptable role; you genuinely want to feel and live the man or woman you seem to be.

Accordingly you need to study yourself as a person—to discover both your image of yourself and what others perceive you to be like. In conjunction with this analysis, make an autobiographical report in which you bring together information relating to your personality, the way it has developed, and the need to strengthen it. (See project 2 at the end of this chapter.)

Although speech training cannot convert you overnight into a dynamic speaker, most of the personality factors with which we are concerned in speech education can be modified. It is no mere accident that dogs given certain types of training by the Army respond by becoming vicious. The same thing was true for the Nazi soldier. Survival in certain situations depends upon the development of a certain type of personality. Objectives in speech education are quite different from those of the Army and the Nazi party, but the same principles apply. Many of the traits of personality which make for effective speech—a better voice, for example—may seem unnatural until you master them as habits or skills.[3] If you carefully define your objectives and apply yourself diligently, you may reasonably expect to develop new traits and acquire new habits. "Who by taking thought can add one cubit to his stature?" was not written of the personality.

Before we proceed to a discussion of some characteristics of personality associated with effective speech let us consider some terms in popular usage about the personality of the speaker. These particular terms are often based on misunderstanding and their use tends to lead to con-

[2] Gordon W. Allport, *Personality*, Holt, Rinehart and Winston, Inc., New York, 1937, chap. 4.

[3] Melba Hind Duncan, "An Experimental Study of Some of the Relationships between Voice and Personality among Students of Speech," *Speech Monographs*, 12:47–60, 1945.

fusion. To say that a speaker should just be natural or just be himself implies that he has no need to change. Practice to change long-followed patterns of behavior is often accompanied by a feeling of awkwardness. To develop new skills does not rob the individual of his self-identity. If he is to learn, he must accept the idea that for a time he may feel unnatural.

When a speaker makes a favorable impression, some people attribute to him the characteristic of sincerity. The word "sincerity," however, is confusing. Confidence men are often described by their victims as "sincere." A dangerous demagogue may be judged sincere by some good people. For this reason we recommend avoidance of the word "sincerity" in describing a speaker. Although an effective speaker must be credible, all credible people are not good speakers. The word "insincere" may be appropriate for behavior which is inconsistent.

A frequently heard bit of criticism is that a person is too sensitive. Nonsense! The more sensitive one is, the better the adjustment one should be able to make. On the other hand there may be little to be gained by becoming highly emotional about what one senses. This may be what the critic means. If so, that is another matter. One should not worry about becoming too sensitive!

Do not expect your study to enable you to speak with ease. The more you study the more you will realize that skillful speaking is seldom easy. This fact should not prevent you from learning to get more enjoyment out of your speaking.

Do not go to the extreme of believing that you must always be well adjusted. If you do, you will be letting other people run your life. Reasonable efforts at conformity are productive, but there may be times when you will need to fight for your point. You will need to decide for yourself what you want to work and fight for. Don't make the mistake of thinking that you can achieve even a moderate success without some struggle.

Improving Your Speaking Personality

How can you effect changes in your personality? You must study your personality, discover your positive traits, and decide what steps you can take to emphasize these positive traits.

1. *Motives.* Analysis of the reasons for which people speak reveals some interesting personality differences. It would be impossible to classify all the speaking motives, but some of the more common ones are:

   a. To satisfy pride, to defend oneself, to attract attention

   b. To avoid action by substituting speech for action when action is difficult *c.* To relieve personal feelings, to release tension (usually visceral or thoracic)

d. To confuse others, to distract attention from a purpose or act

e. To arouse a listener, to cause him to think for himself

f. To facilitate the enjoyment of pleasant social contacts

g. To share in the solution of common problems

h. To inform, clarify, explain, or instruct

i. To influence, control, or dominate others either for socially desirable purposes or for ulterior purposes

You will observe that these motives range from negative and destructive ones to positive ones, aimed at gaining beneficial social effects, and from self-centered motives to socially centered ones. If your motives are usually negative, you should attempt to determine why and to remove the causes for this kind of motivation. Develop your socially useful and acceptable motives.

In insisting that we be genuine and forthright as speakers, that our motives be above reproach, we are dealing with what the ancient rhetoricians called "ethos." Aristotle, whose ideas concerning speech still prevail, stated in his *Rhetoric* that "the instrument of proof is moral character. . . . There is no proof so effective as that of character." Similarly, Quintilian quoting Cato said, "An orator is a *good man* speaking."

In addition to having good moral character, you must display this virtue to your listeners.[4] One cannot be a good speaker by hiding his light under a bushel. Honesty, as a reflection of character, means among other things that you will have a sense of responsibility for what you say. You will avoid willful distortions of fact or sharp practices by which your listeners may be deceived. You will utter nothing that you do not genuinely believe; the proposals you make will be, as far as you know, for the betterment of your fellows. "Responsibility for the well-being of others is implicit in all persuasion." Speech properly understood and applied is thus "a moral force of a high order."[5]

2. *Objectivity.* Objectivity means the ability to observe with a certain detachment yourself, your purposes, and your performances. It means to be aware of the need to have checks on your thinking and other behavior and of the need to have independent confirmation of your status or progress from those qualified to exercise judgment. It means having impersonal standards of operational procedure which can be followed by someone else and checked. Inability to be objective often results in unnecessary frustration, bewilderment, and disorganization, usually because

[4] Franklin S. Haiman, "An Experimental Study of the Effects of Ethos in Public Speaking," *Speech Monographs,* 16:190–202, 1949.

[5] Winston Brembeck and William S. Howell, *Persuasion,* Prentice-Hall, Inc., Englewood Cliffs, N.J., 1952, p. 464.

of lack of perspective. Trigger release of your emotions, which is wasteful of your energies and potentialities, is the result of inability to be objective. True objectivity, on the other hand, enables you to face problems squarely, to take into account the important factors, and to meet the demands of the situation with carefully organized and developed plans.

Your ability to be objective can be measured by your attitude toward friendly criticism. Can you accept criticism calmly, or do you lose self-control or withdraw into yourself? Raising a smoke screen of emotional behavior when you are criticized means that you are not able to be objective about your problems. On the other hand, the student who tries to discipline his personality to accept criticism calmly, who carefully weighs both flattering and derogatory comments, and who profits as best he can is on the way toward progress. The experience of accepting criticism affects the student somewhat as the process of tempering affects steel; the result is the development of habits of good speech and a sound personality. The student of speech who is willing to put himself through an analogous process in class may expect to come out with a tempered objectivity which should enable him to meet most life situations calmly and with poise. If criticism is warranted, he should accept it with thanks; if it is unwarranted, he should not pay undue attention to it.

3. *Intelligence.* Your achievement as a speaker is often assumed to be closely related to your general ability or intelligence. In a group made up of persons with a wide range of intellectual ability, a wide range in speaking ability will appear; but speaking ability does not always vary exactly with intelligence. Students with high IQs may have serious speaking problems. It is true that high ability in some components of the speech process, such as vocabulary, correlates closely with high intelligence. But where the range of intellectual ability in the group is relatively narrow, as in a typical college speech class, little relationship can be found between ratings on short samples of speaking and intelligence. The point is that among students in typical college speech classes, differences in achievement can usually be traced to factors of personality other than intelligence.[6] In other words, you cannot expect to get by on intelligence alone. Some smart men aren't very wise.

4. *Social intelligence.* The extent of a person's speech experience is often an index of his social intelligence or social behavior. The correlation between social intelligence and speaking ability is high because socially experienced speakers demonstrate greater achievement in speech than do individuals with little social experience, and good speakers are sensitive to their listeners, readily become aware of their reactions, and adjust to them. The speaker who lacks social sensitivity rushes blindly

[6] Howard Gilkinson and Franklin H. Knower, "A Study of Standardized Personality Tests and Skill in Speech," *Journal of Educational Psychology*, 32:161–175, 1941.

ahead in pursuit of his own ideas or purposes without concern for the reactions of his listeners. For example, the speaker who finds it difficult to look at his auditors cannot be expected to achieve a very satisfactory adjustment to them.

In order to know and like the people who listen to us, we must study them and develop methods for getting along with different types of people in different situations. The "lone wolf" is not likely to be effective in many speech situations. We should become as much at home as possible with people through repeated oral communication with them.

5. *Development of interests.* The number of types of speech activity in which students are interested and active seems to be an important factor in determining achievement in speech.[7] Students should develop an interest in as many types of speech activity as possible—persuasion, radio speaking, interpretative reading, discussion, debate, business and professional speaking, and others.

6. *Aggressiveness.* The speaker with a certain amount of aggressiveness and persistence is likely to be more effective than the listless speaker who is not motivated toward audience contacts and projection of personality.[8] It is true that some speakers, for example, those who practice high-pressure salesmanship, fail because of overaggressiveness. The success of social aggressiveness is thus better represented by an inverted *j*-curve than by a straight line; up to a certain point, the more dominant the speaker, the more effective his speech; beyond that point, the reaction to aggressiveness becomes negative. Moderately energetic attitudes toward his speech and his audience, however, will help a speaker hold attention, create interest, and evoke constructive responses.

7. *Self-confidence.* Beginning speakers are especially likely to be disconcerted by apparent signs of boredom or disapproval among their listeners. Speakers who lack confidence or have not had pleasant speaking experiences are more inclined to be suspicious of any signs of adverse audience reaction than are good speakers. Actually, the audience's evaluation of a speaker generally approximates the value that the speaker places upon himself. Most audiences want the speaker to succeed. They are pulling for him. The student should cultivate the ability to forget himself—an important aspect of self-confidence. He can be confident without egotism or excessive assertiveness. Beginning speakers err more often in the direction of humility than of overconfidence.[9]

[7] Howard Gilkinson and Franklin H. Knower, "Analysis of a Guidance Questionnaire for Students of Speech," *Journal of Experimental Education,* 9:175–176, 1940.

[8] Howard Gilkinson and Franklin H. Knower, *Psychological Studies of Individual Differences among Students of Speech,* University of Minnesota, Department of Speech, Minneapolis, 1939.

[9] See Chapter Eight, "Developing Confidence."

8. *Emotional thinking.* The intellectual behavior of the speaker reflects his personality. Rational thinking reflects a well-organized personality, and uncontrolled, disorderly thinking reflects disorganized emotional activity.

Avoid the more flagrant tendencies of seasoned as well as beginning speakers to reason or think emotionally.[10] A few of these negative emotional practices are suggestibility, fixed ideas, compartmentalized thinking, rationalization, and avoidance of issues.

Suggestibility is the tendency to react uncritically to stimuli. It is exemplified in the automatic acceptance of an idea without deliberation. When, for example, you yield without reflection to the popular demand to "Support Hendrickson for Class President," you are being governed by suggestion. Especially if you are susceptible to the influence of the crowd, you are likely to succumb to suggestion. "Marked suggestibility and intensification of emotion have been stressed as outstanding features of crowd behavior." [11] Examine reasons for the positions you take, and do not simply echo a few books or people.

What are fixed ideas? All of us have known speakers whose expressions of belief have been uttered with a finality that puts an end to further discussion of the topic. The speaker whose attitudes suggest, "When I speak, let no dog bark," probably has a closed mind, fixed ideas, and obsessions. He may reason logically on false assumptions. He is like the stalwart but unbending farmer in Robert Frost's poem, who would not "go behind" his father's saying, "Good fences make good neighbors."

Often we treat inconsistent beliefs or lines of thought with equal vigor without realizing their inconsistency. This is "compartmentalized thinking." A lawyer is said to have defended a client who was sued for breaking a borrowed vase by advancing three lines of argument: First, the man never borrowed the vase; second, the vase was broken when it was borrowed; and third, the vase was all right when it was returned.

Rationalization is the process of setting up plausible reasons which do not conform to the facts in justifying an emotionally determined position or action. Consider the case of the student who is studying for an important examination and who is invited to participate in a game or to attend a movie. He accepts the invitation and reasons, "All work and no play makes Jack a dull boy." Only if the young man has spent a good deal

[10] Some of these maladjustments in thinking represent types of reactions for which procedures in mental hygiene are often prescribed. See Bryng Bryngelson, "Personality Changes," *Quarterly Journal of Speech*, 16:207–218, 1928; and Wayne L. Morse, "The Mental Hygiene Approach to the Teaching of Speech," *Quarterly Journal of Speech*, 16:543–553, 1928.

[11] Charles Bird, *Social Psychology*, Appleton-Century-Crofts, Inc., New York, 1940, p. 356.

of time working recently can this justification be called rationalism rather than a rationalization.

Students of argumentation and rhetoric label as "ignoring the question" such practices as the substitution of prejudicial statements and attitudes for well-controlled rational approaches to a subject. An illustration is the "scapegoating" technique for absolving oneself of responsibility for the success or failure of an idea or position. Other illustrations are the use of assertions without reasons or justifications, the resort to questions that do not relate to the subject, and the use of completely irrelevant humor or anecdote.

9. *General emotionality.* Societal and family problems exercise marked influence on the manner in which emotions are expressed from infancy onward. As children develop, they are ordinarily rewarded for achieving more and more control over their emotional reactions. Although moderate emotional reactions appear to stimulate intellectual activity, intense emotionality will diminish the clarity and effectiveness of memory and of complex thinking processes. Some persons do not speak or read well because they are cold and emotionally unresponsive. While emotions appear to have biological value in human behavior, they need to be developed in balance and exercised with critical care.

In the study of speech you will find many opportunities for the discussion and analysis of your emotional reactions. If you are not able to analyze and talk about your emotional reactions and thus facilitate their objective evaluation and control, you should take this opportunity for personal growth in this respect.

Concluding Suggestions

If this chapter has given you insight into your particular problems of personality development, you have gained much. If you have acquired new insight into human nature, if you understand a little better than you did earlier the techniques of analyzing and evaluating emotional reactions, you have already achieved something in personality development. The information presented here has been selected with care for its relevance to the problems of the speech student, and it constitutes only an introduction to the tremendous amount of professional literature on the subject. By studying the subject more extensively, you will gain further insight into personality development. In doing so, you will contribute to your personal growth.

Your new understanding of personality development should be accompanied by practice of the desired forms of behavior. As you master specific skills, you should develop desirable attitudes, and new experiences will clarify principles which you understood only partially at the beginning.

No attempt has been made to describe an exact pattern of development or to assure you of great success. Good results will obviously depend somewhat upon your native capacity or aptitudes; upon your real interest in personality improvement; upon the formation of definite and reasonable goals toward which you can make progress; upon your use of appropriate exercises, methods of practice, and learning experiences; upon your willingness to exert the necessary effort, and upon an intelligent review of your achievements.

Personality development is only one facet of the development of general speech skills. You will, we hope, adapt these principles and facts to your particular needs as a speaker. They will contribute to your success as a person and as a speaker who is intellectually well organized, socially intelligent, sincere, and responsible.

Projects and Problems

PROJECT 1: OBSERVATIONAL STUDY OF THE SPEECH PERSONALITY

Review Chapter Two and prepare to make a five-minute report on personality traits you have observed which influenced the speaking of others. Discuss traits which have been helpful as well as detrimental to speech. Prepare to discuss the points raised in this chapter as you report. Raise questions about points which need further elaboration.

PROJECT 2: AUTOBIOGRAPHICAL REPORT

Purposes of this assignment: (a) To develop an objective attitude toward yourself in speaking; (b) to facilitate control of fear reactions in speaking.

Speech material for this project should include: A statement of the number of persons in your family and some personality characteristics of each. Your childhood interests and ideals and changes in them as you have grown older. The principal achievements in and outside your school career. Unusual experiences and social contacts which may have influenced your personality. The use you make of your leisure time. Courses you have liked and disliked in school. Your reasons for wanting a college education. Your principal worries and sensitivities; your characteristic moods. An analysis of your various emotional reactions before and during your public speeches or other public activities.

Procedure: Outline a five-minute report for your instructor including all the factors listed above. Prepare the report so that you can present it without notes. Anticipate questions and prepare to answer them.

Facts and principles useful in fulfilling this assignment: Be frank and honest in presenting your life story. Do not apologize for yourself; most apologies are merely a subconscious request for praise. Be willing to admit mistakes or short-comings as long as you accept them as such. If you can see the funny side of your mistakes, so much the better. All human beings have emotions, and one way to learn to control them is to talk about them.

Learn to use "I" without the appearance of bragging. Use ordinary tact in selecting the incidents of your life story in order to avoid hurting anyone's feelings. You can release much tension in talking about your fear reactions in the speech situation. Learn to describe and simulate fear symptoms. Learn to relate incidents to reasons or motives for conduct. Try to avoid rationalization in statements of reasons for behavior. Beware of a tendency to place any blame upon others for your own conduct. Learn to make comparisons, contrasts, and explanations without praise or blame.

PROJECT 3: DISCUSSION OF SPEECH ETHICS

Purposes of this assignment: (*a*) To develop skill in the socially responsible use of speech; (*b*) to further your insight into the ethics of speech performance.

Subjects:

The social consequences of misrepresenting a subject in speech

Prejudice, tolerance, and the speaker's convictions

Forms of unethical expression in speech

Sincerity and "truth" in speeches

Free speech and social responsibility

Democracy and free speech

Ethics in speaking for different purposes

Speaking to please one's auditors

Twisted interpretations of speech materials

Logic and ethics in speech

Avoiding the misrepresenting of a subject in speech

Preventing the abuse of freedom in forms of social interaction other than speech

My standards for ethical speech

The marks of a demagogue

The "high-pressure" salesman

White and black lies

Defenses against the unethical speaker

Ethics in the citation of authority

The ethics of emotional appeals

Character and the good speaker

Ethics and the specific auditors

Learning to speak in an ethical manner

Ethics and speech delivery

Friendship and honesty

Ethics and speech standards

Procedure: Prepare a five-minute extemporaneous speech on one of these topics. As a part of the preparation read at least one general reference on the subject of ethics. Talk over your speech ideas with at least one friend before you speak.

As you listen to the speeches of others make a list of ideas on speech ethics (*a*) which you would like to discuss and (*b*) which you believe to be worth remembering. Prepare to summarize the discussion of the hour at any point by reviewing these ideas.

References

Allport, Gordon W.: *Personality,* Holt, Rinehart and Winston, Inc., New York, 1937.

Brigance, W. Norwood: *Speech,* Appleton-Century-Crofts, Inc., New York, 1952, chap. 4.

Crocker, Lionel: *Public Speaking for College Students,* 3d ed., American Book Company, New York, 1956, chap. 3.

Diamond, Solomon: *Personality and Temperament,* Harper & Brothers, New York, 1957.

Dickens, Milton: *Speech: Dynamic Communication,* Harcourt, Brace & World, Inc., New York, 1954, chap. 10.

Gray, Giles W., and Waldo W. Braden: *Public Speaking: Principles and Practice,* Harper & Brothers, New York, 1951, chap. 1.

McBurney, James H., and Ernest J. Wrage: *The Art of Good Speech,* Prentice-Hall, Inc., Englewood Cliffs, N.J., 1953, chap. 24.

Oliver, Robert T., Dallas C. Dickey, and Harold P. Zelko: *Communicative Speech,* The Dryden Press, Inc., New York, 1955, chap. 16.

Stagner, Ross: *Psychology of Personality,* McGraw-Hill Book Company, Inc., New York, 1961.

Thonssen, Lester T., and Howard Gilkinson: *Basic Training in Speech,* D. C. Heath and Company, Boston, 1953, chap. 5.

FIFTEEN

Informational and

Critical Listening

IN THIS CHAPTER we are to consider the speech act not from the point of view of the speaker but from the point of view of the listener. Most of our consideration of speech is presented from the point of view of the speaker. We ask, "How can he be more effective?" The speech and the speaker are stimuli in the situation. Our model is largely a target model of speech. Now we are to consider communication from the point of view of the listener. Here we want to get a better understanding of the response to the speech act. This approach to the subject gives us a cafeteria model of communication.

Popular reaction to Orson Welles's broadcast of the mythical invasion from Mars is proof of the fact that many people do not listen effectively. Although the audience was warned in the program that the broadcast was only a play, it created havoc in the New York City–New Jersey area.

Listening is more than hearing; it is an active process of receiving and interpreting messages. Hearing is primarily a matter of sensory capacity; listening has to do with perception, comprehension, and other mental reactions. It is not a matter of placing yourself within earshot. It is not merely waiting until you can get in your word. Many, if not most, persons listen with the attitude that it is the responsibility of the speaker alone to put across the idea. Profitable listening requires much more of you than your presence. You must understand the ideas presented, evaluate and organize them, discover implications they may have, and select from the ideas you hear those you find worth remembering. If you make listening a thoughtful, critical process, you control your own thinking; if you do not listen critically, you are little more than a sponge, and often not a very good one.

The speaker who has a worthy social objective in speaking welcomes active, critical listening. The listener's cooperation makes his task easier. An alert, active response from a dissatisfied listener telegraphs to the speaker the message that he must improve his explanation or his argument. The conscientious and lively speaker then adjusts himself accordingly.

As we use the term here, "listening" includes visual as well as auditory perception. It includes watching the speaker and observing his actions and his use of visual aids as well as hearing what he says.

Nichols[1] found that listeners believed that most of the factors which interfered with listening were personal and psychological rather than physical. Two physical factors were inaudibility of the speaker and listener fatigue. Poor listeners were more sensitive to distraction and less

[1] Ralph G. Nichols, "Factors in Listening Comprehension," *Speech Monographs,* 15:154–163, 1947.

As you listen do you focus on what is being said or does your mind wander to other interesting events of your day? (From one of the educational films produced by McGraw-Hill to accompany this text.)

sensitive to the need for adjustment than were good listeners. Poor listeners tended to project their difficulties and blame the speaker for their faults. Poor listeners knew and applied fewer techniques to facilitate their concentration on the speech. They were more concerned with specific facts and less concerned with main points and generalizations than were the good listeners. Poor listeners showed less interest in the subject, saw less significance in it, and had less experience in listening to difficult expository material. Good listeners had more respect for the speaker and for listening as a method of learning. The study suggested pretty clearly that good listening is a matter of acquiring certain specific techniques and habits.

Witty and Sizemore[2] reviewed a number of studies of listening. The studies tended to show that listeners get more out of concretely presented than abstractly presented materials. Poor listeners are typically less well motivated than good listeners. A combination of reading, visual, and oral presentation of ideas tends to be better than any of these methods alone. Styles of materials most easily read tend to be easiest to listen to.

A study by Knower, Phillips, and Koeppel[3] shows that an average of 60 to 70 per cent learning from listening to college-type lecturers is a good average. Their study supports one by Jones[4] to the effect that listeners learn much more from skilled speakers than from less skillful speakers.

Your Purposes in Listening

The development of good listening habits involves a recognition of specific purposes in listening and of separate listening skills for each purpose. There are many purposes and types of listening. Listening may be a full-time or a part-time mental activity. Many people, for example, listen to the radio while driving or while carrying on housework. Most of us probably listen more frequently to gain support for our interests and convictions than to determine issues and evaluate evidence. When we listen as a pastime, we choose listening which will disturb us as little as possible. We listen because we are lonesome or because we are curious. Listening may be aimless or it may be purposeful. We get most from our listening when it has a purpose.

The three most important aims of listening are (1) to find enjoyment,

[2] Paul A. Witty and Robert A. Sizemore, "Studies in Listening," *Elementary English*, 35:538–552, 1958; 36:58–69, 130–140, 1959.

[3] Franklin H. Knower, David Phillips, and Fern Koeppel, "Studies in Listening to Informative Speaking," *Journal of Abnormal and Social Psychology*, 40:82–88, 1945.

[4] Harold E. Jones, "Experimental Studies in College Teaching," *Archives of Psychology*, 68:10, 1923.

(2) to gain information or inspiration, and (3) to evaluate critically. You may, to be sure, listen with all three purposes in mind. Obviously it is a mistake to form the habit of listening for enjoyment only and thereby miss much useful information. If you listen for enjoyment, sufficient unto the moment is the entertainment therefrom. On the other hand, if you expect to use the information you hear in a speech or in shaping your own ideas, then you must assimilate what you hear and make it your own.

Know what you are listening for. If you listen in a vague general way, you need not expect to get as much from your listening as you will if you listen for a specific purpose. Sometimes you may listen to observe the application of the principles of speech construction. If you are seeking information, on the other hand, the only principles of speech in which you will be interested for the moment are the soundness and relationship of the facts and ideas presented, and what you know about effectiveness of speaking otherwise should not be allowed to interfere with your getting those facts. If you listen not only for information but for critical evaluation of ideas, you will be alert to test the accuracy of the speaker's facts and the inferences.

Knowing what you are listening for will help you to organize your listening. Do not, however, fall into the error of hearing what you want to hear whether it has been said or not. Wishful listening is as harmful a psychological habit as wishful thinking. Knowing what you are listening for should help you not only to hear but to evaluate what you hear.

Your purposes in listening will be influenced by the types of situations in which your listening is done. Recreational listening may be casual or it may be highly focused and systematic. In informal social situations, for example, your listening to and participating in the conversation may not require concentration. On the other hand, even listening to a story for purposes of enjoyment may require concentrated attention; if you miss one point or are distracted, your enjoyment of the entire story may be spoiled. In listening to learn, you can never expect to achieve much satisfaction from incidental or irresponsible attention. It is in listening with a purpose that you may most truly distinguish between listening and hearing.

The Process of Listening

1. *Listen with patience and consideration.* It is a well-known fact that people are most talkative with those in whom they have confidence. And confidence develops out of respect and consideration. Do not disturb speakers with unnecessary noises or interruptions. Attention is really the state of being "at-tension." Allowing the mind to wander is as disastrous

in listening as physical distractions. You can achieve alertness and concentration by taking personal responsibility for getting maximum benefit from what you hear.

2. *Eliminate or ignore distracting elements.* Eliminate wherever possible the many distractions in the environment which interfere with listening. Find a place where you can hear and see the speaker easily. Avoid putting yourself in a position where you might be disturbed by such serious distractions as the sounds through an open door, movements in an aisle, the noise or heat of a radiator pipe, drafts, movements seen through a window, companions who like to attract attention, uncomfortable chairs, or chairs that invite complete relaxation. If you expect to take notes, arrange a convenient place for writing.

Some factors, such as a physical deformity in the speaker, a speech defect, and resemblance of the speaker to a person with whom you have had an unpleasant experience, cannot be eliminated by external control. Learn to dissociate the processes of communication from such distractions by concentrating on the subject under discussion.

3. *Critically evaluate ideas.* You may want to evaluate a speaker's ideas for the purposes of understanding or of forming a judgment which may mean developing or changing your attitude, or you may want to take some action relative to the proposal. Whatever your critical purpose, you need to know that criticism demands the highest objectivity and integrity on your part. In this process you should be willing to discipline your thinking into a system that is defensible. The following system should help whether you are critical merely for your own benefit or for the purpose of making a statement of your criticism for the speaker or for others.

First, you should know the responsibilities, objectives, and methods of the critic. Select the standards you will use in your criticism—the value systems or premises on which you will proceed to evaluate. Even the pirates of old flew the flag of pirates.

Communication can be evaluated on the basis of many different value systems. Do you want to evaluate this speech on the basis of effectiveness, aesthetics, correctness as to fact, logical inferences, or social utility? How does it compare with a norm for its type? Was it better than the last speech made by the same person? Does it conform to the principles of classical rhetoric? You may of course base your criticism on one or more of these value systems, but your value system should not go unrecognized even by yourself. Above all you should be able to justify the value system on the basis of which you act.

Second, decide what elements of the performance you want to criticize. The processes of speaking may provide a cue for these elements. You may criticize on the basis of the parts of rhetoric. You may criticize on the basis of the principles assigned for a particular speech. Was it a good reading? Informative speech? Discussion? The important elements are not always the same.

Finally, you reach a judgment, applying the standards chosen to the elements selected, and formulate a fair and just conclusion. Other systems and parts of systems will be discussed later in this chapter.

Generally, you evaluate ideas in listening in the same way that you evaluate materials for your own speeches. Examine them for clarity, factual correctness, logical reasoning, consistency, and relevance to the topic. Be alert to the sources of the material, for they may provide important cues in evaluation.

We think more critically and independently when alone than when in the company of others. The social environment—the persons with whom we listen and talk—influences our evaluation of what we hear. Most people, for example, respond to humor much more vigorously in a crowd than alone, and some texts in public speaking advise the speaker on the methods of turning an audience into a crowd in order to render listeners less critical of suggestion. These methods include bringing the members of an audience close together—getting them to rise and be seated together, to read aloud and sing together, and to applaud. Some speakers give the impression of gaining universal agreement by telling a joke which brings down the house or by expressing commonplace sentiments which evoke indications of widespread approval. The listener who wishes to maintain his independence of thought should be aware of these techniques for disarming critical reactions.

Aristotle long ago said that there were three things which listeners ordinarily want to know about a speaker: the depth of his wisdom, the quality of his character, and the extent of his good will. How can we fairly test a speaker for these traits in order to avoid judging him merely through prejudice or bias?

Let us begin by considering him as a man. We may know him through personal acquaintances or learn of him through the testimony of others. What is his standing among his business or professional associates and in his own community? What types of people have expressed approval of him, how many, and how consistently? On the basis of what achievement does he stand? What is his record? Does what he says square with the known facts? What are his interests? Whom does he represent? Is he straightforward in presenting his facts? Is he courteous? Does his reasoning, based on common experience, coincide with our good judgment? What are the sources of his ideas? Does he cite them precisely?

If the speaker asks you to accept important facts derived from his personal experience, you will want to evaluate his testimony on the basis of such questions as these: Is he competent to observe the facts? Could he have had the experiences he related? What is the evidence of his mental capacity to perceive the reported data? For example, was he excited? Was he sufficiently educated to handle the situation he described? Was he alert and free from fatigue? Does he have a reputation for good judgment in describing data of the type presented? Are there inconsistencies in his report or his reasoning? Are there any reasons why he might lie about the situation? Does he speak with poise and confidence?

As a listener, you must recognize the need for interpreting what is said in the light of the speaker's purpose in talking. Sometimes this purpose is stated; sometimes the listener must determine it for himself. The speaker's general purpose ordinarily can be more easily recognized than his specific purpose.

Recognize Logical Fallacies and Propaganda

A knowledge of the common logical fallacies and propagandistic tricks is especially important to the listener. To be forewarned is to be forearmed. Hasty generalizations, false analogies, arguing from questionable premises, and the *post hoc* argument—the assumption that because one event follows another it must have been caused by it—are some of the logical fallacies which the listener should guard against.

The Institute for Propaganda Analysis identifies a number of devices as propaganda techniques.[5] *Name calling* is a device for labeling a person or subject as undesirable by associating the person or subject in the reader's mind with an objectionable name or classification of things. Some typical bad names include "Communist," "isolationist," "rabble rouser," "yellow," "traitor," "saboteur," and "slacker." *Glittering generalities* are a device for gaining acceptability for propositions by labeling them with approved verbal sanctions. Typical of such verbal sanctions are the words "freedom," "liberty," "progress," "democracy," "patriotism," "thrifty," "a balanced budget," and "investment." *Transfer* is a technique of using sources of authority, prestige, respect, and reverence to create favorable attitudes toward a proposal. The church, the flag, the home, educational institutions, the Rock of Gibraltar, and the red cross of mercy are examples of sources of emotional approval.

The *testimonial*, in which a famous name is associated with a proposition or product as in advertisements, is so well known it does not need illustration. The *plain-folks* device expounds a proposal in terms of the simple, everyday experiences and personalities that make up our lives. Politicians delight in using this technique for showing that, after all, they are only one of our neighbors and therefore worthy of our trust in

[5] Violet Edwards, *Group Leaders' Guide to Propaganda Analysis,* Institute for Propaganda Analysis, Inc., New York, 1938.

public office. *Card stacking* is a scheme used to deceive by means of evasion, distraction, the careful selection of only the favorable evidence, and false testimony. *Half-truths* are used as a smoke screen to prevent the listener from really facing the facts. The *band-wagon technique* creates an impression of universal approval of an idea; the individual is supposed to consider himself an outsider if he does not approve. "Two million people can't be wrong." "I nominate the next President of the United States. . . ."

Other tricks of propagandists include flattery; appeals to fear, hate, anger, frustration, or discontent growing out of misfortune or lack of opportunity; the creation of devils on which to place blame; repetition; wishful thinking, rationalization, rumor, distrust; identification with the great, the beautiful, and the good; and prophecies and positive suggestion. The use of such techniques does not, of course, imply that the proposal is inherently unworthy. The listener must decide for himself whether or not the conclusions fit the facts. But the careful listener will be at once suspicious of any speaker who seeks to make use of emotions to smother reasonable explanation and evidence.

Listening and Personality

Begin your efforts to improve by testing your listening ability.[6] After you have obtained objective evidence concerning your efficiency as a listener, you can begin to make the psychological adjustments necessary for improvement. This means, first of all, that you must recognize your prejudices and understand their nature, since you can interpret what you hear only against the background of your experiences and convictions. Because what you believe profoundly influences your ability to listen fairly, you need to know the common causes of prejudices.

Why are some persons biased in their interpretations of data? People have difficulty in being objective about those beliefs from which they profit personally, or believe they profit; which have been conventionally accepted for a long period of time; which they have espoused and therefore defend as a matter of personal pride; which are supported by friends or community associates; and which if changed would cause considerable discomfort or inconvenience. Some persons are prejudiced in favor of everything new, always expecting the new to be better than the old; some are prejudiced against what is new because it fails to conform to their own limited experience.

[6] For tests of listening, see James I. Brown and Robert G. Carlson, *Brown-Carlson Listening Comprehension Test*, World Book Company, Yonkers, N.Y., 1953; and Thomas T. Blewitt, "Experiment in Measuring Listening," *Journal of Communication*, 1:50–56, 1951.

Recognizing the dangers of fixed beliefs, some persons go to the opposite extreme and refuse to accept any belief that is not based upon the most vigorously controlled scientific evidence. Open-mindedness does not preclude convictions or loyalties, which are necessary to emotional well-being. The philosophy of postponed decision, if carried to the extreme, would lead to complete inaction.

Snobbishness and egotism often are justified as reflections of alleged higher standards and finer tastes. The man who refuses to listen to the ideas of another simply because he is a foreigner or because he has less wealth, formal education, or social polish has little ground for self-satisfaction.

A famous professor of psychology once had a minor riot carefully rehearsed and sprung on an unsuspecting class in psychology. After the uproar subsided he told the students that they would no doubt be called to account for the event and suggested that they write out an exact description of what happened. In the description which was most nearly correct, 26 per cent of the statements were erroneous, and in that which was least correct, 80 per cent of the statements were inaccurate. That part of the incident which was most exciting was reported with 15 per cent more error than the less emotional part.

Although the excitement and strain were abnormal and excessive in the circumstances of this experiment, similar emotional factors are nevertheless of great significance even in more favorable listening situations. You can develop skills which will enable you to overcome many of the obstacles to good listening.

Projects and Problems

PROJECT 1: LISTENING TO UNDERSTAND

Listen to a public speech and make a brief oral report to the class indicating (*a*) the purpose of the speech, (*b*) the central idea of the speech, (*c*) the adequacy and type of details used to clarify the point, (*d*) the pattern of organization of the material.

If possible, two persons should listen to the same speaker and prepare reports independently. Then let the class make a comparison of the two reports. If the speech is argumentative, avoid taking sides in the report; be strictly objective, reporting what was said as accurately and faithfully as you can.

PROJECT 2: LISTENING TO INSTRUCTIONS

Ask someone a question which requires an answer of at least three or four sentences. Then repeat the answer to see if you have understood it clearly. See how much of the answer you can repeat in the exact words used by the other person. If you do not repeat it correctly the first time, have him restate it until you are able to repeat the instructions accurately. Then stand before the class and carry out this process with a new question. Such questions as the following may be asked: (*a*) How do you start a car in learning to drive? (*b*) How do you saddle and mount a horse? (*c*) How do you get to a distant place in a city? (*d*) How do you operate a certain make of comptometer (or other machine)? (*e*) How do you handle a particular piece of sporting equipment? (*f*) How do you operate a specific laboratory apparatus? (*g*) What is to be done in a specific classroom assignment?

PROJECT 3: LISTENING TO EVALUATE AN ARGUMENT

Listen to a radio, television, or platform public speech which is argumentative in nature. Make a report on the speech indicating: (*a*) The central idea of the speech. (*b*) The main points in the organization of the speech. (*c*) The pattern of logical inferences in the speech. (*d*) The use of persuasive devices. (*e*) The techniques or propaganda devices used. Differentiate the facts from the opinions expressed by the speaker. Evaluate the speech content.

PROJECT 4: LISTENING TO RESTATE AN ARGUMENT

Ask someone for his opinion on a certain proposition and have him elaborate his opinion in three or four sentences. Then ask him to listen to you as you restate his opinion in your own words. Try to restate the argument fairly and completely, but avoid the language used by the other person. If you do not state the argument correctly at first, keep trying until you get his approval of your statement as the equivalent of his. Repeat this for the class.

PROJECT 5: LISTENING FOR ENJOYMENT

Attend a speech, play, or movie strictly for the purpose of relaxation and recreation, and report to the class on the success of your listening. Was the entertainment truly enjoyable? What were the enjoyable features of the performance? Were there any factors in the situation which reduced your enjoyment? If so, what?

PROJECT 6: LISTENING TO LEARN ABOUT SPEAKING, READING, OR PLAYS

Go to a play or listen to the speech performance of a public lecturer or entertainer. Evaluate the performance according to a systematic set of criteria for the type of activity involved. What was well done? What would have improved the performance? Report to the class, pointing out the principles of speaking involved.

PROJECT 7: LISTENING TO PERSONAL CRITICISM

After you have finished speaking in a regular class project, ask some member of the audience for a criticism of your performance. When you have heard this criticism, repeat it carefully and completely. Try to avoid attitudes of apology, defense, or smugness.

References

Brigance, W. Norwood: *Speech,* Appleton-Century-Crofts, Inc., New York, 1952, chap. 5.

McBurney, James H., and Ernest J. Wrage: *The Art of Good Speech,* Prentice-Hall, Inc., Englewood Cliffs, N.J., 1953, chap. 10.

Nichols, Ralph G., and Thomas R. Lewis: *Listening and Speaking,* William C. Brown Company, Dubuque, Iowa, 1954, chaps. 1–6.

——— and Leonard A. Stevens: *Are You Listening?* McGraw-Hill Book Company, Inc., New York, 1957.

Oliver, Robert T., and Rupert L. Cortright: *Effective Speech,* Holt, Rinehart and Winston, Inc., New York, 1961, chap. 4.

———, Dallas C. Dickey, and Harold P. Zelko: *Communicative Speech,* The Dryden Press, Inc., New York, 1955, chap. 4.

White, William H., Jr.: *Is Anybody Listening?* Simon and Schuster, Inc., New York, 1952.

PART THREE

BASIC SPEECH

TYPES

SIXTEEN

Informative Speaking

You PROBABLY speak more often for the purpose of imparting information than for any other purpose. Even in telling a story, you must give a certain amount of background information. Cooperative discussion for the purpose of solving a problem or developing a plan of action depends upon the sharing of information among participants. It is unreasonable to expect others to accept your beliefs and to devote their energies to the action you recommend if you do not present the relevant information clearly and effectively.

By informative speaking, we mean, rather specifically, teaching and learning—the educative process. The teacher spends his days facilitating the learning process. He does much formal and informal informative speaking. He studies educational psychology and the psychology of learning to help him accomplish his goals. Of course students also learn by other means, such as the teaching machine, libraries, and field experiences. The problem of presenting information so that it may be assimilated effectively and efficiently is discussed in many sources. The beginning speaker should learn to use these sources.

Steel,[1] writing about a recent conference on the use of the teaching machine, makes these recommendations:

1. Break down the learning into tiny steps leading from what students already know to what you want them to know.

2. Have them do something.

[1] Many suggestions of this type are adaptable to informative speaking.

3. Don't let them make mistakes—keep the steps tiny and if necessary use clues.

4. If they do make a mistake, have them correct it immediately.

5. If they get the answer right, reinforce immediately by letting them know that they got it right and by giving them another problem.

Types and Principles

Informative speaking takes place in many other circumstances than in the presentation of formally organized speeches. Although the types and principles of informative speeches that we will describe apply best to formally organized speeches, they are also applicable to informal conversation and discussion. Short two- to five-minute talks applying these principles closely resemble conversational and discussional speech. Moreover, many of the principles of delivery in informative speaking are applicable to informative oral reading.

The types of informative speaking are, basically, description, the many types of explanation (by analysis, classification, and definition; by illustration, example, and analogy; by historical narrative; by tracing causal relationships; and by means of visual aids and demonstration of an operation), critical interpretation, and reports.

DESCRIPTION

Effective description depends upon the reproduction in the mind of the listener of the idea in the mind of the speaker. The types of description with which we are primarily concerned here are exact and suggestive rather than impressionistic. Although practical description depends primarily upon visual images, it may also draw upon other types of imagery in creating vivid awareness of the object, event, or relationship in the mind of the listener.

The material to be included in a description will depend upon the purpose to be served by the information rather than upon the many characteristics of the object or event to be described. What is included in a description of a river, for example, will depend upon the purposes the description is to serve. Perhaps the subject is the possibilities of navigation, the river as a source of water power or of drinking water, the danger of spreading contagious disease, the suitability of the river for recreational purposes (bathing, scenic beauty, fishing, or boating), the river as a source of water for irrigation, changes in the river's course or in its bed, flood dangers, rate of current, silt load, an obstacle to be bridged, or the length, width, depth, or temperature of its waters. Some descriptions serve several purposes, and obviously none is exhaustive. Be sure you have a clear idea of the specific purposes to be served by your information before you select and organize it.

Determine whether the information must be exact or only approximate. If the river is to be bridged, it must be measured exactly. If you merely wish to skate on a bayou and determine that its ice is reasonably safe, the exact thickness of the ice will be of little concern to you. The aims of scientific descriptions are both comprehensive and exact. Scientific experiments must be described in such a way as to enable another experimenter to duplicate the significant conditions of the project and verify the results.

Indicate clearly the order in space and time of the aspects of the object or event you describe. Persons in a group photograph are commonly identified from the lower left-hand corner across the page, and row by row up the page. In a small group the most prominent person or persons are placed in the center; identify these persons first, and then those to the left and to the right. Thus the two principal methods of procedure in describing any picture are space order and the order of importance of objects, combined with time order. Time order in this sense is a process of revealing orders in space and importance. If a number of items in the picture or scene are of approximately equal importance, some systematic space order nevertheless should be observed. When one item in a picture is of central significance and others incidental, the order of importance from greatest to least should be followed.

The vividness of the details included is as important as the general outline or organization of the description. Vividness can be achieved by using specific, discriminative, image-evoking words, voice patterns, and visual cues. The action in the statement "He moved" is made more concrete and more vivid in such statements as "He ambled," "He glided," "He wormed his way," "He shoved," "He slid," "He paced," "He scuttled," "He weaved in and out," "He zig-zagged," and "He dived forward."

Suggestive descriptions, as opposed to exact descriptions, make use of figurative language to impute specific qualities to objects. Consider, for example, the cool shadow, the protective shadow, the sinister shadow, and the waning shadow. Use a thesaurus regularly to help build the varied vocabulary necessary for vivid description.

Some descriptions are incomplete until the mood that unifies the scene or event is presented. For example, the line from Poe's "The Raven," "Long I stood there, wondering, fearing," or the lines from Wordsworth's "The Daffodils,"

> And then my heart with pleasure fills,
> And dances with the daffodils.

follow extended descriptions of the details of a scene. They are intended to summarize the scene and suggest the speaker's reaction to the scene as a whole. Both these descriptions consist mainly of the physical characteristics of the scene, but the reactions of the observer become an important part of the scene.

The informative speaker who makes use of description will find it helpful to understand some principles of the psychology of observation.[2] Two people looking at an object do not necessarily see the same details or even the same number of details. Skill in observation can be developed; the student of art sees more in a picture than the artistically uninformed. The bird lover or hunter will observe life in a woodland which goes unnoticed by others. Effective description not only presents a picture; it also calls attention to features to be observed. It interprets the significance of features of the scene to the listener. Excited persons do not observe well; neither do those who are prejudiced. Recognize the possibility of emotional reactions among your auditors and adjust the treatment of your subject to the specific situation.

[2] Leonard Carmichael, H. P. Hogan, and A. A. Walter, "An Experimental Study of the Influence of Language on the Reproduction of Visually Perceived Form," *Journal of Experimental Psychology*, 15:74–82, 1932.

A blackboard is useful in explaining a model of what happens in communication. (From one of the educational films produced by McGraw-Hill to accompany this text.)

EXPLANATION THROUGH ANALYSIS, CLASSIFICATION, AND DEFINITION

In analytical speeches, the topic is divided into parts that are treated as minor wholes or units. The units must be small enough to permit the listener to see them as separate parts of the whole. Since analysis is principally a process of dividing and classifying the data used in the development of the subject, many principles which apply to classification of data as we studied it in Chapters Five and Six also apply to analysis. We analyze a topic to discover its elements. We classify elements in order to make them easier to understand.

Remember and follow these four principles in classifying data logically: First, the units must treat the subject comprehensively. Second, the units should be distinct, that is, free from overlapping. Third, they should be classified upon the basis of a single principle. (For example, it would be illogical to classify the citizens of Middletown as Republicans, engineers, or husbands, because a different principle is illustrated by each of these three nonparallel categories. Such categories as politics, professions, and marital status would be logical, however.) Fourth, classified items should be arranged in some suitable order for comprehension, such as size, sequence of events, cause and effect, functions of parts, or types—for example, the classification of the functions of the government as legislative, executive, and judicial; or the classification of music as vocal and instrumental; or the instruments used in an orchestra as string, woodwind, brass, and percussion.

Many subjects about which we make informative speeches do not lend themselves readily to the rigid requirements of logical classification. In treating such subjects, we may classify data topically rather than logically. The principles of logical classification cannot be rigidly applied in topical classifications. As an example, let us consider the classification of speech processes set forth in Chapter One. These processes are labeled "Ideas," "Organization," "Language," "Voice," "Articulation," "Bodily Activity," and "Speaking Personality." What principles directed this classification? There were four. (1) The units cover the subject quite thoroughly. (2) The units are sufficiently comprehensive to contain fairly large collections of data within each class. (3) Although data within the units overlap to some extent, the units delineate relatively specific aspects of the total speech act. (4) Finally, these labels suggest well-worked-out methods for the study of speech in units. Other principles might apply in classifying the data of another topic, since topical classification of data is developed to fit the needs of the particular subject and the speech purposes.

To clarify the nature of specific features of data, after they have been analyzed and classified, we use definition. Definition circumscribes, localizes, and makes specific the meaning of a word or a phrase. Its function is not to provide an authoritarian interpretation of a word; rather, it is to indicate the meaning with which a word is used at the time. Its purpose is to provide a common ground of understanding between speakers and auditors.[3]

EXPLANATION BY ILLUSTRATION, EXAMPLE, AND ANALOGY

In informative speaking, examples serve many purposes. They clarify principles, general statements of conditions or trends, and types of classifications. Since ordinary conversation deals primarily with particulars and few people develop the mental habits necessary for following abstract thinking, general and abstract statements should be illustrated abundantly. Examples serve to epitomize, crystallize, and concretize meaning. Specific examples have the dramatic and human-interest qualities of events, characters, and the unusual. They also arouse the curiosity of listeners; once listeners have heard the beginning, they are interested in following the story to its conclusion.

There are many types of examples used for informative purposes. General and specific illustrations are two of these types. The speaker who is discussing cooperation, for example, may offer "socialism" as a general illustration of cooperation. If he goes on to say that publicly owned and operated utilities are socialistic, he is offering a general illustration of the operation of socialism. But if he discusses the publicly owned waterworks or the municipally owned light plant in a specific town, he is providing not general illustrations but specific instances or examples—here, cases in point.

Hypothetical illustrations ordinarily begin with a phrase such as, "Suppose we had a case . . . ," or "Imagine a situation in which. . . ." Some real examples should be given fictitious elements to make them more typical, to disguise them, or to protect personalities.

Examples should fit the subject under discussion. When they are not to the point, they confuse rather than clarify. Examples should suit the audience in terms of interest, experience, and level of complexity. Examples from a common area of experience are ordinarily better than examples selected from the experiences of the few. Well-known examples may be referred to briefly; unfamiliar examples should be elaborated. In one of Churchill's speeches, a brief reference to the battle of Gettysburg was as effective as a detailed recounting of another battle.

[3] For a discussion of the methods of using informative definition, see p. 239.

The more fitting the story, the less the speaker needs to say about its application to the subject. Elaborate pointing of the moral may spoil its effectiveness. Although the details of the example should be vivid, they should not be so spectacular that the story overshadows the point.

EXPLANATION BY HISTORICAL NARRATIVE

Our concept of history should be broad enough to include the story of the development of any subject worthy of our attention. Historical exposition is used primarily to throw light on the background of a subject. The method is best exemplified in the doctor's tracing the symptoms of his patient's illness. The account should be accurate and interesting, but it must also be brief, designed primarily to impart information rather than to entertain, and adapted to the purpose of a particular speaking situation. Successful student speeches on the following subjects might well include an explanation by historical narrative: the development of jet aircraft, the history of hybrid corn, changes in the game of basketball, the background of communism. This form of exposition has some of the characteristics of the extended example.

Original sources are more reliable than secondary sources. Moreover, there should be sufficient data on consecutive events to provide a continuous narrative of significant changes or developments. The material should be arranged in sequence. As the exposition proceeds, sources should be identified by author, publication, and date. Questionable facts should be corroborated by two or more sources. The data should be summarized, and the significance of the subject clarified.

Among the qualities to be achieved in methods of delivery are enthusiasm for and interest in the story, effective dramatization and projection, and a conversational tone.

EXPLANATION THROUGH TRACING CAUSAL RELATIONSHIPS

Two of the questions we commonly attempt to answer in informative speech are, "What causes it?" and "What can be done about it?" The tracing of causal relationships is an attempt to answer such questions. It seeks to clarify a situation by identifying the causes which have produced a known effect, or the effects which may result from known causes. When our purpose is to identify causes, we will trace events backward in time; when it is to identify effects, we will trace events forward. We seek to identify causes and effects primarily for the purpose of predicting or controlling future events; and we can control events either by modifying causes or by blocking their normal effects.

In explaining causes, limit the discussion to important events in the sequence. Describe and analyze each step with great care. Complex phenomena have complex or multiple causes; therefore do not oversimplify causes in making an explanation. Beware of mistaking for the cause of a given effect what may be merely another effect of a common cause. The student who has difficulty in speech may report that he does not like speech. It is easy to ascribe his difficulties to his lack of interest, whereas his lack of interest may be merely an effect of his past difficulties in speech. Both difficulty and lack of interest are probably more accurately attributable to the fact that he has not had a favorable opportunity to learn to speak effectively. (See Chapter Six for an analysis of tests of causal reasoning.)

INFORMATIVE SPEAKING WITH VISUAL AIDS

The use of the educational motion picture has recently given renewed emphasis to techniques in informative speaking with visual aids. Not many of us will use motion pictures, but all of us will have occasion to use objects, activities, and pictures in our informative speaking. The materials for visual instruction are pictures, diagrams and graphs drawn on cardboard or on a blackboard or projected on a screen; cartoons; maps; objects and working models; samples; and demonstrative action. When used effectively such materials lend clarity to our ideas; they at-

Executive of the Central Soya Company explains to assistants a traffic plan for an open house at the plant. (Central Soya Company.)

tract the attention and maintain the interest of the audience. They also provide us with an opportunity to use action in our speeches.[4]

THE INFORMATIVE SPEECH OF OPERATION

The operations speech is designed to give precise directions on how to perform an action or carry out a process. You may give instructions for driving a car, preparing a dish, cutting a linoleum block, or casting a fly. If your listeners are not familiar with the activity, you may need to create interest in the process. Define terms with which your listeners are not familiar. Describe objects to be used, explain their functions, and give directions for using them. Compare and contrast objects and steps with similar materials and processes that are familiar.

Explain the steps in the order in which they are to be carried out. Make the significance of each step clear as you proceed. Demonstrate as well as describe the action. Sometimes the listeners can carry out the action along with you—the flip of the wrist in fly casting, for example, or the steps of a dance. Observe and correct the mistakes they make. Indicate acceptable variations in procedure. Anticipate difficulties and explain how they can be overcome. Present a clear picture or description of expected results.

THE CRITICAL INTERPRETATION

This type of speech activity may appear to the reader to be argumentative rather than informative. Since criticism on an intellectual rather than an emotional level is the essence of teaching, however, it is considered here as a type of informative speaking. Criticism in this sense is the interpretation of a product or process in terms of acceptable standards of achievement. If the listener does not agree on what is to be criticized, or on the standard by which the elements are to be evaluated, and if differences of opinion develop on the subject and its evaluation, then the exposition passes over into the field of argument. If both speaker and listener agree during the process of instruction on the elements of the act or product, the standard to be applied, and the application of the standard to the act, then critical interpretation is identical with informative speaking.

The steps to be made in a critical interpretation include (1) the selection of elements or parts of a total to be criticized, (2) the application of appropriate standards in interpreting the facts, (3) the accumulation of information on the product to be evaluated, and (4) the presentation of

---

[4] See Chapter Thirteen for a discussion of action as a means of communicating information.

the evaluation. A simple statement of like or dislike is criticism on an emotional rather than an intellectual basis. If the critic is not known to his listeners, he may well introduce his criticism with an explanation of the amateur or professional capacity in which he serves.

Criticism should take into account the specific purpose of the activity. A piece of work performed for one purpose should not be criticized for failing to accomplish another. Adapt criticism of speech or writing to the personality and background of the performer. Remember that criticism should not be personal, smug, or malicious; it should be objective in content and attitude. Do not elaborate the obvious or dwell upon minor slips or petty flaws. Exercise judgment in arriving at a fair interpretation of the work as a whole, remembering that the critic must accept responsibility for his criticism. Your status as a critic does not grant you license to be irresponsible.

REPORTS

Classes, clubs, committees, community organizations, and business and professional groups often require reports. This type of informative speaking is probably used more than any other. Furthermore, abbreviated reports of various types occur frequently in conversations, interviews, and other small-group, face-to-face situations, as well as in larger or more formal meetings. Consider the answers to such questions as: What did the speaker have to say? What is that book like? Did you have a good trip? What happened? These questions present occasions for report making, and the principles which apply to the formal report also apply to the answers to such questions.

1. *Purpose.* The primary purpose of the report is to present information. Reports may or may not be supplemented by recommendations, although reports by experts or authorities may consist largely of recommendations. Even these reports, however, are based on information which should be presented if requested.

2. *Types.* Reports may be roughly classified into types such as (*a*) the summary report, (*b*) the fact-finding report, and (*c*) the critical report. Examples of summary reports are the radio news review, reports of committees to parent organizations reviewing their activities, and personal-experience reports.

There are many types of fact-finding reports. They may be exploratory, or they may be systematic. The exploratory report is ordinarily made during the early period of fact finding and is intended to determine the desirability of various methods and characteristics of the investigation. It is admittedly tentative. The facts may be sought by observation, by experimentation, by normative survey, or by the study of documents. The form of fact-finding reports will be influenced by the method of securing data.

Critical reports may be presented at various stages of their preparation. The preliminary report is largely confined to plans and limited data. The progress report is concerned with more extensive data, tentative conclusions, and further plans. The achievement report is based on extensive data, comprehensive treatment, and interpretations or recommendations. There is some overlapping of major types of reports in the actual practice of presenting them. That is, many reports summarize available data, present new data uncovered by investigation, and offer a critical evaluation and recommendations.

If an oral report is detailed and extensive, it is wise to provide a copy of the report for each member of the audience. The most common practice in the oral presentation of reports is to point out features of special significance and to summarize orally the data presented in writing.

3. *Principles.* The materials of the report should be carefully organized. Main points should be clearly stated and summarized. Statistical data should be presented visually as well as orally. Transitional statements should indicate definitely when one idea is finished and the next begins.

Making a fetish of completeness in reports can lead to the inclusion of unnecessary detail and consequently to confusion and waste of time. Only most important materials which can be presented in the allotted time should be included. If listeners want more information on certain features of the report, they may request it.

The report should be adapted to the amount of knowledge the listeners already have of the subject. A report by one member of a profession to others may be based on a presumption of the knowledge of many facts which amateurs could not be presumed to know.

Critical interpretation of the material of the report is one of its most difficult features. Among the procedures which may be followed in interpretation are generalizing upon the data; stating the recognized limitations of the data; determining the values, implications, and applications of the data; making comparisons and contrasts with previously accepted facts; correlating findings with objectives; and finally, presenting the essential meaning and significance of the data. Negative findings as well as positive findings are a legitimate outcome of research. If an investigation of telepathy, for instance, produced no evidence of the existence of this phenomenon, the investigator must affirm that as a result of his research no evidence of telepathy was discovered.

REPORTING PROCEDURES

Some common procedures to be followed in making reports can be summarized briefly here.

1. *The personal-experience report.* In reporting on a personal experience, your first step is to orient the listeners. Describe the time, the place, and the situation. Focus attention on essential features of events as they occur in sequence, and interpret events in terms of experiences meaningful to listeners. The explanation of personal reactions is as important in the experience report as the events reported. The purpose for which the experience report is made determines what aspects of the report will be given major emphasis.

2. *Review and comparison of ideas.* Enumerate the main ideas as they are presented, analyzing, defining, and exemplifying them. Interpretations should present qualifications, limitations, and conclusions.

3. *The report on research.* State the immediate cause for the report—the persistence and importance of the problem, the points of view to be integrated, the new contribution to the subject. Sketch briefly the history and background of the topic and the general objective and specific limitations of the study to be undertaken. Set forth specific objectives. Present the data under some well-considered plan of classification. Indicate the sources of data as you proceed. Summarize the data, and evaluate the results of the study.

4. *The report on experimental research.* State the general problem to be investigated. Review the background of and literature on the problem. Explain the particular objectives or purposes of this project. What is new about it? What is to be its scope and limitation? Indicate what hypothesis was tested. Describe the instruments or materials used. Discuss the methods of procedure in conducting the experiment and, if your listeners do not understand the reasons for certain procedures, explain them. Indicate how and why the data were analyzed in a particular way as you present them. Summarize the data and interpret their significance. Make any desirable recommendations for the further study of the problem.

5. *The book report.* Identify the book you are reviewing. Discuss the author and his apparent motivation for this particular book. (Reading the preface may be helpful in understanding the purposes of the author in writing the book.) Classify the book as to specific type within its major classification. Describe the contents. If it is a novel, give the time and setting of the story and discuss the characters, plot, events, points of highest interest, and what happens in the end. If it is nonfiction, discuss the general subject, thesis, or central idea, the main points (which may be sections and chapters), and the important details. If you are re-

viewing a novel, read extensively from exceptionally interesting passages for purposes of illustration. Evaluate the book in terms of favorable and unfavorable features, and as a whole. Discuss its form if it has unusual features.

COMBINATIONS OF METHODS IN INFORMATIVE SPEAKING

The types and principles of informative speaking have been presented in some detail. As you study these types of speeches, remember that they can be combined in a variety of ways. Many aspects of one type of speech can be useful in making speeches of other types.

It may have occurred to you that discussion is also a type of informative speaking. The techniques of sharing information in discussion are presented in Chapter Nineteen.

Projects and Problems

PROJECT 1: USING VISUAL AIDS

Purposes of this assignment: The main purpose of this assignment is to develop skill in using visual aids in expository speaking. You may use such visual aids as a blackboard or cardboard drawing; the demonstration of a pattern of action such as that used in the strokes of tennis, applying splints, or shooting a bow and arrow; or the explanation of an object or model, such as a clarinet.

Suggested subjects for this assignment:

Regrouping of genes in cell division	Climate and air circulation
The operation of an oil-burning turbine	Jujitsu
	First-aid bandages
Sighting a new rifle	The operation of a mechanical corn picker
Newton's laws of motion	
The atomic structure of a chemical compound	Landscape designing
	Word meaning
The city-manager plan of government	A subject assigned by the instructor
Directions on maps	

Procedure: Read the discussion of informative speaking presented in the chapter. Select a topic and assemble materials for a five-minute speech. Organize materials and rehearse the presentation of the speech, using an object or diagrams. Present the speech to your classmates. Be sure you have provided visual-aid materials. Have your classmates rate you on this performance. Conduct a discussion of the speech content and your speech methods.

Questions to consider in evaluation of the use of a drawing:
a. Is the drawing large, in proportion, and clearly labeled? ...... _____
b. Does the drawing simplify without oversimplifying the object? .. _____

c. Are the important parts clearly labeled? .... _____

d. Are all references to the drawing stated clearly and arranged in order? .... _____

e. Is the drawing for the speech done easily, with confidence and poise? .... _____

f. Does the speaker handle the pointer effectively, speak directly to the audience, and avoid action which distracts attention from the diagram? .... _____

g. Are the general processes of language and speech used effectively? .... _____

PROJECT 2: PERFORMANCE OF A PROCESS

Purposes of this assignment: The ability to direct others in the specific operations or activities required in carrying through some process is a useful skill. Can you present such directions clearly and effectively? If not, this project should help you improve your skill in making this type of informative speech.

Suggested subjects for this assignment:

Flying by instrument	Making a blue print
Preparing a speech	Using the library
How to study	Fly casting
Designing a stage set	A political convention
Making a steel casting	How to float on the water
The peacetime uses of radar	Skin diving
Artificial respiration	

Procedure: Read the section of this chapter entitled "Informative Speaking with Visual Aids." Prepare a five-minute speech with visual aids and present it to your classmates. Have them rate your speech performance. Conduct a discussion of the speech and of your presentation.

Questions to consider in evaluation:

a. Were listeners clearly oriented toward the activity? .... _____

b. Were the elements of the process described precisely? .... _____

c. Did the speaker present the important steps in consecutive order? .... _____

d. Are listeners left free from any uncertainty about the operation of the process? .... _____

PROJECT 3: DESCRIPTION OF SCENES, OBJECTS, AND EVENTS

Purposes of this assignment: Can you make yourself clearly understood when you describe a house or a room? Can you look at a contour map and describe the country represented? How well do you describe such objects as a piece of machinery, a kitchen or workbench tool, a slide rule, a car, or a boat? Can you describe sounds, tastes, odors, movement, and moods? Do you describe persons precisely? Work on description should help you analyze and talk about such matters more clearly.

Suggested subjects for this speech:

A radio studio	The scene of the crime
A wet-bulb thermometer	A famous battle in history
The South Sea Island native	Night life in the jungle
My dream air flivver	The art of Grandma Moses
A power lathe	The surveyor's transit
The Alcan Highway	A jet engine
Standards for judging purebred horses	Space flight
The bazooka	

Procedure: Read the discussion of descriptive speaking in this chapter. Select a subject with which you have had experience and on which descriptive information is useful. Develop the outline for the speech using the principles of description. Rehearse the speech and present it to the class. Have your associates rate your speaking in this performance. Conduct a discussion of the speech content and your speech technique.

Questions to consider in evaluation:

a. Did the speaker orient his listeners to the object or scene described? . . . . ———

b. Were the details of the picture well selected? . . . . ———

c. Was the description vivid? . . . . ———

d. Was the order of presenting items effective? . . . . ———

e. Were minor parts of the picture subordinated to major parts? . . ———

f. Were details interpreted and synthesized into the picture as a whole? . . . . ———

g. Was the description as a whole effective for the purposes it was intended to serve? . . . . ———

PROJECT 4: THE HISTORICAL NARRATIVE

Purposes of this assignment: The historical narrative informs and explains by presenting the background and development of a principle, institution, or object. It answers the questions: What is the origin and development of this idea? Have you wondered about the development of this idea? Have you wondered about the development of protective armor, the modern college, public health measures, the professions of medicine, law, or personnel management? Do you know the history of railroads, the Flying Fortress, free speech, the mining of iron ore, Percheron horses, or realism in the theatre? Such subjects are appropriate for learning to use the historical narrative in informative speaking.

Suggested subjects for this assignment:

The modern battleship	The microscope
The fight against yellow fever	The use of electricity
Group medicine	The liberal arts college

The cultivation of wheat	The modern novel
The study of speech	Democratic government
Popular music	The practice of dentistry
The rise of Hitler	Educational television
The production of quinine	The Berlin crisis
Conquest of space	

Procedure: Study the principles of the historical narrative in informative speaking. Select a topic for a historical narrative in which you can apply these principles. Prepare a ten-minute speech and deliver it to your associates. Have them rate your speech on a rating scale. Conduct a discussion of the speech content and your presentation of this speech.

Questions to consider in evaluation:
a. Did the speech begin at an appropriate place in the development of the story? . . . .   _____
b. Were the incidents which indicate changes well selected? . . . .   _____
c. Were the facts accurately represented? . . . .   _____
d. Were technical or new words clearly defined? . . . .   _____
e. Were scenes and persons clearly and interestingly described? . .   _____
f. Did the speaker point out connections between events? . . . . .   _____
g. Did the story move steadily to its conclusions? . . . .   _____
h. Was the speaker interested in his story? . . . .   _____

PROJECT 5: ANALYSIS, CLASSIFICATION, AND DIVISION

Purposes of this assignment: Occasionally you will find it necessary to use words which are new or which may mean different things to different people. These words must be defined. To formulate effective definitions requires practice. The new is explained by relating it to the familiar. One method of relating a new idea to an old one is to classify the new idea. In what class does the new idea belong? How does it differ from other ideas in the same class? The processes of definition and classification serve to analyze the subject, to break it down into its significant parts so that you may think about one at a time. This assignment should help you explain your ideas through definition, classification, and analysis.

Suggested subjects for this speech:

Weather	Lincoln's ideas of the evil of slavery
Words and their meaning	Developing concepts of democracy
Synthetic rubber	Dictatorships
The pioneer movement	The idea of human rights
The skyscraper	Imperialism
Conservation of natural resources	Theories of communication
The four freedoms	Theories of learning

Procedure: Study the principles of informative speaking presented earlier in this chapter. Select a topic for an instructional speech in which you can apply these principles. Prepare a five- to six-minute speech, and deliver it to your associates. Have your associates rate your speech on a rating scale. Conduct a discussion of the speech content and your speech methods.

Questions to consider in evaluation:
a. Was the analysis of the topic into parts clear and effective? ... _____
b. Was the classification of data logical or topical? .... _____
c. Can you suggest improvements in the classification of data? ... _____
d. What principles were used in classifying the data? .... _____
e. Were the words and phrases clearly defined? .... _____
f. Would a better use of definition have clarified the subject? .... _____

PROJECT 6: ILLUSTRATION, EXAMPLE, AND ANALOGY

Purposes of this assignment: Informative speaking often involves the consideration of general ideas, principles, and abstractions. When we explain the concepts of speech standards, illustrations probably do more to clarify principles than do general statements. We use examples and analogies to get the audience's attention, keep their interest, crystallize abstractions, demonstrate the working of principles, and facilitate memory for facts. The speech student should learn how to explain his ideas by the use of this method.

Suggested subjects: (*a*) A principle of government illustrated by examples from history. (*b*) A principle of the development of industry. (*c*) A principle of military action. (*d*) A social problem or trend. (*e*) Application of historical examples to current events.

Procedure: Read the discussion on use of examples in speaking in this chapter. Select a topic which can be effectively developed by use of examples. Use general illustrations, specific examples, and analogies in developing the material. Outline the speech and prepare to present it to the class. Make it a point to present your material in an instructional rather than an argumentative mood. Make the speech to a group of associates who rate you on the performance. Conduct a discussion of the speech content and your speech technique.

Questions to consider in evaluation:
a. Did the examples used fit naturally into the subject? .... _____
b. Were the examples clear and interesting? .... _____
c. Were they appropriately elaborated and related to main ideas? . _____
d. Did the speaker use too many or too few examples? .... _____
e. Could the speaker's presentation of his examples have been improved? .... _____

PROJECT 7: TRACING CAUSAL RELATIONSHIPS

Purposes of this assignment: The answers to many requests for information begin with the word "because." The importance of causal relationships justifies careful study of this type of informative speaking. If causes or effects cited are complex or difficult to trace, you should understand the methods by which causal relationships are traced and how such relationships are tested. This assignment should help you to improve your causal explanations.

Suggested topics for this assignment:

Causes of World War I

The effects of soil erosion

Why Japanese soldiers died fighting

Causes of juvenile delinquency

Subsidized industry

Effects of the Versailles Treaty

The significance of free enterprise in the United States

Foreign aid programs

The failure of the League of Nations

The effects of bureaucratic government

Words are weapons

Why we behave like human beings

The values of education

The new wonder drugs

Procedure: Read the discussion of informative speaking in this chapter. Select a subject appropriate for this assignment. Assemble and outline material for a speech. Rehearse the speech and present it to the class. Have your associates rate your speaking in this performance. Conduct a discussion of the speech content and your presentation of the speech.

Questions to consider in evaluation:

a. Is the central idea clearly stated? . . . .   _____

b. Are the causes or effects specifically identified and distinguished? . . . .   _____

c. Are the causes cited sufficient to produce the effect? . . . .   _____

d. Is it improbable that other causes or effects provide the explanation? . . . .   _____

e. Did alleged causes actually operate? . . . .   _____

f. Are the relative influences of various causes and effects revealed? . . . .   _____

g. Are the causes or effects cited the most important ones? . . . . . .   _____

h. Is the presentation of the explanation effective? . . . .   _____

PROJECT 8: THE INFORMAL REPORT OR REVIEW OF IDEAS

Purposes of this assignment: Can you briefly review the early discussions of a group for a latecomer? How well can you report on the content of a chapter in a book or short article you have read? This project is designed to improve your achievement in this kind of reporting.

Suggested subjects: (*a*) The contents of this chapter of the book. (*b*) The ideas discussed in our last "bull session." (*c*) Something I have made. (*d*) The contents of an article I have recently read. (*e*) My recollections of London. (*f*) A subject designated by the instructor.

Procedure: The members of the group lounge informally in comfortable positions. Each member selects a subject to contribute and takes his turn presenting it. The group chairman appoints a critic to evaluate performances when all have taken turns. He may call on members at any time to review what has been said. Write a brief report on your self-evaluation of your achievement.

PROJECT 9: THE BOOK REVIEW

Purposes of this assignment: You have read a book and have definite reactions to it. You are asked by business associates or members of a club to review the book for them. Do you understand what is involved in such a review or interpretation? This assignment should help you make such a report Suggested subjects for this assignment are the books available to you and your associates.

Procedure: Read the section on the principles of the book review in this chapter. Select a book and read it carefully for the purposes of presenting a review. Present the review in accordance with the principles of book reviewing. Have your colleagues rate your speech performance. Discuss the contents of the book and your technique of reporting.

Questions to consider in evaluation:
a. Was the book review effectively introduced? . . . . _____
b. Were the main characters, events, and subjects of the book clearly reviewed? . . . . _____
c. Is the nature and thought of the book as a whole fairly interpreted? . . . . _____
d. Can you offer any suggestions for improving the book reviewed? _____

PROJECT 10: THE RESEARCH OR FACT-FINDING REPORT

Purposes of this assignment: This is the kind of formal report which anyone may be expected to make many times during his life. Members of a school board, religious, civic, or fraternal organization; students; officers of groups; business representatives; and others investigate and report on the facts of a problem. Experience with this project should help you in collecting, interpreting, and presenting the data of such reports.

Suggested subjects for this project:

Industrial morale
Cooperatives
City X as a new factory site
The manufacture of artificial rubber
The National Recovery Act
The struggle for freedom of the press
Plans for a new school building
The psychology of thought

Buddhism
Literature as art
Social security measures
Sales taxes
Leadership
The hidden persuaders
Developments in photography

Procedure: Read the discussion on reporting the research project in this chapter. Select a topic and specific purpose for making the report. Gather and organize material for the report. Prepare and present the report to your associates. Have them rate your performance in this report. Conduct a discussion of the content of the report and your presentation of it.

Questions to consider in evaluation:
  a. Was the report clearly introduced? .... _____
  b. Were the sources of the information indicated precisely? ..... _____
  c. Were the facts secured by the best methods? .... _____
  d. Were the facts clearly and accurately presented? .... _____
  e. Did the speaker use the best methods of presenting materials? . _____
  f. Were the speaker's interpretations of facts reasonable? .... _____
  g. Was the report adequate for the purposes it was expected to
accomplish? .... _____

PROJECT 11: CRITICAL EXPOSITION AND REVIEWING

Purposes of this project: Critical exposition differs from argument in that argument expresses a feeling or conviction for or against a contention, whereas criticism selects a standard or standards and relates the object or event criticized to these criteria. Argument is personal; criticism is impersonal. Argument expresses an affirmation or an objection; criticism seeks merely to clarify the relationship between the facts criticized and the accepted bases of criticism. When criticism is subject to controversy, it ceases to be mere exposition and becomes argument. The purpose of this project is to develop skill in critical exposition and to learn the methods of criticism which enable one to be critical without being argumentative.

Critical exposition is organized to present an interpretation of the quality of an object or performance in terms of accepted standards. Was the play well produced? Is the book worth reading? Is the plan a practical one? Is the painting a work of art? To answer such questions, one must understand a standard or set of principles on which the criticism is based. The exposition must set forth these standards, relate them to what is criticized, and draw conclusions.

Suggested subjects for this assignment:

A radio speech I recently heard
A visiting speaker in camp
The agriculture of India
The play of the Cleveland Indians
The statuary of Italy
The business practices of chain stores
The government in business
The Fordson tractor
The Spitfire and the Thunderbolt

The policies of Senator Blank
The music of Cab Calloway
The humor of Bob Hope
The Japanese and the German soldier
A university play
The John Birch Society
The Un-American Activities Committee

Procedure: Read the section of this chapter which discusses critical exposition. Select the subject for your criticism. Determine the standards you will use in the criticism. Formulate the judgment you will expound in the criticism. Prepare and present the speech to meet the criteria of good criticism presented below.

Questions to consider in evaluation:

a. Is the criticism objective and factual, or prejudiced and argumentative? . . . .   _____

b. Are the standards used in criticism explained? . . . .   _____

c. Is the criticism concerned with the important aspect of the subject? . . . .   _____

d. Does the criticism take into consideration the inherent purpose and limitations of the object or activity criticized? . . . .   _____

e. Is the criticism adapted to the listeners? . . . .   _____

References

Gilman, Wilbur E., Bower Aly, and Loren D. Reid: *The Fundamentals of Speaking*, The Macmillan Company, New York, 1951, chap. 15.

Gray, Giles W., and Waldo W. Braden: *Public Speaking: Principles and Practice*, Harper & Brothers, New York, 1951, chap. 8.

McBurney, James H., and Ernest J. Wrage: *The Art of Good Speech*, Prentice-Hall, Inc., Englewood Cliffs, N.J., 1953, chap. 14.

Monroe, Alan H.: *Principles and Types of Speech*, 4th ed. Scott, Foresman and Company, Chicago, 1955, chap. 20.

Oliver, Robert T., and Rupert L. Cortright, *Effective Speech*, Holt, Rinehart and Winston, Inc., New York, 1961, chap. 16.

————, Dallas C. Dickey, and Harold P. Zelko: *Communicative Speech*, The Dryden Press, Inc., New York, 1955, chap. 11.

Thonssen, Lester T., and Ross Scanlon: *Speech Preparation and Delivery*, J. B. Lippincott Company, Philadelphia, 1942, chap. 8.

SEVENTEEN

Argumentative Speaking

No SMALL PART of our speaking during the past twenty-four hours has been controversial. Even though much of it has had to do with personal, comparatively trivial problems, such as whether to elect a certain course, our concern is also often with more important issues that both we and our community face. Because we and society are always engaged in a common effort at mutual adjustment, because we cannot and do not wish to escape from the social-political-economic-occupational world of continual conflict, and yet because we have numerous desires and needs that must be fulfilled if we are to get on or even survive, we find ourselves always in this world of controversy.

Our identification with community fortunes engulfs us in this common effort to solve the persistent problems of war, peace, taxation, legislative action, and so on. These issues, we agree, need to be solved if society is to progress. We agree, furthermore, that in talking about these problems we must have free speech and freedom of choice. We also agree that the wisdom of our free choices will depend on our education. Colleges, therefore, are training centers for intelligent problem solving. And such intelligent problem solving in turn depends heavily on methodical sound thinking.

Typical talk in such controversy is argumentation. Argumentative speaking is the art of influencing others to think and act in a specific way. It requires a clear statement of the problem, analysis of the important issues which divide speakers and some part of the audience, the summoning of evidence, the use of inference, and refutation as further defense of the speaker's propositions and assurance of his success.

What is the relation of the aim and method of argumentative speaking to speaking in general? Basically both focus on the speaker, audience, occasion, and speech itself, including the seven fundamentals with which this book deals.

How does argumentative speaking differ from persuasion? The two are almost identical except that argumentative discourse concentrates more directly on logic and evidence, with relatively less stress on suggestion, emotional and imaginative coloring, verbal pictures, connotative language, and sentence structure. Argument does require such motivative elements, but they are not dominant. Persuasion, on its part, certainly does not minimize fact and inference, but usually the more eloquent speeches have greater emotional content. Chapter Eighteen deals specifically with "Persuasive Speaking."

How is argumentative speaking different from discussion? Discussion involves a group whose purpose is to solve a problem cooperatively. The discussant, like the arguer, adheres to a logical pattern of thinking. He recognizes the problem, focuses on the definition of terms used in the controversy, analyzes the factors that combine to create the disturbing situation, states clearly the various hypotheses or representative solutions, weighs in turn the advantages and disadvantages of each solution, selects the outcome that seems most feasible to the group, and finally frames a program for carrying out the solution as determined.

Different from the arguer, the discussant ignores almost entirely the techniques of persuasion. He aims at a consensus of judgment theoretically based on reason alone. This discussional approach thus sets the speaker off sharply from the debater, the salesman, or the typical arguer in the classroom or elsewhere. For detailed treatment of discussion, see Chapter Nineteen.

How is argumentative speaking related to debate? Debate is a type of argument regulated by time limits and other parliamentary or forensic rules. Procedures on the floor of the United States Senate, like courtroom procedures, are circumscribed by rules and by the gavel of the presiding officer, the symbol of the deliberative body. Argumentative speaking in these situations may also be referred to as debate. School and college debate is simply argumentative speaking in which each side is usually represented by two persons who speak in a specified order and for a specified length of time. Although in this chapter we will explain these procedures in some detail under "Conducting a Debate," most of our discussion will apply to both argumentative speaking and debate.

The Proposition

All argumentative speaking is based upon propositions. A proposition is a problem formally stated: If you are arguing the question of the ballot for eighteen-year-olds, your proposition will read, "*Resolved,* that (you may omit these two preliminary words if the occasion is informal) in local, state, and national elections in the United States the legal voting age should be lowered to eighteen years." Or you may put the statement in the form of an impartial question: "In local, state, and national elections in the United States, should the legal voting age be lowered to eighteen years?" The resolution type of statement is to be preferred unless the speaking situation is extremely informal. Exact statement, however, should be the aim, whatever the sentence type.

Limit the scope of your proposition. If the speaking time is five minutes, weigh your subject carefully and limit your proposition to only one phase —for example, the educational qualifications of the young voter. Thus the proposition would be worded: "*Resolved,* that the eighteen-year-old is educationally qualified to vote."

Phrase the proposition in a simple rather than a compound sentence. See that it is free from ambiguous, vague, or question-begging terms. If it is proposed for a school or college debate, construct it so as to give the affirmative the "burden of proof." This term, borrowed from courtroom parlance, simply means that the resolution should advocate a change from the existing order or a continuation of the existing order in the rare cases in which it is clear that the overwhelming sentiment of the audience is opposed to the *status quo.* Thus the speakers opposed to the proposition should have a majority of the audience on their side before the argument starts. Word the statement, then, so that it proposes a change or proposes a policy counter to audience opinion.

PROPOSITIONS OF FACT AND OF POLICY

A proposition of fact deals with the question of whether an alleged "physical or mental event, situation, or existence" can be verified by testimony and inference. Such a proposition asserts the truth or falsity of the alleged claim to "truth" or "veracity." The conclusion calls for mental endorsement of the statement rather than for action. Obviously, some disputed questions of fact, such as "James Jederkoft's illness is due to smallpox," can be more directly proved than others, such as "Nikita Khrushchev does not want war." The ability to summon concrete evidence and draw specific conclusions varies all the way from "This conclusion is certain" (that is, endorsed by almost everybody who examines the evidence and logic) to "This conclusion is almost certain," or "This conclusion is probable."

Typical propositions of fact are (1) Fluoridation of the water-supply system in my city will decrease tooth decay over the next ten years. (This proposition will presumably be pretty well established or rejected after several years' examination of the evidence.) (2) The local chapter of the Bi-Alpha fraternity has a policy of excluding Negroes. (Despite the ambiguity of the word "policy," the truth or falsity of the proposition can no doubt be demonstrated by proper research.) (3) Franklin D. Roosevelt was the leading American orator of the period 1900 to 1950. (Aside from the span of years involved, and the need for considering the strength and weakness of comparable speakers, the question is further complicated by the question of whether only political speakers are included.)

This third example of alleged "fact" is often labeled a proposition of "value." Such a proposition relies heavily on "opinion" in the absence of concrete proof. Examples are (1) Television is ruining the reading habit. (2) Religion is losing its influence on the moral conduct of Americans. Such propositions of value express judgments of the worth or worthlessness, justice or injustice, importance or unimportance of things, concepts, persons, institutions. The factor of speculation is considerable. We never-

Our American democracy is dependent upon the ability of representatives to speak effectively in our interests as are these members of the House of the state of Ohio. (Ohio State University Department of Photography.)

theless give to these value judgments as much verifiability as possible and classify them as propositions of fact.

A proposition of policy places the emphasis on action rather than on belief. The differences between propositions of fact and of policy can be illustrated by restating the subjects of the propositions of fact above as those of policy. Note how approval is changed to a call for action in these propositions: (1) My city should adopt a program of fluoridation of the water-supply system. (2) the local chapter of Bi-Alpha fraternity should be condemned for its exclusion of Negroes. (3) In the study of outstanding orators of the United States from 1900 to 1950, first place should be given to Franklin D. Roosevelt.

DEFINING TERMS IN YOUR PROPOSITION

Although all types of speaking call for a clear explanation to your audience of what you are talking about, your obligation to interpret any words or terms that might confuse is especially important in argumentative speaking. Much of the follow-up action or mental approval (or rejection) may hinge on the understanding of the key terms of the resolution.

Although the introduction of a five- or six-minute argumentative speech should not be loaded with technical definitions, you will nevertheless take sufficient time to clarify any terms that might confuse and sidetrack the thinking of your audience. At the beginning you will clear the air of language complexities, and you will retain such clarity to the end.

How will you define your words? Dictionaries may be a starting point. But often the problem is one of explaining a term rather than a word. "Socialistic control offers a remedy for the present economic-political instability in the United States" immediately demands that the terms "socialistic control" and "present economic-political instability" be defined. The attempt to grapple with these formidable terms will no doubt lead the reasoner to recast the entire proposition in more understandable language.

In addition to dictionary and encyclopedia definitions, you will find helpful such well-established explanatory methods as the following: (1) Quote an authority on the subject. ("Jules Beckman, professor of economics at New York University, defines price control as action which is deliberately undertaken for the purpose of affecting, limiting the movements of, or setting prices.") (2) Use analogy or comparisons. ("We propose to define cabinet government by comparing it with congressional government.") (3) Give the history of the term. ("Pan-Americanism has evolved as follows: . . . .") (4) State the purpose or function of the concept. ("Disarmament means the universal abolition of peacetime military training.") (5) Give an operational description. ("This is how it works.") (6) List the details of the concept. ("These are its special parts.") (7) Give the common usage of the term. ("By ethics we mean those standards of public and private conduct recognized and supported in our community.") (8) Use a combination of such methods.

Most of the disputations and misunderstandings in argumentative and discussional discourse would not arise if speakers cleared up the language difficulties at every stage.

ANALYZING THE PROPOSITION

Analysis is the process of dividing the problem into its main and subordinate divisions. To analyze a proposition, discover and state the issues—the controversial points whose answers will make up the pattern of the argument. State the issues as impartial questions. Thus, on the subject of the ballot for eighteen-year-olds, the chief issues might be: Do eighteen-year-olds have enough education to vote? Are they sufficiently experienced to vote? Have they had sufficient political experience? Each of these issues should in turn be divided into subquestions.

In the analysis of a proposition of policy, the central questions usually arise from a cause-and-effect analysis of the problem. What will be the alleged results of its establishment or application? These questions involve several apparent subissues: (1) What factors call for a change or for action? (2) Will the establishment of the proposal produce satisfactory results? Will the difficulties be removed? Will positive benefits result? (3) Is the proposal practicable? Can the organization or machinery necessary for its success be established? Has it demonstrated its successful operation in other places or areas? Is it to be preferred to other proposed solutions?

These questions represent "stock issues" and are familiar to students of argumentation. The inquiries are mechanical; they should be applied only as a means of helping you to focus on the outstanding lines of investigation. Other pertinent questions can be added to this list—for example, (4) Is the proposal just to the groups that have a stake in the problem?

To understand the process better, consider the problem, "Shall we start a new political party in the United States?" Following the pattern above reveals these issues: (1) Are there important problems that the political parties should deal with and attempt to settle? If so, do the major political parties face these problems squarely? (The affirmative answers "no," the negative, "yes.") (2) Would the creation of a new major political party facilitate the settlement of such important problems? (3) Would the establishment of a new major political party be practicable? Stock issues are helpful, therefore, in the formulation of specific inquiries.

Stock questions are useful also in the analysis of a proposition of fact. The proposition, "*Resolved*, that Eastward College offers better general liberal arts training than Middlesex College," requires a classification of the kinds of education presented in a liberal arts college and the aims of this type of education—for example (1) self-realization through thinking, etc., (2) social aims, (3) political aims, (4) economic aims, (5) moral aims. Is Eastward College more effective in teaching students how to think? In providing a view of history, literature, the social and physical sciences? In emphasizing political concepts and training? In providing training in human relations? In ethical and moral training?

Other methods of discovering the issues involved in a proposition include analysis of (1) the forms of proof (evidence, authority, causal relations, comparisons, instances); (2) historical periods; and (3) the parties involved (students, faculty, the college in general). The classificational method of analysis suggested above is perhaps the most convenient, although you will frequently apply the principle of causes and results of a policy, event, or situation.

ORGANIZATION

The argumentative speech should provide the answers, with reasons and evidence to support these answers, to the questions or issues raised in the analysis of the problem. Thus analysis enables the speaker to state the points he intends to develop in support of or in denial of the proposition. Note the following issues:

Resolved: that Congress should pass legislation providing for a Federal sales tax.

    I. Does the need for raising further Federal revenue demand some modification of our present Federal tax program?

   II. If so, would a further increase in any or all of our existing sources of Federal taxation, exclusive of a sales tax, raise the necessary revenue, or would measures other than a Federal sales tax provide a satisfactory solution of the problem?

  III. Would the Federal sales tax be a significant means of meeting the alleged need for further Federal revenue?

  IV. Would a Federal sales tax be practicable?

   V. Would the sales tax be fair to the lower income groups?

If the speaker wishes to argue that the passage of a Federal sales tax at this time would be objectionable, his contentions or points to be developed would be the following:

    I. An increase in income taxes and a further curtailing of Federal expenses would make unnecessary the proposed Federal sales tax.

II. The insufficient additional revenue raised by such a tax would not justify its establishment.
III. A Federal sales tax would be impractical. (It would increase the cost of living and would cost too much to administer.)
IV. The tax burden would fall largely on those least able to pay.

The argumentative speech which presents these issues and contentions should have an introduction, a main body or argument proper, and a conclusion. Although these three divisions are flexible and should not be rigidly adhered to at the risk of boring the audience, this standard pattern is of advantage to both the speaker and the listener.

Usually, in your introduction: (1) State the reasons for the discussion and the immediate cause of the controversy. (In the case of the resolution above, a revenue bill may recently have been introduced in the House of Representatives.) (2) Explain briefly the terms. (In this case, explain the Federal sales tax.) (3) State the issues. (4) Enumerate the points or contentions to be established.

The main body or argument proper should be a comprehensive treatment of each contention or proposition. Do not attempt to deal with more major ideas than time will permit. Think of each argument as a speech in itself, with its introduction, main body, and conclusion. If you are arguing a proposition of policy, be sure to discuss (1) the necessity (or lack of necessity) of the proposal, (2) its benefits (or evils), and (3) its practicability (or impracticability). In arguing a proposition of fact, you will make each phase of your classification a heading in your main body.

The purpose of the conclusion is to summarize and reinforce your points and to appeal for cooperation or action. You may insert a series of persuasive questions, or you may refer again to the occasion.

OUTLINING

Your argument should be carefully outlined in an "argumentative brief." Developing your outline in this complete form will clarify your thinking, test the logical consistency and factual completeness of your ideas, and increase the clarity and convincingness of your case.

Review the principles of outlining in Chapter Five, noting especially the requirement of complete sentences, impersonal language, suitable symbols and indentations, the inclusion of specific evidence, and the listing of sources of data and ideas.

Note that the brief proper should be developed by a series of reasons, with "for" as the typical connective between main ideas and subideas. ("For" is a synonym for "because.")

The brief below illustrates the typical form (I, A, 1, etc.); margins and indentations; the use of complete sentences; the insertion of "for" in the body to develop proof; the inclusion of specific evidence; the three parts of the speech; and the citation of sources.

Resolved: that we should support a policy of further development of educational television.

Introduction

I. The question is important and timely.
  A. Paul Walker, former Chairman of the Federal Communications Commission, declared that the opportunity offered by television equals that which came to mankind about five hundred years ago with the invention of printing.
  B. Progress in television after 1952 made it possible to bring to all homes and schools the benefits of sight-and-sound techniques in communication.
    1. The FCC reserved 242 channels for educational use.
    2. The communities that appropriated these channels opened wonderful opportunities for community progress.
II. The following explanations are pertinent:
  A. *Educational television* applies to talks and demonstrative aids that provide informational, impressive, and thought-provoking programs to supply fresh knowledge, appreciation of art, literature, and other aesthetic interests, current social-political-economic-educational problems, and to the systematic presentation of school, college, and adult learning courses and projects.
  B. *To support a policy* means to cooperate actively with private and public agencies that aim to promote education through the establishment of independent educational television stations and to influence commercial stations to give more broadcasting time to educational programs.
III. The issues are thus suggested:
  A. Do present commercial television stations on the whole offer adequate educational programs?
  B. If not, can educational television achieve both effective audience appeal and sound learning results?
  C. Is the wide development of educational television practicable?

Body

I. Wider support of educational television is needed, for
  A. The claim that the educational needs should be handled exclusively by commercial stations is not justified, for
    1. Few commercial stations can afford to devote much of their

daytime service and their best evening hours to nonprofit educational shows, for

   a. Their aim is primarily to sell goods and services.

   b. Their appeal is to the mass mind and interests, with entertainment the dominant method.

   c. They depend on mass markets for their financial survival and progress.

  2. A survey by the National Association of Educational Broadcasters of seven television stations in New York showed the large percentage of total time per week taken up by non-educational programs.

II. Educational television can achieve effective audience appeal, for

  A. "The Johns Hopkins Science Review," given over a commercial station, was a demonstrated success.

  B. Western Reserve, Syracuse, Columbia, and other colleges produced programs over commercial stations that were also highly commended.[1]

  C. "Really great teachers were as effective on television as in the classroom."

  D. Rich material for television programs resides in every community, great and small, for

    1. Lectures by the nation's really great teachers are available.

    2. Public libraries have developed exceptional storytelling hours.

    3. Towns have built up successful art courses.

    4. In nearly all states are extensive film libraries of significant educational films, for

      a. The University of Kansas has about twenty thousand films available.

      b. Ohio State has produced motion pictures.

      c. The University of Houston has produced full-length plays of merit.

III. Wider development of educational television is practicable, for

  A. Many high-level programs have been and can be developed by educational television stations, for

    1. Stations can exchange good programs.

    2. The Educational Television and Radio Center, with an initial grant from the Fund for Adult Education, is a center for testing programs and for exchange of television films.

  B. The cost of establishing and maintaining such stations is not prohibitive, for

[1] Data drawn chiefly from "Educational Television," National Citizens Committee for Educational Television, Washington, D.C., n.d.

1. The best electronic equipment has been estimated to cost about $300,000.
2. A building would cost $150,000 or $200,000.
3. Operating cost would be $200,000 or $300,000 per year.
4. The National Citizens Committee for Educational Television has published this statement: "Educational television can be brought to the home for just pennies per day per home."

Conclusion

I. Educational television is known to be useful, interesting, and practicable.
II. We must find a way to extend it in this country.

Sources

1. The *National Association of Educational Broadcasters Journal*, 20:14–20, 1961.
2. Philip Lewis, *Educational Television Guidebook*, McGraw-Hill Book Company, Inc., New York, 1961, 238 pp.

From the argumentative brief you may draft speaker's notes to be used as you talk. If you follow the logical brief rigidly in delivery, you will probably give a mechanical and uninteresting presentation. But if you use your notes, adjust your speech to the time available to you, and adapt yourself to your audience, you will utilize well your carefully prepared argument.

EVIDENCE

To convince the listener to think and act as you wish him to, you will appeal to him through facts.

What are facts? They have to do with the existence of things, the occurrence of events, the classification of data, and the character of phenomena. They are the concrete or abstract materials out of which we attempt to weave conclusions or from which we try to draw inferences. They are the examples, instances, testimony which constitute the forms of support for informational speeches. In the context of argument and persuasion, however, these basic materials must be especially examined. If through informational speeches, we attempt to add to the listener's knowledge, through argument, we, in addition, seek to influence him to change his opinions and to act.

What is evidence? It is those matters of fact that support an argument. Evidence may consist of the objects or things themselves and/or the verbal evidence, statements of the observer who reacts to the situation by sight, sound, and other sensory stimuli. In "direct" evidence the witness testifies concerning what he saw of the event itself (e.g., he saw the murder). In "indirect" evidence he testifies concerning facts which point to a conclusion (the murder). In the latter case, the witness did not see the murder, but he testifies that the accused was near the scene at the time, that his clothing was bloodstained, that his revolver was smoking, and that other items identified with the scene all point to his guilt.

Be sure to verify your facts. Your confidence in them will give your delivery convincingness. Test your supporting materials by asking yourself these questions:

1. Are the facts in my argument accurate? (Figures show that Corporation XY in the current year "lost money." Are figures of "lost money" accurate?)

2. Have I included enough facts? A single fact may not be enough to convince listeners; the case may be an exceptional one. ("The students of that college are reckless and irresponsible, for freshman Gearhart last night was caught for speeding.") Is one case enough?

3. Are my facts recent? (Middleton's population, its reading habits, leisure-time activities, and other facts pertaining to that city in 1950 no longer apply in the 1960s. Is this the most recent information available?)

4. Are my facts stated in simple, clear language? (Did "millions listen," or was it actually "thousands"?)

5. Are my facts backed by specific sources or authorities? ("The source for the statement that Woodrow Wilson at Princeton year after year was voted the most popular professor by the students was cited from Ray Stannard Baker's *Woodrow Wilson, Life and Letters,* volume 2, page 13.")

6. Are my authorities competent to testify; are they unprejudiced and intellectually honest? (Is Goren an able authority on international affairs? Adlai Stevenson on Latin American affairs? Is Richard Nixon an unprejudiced authority in assessing the domestic policies of the Kennedy presidential administration? Is the *New York Times* unbiased in its general reporting and analysis of union labor's affairs and policies?)

7. Do the sources have special knowledge of the field of their testimony?

8. Is the source a primary one? (*Reader's Digest* tells us that "established churches in thirty major cities conduct special healing services apart from their regular ritual.") What is a more exact source? (An article, "The Facts about Faith Healing," appeared in *Reader's Digest* in September, 1960, on page 49. It was written by Jhan and June Robbins. The authors got their information from a survey made by the National Council of Churches, which was printed as a pamphlet by the Council's New York office in 1960. The pamphlet is a primary source.)

9. Is the source corroborated by other sources?

10. Are the facts reasonable according to the tests of logic, including causation? Does common sense indicate acceptance of the materials and their sources?

ARGUMENT

Our practical problem in argumentation is to select and arrange inferences, buttressed by facts, that together lead to a dependable conclusion. This process of reasoning relates direct sense-perception experiences and testimony to supposed truths or generalizations. Reason occurs when we mentally explore and arrive at a position in a hitherto undiscovered region. This thought movement, however, is controlled by a careful inspection of the facts and principles at hand and by a cautious examination of those not so clearly seen. It is guessing, but intelligent guessing. It is judicious guessing, based not on "hunches" but on a methodical survey of the probabilities and hazards accompanying the new stand. How do we know that the reasoning is sound? Our repeated testing indicates its soundness. Our assumption, which our experience continually verifies, is that what has worked will continue to do so. Behind that assumption is another: The universe is an orderly one. "Inference is possible because the world is orderly. . . . The uniformity of nature, the conviction that things will continually occur in the same manner as they have hitherto, is undoubtedly the best grounded generalization in the whole range of human existence." [2]

Two general logical patterns have been recognized: inductive and deductive. If you start with concrete objects or details or cases and make the transition to a general conclusion, your method is inductive. If, on the contrary, you concentrate first on a general concept or conclusion and proceed to a specific event or object, your method is deductive.

The two modes, though superficially different, are in reality closely articulated. They are complementary. Inductive reasoning assumes certain general hypotheses or assumptions. Deductive reasoning, on the other hand, although it begins with major premises, takes for granted that these, too, have been checked or verified by common experience and repeated demonstration (induction). The order in which the generalization is stated does not make the difference between induction and deduction. The important distinction lies in what is given and what is to be the conclusion.

---

[2] Columbia Associates in Philosophy, *An Introduction to Reflective Thinking*, Houghton Mifflin Company, Boston, 1923, p. 93, quoted in A. Craig Baird, *Argumentation, Discussion, and Debate*, McGraw-Hill Book Company, Inc., New York, 1950, p. 46.

Your argument will ordinarily use one or more of the representative types of inductive and deductive inference: specific instance, analogy, causation, authority, and general propositions. Note that specific instance is inductive; analogy, cause, reasoning, and authority are both deductive and inductive. Each of these types, to repeat, represents two-way reasoning—from specific to general and from general to specific.

1. *Argument from specific instances* (*argument by generalization*). In reasoning from specific instances, you are expected to make an inductive hazard, that is, to extend your conclusion beyond the immediate data. Your proposition, for example, is that representative South American countries are moving toward adoption of the Castro-Cuban Communist form of government. Your evidence unfolds somewhat as follows: Brazil indicates such a leftist movement (in agricultural and industrial confiscation, in denunciation of Yankee imperialism, in repudiation of upper-class, supremacy, in support of semi-Communist leadership). Chile shows similar trends. So does Colombia; so does Venezuela. Your examination of these cases or instances leads you to draw a statement that covers the entire field, including those states which you have not inspected—Argentina, Paraguay, Ecuador, Bolivia, Uruguay, and others. The generalization becomes "hasty," or questionable.

How can you check your own thinking and that of others as you thus generalize from instances?

a. You must see that the cases are sufficient in number. To prove that the students of your campus in general will vote against a proposal for self-government you must do much more than poll twenty students in your dormitory.

Can we prove that all members of the freshman class at the State University of Iowa are over seventeen years of age? Obviously, we cannot until we have checked every one of the 2,000. But we can conclude that, in general, the freshmen are readers of the *Daily Iowan* (student paper) even though our questionnaire was filled out by only 100 or so (random sampling). A larger sample might give more accurate results, but it is unnecessary in this case to collect 1,000 cases. It is one thing to generalize concerning the assumption that all are over seventeen years of age and another to infer that the group in general reads the university daily.

b. You must note whether the cases are representative or typical. The former *Literary Digest* conducted a poll in 1936 to predict the presidential election results of that year. Although large numbers were questioned, the poll was limited to persons listed in telephone directories. This biased sample bypassed millions of voters in the lower economic group. The illogical conclusion of the poll was that Landon would be the winner. In the election, however, he received 8 electoral votes and Franklin Roosevelt received 523 (against a *Literary Digest* prediction of about 160).

If you wish to prove that the leaders of the Republican party are on the whole "conservatives," you will in fairness not limit your instances to the "old guard" or to those over seventy; you will include the young Republican governors and congressmen and you will study a cross section of the party leadership.

c. You must look closely to the sources of your facts—to yourself as observer and collector or to official or unofficial printed sources from which you quote. You will check the character, authority, reliability, and corroborative value of your sources.

Review again the tests of evidence and of the sources of evidence. Avoid the vague statement, "The *Congressional Record* states on page 1051. . . ." Who says it? When? Is the speaker a Senator? If so, is he an expert on this subject? Is he a "biased Republican"? An "old-line Democrat"? And have you quoted him accurately? [3]

2. *Argument from analogy.* A second type of inference is that from analogy (inference by comparison). The isolated facts, cases, objects, or relationships between such objects are compared with other similar facts, objects, cases, or relationships about which our information is relatively hazy. From such matching and contrast we may draw conclusions concerning these relatively unknown situations, facts, objects, or relationships. By analogy we compare the democratic ways of the American with those of the Englishman, about whose democratic ways we are less sure, and we conclude that the Englishman is also a supporter of democratic principles.

Analogy, although it limits itself to a comparison of objects or relationships, does assume a general statement and therefore is really a combination of the inductive and deductive methods. Thus: "Five seniors at Shakestown University were selected for National Science Foundation scholarships. It is therefore probable that about five seniors at Portland University were also selected."

The comparison is between two universities about each of which much is known. Our data show that the seniors at Shakestown have achieved certain results. Although we know nothing of the similar testing results and awards at Portland, we do know that many similarities exist between the comparable senior classes. We therefore conclude that similar testing results would occur. The assumption underlying this comparison is that "all institutions that have characteristics essentially like those of Shakestown University would be expected to achieve similar results in such testing."

The worth of the analogies or comparisons will obviously depend on

---

[3] For further treatment of "generalization and evidence," see Baird, *ibid.,* chap. 10.

the accuracy with which the factors of similarity are carried out. We ask:

a. Do the objects or relationships under comparison actually have a significant number of items in common?

b. Are the two objects or relationships under comparison alike in significant details? In 1961 and later some Americans argued that the United Nations with its 100-odd members should be reorganized into a world government, just as the thirteen colonies in 1787 banded together to form the United States. But were these two historical cases parallel in those factors having to do with the success or failure of world government? Impartial readers and listeners found it difficult to accept the validity of the analogy. Many details were significantly different. Even Shakestown and Portland Universities, in the example above, differed much in spite of surface similarities relating to the selection of scientific scholarship awards.

c. Are the points of resemblance sufficiently numerous? To say that directing the destiny of the United States is similar to navigating a ship or airplane would be an interesting statement. But the comparison involves methods or agencies that have nothing directly in common. This illustration is one of "figurative analogy," effective for illustration but hardly a substitute for sound logical method.

d. Do important differences exist? The argument often advanced is that the democratic government of the United States works effectively. Therefore a similar political structure would work well in the Republic of the Congo and in other newly created African states. The obvious differences in history, cultural development, climate, and other factors would qualify the quick claims to the validity of this comparison. Democratic states, we believe, will succeed in Africa—but not simply because the democratic system has prospered in the United States.

e. Are the alleged factors on which the comparisons are based fully established and stated? If we infer that the scholarship of the student population in a given university is high because that institution "won a national intercollegiate football championship," are the facts underlying this comparison accurate? Is it true that that university, or any other, actually won a "national football championship"? No "national football championship" contests have been held, even though Rose Bowl, Sugar Bowl, Orange Bowl, and various other contests are annually staged.

f. Can the alleged comparison or conclusion be verified by argument from generalization, causal reasoning, or testimony?

3. *Argument from causation.* A basic form of inference is that of reasoning from causation. We conclude that assumed facts affect alleged results (cause-to-effect reasoning). Or we focus our attention on these same instances or cases and attempt to describe other factors, cases, or

situations that may have produced them (effect-to-cause reasoning). Like analogy, such inference attempts to establish relationships between particulars.

Like analogy, the causal connections assume a general law or principle, and so represent a combination of induction and deduction.

Causal reasoning deals not only with particulars and with both induction and deduction, but it is interactionary. For convenience we describe causation as existing when a single act or phenomenon acts upon another. We describe this relation in a time sequence. One event succeeds another in time. Causality, however, cannot always be explained so easily. The truth is that the particulars mutually react to each other: "Action and reaction are equal and opposite." Is it true that sulfanilamide (cause) cures pneumonia (result)? Certainly if the organism of the victim did not react in some *reciprocal fashion* to the compound there would be no cure. "Cause and effect are simultaneous; the effect is not contained in the cause; there is a passive factor." [4]

Furthermore, causes and effects are so numerous that it is impossible —or difficult—to describe these relations in terms of sharp separation between a single cause and a single effect. Diphtheria germ may cause death, but circumstances operating in a particular case make it inaccurate to isolate one cause (this germ) as completely responsible for this one effect (death). Age, previous illnesses, effect of other drugs at time, character of the nursing, and physical stamina are to be reckoned with. We single out one unit and call it a cause; another, effect. We need to test carefully these relationships and use much care and qualified language in framing our conclusions.

What are the tests of such reasoning? Almost every argument will contain inferences from the causal relations—either specific arguments within a section or large arguments encompassing the entire proposition. How shall we analyze their validity? We may ask six principal questions:

a. Does a genuine connection appear between the antecedent (prior fact, event, situation) and the consequent (subsequent fact, event, situation)? Coincidence is often mistaken for causal connection. Because one event follows another, we cannot assume direct connection. Even droughts and earthquakes (results) have been connected with the acts of certain political parties (alleged cause) merely because the events have been chronologically together. The fallacy is that of *post hoc, ergo propter hoc* —after this, therefore because of this.

Note the fallacies: "Breaking a mirror brings bad luck." "Don't go under a raised ladder." "We had thirteen at our table. The next day I lost five dollars on a bet." "This summer's Midwest drought is bad, with dust

[4] F. R. Tennant, "Cause," in James Hastings et al. (eds.), *Encyclopedia of Religion and Ethics*, 12 vols., Charles Scribner's Sons, New York, 1911, vol. 3.

storms, grasshoppers, and ruined wheat. Why? The Democratic party has been in power since January."

b. If there is a connection, is the alleged cause adequate to produce the alleged effect, or is the alleged effect determined by the alleged cause? "Jones will certainly succeed as a lawyer, because he has brains." But he may have his brilliant legal prospects interfered with by years of severe tuberculosis. "The world will not see a World War II, because atomic power development makes such a war impossible." But hair-trigger dictators in possession of nuclear weapons may touch off such a war.

A given situation may be traceable to numerous causes. The problem is to recognize the "plurality of causes," but to concentrate on one that stands out as a cause without asserting it as the sole explanation of what occurs.

c. Even if the alleged cause is sufficient to determine the results, do not intervening factors cancel or minimize the controlling influence of the connection? It is asserted, "The steelworkers have been granted higher wages. We are in for higher prices in general." But Federal legislation, various Federal and other agencies, the cooperation of the steel industry in maintaining former prices, and other factors might well counteract inflationary effects.

d. Have the alleged facts in this case been fully verified? These "facts" in debate or elsewhere we too often assume as correct. In the discovery of the planet Pluto, for example, the first task of the investigators was to verify reports concerning the irregularities of Neptune and Uranus—the basis of the entire logical application.

4. *Argument from authority.* Still another method of inference is to cite authorities or expert sources for verification of your idea. The gist of such inference is that "so-and-so is true, because Mr. X so states." Here you identify an authority with an alleged conclusion. The reasoning really amounts to the assumption that whatever Mr. X has to say on his subject is sound. You may test the assumption by means of these questions: (*a*) Is the source accurately quoted? (*b*) Are the facts (if facts are given) properly reported? (*c*) Is the source especially qualified on this subject? (*d*) Is he unbiased? (*e*) Is the testimony offered contrary to the interests of the authority? (*f*) Does other testimony confirm this evidence under examination? (*g*) Does reasoning from causal relation, analogy, generalization, and specific instance confirm this particular conclusion or assumption?

5. *Argument from general propositions.* Another type of reasoning you will use constantly is inference from general propositions or statements. This is argument from deduction. The usual advice of teachers of communication is to organize a speech deductively. Such development is no doubt a help in clarity. For persuasion it is often preferable to begin a

speech with details and point the way toward general conclusions. More often, however, we proceed deductively.

What is the deductive pattern? It is a series of assumptions, of opinions stated with their soundness usually taken for granted, and of general propositions that sometimes are unproved.

To logicians the typical form of deduction is the syllogism, in which the first proposition (assumption, hypothesis) is labeled the major premise; the related and more specific proposition, the minor premise; and the connecting proposition, the conclusion. The following statements, with the three propositions and the three terms, constitute a typical categorical syllogism:

I. Major premise: Whatever steps should be taken to minimize tooth decay of the citizens of our community should be adopted.
II. Minor premise: Fluoridation of the water supply of our city would minimize tooth decay of our citizens.
III. Conclusion: Fluoridation of the water supply of our city should be adopted.

Inferences, framed so as to include three propositions, are of two general types: categorical and conditional. The conditional type is again subdivided into the disjunctive and the hypothetical types.

In the categorical type, the assumption is an unqualified affirmation. In the disjunctive, the assumption states choices or alternatives:

I. Either we have a program of free trade or we shall suffer great loss in international economic competition.
II. We shall adopt a policy of free trade. We shall not suffer great loss in international economic competition.

In the hypothetical type, the major premise or assumption is a condition. To illustrate:

I. If several American-launched missile-alarm satellites circle the globe, this nation will have adequate warning against nuclear surprise attacks.
II. Several American-launched missile-alarm satellites are circling the globe.
III. This nation will have adequate warning against nuclear surprise attacks.

You will use freely such reasoning, with the following qualifications or tests:

a. Logical syllogisms (those with three propositions expressed) almost never exist in argument. They generally take the form of "rhetorical" syllogisms (with one proposition assumed). For your own benefit, or for others, you may recast the statement in the full logical form in order to see more clearly what is implied in the argument.

b. Be sure that the main premise is a proposition properly proved and not merely an unwarranted assumption. It is interesting and instructive to see how frequently we utilize such a major premise without bothering to express it.

For example, each time we use an authority we have a telescoped syllogism. To illustrate: "The *New York Times* declared editorially on July 9, 1961, that outdoor advertising along the new interstate highways would produce a landscape cluttered by a garish claptrap, and insensitive commercialism that has already ruined . . . so much of our loveliest scenery." Fully expanded the statement would read:

I. Whatever this source states on the topic of advertising and interstate highways is to be accepted as authoritative.
II. This is an instance in which the *New York Times* gives a statement on this specific topic (e.g., the effect of billboard advertising on interstate highways).
III. This statement by the *Times* should be accepted as authoritative.

Examine again the major premises of the examples given above concerning fluoridation and tooth decay, free trade and international economic competition, and the authority of the *New York Times* in billboard advertising. Many critics would attack the validity of these premises and demand full proof of each. In the matter of free trade, for example, it might be argued that even though we should adopt such a policy, the Communist nations with their combined solidarity might underbid us and so cause us to have economic losses.

c. Use the word "some" or another equivalent qualifying term in the so-called "categorical statements." Avoid the all-inclusive propositions, such as, "*All* Americans are democratic." Your argument will be sound if you content yourself with the statement that "Americans in general are democratic." (Naturally you will earlier define "democratic.")

d. Use evidence and proofs to verify each of the three propositions. Constantly verify all facts appearing in the inference. Deductive reasoning is thus a combined process of establishing the validity of the reasoning employed (logical connection between the three propositions) and the truth of the reasoning as demonstrated by examination of the detailed evidence and arguments of these propositions.

Obstacles to Straight Thinking

The brief review of argumentative speaking above reminds you of the need for straight thinking. The questions raised under the various divisions of argument and logic aim to prevent or minimize fallacious logic. You will review your facts to ensure their reliability; see that your generalizations are not "hasty"; that your analogies are not false; that your causal reasoning reflects proper interpretation of connection between alleged phenomena; that your authorities are properly weighed; that your general propositions do not "beg the question," in which you merely move from premise to premise without any logical progress; and that in your argumentative speaking you keep to logical lines rather than resort to name calling or other propagandistic devices that substitute emotional appeals for evidence and argument.

Conducting a Debate

Rules. Let us assume that you are to take part in a debate—to argue according to specific rules. What are the rules and regulations of formal debates?

Time limits are imposed on debaters. Intercollegiate debates, for example, usually last one hour. During this time, each of the four speakers speaks twice. Each speaker makes a "constructive" speech ten minutes long, and each is allowed five minutes for rebuttal to ensure review of the arguments presented. Thus the distribution of debating time is usually as follows:

Constructive Speeches

First Affirmative	10 minutes
First Negative	10 minutes
Second Affirmative	10 minutes
Second Negative	10 minutes

Rebuttal Speeches

First Negative	5 minutes
First Affirmative	5 minutes
Second Negative	5 minutes
Second Affirmative	5 minutes

The argument is conducted according to parliamentary rules, the purpose of which is to guarantee to the two sides equal protection and opportunity. The affirmative opens and closes the debate, and the negative speaks first in rebuttal. The subject is phrased in resolution form, and at the conclusion a vote is taken on the "merits of the question."

The purpose of debating is to arrive at and record a decision. In student debates, engaged in for learning purposes, the critic judge decides in favor of the team that "does the most effective debating."

Preparation and presentation. In your debates as a student of speech, you will work under the close supervision of your debate or speech instructor. With your fellow speakers, select a topic that is of interest to you and word it carefully. Prepare or secure a list of references on your topic, and take notes carefully on the material you read. Draw up a tentative brief and submit it to your instructor or adviser for criticism. Revise this brief repeatedly as your command of your material develops.

In preliminary occasions with your team mates, report to one another on your readings, analyze the problems, and frame the issues. Decide upon your team case—the series of propositions that you want the judges and the audiences to accept as your argument. For example, the case for an affirmative proposition of policy would follow closely the "stock issue" propositions.

First Affirmative

I. The present situation is unsatisfactory.
II. Defects are inherent in the present system. [These two contentions prove the contention of the second affirmative that the proposition is necessary.]

Second Affirmative

I. The proposal will remedy these defects.
II. It is a practicable proposal.
III. It is preferable to other remedies. [These three contentions prove the advantages and practicality of the proposal.]

For the negative, the case might be exactly the reverse:

CASE A
First Negative

I. The present situation is satisfactory.
II. The alleged defects can be corrected without destroying the present policy.

Second Negative

III. The proposal will be detrimental.
IV. The proposal is impracticable.

The negative may vary these "cases" by some such plan as the following:

CASE B
First Negative

I. The proposal is impracticable.
II. The proposal is detrimental.

Second Negative

III. The proposal is not needed.

Case C

First Negative

I. The plan is unworkable.
II. The plan is detrimental.

Second Negative

III. A better plan is proposed.

Other choices of "case" are also open to the negative. The case for a proposition of fact resolves itself into a series of statements that usually reflect (1) causes and results or (2) classification of the arguments or evidence. To illustrate:

Resolved: that the liberal arts colleges are a failure.

I. The students do not receive sufficient training in critical thinking.
II. The students do not receive sufficient training in the social sciences.
III. The students do not receive sufficient training in philosophy or ethics.
IV. The students do not receive sufficient training in oral and written communication.

The first affirmative would cover the first two of these statements, and the negative would be developed similarly. In the example above, each of the two negative speakers would develop two of the four main points. (Note that the division is based upon a classification of the aims of the liberal arts education.)

Write your debate speech as a means of achieving effective condensation, clarity, and persuasiveness. But leave your written speech at home.

Practice rebuttal. You can improve your technique in rebuttal by studying both sides and by collecting and classifying rebuttal cards in advance. In order to refute your opponents' ideas, listen attentively and take down the substance of their arguments. Then, in rebuttal, state clearly the idea to be refuted. Refute the central ideas, and avoid refuting points not made. Refute your opponents' ideas by attacking the accuracy of the facts, the weakness of their authorities, and the weakness of their arguments based on generalization, false analogy, and false causation. Then summarize your own case to indicate its superiority to your opponents' case.

When you are preparing to debate, practice delivery each day, even if a vacant chair is the only audience available to address. Your delivery style in debate should be direct and conversational, free from bombast and insincerity. Finally, observe the conventions of debating courtesy; remember to recognize the chairman at the beginning of each speech. In the debate itself, invariably be courteous to the other teams. Let your attitude at every stage be friendly and gentlemanly. While others are speaking, listen closely. Accept your responsibilities for genuine sportsmanship.

Projects and Problems

PROJECT 1

Write a 300-word introduction for an argument to be delivered before a college audience. Explain at the end of the composition what analytical steps you included.

PROJECT 2

Prepare an argumentative brief on the national high school debate proposition for the current year.

PROJECT 3

Make a brief for an argumentative speech delivered in recent years.

PROJECT 4

Develop a short argumentative speech (four minutes) in which you (*a*) explain in one or two paragraphs the causes of a social, political, or economic condition or situation that needs correction, and (*b*) in one or two more paragraphs, review the probable consequences of that situation if it is not corrected.

PROJECT 5

Refute in a four-minute speech a representative argument found in your recent reading. Be sure to state the exact source of the material you refuted. Try to use more than one of the special methods of refutation mentioned in this chapter.

PROJECT 6

(For the instructor) Develop a program of classroom debates on important campus or local problems of policy. Divide the class into one-man "teams," each assigned to an affirmative or to a negative side. Divide the speaking time equally: for example, allow the affirmative seven minutes for its constructive speech, the negative ten minutes, and the affirmative three minutes for rebuttal.

References

Aristotle: *Rhetoric and Poetics of Aristotle,* introduction and notes by Friedrich Solmsen, The Modern Library, Random House, New York, 1954.

Baird, A. Craig: *Argumentation, Discussion, and Debate,* McGraw-Hill Book Company, Inc., New York, 1950.

Beardsley, Monroe C.: *Thinking Straight,* Prentice-Hall, Inc., Englewood Cliffs, N.J., 1950.

Behl, W. A.: *Discussion and Debate,* The Ronald Press Company, New York, 1953.

Black, Max: *Critical Thinking,* Prentice-Hall, Inc., Englewood Cliffs, N.J., 1952.

Braden, Waldo W., and Ernest Brandenburg: *Oral Decision Making: Principles of Discussion and Debate,* Harper & Brothers, New York, 1955.

Brembeck, Winston L., and William S. Howell: *Persuasion,* Prentice-Hall, Inc., Englewood Cliffs, N.J., 1952.

Chase, Stuart: *Guides to Straight Thinking,* Harper & Brothers, New York, 1956.

Crocker, Lionel: *Argumentation and Debate,* American Book Company, New York, 1944.

Dewey, John: *How We Think,* D. C. Heath and Company, Boston, 1933.

Ewbank, Henry H., and J. J. Auer: *Discussion and Debate,* Appleton-Century-Crofts, Inc., New York, 1951.

Gulley, Halbert E.: *Essentials of Discussion and Debate,* Holt, Rinehart and Winston, Inc., New York, 1955.

Kruger, Arthur M.: *Modern Debate: Its Logic and Strategy,* McGraw-Hill Book Company, Inc., New York, 1960.

Potter, David (ed.): *Argumentation and Debate,* Holt, Rinehart and Winston, Inc., New York, 1954.

Thouless, Robert H.: *How to Think Straight,* Simon and Schuster, Inc., New York, 1941.

Toulmin, Stephen E.: *The Uses of Argument,* Cambridge University Press, New York, 1958, part III.

EIGHTEEN

Persuasive Speaking

In our study of argumentative speaking we have stressed the logical processes involved in this type of speaking. In studying persuasive speaking, we shall consider psychological principles and techniques almost exclusively.

Persuasion is "the conscious attempt to modify thought and action by manipulating the motives of men toward predetermined ends."[1] Etymologically, the word "persuasion" developed from *per suasio*, "through sweetness." In modern usage the term refers to the process of appealing to a variety of motives to influence attitudes and conduct. It is also explained by some as a form of learning.[2]

Persuasion Analyzed

Persuasion, as we use the term here, is the attempt to influence others by motivational appeal as well as by logic, facts, and opinion of authorities. Persuasive techniques are especially applicable in argumentative speaking; in the same way, logic, fact, and opinions of authorities—the tools of argumentation—often form a strong part of the subject matter of persuasive speeches. Both types of talks must be both logical and per-

---

[1] W. L. Brembeck and W. S. Howell, *Persuasion*, Prentice-Hall, Inc., Englewood Cliffs, N.J., 1952, p. 24.

[2] Carl I. Hovland and others, *Communication and Persuasion*, Yale University Press, New Haven, Conn., 1953.

suasive. Aristotle stressed the importance of combining the two elements: Sound reasoning and dependable evidence, he said, must be buttressed by *ethical* and *pathetic* proofs. Ethical proof consists of those types of proof that demonstrate the good will, wisdom, and character of the speaker; we might relate this type of proof to the speaker's candor in presenting the truth as he sees it. Pathetic proof involves the relationship of the subject to the attitudes and emotions of the auditors; that is, the "truth" can only be presented in terms which will be comprehensible and palatable to the auditors. Modern psychological experimentation has shown that prestige suggestions by a speaker and his established credibility make a difference in audience response.

It is a mistake to assume that logical and emotional elements are mutually exclusive, or that a speech can consist of only one of these elements, although it may be preponderately one or the other. We can illustrate ways in which these two elements are interrelated by indicating them on two continua which cross at some point, as illustrated in the following diagrams. Number 1 on each continuum indicates the near absence of that factor, and number 7 indicates its presence in the highest degree.

In the diagrams, one line represents logic and the other persuasion. Speech I, therefore, is weak: Although it is strong in persuasion, it is weak in logic, since the point of intersection comes at 7 on the persuasion continuum and 1 on the logic continuum. Speech II is a relatively useless speech: It is weak both in persuasion (1) and in logic (1). Speech III is strong in logic (7), but highly deficient in persuasion (1) —an ineffectual speech. Speech IV is best in that both the logical (7) and emotional values (7) are strong.

In speech making, as in our daily lives, we must establish a balance

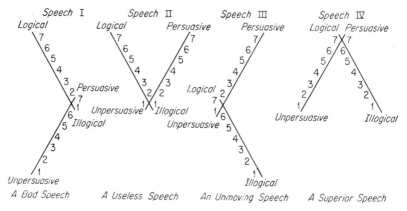

Coordinate continua of logic and persuasion

between logic and emotion. John Dewey has given us an excellent description of the place of emotion in our lives.[3]

The conclusion is not that the emotional, passionate phase of action can be or should be eliminated in behalf of a bloodless reason. More "passions," not fewer, is the answer. To check the influence of hate, there must be sympathy, while to rationalize sympathy there are needed motions of curiosity, caution, respect for the freedom of others—dispositions to which evoke objects which balance those called up by sympathy, and prevent its degeneration into maudlin sentiment and meddling interference. Rationality, once more, is not a force to evoke against impulse and habit. It is the attainment of a working harmony among diverse desires.

Some of the highest achievements of man have their foundations not in coldly and closely reasoned logic, but in feelings, attitudes, loyalties, sentiments, aspirations, and social ideals. There are many roads to the good and the true. They are exemplified in the persuasion of drama, poetry, painting, and religion. Persuasion provides a means of ordering these motives, a means never opened to the narrowly logical mind. There is perhaps as much immorality in indifference and inaction as in the use of bogus appeals to action.

Most of us are aware of the value in our lives of emotions which stabilize and help our society to maintain our value systems. But what has this to do, we ask, with our use of emotional appeals? The words "emotion" and "motivated" come from the same root as the word "motion." An emotionally stimulated response is an energized response, at least for all the emotions associated with approach to or withdrawal from the stimulus object. When the organism responds emotionally, glycogen is released from the liver into the blood stream. The energy provided in this way prepares the individual for action. It is therefore no mere accident that the persuasive speaker has found the appeal to the emotions as a practical device for stirring the listener to action. It is only when the listener's emotions have been conditioned to his logical-thinking behavior that the logical appeal results in action. Thus even the use of logic to produce action is dependent ultimately upon the emotions.

Evaluation of Persuasive Appeals

We have already pointed out the importance to intelligent listening of evaluation of persuasive appeals. From the point of view of validity, there are three types of persuasive appeals: valid, marginal, and bogus.

1. *Valid appeals.* Valid appeals to action are directed toward worthy

[3] John Dewey, *Human Nature and Conduct*, Holt, Rinehart and Winston, Inc., New York, 1922, pp. 195–196.

motives which have a reasonable prospect of satisfaction in the action proposed. Few satisfactions are absolutely certain, but only those which are free from reasonable doubt should be proposed. An example of such an appeal was the request by President Kennedy for the money to strengthen our forces in light of a growing Berlin crisis in 1961.

2. *Marginal appeals.* Marginal appeals are proposals in which the satisfactions suggested may be real but are of minor or incidental value. These short-term appeals to action may be accepted as appropriate for needs to which they appeal; they can scarcely be approved for use in connection with the satisfaction of more permanent and important needs. For example, "Buy this insurance policy and receive a new billfold free."

3. *Bogus appeals.* Appeals which foment hasty and ill-considered action or which offer false and improbable claims of satisfaction through the action proposed are bogus. They include appeals which frustrate the higher codes of society by arousing the baser emotions. Most of the abuses of persuasion belong to this class. Patent-medicine advertisements are an example: "Restore your health with a bottle of Zixolon." (Review Chapter Fifteen for more detailed discussion of propaganda and emotional appeals.)

Theories and Techniques of Persuasion

Techniques of persuasion are not so simple as the tricks of the propagandist described in Chapter Fifteen. Genuine persuasion depends upon winning the good will of your listeners, focusing their attention and interest on your ideas, and stimulating an active response.

ESTABLISHING GOOD WILL AND CREDIBILITY

The good will of the speaker toward the audience is essential in persuasive speaking. But it is not sufficient that the speaker be a person of good will; he must communicate his attitude to his audience. He must avoid inconsistency of expression that would make him seem incredible.[4] The discussion of the speaker's personality in Chapter Fourteen will be helpful in connection with persuasive speaking. Here we shall discuss some of the habits which a speaker should cultivate for effective persuasive speaking.

1. *Know your audience, and plan and word your appeals to take into account the audience's known experience, interests, and attitudes.* Recognition of the right to disagree must be the basis of any attempt at persuasion, for the persuaded person must be won, not pushed, to agreement. Recognition of this right is part of your respect for your listeners and

[4] Hovland and others, *op. cit.,* chap. 2.

their ability to make a wise decision. Even though you will disagree with them on major issues—if you did not you would not be making a persuasive speech—you must yield to their views in some respects in order to win their acceptance of your views in other respects. Sometimes you can do this by praising what the listener approves or condemning what he hates. But if you cannot do these things in honest respect, you should not do them at all.

2. *Demonstrate your mastery of your subject.* Evidence of your knowledge of and ability to handle the materials of your subject—to interpret soundly and organize well—will influence your audience strongly.[5] When talking to an educated and capable audience it is helpful to give evidence that you know different sides of an argument.[6] There may be two sides, you know, or even three or more. You must be fair and just even to those arguments you reject. If you can demonstrate your ability to solve problems and resolve conflicts through unusual insight, you will win your audience's respect and admiration. Avoid dogmatism, often a defensive attitude suggesting weakness. Evidence that your experience has contributed successfully to the needs of others in similar situations is highly persuasive.

3. *Give evidence that you are a worthy leader.* The record of your achievements, if it is well presented, will add to your prestige. It is difficult to prove your ability to your audience tactfully, but if you solicit the support of others, you must indicate to them that you are a good leader. Courage to fight for your convictions, the ability to meet tests, and evidence of past successes are evidence to your audience of your capacity for future successes. Learn to use your record without a vulgar parade of egotism and conceit.

4. *Your character will influence your audience.* In the opinion of your listeners, character means a record of conformity with the virtues they recognize. As a persuasive speaker, you must identify your character with the just and virtuous, with deeds of altruism and magnanimity. Where character is in doubt, other qualities of personality are useless.

Certain personality traits can be depended upon to contribute to persuasive speaking. Modesty, restraint, understatement, and temperate demands are to be preferred to egotism, lack of control, exaggeration, and unreasonableness. Develop the ability to adapt your moods to listeners— to be earnest, to be good-humored, to joke, to be forgiving, or to be uncompromising concerning ideals.[7]

Good will toward your subject may be created by showing its altruistic

[5] Carl I. Hovland and others, *The Order of Presentation in Persuasion,* Yale University Press, New Haven, Conn., 1953.

[6] Hovland and others, *Communication and Persuasion.*

[7] *Ibid.,* chap. 6.

nature, the personal benefits it will provide to your listeners, and its practical advantages. Although the other sides of the argument must be taken into account and duly eliminated, they should not be heavily stressed. Keep the true strength of the proposal in focus by emphasizing its benefits. Lead your listeners to the desired conclusion by placing the necessary information in their hands and encouraging them to make their own decisions.

GETTING ATTENTION AND CREATING INTEREST

William James's theory of persuasion was that what holds attention determines action.[8] If this theory is true, your ability to hold your audience's attention will determine your success as a persuasive speaker. You must keep the attention of the audience focused upon the job to be done. Man's attention span is limited, because attention involves tension which must be relaxed occasionally. If the speaker does not give his listeners opportunity to relax occasionally, they may cease to follow him. The speaker must make it easy for his audience to be attentive.

1. *Show the significance of the proposal.* Presenting an idea as something vital to the listener is the most important way of maintaining interest. The listener must be well motivated to be attentive. Your proposal must appeal to important wants, desires, and needs. By focusing your audience's attention upon the benefits to be derived from your proposal, you can arouse responses of anticipation, acceptance, and approach— responses which are only a short step from action.

2. *Make use of conflict concerning your proposal.* When man's goals are threatened, his energies are renewed. To direct this energy through your persuasive speech, show the dangers which threaten the listeners' understanding, ideals, and standards if they do not accept your proposal. If members of your audience feel that their cherished ideals are threatened and that your proposal will protect those ideals, they will identify themselves with you as a person and endorse your proposal.

Rosenberg's[9] recent book sets forth experimental evidence to show that audience responses may be explained as a need for consistency. Attitudinal states are conceived as constellations of affects or feelings, cognitions or understandings, and more overt patterns of behavior. Stimuli which induce changes in one or more of these parts tend also to induce the organism to change other parts to achieve consistency. Festinger[10]

[8] See William James, *Psychology, Briefer Course,* Holt, Rinehart and Winston, Inc., New York, 1900, p. 448.

[9] Milton J. Rosenberg, *Attitude, Organization, and Change,* Yale University Press, New Haven, Conn., 1960.

[10] Leon Festinger, *A Theory of Cognitive Dissonance,* Row, Peterson & Company, Evanston, Ill., 1957.

has developed a similar theory as it affects cognition or understanding. Certainly conflict plays a central part in these theories of persuasion.

3. *Shock the listener.* If the listener accepts his goals as a matter of course, he may need to be jolted out of his complacency. Pearl Harbor was a shock which awakened many Americans to the need to fight to preserve our way of life. Many drivers are more careful after witnessing an automobile wreck. The introduction of surprise has in it elements of the shock response. Use this technique carefully in order to avoid creating resentment which will damage your cause rather than help it.

4. *Arouse curiosity.* It is human nature to want to complete an attractive or habitual pattern once the act has been begun. Arouse the curiosity of the listener by telling a story which has a conclusion that is pertinent to your cause. Expound causes which will arouse the audience's curiosity concerning the effects. An unexpected pause attracts attention. When you use these techniques, be sure to show the significance for your speech of the materials in which you use them.

5. *Make your speech easy to follow.* A proposal which puts a strain on attention will meet with resistance. Make attention easy for your listeners by appealing to the various senses—visual, auditory, kinetic, olfactory, gustatory, and others. Organize your proposal so that main points are arranged in a natural and easy-to-remember sequence. Repeat and restate your ideas so that there can be no chance of confusion. Provide adequate transition from point to point.

6. *Use variety.* A speech in which the new is balanced with the familiar is more interesting than a speech in which all the materials are completely new or completely familiar. Movement which appeals to the eye; variations in rate, loudness, pitch, and quality of voice which appeal to the ear; and changes in sentence length and form are methods of achieving variety which we have discussed in earlier chapters.

Attention is contagious and cumulative in an audience, and it can be increased by the deliberate use of the methods we have suggested. But beware of attention-getting devices which call attention to themselves; "ham" acting is not good speaking. To acquire skill in the use of attention-getting techniques requires a finesse not ordinarily achieved without much practice.

STIMULATING FAVORABLE FEELINGS AND EMOTIONAL ENERGIES

1. *Appeal to dominant motives.* Good persuasion is in effect the successful appeal to motives. This appeal must achieve a close harmony between the proposal and the dominant motives of the listener. Motives are usually complex and variable. Behavior is organized through an arrangement of the motives of the moment in a hierarchy of values; motives

dominant at one time may play a subordinate role in influencing behavior at a later time. Different persons do the same thing for different reasons.

Many attempts have been made to catalogue human motives, and the various classifications differ greatly with regard to the nature and value of the motives. We do not maintain that the following classification is complete. The student may add to this list as his knowledge and experience warrant. The four different types of drives, which overlap in some degree, are (*a*) the biological drives, (*b*) the ego drives, (*c*) the social drives, and (*d*) the drives of habit.[11]

Many of the *biological* drives may be called hungers. They are cyclical in nature, and their force depends upon the state of the organism. The desire for food and shelter is basic to life. Our efforts to acquire and retain these necessities consume much of our energy. The particular forms in which we satisfy these drives are largely matters of habit. These are among the strongest of the drives. Closely related to them is the desire to avoid danger. The sex drive, also a strong drive, may or may not, depending upon the person, be identical with the desire to care for and rear children. The desire for freedom from restraints on action appears to be of biological origin: The newborn babe struggles when held too tightly; the adult seeks personal freedom of belief and action. There appears also to be a drive for ease and economy of action. We strive to release emotional tension in the exercise of pleasant sensations and emotions, and we attempt to avoid unpleasant sensations and emotions.

The biological drives are stronger and more primitive than most others. They are commonly considered the baser motives to action.

Desires for self-respect, pride, and dignity can be classified as *ego* drives. Professor Wendell White has called these drives the desire for a feeling of personal worth.[12] Men commonly seek to excel, to gain power, to control, to create, to meet the challenges to their abilities. Property is one of the ways in which this drive finds expression at an early age. The care of one's appearance is no doubt a function of the desire for self-respect. The attainment of self-images and ideals is a process involving great struggle. These drives are also subject to modification by experience and learning, and they constitute a type of motive which combines the biological and the social.

The *social* drives are to a great extent the product of experience. They may be largely habitual. They appear in the desire for conformity, favorable attention, and status. We like to be approved by our associates. As a result, we are stimulated by praise and reproof, by social sanctions

---

[11] Hovland and others, *Communication and Persuasion*, chaps. 3 and 4.

[12] Wendell White, *The Psychology of Dealing with People*, The Macmillan Company, New York, 1936, chap. 4.

and taboos. The self may be sublimated to serve the social virtues of trust, integrity, loyalty, precedent, fair play, good sportsmanship, and justice. Someone has said that everyone wants an audience, and the kind of person he is reflects the type of audience he wants. These drives are altruistic and unselfish as contrasted with the more immediately selfish desires; for this reason they are sometimes called the higher motives. They offer long-term appeals to enlightened selfishness.

The drives of *habit* include the desire for maintenance of tastes, interests and preferences, work habits, and intellectual and emotional habits. They also involve the search for new experience, adventure, and growth as well as the preferences for the traditional, the familiar, and the maintenance of the *status quo*. We often retain for years habits that have ceased to serve their original purpose.

Word the main ideas of your persuasive speech so that they contain appeals to the dominant motives of your audience, and use supporting materials which show the relationships of the proposition to the motive. The following diagram presents the main ideas of a student speech. The first point is introductory, but it seeks to arouse the egotistical reactions as well as the higher social motives which create action. The second point appeals to the biological drives by creating an emphatic reaction against deprivation of food, shelter, and care. The third point returns to social interests and habit drives for maintaining the democratic way of life. The final appeal is to the biological drive for safety of self and family and to the habit drives for the development of social ideals.

2. *Meet objections.* Persuasion cannot be expected to work where action is inhibited by conflicting drives. The causes of objection to action may be met by strengthening favorable drives and reducing the strength of competing drives. Competing drives can be eliminated by showing

Impelling motives as main ideas

that they do not apply to the proposal or that they may be satisfied in other ways. If the drives that inhibit action are successfully removed, a proposal for action which stimulates a dominant motive develops and releases the energy necessary for action.

3. *Adapt to the situation.* Make use of the total situational context to support action. Rhetoric was originally defined as "finding within a subject the available means of persuasion." If we substitute the word "situation" for "subject" we have a good definition of this theory. In some ways it is also an extension of the theories reported by Festinger and Rosenberg. We must recognize that people respond to many stimuli in every situation. Some of these factors are their memory of the past of the stimuli; their hopes, interests, desires, or wishes for the future; the resources for responses from which a choice is made; the environment in which a stimulus is presented, including the people present; their cultural patterns, including conventions, customs, and mores; the degree of their frustration or conflict of motives; their attachments to particular stimuli; their habits; their transient and more permanent emotional conditions; the depth of their understandings; and many other factors. Although there is no inevitable stimulus for action for most people, the greater the stimulus conforms to all potential conditions for action the greater the probability of response.

CONCILIATION AND RESTRAINT OF ACTION

Conciliation as a type of persuasion differs from persuasion as we have described it in this chapter in that, instead of stimulating interest, conviction, or action, conciliation seeks to create disinterest, doubt, and the cessation of action. Many of the principles we have discussed apply in reverse to conciliation, because the purpose of conciliation is to stop action, to create doubt, and to conciliate opposition. To achieve these things, the speaker seeks to reduce the intensity of motivation. Persuasion cannot be expected to work where action is inhibited by conflicting drives. The causes of objection to action may be met by strengthening favorable drives and reducing the strength of competing drives. Competing drives may be eliminated by showing that they do not apply to the proposal or that they may be satisfied in other ways. If the drives that inhibit action are successfully removed, a proposal for action which stimulates a dominant motive develops and releases the energy necessary for action.

As a conciliatory speaker, you must create good will. An objective and impersonal manner provides little opportunity for positive emotional response. Keep the attention of the listener pleasantly distracted and focused on inaction. Delay action by appealing to motives that conflict with those which are aroused. Pit motive against motive to create doubt, uncertainty, frustration. Concede on some issues as an appeal to pride and tolerance, and emphasize pertinent grounds of agreement. Show that similar ventures were frustrating and unsuccessful. Reduce tension and strain by finding harmless opportunities for action. Otherwise the repression of active drives may intensify them, making their release more explosive. Make immediate action difficult, and initiate minor patterns of action inconsistent with the dominant trend. Break up larger groups into smaller ones. Show better ways of satisfying the motives for action, and appeal to the higher and more critical motives. The techniques of conciliation are in many respects the opposite of those of persuasion.

PRESENT A PRACTICAL PLAN OF ACTION

The persuasive speech derives much of its force from the presentation of a practical plan of action. The plan may be the deciding element in persuasion when powerful motives and drives are closely associated with the proposal in the mind of the audience but lack direction and organization. Emphasis on the benefits to be derived from carrying out the plan serves to strengthen the relationship between desire and method.

We have considered persuasion as techniques of motivation added to the evidence and logic of argumentation in appeals to action. The persuasive speaker should carefully consider his appeals to motives to assure himself of their validity. The techniques of persuasion involve such processes as creating good will, getting attention and maintaining interest, and showing the relationship of the proposal to the dominant motives of listeners. Although most persuasion is designed to release the energies in action, occasionally the situation calls for inhibition or cessation of action. Under these circumstances appeals are directed to conciliation and demotivation.

Projects and Problems

PROJECT 1: THE STUDY OF SLANTING IN PERSUASION

Read one of the speeches employing persuasive technique in Baird's *Representative American Speeches* or in *Vital Speeches* and make a report to the class on (*a*) attention-getting devices, (*b*) slanting, (*c*) the quality of emotional appeals.

PROJECT 2: DEVELOPMENT OF INTEREST IN THE SUBJECT

Purposes of this assignment: (*a*) To develop knowledge of the techniques of making speeches interesting; (*b*) to develop skill in arousing interest.

Procedure: Select a topic, word a central idea for an informative speech, and outline two or three main points to support the central idea. Develop your main points by using material which applies one or more of the principles for making material interesting (see pages 286ff.). Plan the appropriate methods of delivery for making your speech interesting.

Methods of creating interest: Create interest through selection and development of materials. Show how your subject and materials are important to your audience. Put your material in a narrative form which arouses curiosity about the outcome of the conflicts. Use illustrations in which you can draw vivid word pictures for your audience. Relate the unknown to the known by sharp comparison and contrast. Tell your listeners just enough to suggest the idea with the implication that they can reach the proper conclusion without being told. Use language forms which express feelings and emotions as well as intellectual ideas. Find a humorous side to your material. Keep the development of the main idea obviously moving forward.

Use methods of delivery for creating interest. Be alert, active, and direct. Dramatize, illustrate, visualize with or without use of blackboard and chalk or other materials. Speak forcefully enough and at a proper rate to be clearly and easily understood. Use a voice which responds to the specific moods of your material. Show your own interest in the ideas you are presenting.

Make use of general principles for the development of interest. No topic is inherently dull; speakers sometimes do not take the trouble to help themselves. Never use an interest technique which calls more attention to itself than to the idea to be developed. Audiences may pay attention to sheer noise, anticlimax, highly personal reference in public speeches, unfairness, discourtesy, and other evidence of bad taste or manners, but they will also be irritated. Do not be obvious, trivial, repetitious, or ponderous, and do not go into endless detail.

Standards for judging this project:
  a. Were the materials selected and developed to create interest? . _____
  b. Was the technique of delivery effective in creating interest? . . . _____
  c. Did the techniques of interest force attention to the ideas to be emphasized? . . . . _____
  d. Was the speech logically sound? . . . . _____

PROJECT 3: THE PERSUASIVE APPEAL TO ACTION

Purposes of this assignment: The persuasive appeal to action adds the use of emotional appeal to evidence and logic. Although illogical appeals to action are sometimes made in argument, there is no justification for the use of illogical emotional appeals or for the assumption that emotional appeals must be illogical. Emotional appeals add interest to argument and stir up and release the energies necessary for action on propositions of policy. The student not only should know the technique of appeal to the basic human drives and emotions, but should also learn to apply the principles for creating interest, the devices for achieving emphasis in argument, and the procedures for using language persuasively. Careful selection of a few persuasive techniques adapted to particular listeners or readers is a better method of persuasion than the attempt to use a large number of such devices in a particular argument.

Subjects for this speech:

Buy government bonds	Learn to swim
Join a hobby club	Drive carefully
Sign this petition	Become a church member
Have an annual health examination	Buy a school paper
Read this book	Form new study habits
Keep a budget	Take a course in psychology
Buy Christmas seals	Make government service a lifework
Keep to the campus walks	Contribute to the Red Cross
Write your letters with Scripture ink	

Standards for judging the persuasive appeal to action:

a. Did the argument catch attention and create interest? .... _____

b. Did the reasons offered provide logical as well as emotional appeals? .... _____

c. Did the appeals emphasize long-term rather than short-term drives? ....⟨.. _____

d. Was the speech free from bogus appeals to action? .... _____

e. Did the speaker or writer create respect for himself as a person? _____

f. Were the emotional appeals adapted to particular listeners and readers? .... _____

g. Was the material presented with effective emphasis on important points? .... _____

h. Was the language well chosen for persuasive effects? .... _____

i. Did the argument contain an appealing plan of action? ...... _____

PROJECT 4: THE SPEECH TO RESTRAIN ACTION

Purposes of this project: The speech designed to inhibit or restrain action operates on principles which are quite dissimilar to those which arouse action. It seeks to quiet emotion, create doubt, distract attention, arouse awareness of difficulty, release energies through other channels than that already proposed, and postpone action. It is essentially the refutation of the emotional appeal. Work on these techniques in a three-minute speech.

Subjects for this assignment:

Break the smoking habit	Some don't's of human relationships
Learn to control your temper	Don't take advantage of the little fel-
Don't spend money foolishly	low
Don't speed	Don't walk on the grass
Stop drifting	Curb a licentious tongue

Standards for judging this project:

a. Were the techniques for releasing tensions clearly set forth? ... _____

b. Did the speaker create a desire to avoid action? .... _____

c. Were the reasons logical as well as persuasive? .... _____

PROJECT 5: THE SPEECH OF CONCILIATION

Purposes of this project: The techniques of conciliation in argument are aimed at the attention of the antagonistic listener or reader or the person who has a closed mind on the subject. In the development of the idea and its support, these techniques function not as a substitute for evidence and reasoning, but as a method of handling evidence for a particular type of purpose.

Subjects for this assignment:
Southerners are responsible for the plight of the Negro in the South.
Racial prejudice against minority groups is to be deplored.
Compulsory teacher oaths will not produce better democracy.
The rights of labor must be preserved.
Modern society demands some governmental control of business.
Civil liberties do not excuse citizens from social responsibilities.
Conscientious objectors are not necessarily cowards.
American democracy can be improved.
Religious freedom does not include the right to prevent compulsory vaccination of children.
War crimes cannot be punished as ordinary crimes are punished within a nation.
Progressive education is not a panacea.
New ideas and practices do not always mean progress.
The various Christian denominations have much to learn from one another.
Someone in a position of authority over you has emphatically denied a request. You do not consider the case closed. How would you get a hearing?
A friend takes offense because of some imagined insult. Straighten out the misunderstanding.
You are accused unfairly and maliciously of an act you did not commit. How will you square yourself?
As a committee chairman, you are to present a request to a group in which there is tension and irritation toward the proposal. How will you get a favorable hearing?

Facts and principles you should know to succeed in this assignment: Some of the principal means of arguing in this situation are indicated by the following rules. First, take special care to present your argument in an objective and impersonal manner. Argue calmly, frankly, and simply. These are the facts and this is the way to reason about them to reach this conclusion. Personal interests and wishes are unimportant. Limit your objectives. It is a mistake to try to accomplish too much at once. If a man's mind is closed, the attempt to yank it open may only result in wedging it more tightly shut. Show understanding of and respect for opposite opinions and the persons who hold them. There is no place in this type of argument for blame or censure. Be calm, patient, friendly, and agreeable. Make use of humor if you can without being flippant. Finally, find an indirect way to present your argument. Use arguments which suggest rather than state your conclusion directly. Show personal benefits for your listener which he may have overlooked. Select your subject or situation and proceed to prepare your material. Know your procedure thoroughly and present the speech in a fair and effective manner.

Standards for judging conciliatory argument:
a. Was the case argued objectively and impersonally? . . . . _____
b. Was the argument properly limited for a single argument? . . . . _____
c. Did the argument show respect for those who disagree? . . . . . . _____
d. Was the argument presented in a calm and friendly tone? . . . . _____
e. Were indirect forms of argument used successfully? . . . . _____

References

Brembeck, Winston L., and William S. Howell: *Persuasion,* Prentice-Hall, Inc., Englewood Cliffs, N.J., 1952.

Brigance, W. Norwood: *Speech,* Appleton-Century-Crofts, Inc., New York, 1952, chap. 19.

Bryant, Donald C., and Karl R. Wallace: *The Fundamentals of Public Speaking,* 3d ed., Appleton-Century-Crofts, Inc., New York, 1960, chaps. 17, 19, and 20.

Festinger, Leon: *A Theory of Cognitive Dissonance,* Row, Peterson & Company, Evanston, Ill., 1957.

Gilman, Wilbur E., Bower Aly, and Loren D. Reid: *The Fundamentals of Speaking,* The Macmillan Company, New York, 1951, chaps. 16 and 20.

Hovland, Carl L., Irving L. Janis, and Harold Kelley: *Communication and Persuasion,* Yale University Press, New Haven, Conn., 1953.

Hovland, Carl L., and others: *The Order of Presentation in Persuasion,* Yale University Press, New Haven, Conn., 1957.

Janis, Irving L., and others: *Personality and Persuasibility,* Yale University Press, New Haven, Conn., 1960.

McBurney, James H., and Ernest J. Wrage: *The Art of Good Speech,* Prentice-Hall, Inc., Englewood Cliffs, N.J., 1953, chap. 16.

Minnich, Wayne C.: *The Art of Persuasion,* Houghton Mifflin Company, Boston, 1957.

Monroe, Alan H.: *Principles and Types of Speech,* 4th ed., Scott, Foresman and Company, Chicago, 1955, chap. 21.

Oliver, Robert T.: *The Psychology of Persuasive Speaking,* Longmans, Green & Co., Inc., New York, 1957.

———— and Rupert L. Cortright: *Effective Speech,* Holt, Rinehart and Winston, Inc., New York, 1961, chaps. 20 and 21.

Rosenberg, Milton J., and others: *Attitude, Organization, and Change,* Yale University Press, New Haven, Conn., 1960.

Sherif, Musafer, and Carl L. Hovland: *Social Judgment: Assimilation and Contrast Effects in Communication and Attitude Change,* Yale University Press, New Haven, Conn., 1961.

Thonssen, Lester T., and Howard Gilkinson: *Basic Training in Speech,* D. C. Heath and Company, Boston, 1953, chap. 25.

Young, Paul Thomas: *Motivation and Emotion,* John Wiley & Sons, Inc., New York 1961.

NINETEEN

Discussional Speaking

As YOU DOUBTLESS know, grades, electives, the merits and demerits of Professor C, the outcome of the presidential election, the man-in-space flights, a possible World War III, and any one of a number of other subjects can provoke a spontaneous discussion among students. In the classroom, too, you and your course mates hold discussions, either as part of a recitation or as a spontaneous reaction to a lecture.

Discussion plays an important role in business and industry. In the active management of a corporation, for example, committee systems hold executive sessions and conferences for mutual information and for policy determination. Business discussions are also carried out in sales-promotion meetings, national and regional conferences, conventions of trade associations with common problems.

Participants in community chest and other drives discuss the organization and direction of their campaigns. Community organizations, such as reading clubs, adult study groups, community forums, interracial councils, labor unions, the League of Women Voters, the Young Republican and Young Democratic clubs, constantly employ various types of discussion.

America, more perhaps than any other nation, is organization-minded. Conferences of organizations—educational, industrial, legal, scientific, religious, social, literary—are almost without number. American youth congresses and conferences of college librarians, governors, mayors, church

296

unions, and promoters of higher education, mental health, and art education are illustrative.[1]

Radio and television, too, have been agencies for establishing and extending the popularity of panels, round tables, and audience-participation programs. "Meet the Press," "Youth Faces the Nation," and many other programs have stimulated the discussion of current problems among the millions.

Discussion is important to us mainly because it is a means by which we attempt to solve our public problems. Talking is an essential tool of our democracy. As Macaulay put it, "Men are never so likely to settle a question rightly as when they discuss it freely." [2] The secret ballot by which our public officials are elected is based on free speech, free press, free assembly, and open discussion. As John Stuart Mill stated, "Liberty, as a principle, has no application to any state of things anterior to the time when mankind have become capable of being improved by free and equal discussion." [3]

Modern political discussion developed with the rise of the British parliamentary system, its extension during the seventeenth and eighteenth centuries in Great Britain, and its extension since the late eighteenth century in American local, state, and national legislative bodies. Although critics are rightly alarmed at the threats to our freedom of speech, discussion and debate have steadily advanced in general popularity. The most practicable way to deal with our domestic problems of inflation and deflation, agriculture, labor, industry, social security, and national defense has been to discuss these problems freely both locally and nationally. No tyranny of the majority or gestapolike pressures from certain organizations have diminished or damaged this democratic habit.

On the international front, the United States and the other members of the United Nations have constantly utilized group deliberation. The Austrian peace treaty, the Korean armistice, the North and South Vietnam and the Laos negotiations, the Geneva disarmament discussions, and many other diplomatic and political negotiations have been conducted by discussion and conference, sometimes with constructive results.

What Is Discussion?

Discussion is not mere talking. Conversation serves a useful purpose in promoting good fellowship and exchanging ideas and attitudes, but it does not systematically focus on specific ideas or necessarily solve prob-

[1] See Halbert Gulley, *Discussion, Conference, and Group Process*, Holt, Rinehart and Winston, Inc., New York, 1960, p. 20.

[2] Thomas Babington Macaulay, *Southey's Colloquies*, 1930.

[3] John Stuart Mill, *On Liberty*, Ticknor and Fields, Boston, 1863, p. 8.

lems. Discussion, moreover, is not debate. The debater or arguer, before he faces his audience, has already analyzed the subject, framed his arguments, and made up his mind. He sets out to influence others to accept his proposition.

Discussion, by contrast, has the following distinctive characteristics: (1) Its purpose is to analyze and solve a problem; (2) the method is primarily that of a group activity; (3) it evokes reflective thinking rather than casual emotional reactions; (4) it is deliberative rather than advocative; and (5) it is usually oral communication.

1. *Discussion aims to analyze and solve a problem.* Discussion, distinct from exposition or narration, deals with questions about which people have not made up their minds. The issue may be one of seeking information rather than a pattern of action. "Is manned flight to the moon probable within the next ten years?" is a problem looking for information. This particular question, we admit, covers a wide range of scientific material and can presumably be properly grappled with only by meteorological, astrophysical, geological, and other experts. A simpler question of fact for discussion would be, "Are too many students now being admitted to my college?" (How do we define "too many"?) or "Are we now in for inflation?" (What is "inflation"?) Broad political, literary, and other academic questions of fact are often discussed, such as "Is the Federal Constitution too difficult to amend?" (What is meant by "too difficult"?) "Is C. P. Snow a more important novelist than Ernest Hemingway?" (What is meant by "more important"?)

The issue may necessitate a call for action, such as, "How can we best promote interracial good will in our community?" "What action, if any, shall we take to alleviate the parking congestion at the university?" Note that questions of policy involve also questions of fact. The factual answers in turn lead to the decision-making phase of the discussion.

Several steps are involved in the discussional process. The procedure is to determine and define the difficulty or problematic situation; analyze the most reasonable methods of dealing with it; weigh each proposed solution judiciously; concentrate on that answer which the group regards as the preferred one; and if the problem is one of policy, map out a course of action which reflects the group's conclusions. The aim and method are thus practical.

2. *Discussion is primarily a group activity.* Discussion requires the association of several minds in thinking and acting. The assumption is that group judgments are superior to those of one individual because they are enlightened by the judgments of many individuals. The personality of each individual involved is thus emphasized rather than submerged as individual judgments are inspected and diagnosed objectively. The out-

come of a discussion is thus the result of the collective behavior and performance of the entire participating group. What the group accomplishes as a unit rather than what some especially brilliant individual contributes should be the measure of its success.

Group expression must result from group interaction. All members of the group must participate and mutually react. If you are to chart satisfactory communicative exchange, you should draw lines between all members, rather than simply between the members and the chairman.

For a round table of some six discussants, we would chart unsatisfactory and satisfactory communication thus:

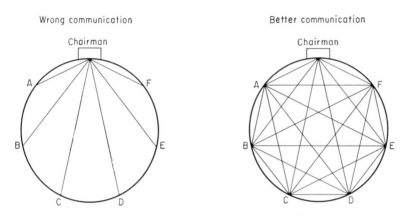

The climate must be one of freedom for each discussant. Not only must there be sustained group interaction, but there also must be a common interdependence and respect for the interests of each discussant. Group decision making should not be a case of "majority rule" but rather of consensus. Although the group is made of individuals, each with his own needs and attitudes, societal objectives must inhere in the judgments. The decisiveness of a few individuals must not dominate the scene and so govern the outcome. Implied in satisfactory group orientation is mutual respect, understanding of the mind and attitudes of the other members, commitment to a principle of equilibrium between individual and group interests, and the resulting consensus.

3. *Discussion evokes reflective thinking as contrasted with undirected emotional responses.* The atmosphere of discussion encourages intellectual activity; it rules out disorganized and aimless mental responses. The purposeful reflective thinker distinguishes assumptions from facts, studies contexts and backgrounds, notes causes and effects, tests authorities and testimony, generalizes in view of the facts, checks his own tendency, and that of others, to mistake assertions for proof and to substitute biases and

prejudices for well-reasoned conclusions. Reflective thinking is characterized by a disciplined attitude and an orderly testing of evidence and argument.

4. *Discussion inquires rather than advocates.* In a mood of inquiry, problems are explored for the purposes of gaining information and achieving subsequent action. The advocate (in argument, debate, persuasion) begins with a proposition and persuades groups to his point of view. Discussion as deliberation is thus entirely different in spirit and method from argument. The advocate is typically a debater or persuader. The discussant, somewhat like the scientist, is typically an inquirer.

We are not here condemning debate. Its purpose and method are different from those of discussion. Once the group arrives at a point where discussion is no longer fruitful, debate may take over in the attempt to secure parliamentary action. Once the debating conclusions are arrived at, discussion may again ensue.

To illustrate the relationship note the following comparison:

Discussion

(The more likely points of conflict, variant conviction, and so of debate are indicated by asterisks.)

1. Explanation of terms.	*Discussion may end and debate ensue.
2. Goals in analyzing and solving the problem.	*Discussion may end and debate ensue.
3. Analysis of the "felt difficulty" or problem—including description of the disturbing phenomena, their causes and results.	*Discussion may end and debate ensue.
4. Statement of hypotheses or probable solutions to be listed.	*Discussion may end and debate ensue.
5. Weighing of solution A.	Discussion may end and debate ensue.
6. Weighing of solution B.	Discussion may end and debate ensue.
7. Weighing of solution C.	Discussion may end and debate ensue.
8. Validation of the preferred solution (A or B or C).	Discussion may end and debate ensue.
9. Determination of a program to implement the solution preferred.	Discussion may end and debate ensue.

5. *Discussion is an oral form of communication.* Discussion is group experience in socialization of thinking accomplished by oral communication. Although oral communication is cheaper and more expedient than

written communication, it is often less carefully thought out. Its advantages are nevertheless obvious for occasions where decisions must be made quickly. By means of discussion, Congress was able to make a declaration of war within a few hours after Pearl Harbor. Because discussion is an oral form of communication, discussants, like other speechmakers, must cultivate vocal skills and visual aids to good speech making.

Typical Forms of Discussion

As we suggested above, discussions occur everywhere—in schools, colleges, churches, business gatherings, community clubs, and over the air—and the term is popularly used to refer to casual conversation as well as to formal group exchanges. In formulating our definition of discussion, however, we have made a distinction between casual conversation and discussion. Now we shall describe seven specific types of discussion with which the student should be familiar and in which he will often engage.

1. *Round-table or informal discussion.* A discussion in which perhaps five to ten people participate without a contributing audience and in an atmosphere of casualness can be called a round table. Although there may be a chairman, he does not function formally. The participants should understand discussion techniques and the purpose of the specific discussion.

Round tables include study groups, the purpose of which is to gain a better understanding of "great books," schools, or colleges; professional groups which convene systematically and regularly for "workshops," with the aim of improving their methods of getting practical results; and business and other briefing sessions, which, however, are often unduly dominated by the chairman of the round table.

2. *Committee discussion.* The purpose of committee discussions is to prepare a report to the larger organization. The discussion is conducted like a round table, but because of the purpose of the discussion, the chairman exercises more control. He sees that the agenda is closely followed, that a secretary records the proceedings, and that the report itself is completed and accepted by the members of the committee. At times he has the members of the group vote in order to determine group wishes. Committee discussions usually have specific purposes.

3. *Panel discussion.* A panel is made up of a chairman and a small group, usually seated around a table, who carry on a discussion before a relatively small audience. The members of the audience should be seated near the panel so that they can hear well. After the panel has completed its main discussion, the audience should participate by asking questions and making comments. At least half of the total time should be given to remarks from the floor, but each of these contributions and its reply by a

member of the panel should be brief. At the end, the chairman summarizes. The success of the occasion will depend partly on the extent to which the audience participates in group thinking.

4. *Dialogue.* In a dialogue, two communicators have a discussion. Informal conversation prevails, but the format is well planned in advance. Again the audience contributes, as in a panel discussion.

5. *Symposium.* A symposium consists of three or four speakers, each of whom is given at least five minutes in which to deliver a prepared speech on a specific phase of a problem. Each speaker must adjust his prepared remarks to the preceding contributions. The purpose of the speakers is chiefly to contribute information and to analyze the issues. After this standardized part of the program is concluded, the chairman and discussion leader will engineer the meeting so that the audience, as in the panel situation, dominates the thinking and discussion. The "American Forum of the Air" approximates this type of discussion.

6. *Public forums.* The panel and the symposium are conducted with small audiences of perhaps 100 or 200. The public forum may have an audience of as many as 2,000 or 3,000. It is difficult to maintain a public discussion with this number of people. The speaker must be an energetic and experienced public speaker who lectures for perhaps thirty minutes, creates an atmosphere of open inquiry, and then invites analysis by the audience (although the chairman may offer the actual invitation) of the issues on which he has lectured. The speaker must create an atmosphere of discussion; if he is a rabid protagonist for a cause or if he propagandizes his audience, the discussion will probably not be very fruitful.

Variations of the forum are the debate forum, in which two sides of the issue are presented; the colloquy or interview forum, in which two spokesmen carry on a dialogue to initiate the discussion with the audience; the symposium in which a number of speakers talk on different phases of a subject before a forum audience; and the film forum, in which a film is followed by audience discussion. Some of the broadcasts of the "New York Town Meeting of the Air" were good examples of the public-forum discussion. Occasionally, however, the broadcasts developed into heated debates and so lost the atmosphere characteristic of reflective group thinking.

7. *Radio and television discussion.* Discussions over the air are not distinct in form or content from the types of discussion we have described; they may take the form of the round table, the symposium, the panel, or the interview. Even the forum can be televised to show the "live" audience in action. However, broadcasting mechanisms and techniques impose limitations and require adaptations that modify the spirit of the discussion. Time limitations, the selection (on some programs) of audience participants, and preliminary rehearsals tend to remove the

element of spontaneity from the discussion. (See Chapter Twenty-one, "Radio and Television Speaking.")

Selecting and Wording the Discussion Question

Subjects for discussion should be of interest and concern to all the discussants. Since the object of discussion is to reach a group decision or to further group thinking, the subject should concern a problem about which the participants must eventually reach a decision. Remember the following principles in selecting subjects:

1. *Select an important question.* For a learning group the educational problem is that of choosing a question that will both interest and educate. Should hours of talk be given to a trivial topic? Mid-week dances or the merits of a "dry" night club are hardly worth the time and energy involved. High school and university students will profit more by grappling with the major issues of war, peace, transportation, and government.

2. *Select a timely question.* In late 1961 the problems much talked about in schools and colleges, over the air, in the press, and in various professional and governmental circles included: Shall the United States vote to admit Red China to the United Nations? Shall the Federal government enact legislation providing substantial aid to public secondary and primary schools? Shall medical care for older citizens be provided as part of the Social Security program? Shall Great Britain, France, and the United States resist by all means the Khrushchev policy of making a separate peace treaty with East Germany?

3. *Select a controversial question.* Be sure that there are at least two defensible points of view connected with the problem. Subjects on which no real difference of opinion exists are expository and do not make for interesting discussions. Avoid also those topics about which debaters long ago made up their minds unanimously.

4. *Select a question either of fact or of policy.* If we argue a question of an event or situation, we aim to establish in our minds the truth or falsity of the alleged fact. Or our practical inquiry may be an attempt to organize a program for solving a given problem. In the first case our interrogation is obviously one of fact; in the second, one of policy. Questions of fact are of two types: those susceptible of proof through objective evidence, and those based largely on subjective judgment. "To what extent does insulin increase the longevity of the diabetic" is a problem settled by gathering and interpreting reliable data. When the investigators penetrate into the political-social-philosophical realm, however, the answers often rest upon value judgments. The significance of alleged evidence and inference will hark back to the discussant's evaluation of justice and injustice, expediency and inexpediency, right and wrong.

These questions of fact concern themselves with the meaning of terms ("What is democracy?"), with comparisons or relationships ("Is congressional government better adapted to a democratic Anglo-Saxon nation than is the parliamentary type?"), or with cause and effect ("Is Soviet propaganda successfully defeating the anticommunistic policies of the United States?").

Questions of policy are of two types: those which focus on general policy-forming principles ("Is the proposal based on sound principles? Is the proposal theoretically advisable?"), and those which by general agreement deal with the specific action ("Shall the United Nations be presided over by a three-member administrative committee?" "Should Johnson County, Iowa, reduce its real and personal property taxes?")

5. *Select a question adapted to the learning level and interests of the group.* Creative writers usually consider problems of composition; committees of the General Assembly of the United Nations consider problems assigned to them for analysis and recommendation; college discussants often deal with a problem determined for them by an intercollegiate forensic association. A town meeting, a unit of the armed forces, a state legislature, or a high school forensic group—all select problems closely related to their interests.

6. *The question should usually be capable of solution.* "Should my fraternity raise its monthly bill of $10?" can be specifically settled on the basis of concrete evidence. Because of our general curiosity and our long-range view of political and other problems, we are also justified in evaluating problems that are less tangible—those in the realm of value judgment.

7. *If possible, select a problem that the group itself can help solve.* Subjects that result in proposed solutions or in action have a great deal of appeal for discussants. If the students believe that college mathematics should be an elective and if the issue confronts the faculty, then a committee of the student council, after deliberation, might frame its opinions as a proposal and consult the faculty curriculum committee. Subjects that evoke extended analysis seem to be of less immediate importance to most discussants and to most audiences.

8. *Limit the question.* Many discussions are futile because the issue is too broad or is vaguely stated. The factor of time may limit the choice of a problem.

A problem such as, "How, if at all, shall the liberal arts program of my university be reorganized?" should be limited to some specific aspect, such as, "Shall courses in plane and solid geometry and college algebra be required of every student in the liberal arts college of my university who has not completed satisfactorily such a course or courses in a secondary school or in another college?" Narrower subjects require more specific information, but they produce better results in discussion.

9. *Always state the issue as an impartial question.* The question form is symbolic of the discussion process and sharpens the direction of the thinking.

10. *Frame the issue clearly.* Vague or ambiguous terms are likely to occur in the phrasing unless an effort at clarity is constantly exercised. "Should my state adopt loyalty as a test of voters?" (What is "loyalty"?) Note the vagueness or ambiguity of the italicized words in the following queries: "Is the Democratic party *distinctly socialistic* in its political policies?" "Are the Republicans on the whole committed to *rank conservatism?*" "Should *fraternal life* be ended on my campus?"

Sometimes the terms beg the question. "Can we *honestly say* that smoking cigarettes is harmful to the lungs?"

Even carefully worded questions sometimes present a problem in word meaning. Many discussions have failed because the terms, seemingly sensible, led to widely different interpretations.

The Framework of Discussion

The typical discussion follows a definite organizational pattern. This arrangement includes six steps which answer the following questions:

1. What do the terms mean?
2. What is the nature of the problem and what are its causes?
3. What conditions will result if the problem is not solved?
4. What are the advantages and disadvantages of each solution?
5. What is the preferred solution? (Synthesize the conclusions arrived at after examination of each solution and emphasize the advantages of the preferred one.)
6. How can this solution be put into practice? (Present a program for putting the preferred solution into action.)

These six questions constitute a plan of development for a question of policy ("What program is to be carried out?"). For a question of fact ("Is cigarette smoking a major cause of lung cancer?"), step 6 should obviously be omitted. This plan of development can be used in any one of the forms of discussion.

Outlining the Discussion

The following skeleton outline for a discussion illustrates how this pattern of organization can be applied to a problem of policy.

The question is: . . .

I. What explanations are needed?
   A. What is meant by . . . ?
   B. What is meant by . . . ?
   C. What is meant by . . . ?
II. Does this question constitute a major economic, social, and political problem that calls for solution?
   A. What are the chief facts or events that created the problem?
   B. What are the chief causes of these disturbing facts or events?
      1. What are the alleged economic causes?
      2. What are the alleged political causes?
      3. What are the alleged social causes?
   C. What are the alleged economic, political, social results of the problem?
III. What are the proposed solutions?
   A. What is solution A?
   B. What is solution B?
   C. What is solution C?
IV. Are the suggested solutions for dealing with this problem satisfactory?
   A. What are the alleged advantages and disadvantages of solution A?
      1. What are the alleged advantages?
      2. What are the alleged disadvantages?
   B. What are the alleged advantages and disadvantages of solution B?
      1. What are the alleged advantages?
      2. What are the alleged disadvantages?
   C. What are the alleged advantages and disadvantages of solution C?
      1. What are the alleged advantages?
      2. What are the alleged disadvantages?
 V. In view of the discussion above, what solution is, on the whole, preferable?
   A. What are the advantages of this solution that indicate its superiority over others?
   B. Does the operation of this preferred solution justify its selection on grounds of practicability?
VI. What program for putting the proposed solution into operation should be set up?

SAMPLE DISCUSSION OUTLINE

Should we endorse the trend toward automation in American industry?

> *Introduction*

I. Is the question important?
   A. Have the rapid advances in electronics and technology made this question important?
   B. Does the recent trend toward mechanization of what was previously accomplished by men's minds and muscles make this question significant?
   C. Has the adoption of automatic devices in wholesale and retail trade, in transportation and communication, in agriculture, in offices, in households, in assembly plants, in data-processing systems brought this question to the fore?
II. What explanations are essential in this discussion?
   A. What is "automation"?
      1. Is it the mechanization of everything that was previously done by muscles and mental activity?
      2. Is it the science of operating or controlling a mechanical process by highly automatic means?
      3. Is it the supervision and regulation of the production process by self-operating mechanical, hydraulic, pneumatic, chemical, electrical, or electronic devices?
   B. What is implied in "endorsement"?
      1. Does it mean approval by those who participate in this discussion?
      2. Does it also imply that this group will support, by speaking, writing, and action, the representative means by which automation is extended throughout American life?
III. Does automation constitute a major problem that calls for solution?
   A. What economic-social-political aims indicate the need for automation?
      1. Is our economic-political goal one of progress?
      2. Is progress dependent on a rising standard of living?
      3. Is a rising standard of living dependent on increased productivity?
      4. Is increased productivity dependent on automation of our industrial life?
   B. What factors contribute to the problem of increased productivity?
      1. Does our increasing population call for increased production?
      2. Are real wages rising?

3. Is consumption increasing through increased purchasing power?
4. Does the cold war stimulate the demand for automation?
5. Do trends in research by both governmental and private agencies contribute to automation?
6. Is the demand for the results of productivity increasing so rapidly that it cannot be met without automation?
7. Is all-out automation necessary in the United States in order to maintain our world leadership?

C. Will means other than automation increase productivity sufficiently to permit us to continue to raise our standards of living?
1. Will the incentive of wage increases (including annual wages) be sufficient for satisfactory productivity?
2. Will improved managerial efficiency, short of all-out automation, be sufficient to ensure increased productivity?
3. Will longer hours for labor increase productivity?
4. Will the leveling off of population, and thus a decrease in demand for goods, be a satisfactory substitute for automation?

IV. Is automation a satisfactory solution of this problem?
A. Will automation be advantageous (or disadvantageous) to management and business?
1. Will automatic machinery diminish costs of production?
2. Will less capital per unit of output result?
3. Will less waste of materials result?
4. Will the products themselves be superior in quality to those otherwise produced?
5. Will only the wealthy corporations be able to afford the change-over to automation?
6. Will less well financed corporations and businesses be ruined?
7. Will automation machinery quickly become obsolete?
8. Will strikes by a few hold up an entire plant more decisively than now?

B. Will automation be advantageous (or disadvantageous) to labor?
1. Will it lead to large-scale unemployment?
2. Will it make man the slave of the machine?
3. Will it reduce seasonal unemployment?
4. Will it reduce worker fatigue?
5. Will the demand for unskilled labor decline?
6. Will it give time for more leisure?

C. Will automation be advantageous (or disadvantageous) to the economic and political interests of the public?
1. Will it increase the standards of living?

2. Will it increase purchasing power and general prosperity?
3. Will it lead to deflation?
4. Will arts and crafts be priced out of existence?
5. Will it promote scientific and technological research?
6. Will it lead to governmental regulation and to dictatorships?
D. Will automation be advantageous (or disadvantageous) to national defense?
   1. Will it improve the equipment and efficiency of our fighting forces?
   2. Will it enhance our military strength as compared with that of the Iron Curtain nations?
E. Will it be advantageous (or disadvantageous) to other countries?
   1. Will it assist in the improvement of underdeveloped nations?
   2. Will automation in the U.S.S.R. and its satellites permit it to capture the world markets?
V. In view of this discussion, is automation, as compared with other solutions of the productivity problem, the most practicable solution?
A. Do the advantages of this solution point to its superiority over other proposals?
B. Is automation on the whole a practicable policy?
VI. What program for putting the proposed solution into operation should be set up (if the policy is approved)?

A Few References

Buckingham, W. S., *Automation,* Harper & Brothers, New York, 1961.

Diebold, John, *Automation: The Advent of the Automatic Factory,* D. Van Nostrand Company, Inc., Princeton, N.J., 1952.

Einzig, Paul, *The Economic Consequences of Automation,* W. W. Norton & Company, Inc., New York, 1957.

Goldberg, A. J., "Challenge of Industrial Revolution II," *The New York Times Magazine,* April 2, 1961, p. 11.

Steele, G., and Kircher, P., *The Crises We Face,* McGraw-Hill Book Company, Inc., New York, 1960.

Woodbury, David O., *Let Erma Do It,* Harcourt, Brace & World, Inc., New York, 1956.

Naturally these steps need not be followed slavishly. You may pass over any step on which all the discussants agree; and you may thoroughly investigate any which represent a significant aspect of your problem.

In your preparation, draw up an individual outline for your private help, answering each of these questions in some detail. This organized preview of the ground that may be covered will give you added insight into what takes place in the group.

Leadership in Discussion

Discussion develops from the participation on an equal footing of the individuals who make up the group. There are no official titles of distinction, no priority in seating arrangements, no set order of speaking, no timing of speeches. Because discussion often requires administration, many groups choose or appoint a leader.

The function of the chairman-leader is to guarantee genuine discussion and to prevent any discussant from impeding the free flow of ideas. Actually, every discussant should be qualified to act as moderator. What special qualifications should a moderator have? He should (1) know the subject to be discussed, (2) be familiar with general discussion techniques and the special techniques required for this meeting, (3) know the audience and understand how small and large audiences behave, (4) have the personal qualities of a successful group leader, (5) be able to extemporize freely, (6) know the discussants and see that a group outline is in their hands before the meeting, (7) create a favorable climate for the discussion, (8) properly introduce the subject, (9) help develop the discussion pattern, (10) use frequent summaries and transitions, and (11) draw out nontalkers and control overly aggressive discussants.

1. *Know the subject.* The discussion chairman must be much more than a figurehead. As chairman, you must know whether the facts are accurately reported and be able to evaluate ideas. You must prepare as thoroughly as the discussants, for it will be your duty to recall the speakers from their byways and to clarify definitions and ideas that become confused or obscured in the discussion.

2. *Know discussion techniques.* Under your guidance, the discussants must function as a unit, focusing in turn on each step of the analysis and demonstrating the values of group thinking. It will be your duty to discourage long-drawn-out questions and replies, to draw out contributors who are worth listening to, and to keep both the speakers and the audience active throughout the discussion.[4]

3. *Know the audience.* Whether you are dealing with an audience of 100 or of 1,000, learn as much as you can about your listeners' ages, sex, occupational interests, education, affiliation with social or professional organizations, probable attitudes toward the subject, fixed beliefs and

---

[4] For a detailed discussion of these techniques, consult, for example, A. Craig Baird, *Argumentation, Discussion, and Debate,* McGraw-Hill Book Company, Inc., New York, 1950, chaps. 20–23.

motives, and training in discussion. This information will enable you to gauge more effectively what is happening during the talking and enable you to bridge the gap between speakers who are specialists and an audience of laymen.

4. *Cultivate personal qualities of leadership.* At the outset you may lead merely because fate or some authority has committed the group to your charge. Ultimately, however, you will remain the leader only if the group has confidence in you, for artificial efforts to govern quickly collapse. Thus, your group must be able to respect your knowledge of the subject and your demonstrated ability to run the meeting. Perhaps even more important is your genuine interest in and understanding of the group's interests.

If the group is small, learn the name of each person present and put him at ease. Introduce the members of the group. Avoid behaving like a monitor.

In addition to being tactful, be open-minded. You need not be a "yes man," but you must give each discussant opportunity to state his ideas. Review in advance the various points of view on the subject, and be tolerant of those you cannot accept.

Purposefulness and enthusiasm for the subject are important qualities in leaders. Listlessness on the part of the leader will engender general stagnation, whereas audiences respond in kind to earnestness and enthusiasm. Do not accept a chairmanship assignment if you are not interested in the problem to be discussed.

Be genial and pleasant, but do not joke. Cooperation and good will thrive in a genial atmosphere.

5. *Practice extempore speaking.* As a discussion leader you will often be called upon for impromptu remarks. You will be required to introduce speakers and answer unexpected questions; you must be able to repeat accurately the queries addressed to a speaker and to amplify both question and answer. You must be able to summarize completely and accurately a meandering one-hour speech.

6. *Learn what you can beforehand about the members of the group; prior to the meeting prepare with them or with a committee of them a group outline to be used as a basis for the discussion session.* Get the names of the speakers and learn as much as you can about them.

7. *Create a favorable climate for the discussion.* Provide favorable physical conditions; arrange the lighting and furniture so that members of the group will be comfortable and in close association with one another.

8. *Introduce your round table or panel to the audience.* If a large audience is present, it is sometimes advisable to place a name tag before each participant (as is often done in television).

9. *Properly introduce the subject.* Show the importance and immediate interest of the topic. Relate a case history or use visual aids to stimulate interest and discussion.

10. *Help develop the discussion pattern.* Limit the problem. See that terms are defined, that the problem is fully analyzed, that goals are clear, that representative solutions are clearly stated and analyzed, that differences of opinion are aired, and that group synthesis is achieved or at least intelligently attempted at the end.

11. *Use frequent summaries and transitions.* Keep your eye on the clock and make the best use of the time at your disposal. Keep the talkers on the subject and use judgment in the amount of time given to each phase of discussion.

12. *Let the discussants do most of the talking.* Good discussion means that all points of view are fully aired.

13. *Draw out the nontalkers and tactfully control the overtalkative and belligerent ones.* It is proper for the critic-observer to note the amount of talking done by each participant. Some have practically nothing to say, but others who are well prepared can contribute much. Equal distribution of time to each participant is often unwise in a round table.

The overtalkative speaker needs checking. The leader may tactfully interpose with, "Since we have only a limited time, will you please condense your point of view?" The comparatively silent one may be drawn out by, "Ralph, can you add anything to what Marilyn has said?"

14. *Continually attempt to relate remarks to evidence and related inferences.* Tactfully call for facts and the sources of facts to support broad statements. Tactfully put to the group the questions concerning the analogies, authorities, generalizations, and causal connections raised by any participant's remarks.

Participation in Discussion

What distinction may we make between the leader and the other discussants? In round tables, the difference is negligible; all are leaders. However, if an audience is created apart from the nucleus of speakers and is definitely separated in seating arrangements and composition from the speakers, then the duties and importance of the leader-chairman become apparent. He is to direct a panel, or introduce a symposium, or control a large audience.

1. *Share in the selection and tentative wording of the subject.* As a panel member, committee member, or forum speaker, you will rightly share in deciding what is to be talked about. Use your influence to limit the subject. If the discussion occupies several periods, as is sometimes the case in learning situations, you will help to reword the issue.

2. *Prepare thoroughly.* Patronize the library. Collect and digest several books and many articles on your topic. Take diligent notes that may be read by others, for no substitute yet has been found for the orderly recording on paper of the gist of your systematic reading.

3. *Prepare an individual outline and, if your group so proposes, a group outline.* At an early point in your study, crystallize your findings and thinking in the form of an individual outline that conforms to the structure and details illustrated in this chapter. This skeleton pattern should be supplemented by a group outline, the product of the panel rather than of a single spokesman.

4. *In the discussion itself cultivate open-mindedness, tolerance, group sensitivity, and cooperation.* Only in an atmosphere of open-mindedness, free from prejudice and dogmatism, will discussion be profitable. Analyze your own attitude as you enter into a situation and abstain unless you have adopted a mood favorable to genuine discussion.

5. *Contribute relevant evidence.* Insist on mustering a sufficient number of pertinent facts to illustrate the point fully and to justify the individual and group generalizations. Check your facts constantly with those of your colleagues. Cite sources easily but without boring details. Don't flounder among your notes.

6. *At every stage reflect principles and methods of sound argument.* Explain why facts and situations are so. Develop your ideas by generalization, analogy, authority, deductive proposition. Question arguments and ideas that seem to you fallacious, but do so with some calmness and tact and with counterevidence. Help to expose bad propaganda. As the discussion evolves, modify your original stand (if you have honestly changed).

7. *Contribute to the organization of the discussional thinking.* Like the leader, you will become a sponsor of the logical pattern outlined in this chapter. You, too, will insist upon definitions, upon statements of goals, upon tracing causes and effects, and upon testing panaceas and specific programs, exposing their weaknesses, validating their foundations. Your summaries, introductory statements, and citation of facts will be an index of your cooperativeness.

8. *Adjust your oral style to that of the group.* You may know other members of the group well enough to use first names. How much you incorporate broken sentences, personal pronouns, and interruptions will depend on the occasion. You will avoid dissolute grammar and mangled syntax. Your language will be free from bromidic triteness or irritating positiveness.

9. *Your delivery should rate well.* Round-table contributors often assume that their discourse is strictly private and that it may be excused from vocal excellence. On the contrary you will have good voice quality.

sufficient loudness, a lively sense of communication, and clear articulation and enunciation; these are the other determinants of desirable delivery. As you move from a private round table to a more public situation —panel, symposium, or larger forum—the demands will be greater. But you will continue to exercise the basic qualities of proper communication before this larger audience.

10. *Be a good listener.* Just as fluent speaking is required, so is genuine listening. Listening does not mean silence. It means active cooperation. You are engaged in a dialogue—or rather a succession of dialogues—as each member of the group speaks and speaks again. Though you are inaudible, you are constantly "feeding back." You should be able to summarize the discussion at any moment.

11. *Ask sensible questions.* Intelligent listening is accompanied by intelligent questioning. Questioning takes place both in the constant give-and-take of a closed discussion session and in the "questions from the floor" by a panel or forum audience. Your interrogations in any case should be short and simply framed. You may call for further information, repetition of a statement, inference from certain data, or additional citation by expert testimony; you may invite a speaker to summarize the state of the controversy; or you may ask specifically, "What should be done about this problem?"

Evaluation of Discussion

How is discussion to be evaluated? What tests do you apply to yourself? How do you judge your skill in analysis, evidence, logic, language, interpersonal relations with the group, and oral communication? How do you measure your general effectiveness? Having a sound knowledge of the problem under discussion, understanding your role as an inquirer after truth and as a cooperative thinker with your colleagues, being able to handle facts skillfully, to reason soundly, and to adjust your delivery and speaking personality to discussion rather than to strong persuasion or debate will make you a highly satisfactory participant or leader in discussional speaking.

Projects and Problems

PROJECT 1

Collect, from printed sources, five or six representative statements from national leaders—educational, political, religious, or otherwise—concerning the value of discussion. Or solicit from former university students testimony of this type. Present your findings in a four-minute report to the group.

PROJECT 2

Topic for informal classroom discussion: What is the place of discussion in our American political society?

PROJECT 3

Topic for classroom discussion: Should we prefer debate to discussion? Or should we endorse and participate in both? Or should we support discussion only?

PROJECT 4

Draw up the outline for a group discussion on a comparatively familiar subject, such as "Shall university dailies refrain from editorial comment on local, state, and national problems?"

PROJECT 5

Suggestion for the instructor: Assign four or five members of the group an informal discussion to demonstrate the principles of group discussion. Allow sufficient time during the hour for class comment on the demonstration.

PROJECT 6

Repeat project 5, assigning to three or four speakers the topics for a symposium.

PROJECT 7

Suggestion for the instructor: Divide the class into discussion groups of five each. Assign a common topic. Have half the class carry out a full-length discussion; have the others serve as critics. At the following meeting reverse the process so that in two meetings each student will have discussed and will have served as a critic.

PROJECT 8

Suggestion for the instructor: Have the class prepare to discuss a currently significant problem. Organization should follow a logical framework: The first hour will be given to (*a*) definitions, goals, and analysis of the problem; the second hour to (*b*) solution A; the third hour to (*c*) another representative solution; and the fourth hour to (*d*) a statement by each student of his solution. The groups will meet simultaneously in several rooms with at least one critic present. A final meeting of the combined groups may be held for application of the "action" step.

PROJECT 9

Suggestion for the instructor: Have the class organize a forum. Let two members present the problem briefly. Have an experienced moderator (if necessary, the instructor) receive and direct remarks and questions from the floor. Observe the techniques and procedures of a large community forum.

PROJECT 10

Suggestion for the instructor: Obtain time on the radio and reproduce over the air the best of the discussions in the projects assigned above.

PROJECT 11

Suggestion for the instructor: Assign a topic to the entire class and have each of six or seven groups prepare an outline. After each group has worked out its outline, have the class confer as a unit and synthesize the outlines. Use the resulting group outline for a classroom forum or panel discussion.

PROJECT 12

Attend a college public-discussion program. Submit to your instructor a 200-word criticism of the leader and of the participants.

PROJECT 13

You have been chosen to organize and prepare a community group for a single discussion on a timely topic. Explain the steps and procedures you would follow.

PROJECT 14

Listen to a radio discussion by your college or university colleagues or by speakers from some other institution. Submit your written criticism to the instructor. Criticize especially the "discussion pattern" of the performance.

References

Baird, A. Craig: *Discussion: Principles and Types,* McGraw-Hill Book Company, Inc., New York, 1943.

Brigance, W. Norwood: *Speech,* Appleton-Century-Crofts, Inc., New York, 1952, chap. 18.

Cortright, Rupert L., and George L. Hinds: *Creative Discussion,* The Macmillan Company, New York, 1959.

Gilman, Wilbur E., Bower Aly, and Loren D. Reid: *The Fundamentals of Speaking,* The Macmillan Company, New York, 1951, chap. 23.

Gulley, Halbert E.: *Discussion, Conference, and Group Process*, Holt, Rinehart and Winston, Inc., New York, 1960.

Haiman, F. S.: *Group Leadership and Democratic Action*, Houghton Mifflin Company, Boston, 1951.

Howell, William S., and Donald K. Somter: *Discussion*, The Macmillan Company, New York, 1956.

Keltner, John W.: *Group Discussion Processes*, Longmans, Green & Co., Inc., New York, 1957.

McBurney, James H., and K. G. Hance: *Discussion in Human Affairs*, Harper & Brothers, New York, 1950.

Monroe, Alan H.: *Principles and Types of Speech*, 4th ed., Scott, Foresman and Company, Chicago, 1955, chaps. 30 and 32.

Oliver, Robert T., Dallas C. Dickey, and Harold P. Zelko: *Communicative Speech*, The Dryden Press, Inc., New York, 1955, chaps. 14 and 15.

Potter, David (ed.): *Argumentation and Debate*, Holt, Rinehart and Winston, Inc., New York, 1954.

Sandford, William P., and W. Hayes Yeager: *Principles of Effective Speaking*, The Ronald Press Company, New York, 1950, chaps. 17 and 18.

Sattler, William, and Edd. Miller: *Discussion and Conference*, Prentice-Hall, Inc., Englewood Cliffs, N.J., 1954.

Thonssen, Lester T., and Howard Gilkinson: *Basic Training in Speech*, D. C. Heath and Company, Boston, 1953, chap. 24.

Utterback, William E.: *Group Thinking and Conference Leadership*, Holt, Rinehart and Winston, Inc., New York, 1950.

Wagner, Russell, and Carroll Arnold: *Handbook of Group Discussion*, Houghton Mifflin Company, Boston, 1950.

TWENTY

Oral Reading

MANY PERSONS speak well and read poorly; others read well but speak poorly. Yet effective oral reading depends upon many of the same factors that produce effective speech. Articulation, voice control, confidence, physical expression, and directness play their parts in both activities. The crucial difference between the two appears to center around the speaker's ability to communicate ideas from another source.

The source of the ideas one expresses in speaking is recollection and the creative imagination. The source of the ideas one expresses in reading is the printed page. Some persons find it easier to express their own ideas. Others, freed from the responsibility of determining what words to use, find it easier to transmit ideas that are already expressed on the printed page. Effective communication requires skills of both the creative and the interpretative types.

Principles of Oral Reading

1. *Understand the common reasons for failure to develop skill in oral reading.* Many difficulties in reading aloud are traceable to the faulty methods by which reading is taught. Monotonous and laborious word-by-word reading often results from learning to read by the flash-card or some similar method. Words are printed on cards, and the student learns what the word looks like on each card; when the word is exposed, he says it aloud. Soon the cards are placed together to form a sentence, and the

student reads the sentence by naming the word on each card. As soon as the student is able to recognize words, oral reading is discontinued in favor of more rapid and less noisy silent reading. The pattern of oral reading followed by persons who learned to read by this method resembles a first experience with printed words. Good oral reading is not a matter of pronouncing individual words.

Other difficulties have their origin in the failure to distinguish between silent and oral reading. Silent reading is often a process of skimming a paragraph or page to get the meaning of a passage as a whole. If the meaning of a word or phrase is not readily apparent, the reader may hurry over it with the hope of getting the meaning from the context. Moreover, much silent reading is recreational reading of light material which can be grasped at a faster rate than more serious instructional material. Although these habits may be appropriate to silent reading, depending upon the reader's purpose, they are destructive to good oral reading when they appear as racing, running words together, and mumbling. Since the listener does not have the benefit of punctuation marks, the oral reader must use techniques of phrasing and inflection to take their place. Rapid and monotonous oral reading often fails completely to convey the intended meaning.

Oral reading differs from silent reading in many ways. In silent reading we are concerned only with getting the meaning for ourselves. In oral reading we wish to share the meaning with others, yet we often assume they will get the same reaction from our saying the words that we get from a well-styled printed page. Oral reading ordinarily requires a slower rate for comprehension than silent reading. The reading speed must, therefore, be adjusted to the distractions and responses of listeners. If we are reading silently and do not immediately understand a word or passage, we can go back and study it. But if we are reading orally, the words must be instantly intelligible to listeners; otherwise the meaning will be lost. If they miss much of a passage, their interest wanes and reading ceases to be communication.

2. *Study the meaning of the material you are to read.* Before you can share ideas, you must understand them. The first step is learning the meaning of unfamiliar words. Remember that many words have more than one meaning and that you must therefore determine the appropriate meaning on the basis of the context. Read with a provisional interpretation of the meaning until the exact meaning is clarified by the context. Study each sentence to find the methods of phrasing which make the meaning clear. Phrasing or word grouping within the sentence is often— but not always—revealed by punctuation. Consider the differences in meaning of the two ways of punctuating or phrasing the following sentence:

The Captain said the mate was drunk today.
"The Captain," said the mate, "was drunk today."

Find the central idea of the passage and keep it in mind as you read. Analyze the purpose for which the material was written. Purpose is frequently revealed by the attitude or mood of the material when it is not clarified by exact statement, and even simple informative prose reveals a great variety of attitudes or moods. The reader must understand and express these prevailing moods if he is to interpret meaning clearly. In studying material to be read, ask yourself if the writer is frank, puzzled, pontifical, cautious, picayune, angry, smug, concerned, sarcastic, flippant, facetious, whimsical, cordial, confidential, sympathetic, fawning, modest, disappointed, aggrieved.

Analyze and evaluate the ideas presented, and judge for yourself the soundness of the causal relationships involved. Ask yourself if the generalizations fit the evidence. Relate the ideas to your own experience in order to interpret their meaning.

Preparation for oral reading should do justice to the importance of the material. Sometimes, however, we find it necessary to read with minimum preparation or at sight. The techniques of analysis which we have discussed apply even to reading on short notice. A brief glance may orient the reader to the more significant aspects of the material. The beginner, however, cannot expect to read well without devoting considerable time to preparation.

3. *Develop an appropriate and flexible rate of reading.* The rate of oral reading must be slow enough for clear comprehension but fast enough so that the listener's attention does not lag. According to one study, the average oral-reading rate for simple informative prose is about 165 words a minute.[1] Experience in observing untrained readers warrants the conclusion that more of them read too fast than too slowly. Reading rates should vary with the reading situation: Light or simple material may be read faster than heavy or complex material; but if the reader's purpose is to give the audience a thorough or exact understanding of the material, the rate should be slower than the rate of reading for amusement. For a large or formal audience, the rate should be slower than for a small informal one. The rate should be adapted to the style, the mood revealed by the material, and the importance of the idea expressed.

4. *Phrase or group the words within sentences to make the meaning clear.* There are three important reasons for careful phrasing. First, units of meaning in oral communication are ordinarily derived from phrases rather than from words or sentences. Second, the shortness of the listener's

---

[1] Frederic L. Darley, "A Normative Study of Oral-reading Rate," unpublished master's thesis, State University of Iowa, Iowa City, 1940.

span of attention may permit him to keep in mind only a limited number of words at one time. If the phrases are long, he may lose track of the sequence of ideas. Third, phrasing helps the oral reader maintain effective control of his breathing for vocalization. Although the first of these reasons is the most important one, the others are also significant.

Phrasing is essentially a process of grouping words together. This is usually done by means of the pause, but other vocal processes, such as varying the rate, pitch, quality, and loudness of different phrases, are also useful in making meaning clear. The pause for phrasing cannot be clearly differentiated from the emphatic pause, since both are used to clarify meaning; but length of the phrasal pause should be adjusted to suggest variations in meaning as revealed by differences in punctuation. Consider the length of various phrasal pauses in the following sentence: "He spoke sharply, but with consideration, to the prisoner; quietly, but with feeling, to his mother; and confidently, but with deference, to the captain." Rules for phrasing cannot be based precisely on punctuation, although the careful study of punctuation will suggest the proper phrasing of many sentences. Overphrasing, or the mechanical breaking up of the sentence into minor units, will only confuse the meaning. Underphrasing is, however, a more common fault than overphrasing.

5. *Effective oral reading requires skill in emphasizing and subordinating ideas.* In spite of the fact that the ideas in any reading passage vary in importance, one of the most common weaknesses or faults of oral reading is monotony. Boredom results from monotony of rate, force, and pitch. The hypnotist uses monotony to put his subject into a trance. The chief purpose of vocal variation, however, is not to catch attention, but to clarify meaning. Rhythmical variations in voice which produce a sing-song pattern may be as monotonous as complete lack of variation. Arbitrary variations for the sake of arousing attention are confusing. The student of oral reading should make a careful study of vocal variation as presented in Chapter Eleven.

Use vocal emphasis to make transitions clear. Climax is achieved by using minor vocal variations in the introduction and more radical variations near the point of greatest emphasis. Descending cadences, moderation of tempo, and softening of intensity are difficult but important techniques for indicating that the conclusion is near. Beware of overemphasis; shouting only irritates and tires the listener. Remember that the repetition of a phrase or sentence in oral reading, as elsewhere, is a good technique for emphasis.

6. *Read loudly enough to be heard easily.* The level of intensity of a bedtime story is not adequate for group reading. Concert pianos are tuned to a higher pitch than chamber pianos to increase the effectiveness of projection. Some sounds in the English language are difficult to hear un-

less the reader uses sufficient force to project them clearly and sharply. Such unvoiced sounds as *f*, *t*, *p*, and initial *th* are especially difficult.

7. *Read fluently and precisely, and pronounce words clearly.* Stumbling over words, reading hesitantly, and random repeating of words or phrases confuse the listener. Learn to anticipate meaning and the inflectional changes necessary to communicate it. Focus words sharply so that you do not fall into the habit of making wrong and confusing guesses at their importance and meaning. Learn to follow the lines of type even as you look up at your listeners. It is better to pause briefly to scan a line than to guess wildly and then find it necessary to repeat and correct the inflections or phrasing.

8. *Learn to read factual materials conversationally and more emotional materials in the appropriate mood.* If you have ever listened to an inexperienced person read from a script in responding to the questions of a radio interviewer you should have a good idea of the objective of this principle. Conversational reading is difficult, but it is a skill which can be developed with practice. The principle of first importance is to keep your mind clearly focused on the meaning to be communicated. Work to respond actively to the ideas you are reading.

Variations in rate, pitch, and loudness will contribute to a conversa-

Two students about to go on the air in a radio broadcast are awaiting their cue to read from manuscript.

tional tone. One phrase may be slowed down and uttered in a light, soft voice; the next may be speeded up, with a marked change in pitch and tonal vigor. All changes must reflect the meaning and mood of the ideas involved.

9. *Good oral reading requires effective adjustments to the materials and situation.* Learn to hold the reading material up so that you can see it clearly and can avoid constriction in your jaw and throat. Do not hold a paper or book in such a way that your face is hidden from your listeners. Be sure that you have adequate light. Practice reading with and without a reading stand. But do not become so engrossed in your materials that you act them out. Respond with facial expression and bodily action to ideas, but avoid distracting mannerisms. Learn to respond effectively to humor without conspicuously laughing at your own jokes. It is possible to read emotionally toned materials in a manner which reveals the mood without immersing yourself in the emotion. Read informative materials sympathetically but objectively; your manner of reading emotionally toned materials will not seem convincing, however, unless you respond to their mood. For example, a ritual would not be effective if read like the routine of a radio comedian.

10. *Adjust the processes of oral reading to your listeners.* The ultimate objective of oral reading is to affect your listeners. Good reading is not exhibitionistic or elocutionary. Keep the social purpose of your reading in mind, and develop the techniques which will achieve it. Think of your work as projection *to listeners* rather than merely reading *from a manuscript.* If your material needs introduction, orient your listeners before you start; do not plunge in and expect them to catch up with you. On the other hand, if some factor in the situation has operated as an introduction and your listeners are ready to hear what you are to read, you do not need an introduction.

Projects and Problems

PROJECT 1: THE ELEMENTARY PRINCIPLES OF ORAL READING

Try reading the following passages aloud in the four different ways suggested. This project should help you to understand better the need for work on the elementary principles of oral reading.

a. Read by saying each word as a separate and distinct entity as if you were showing your ability to recognize each word on a flash card. Observe whether the passage makes sense read in this way.

The — statute — in — question — cannot — be — justified — by — reason — of — the — fact — that — the — publisher — is — permitted — to — show, — before — injunction — issues, — that — the — matter — published

— is — true — and — is — published — with — good — intentions — and — for — justifiable — ends.

b. Read by uttering the words in phrases, pausing only where a slant interrupts the line of print:

If such/ a statute, authorizing/ suppression and/ injunction on such/ a basis, is constitutionally/ valid, it would be equally/ permissible for the/ legislature to provide/ that at/ any time the publishers/ of any newspaper could be/ brought before/ a court, or even an/ administrative officer (as the/ constitutional/ protection may/ not be regarded as/ resting/ on mere procedural/ details) and required/ to produce proof/ of the/ truth/ of his publication, or/ of what he/ intended to/ publish, and/ of his motives, to/ provide/ machinery for/ determining in the complete/ exercise of its/ discretion what/ are justifiable ends and/ to restrain publication/ accordingly.

c. Read as fast as you can without consideration of pauses or inflection:

And it would be but a step to a complete system of censorship. The recognition of authority to impose previous restraint upon publication in order to protect the community against the circulation of charges of misconduct, and especially of official misconduct, necessarily would carry with it the admission of the authority of the censor against which the constitutional barrier exists.

d. Read the following passage with short pauses for single slants and longer pauses for double slants. Read the passage a second time giving slight emphasis to words italicized and greater emphasis to words in boldface type. (Which of the two readings makes the meaning clearer?)

The **preliminary** *freedom,*/ by *virtue* of the *very reason* for its *existence,*// does **not** *depend,*/ as the *Court* has said,/ on **proof** of *truth.*// **Equally** unavailing/ is the *insistence* that the *statute* is designed to **prevent** the circulation of *scandal*/ which tends to *disturb* the *public* peace/ and to provoke assaults/ and the commission of *crime.*// *Charges* of reprehensible *conduct,*/ and in **particular**/ of official **malfeasance,**// **unquestionably** *create* a public *scandal,*// but the **theory** of the *constitutional* **guaranty**/ is that *even* a *more* **serious** public evil/ would be *caused* by *authority* to **prevent** *publication.*

PROJECT 2: THE BASIC SKILLS IN READING ALOUD

Purposes of this assignment: (*a*) To obtain a better understanding of the standards of effective reading; (*b*) to develop skill in reading aloud; (*c*) to provide practice in working on voice problems.

Procedure: Study the material suggested for this assignment until you understand clearly the meaning of the selection as a whole. Look up the meaning and pronunciation of any unfamiliar words. If you have difficulty with phrasing,/ mark off the words/ that are to be grouped together/ as you find them in this sentence. Decide which words in each sentence are to receive emphasis; draw a solid line under words which are to receive strong emphasis and a broken line under words which should be stressed lightly, as has been done in this sentence. Practice reading the selection with a full resonant voice, clear articulation, and a rate which makes it easy to understand the meaning of the passage. When you read in class, concentrate on the meaning of the passage to be communicated to the class.

Materials to be read: Select one to two pages of simple informative prose. It should express an idea you think worth sharing with others.

Facts and principles to be understood to fulfill this assignment: Good reading should sound like good speech. It should have conversational phrasing, rate, and emphasis. The unit of meaning in speech is the phrase; therefore words must be grouped together in phrases by pauses and inflectional changes in a manner which makes each phrase a unit. Learn how to look along the line you read to find the units of meaning, and phrase accordingly. Stumbling, blocking, and distracting repetition can be reduced by good phrasing.

It takes a very good reader to read intelligibly at a rate faster than normal speech. It is better for the inexperienced oral reader to read too slowly than too fast. Remember in oral reading that you are reading for others to understand, not merely to complete the selection. Experiment with varying the rate of different phrases to make your reading sound conversational. A common fault in reading is monotony. Therefore, use the devices of changes in intensity, rate, and inflection to stress important ideas in what you read. Hold your paper out from your body and near the line of your chin or mouth to keep from cramping the articulatory organs. Work on the process of reading to communicate the mood and spirit as well as the exact denotations of the words.

PROJECT 3: PROJECTION

Purposes of this assignment: (*a*) To gain further skill in applying the elementary principles of oral reading; (*b*) to learn to correct points of criticism in your first reading performance; (*c*) to work specifically on effective projection to the audience.

Procedure: Select a passage written to be read or spoken which you have not read aloud before. Be prepared to read about one page. Study the passage carefully so that you understand clearly what it means. Look up unfamiliar words for pronunciation and meaning. Read the passage aloud to work on phrasing, emphasis, and inflection of the sentence, and concentrate on the meaning of the passage as you read. Practice on long words and words or phrases of difficult sound combinations until you can say them clearly and forcefully. If you have a special reading problem, practice to improve your reading in that particular factor. Apply the methods of effective projection to your audience.

Subject: A selection of informative prose of moderate difficulty.

Facts and principles on the projection of material to an audience: Get into a communicative frame of mind by preparing a brief introduction to the selection you are to read to your audience. Good projection requires forceful speech. Learn to throw your energies into your reading without shouting. Effective projection is speech directed at the audience; therefore, keep your chin up. Open your mouth when you speak, and learn to look up from the page at your audience from time to time. Well-projected material is instantly intelligible, hence one should read at a rate which makes it easy for the listener to follow the idea. Be sure to phrase and inflect the sentences carefully and work on emphasis of main ideas by changes in force, rate, quality, and pitch.

PROJECT 4: THE ORAL READING OF CONNOTATIVE LITERATURE

Purposes of this project: (*a*) To learn to interpret the emotional and implied, as well as the intellectual and direct, meaning of a piece of literature; (*b*) to develop a relatively high standard of skill in the oral interpretation of literature.

Subject: Select poetry, an essay, a play, an editorial, or a part of a speech which expresses a deep feeling or emotional attitude.

Procedure: Carefully analyze your rating on earlier reading and practice to eliminate any weaknesses indicated on those reports in your preparation of this project. Study carefully to know the meaning and pronunciation of all words and the implication of references. Analyze the dominant motive of the author in this piece of writing and work to interpret it precisely and fully in reading. In interpreting emotional literature, the voice should be made to respond in force, quality, pitch, and time. An effective interpretation of emotional literature ordinarily requires a response in bodily action which is suggestive of the mood to be interpreted. It will be necessary to use basic skills of fluency, phrasing, timing, and intensity in careful coordination.

Good oral interpretation requires the reader to maintain his own identity as a reader and to avoid exaggeration in his suggestive use of voice and action. To read well, the reader must have assimilated the meaning to be interpreted and have a sincere desire to share the moods of the piece with his audience. He should introduce his reading with a few comments selected to orient the audience toward what is to be read.

Facts and principles which should be understood in fulfilling this assignment: The ability to make a total bodily response while maintaining reserve will contribute to your effectiveness. Vivid awareness of material and responsiveness to your audience will help you attain the goal of this project.

PROJECT 5: HEALTHFUL EXERCISE IN READING WITH EFFECTIVE ORAL PUNCTUATION

Practice reading the following sentences as a study in adapting oral reading to punctuation marks. Your reading material may not always be well written or punctuated. You must determine the intended meaning and punctuate it orally.

The doe was seen four nights running in the woods.
The teacher, said Earl, taught the class skillfully.
The teacher said Earl taught the class skillfully.
Can you pull, Tim?
Can you pull Tim?
The pilot without his life jacket is poorly equipped.

The pilot, without his life jacket, is poorly equipped.

The firing continued, as the tank plunged across the ditch, to hit the mark.

Normal speech requires two or more persons, writing, but one.

Those courses which are not well prepared should be eliminated.

Do your best; it is all we expect of any man.

I will take the duffel—blanket, mattresses, food, and fishing tackle—in the canoe.

You call it propaganda! Better say deceit, exploitation, murder!

He was a tactful (!) man in his thievery.

What in the name of common sense are you doing!

Are these the supermen!

"Why stand we here idle?"

"To err is human—To forgive, divine."

Defeat should teach you the strength of democracy; defeat should give you—but it's utterly useless to expect you to understand it.

Our strength—we must remember—is in our tolerance.

That faraway look in his eyes disturbs me.

His holier-than-thou attitude was certainly not Christian.

He has that "I told you so" smirk of condescension.

PROJECT 6: PRACTICE IN ORAL READING

In consultation with your instructor, choose one or more of the following selections for oral reading before the class. Keep in mind, in preparing and presenting the selection, the exact meaning of the material, the author's philosophy, the background and setting of the reading, the intellectual and emotional mood and purpose of the passage. Be flexible in your rate of reading; phrase the words within sentences to make the meaning clear; properly emphasize and subordinate the ideas; control your loudness level; read fluently and precisely; articulate and pronounce clearly; project rather than merely read; and make the necessary adjustments to the light and other physical conditions.

For most of the speeches listed below, see A. Craig Baird, *American Public Addresses: 1740–1952*, McGraw-Hill Book Company, Inc., New York, 1956.

(a)   The world is too much with us; late and soon,
            Getting and spending, we lay waste our powers:
            Little we see in Nature that is ours;
            We have given our hearts away, a sordid boon!
            The Sea that bares her bosom to the moon;
            The winds that will be howling at all hours,
            And are up-gathered now like sleeping flowers;
            For this, for everything, we are out of tune;
            It moves us not.—Great God! I'd rather be
            A Pagan suckled in a creed outworn;
            So might I, standing on this pleasant lea,
            Have glimpses that would make me less forlorn;

Have sight of Proteus rising from the sea;
Or hear old Triton blow his wreathed horn.
—WILLIAM WORDSWORTH, "The World Is Too Much With Us."

(*b*)   I am loath to close. We are not enemies, but friends. We must not be enemies. Though passion may have strained, it must not break, our bonds of affection. The mystic chords of memory, stretching from every battle-field and patriot grave to every living heart and hearthstone all over this broad land, will yet swell the chorus of the Union when again touched, as surely they will be, by the better angels of our nature.
—ABRAHAM LINCOLN, *First Inaugural Address*, March 4, 1861.

(*c*)   The theory of books is noble. The scholar of the first age received into him the world around; brooded thereon; gave it the new arrangement of his own mind, and uttered it again. It came into him life; it went out from him truth. It came to him short-lived actions; it went out from him immortal thoughts. It came to him business; it went from him poetry. It was dead fact; now, it is quick thought. It can stand, and it can go. It now endures, it now flies, it now inspires. Precisely in proportion to the depth of mind from which it issued, so high does it soar, so long does it sing.
—RALPH WALDO EMERSON, *The American Scholar*, August 31, 1837.

(*d*)   We cannot reconcile Jesus Christ and war—that is the essence of the matter. That is the challenge which today should stir the conscience of Christendom. War is the most colossal and ruinous social sin that afflicts mankind; it is utterly and irremediably unchristian; in its total method and effect it means everything that Jesus did not mean and it means nothing that He did mean; it is a more blatant denial of every Christian doctrine about God and man than all the theoretical atheists on earth ever could devise. It would be worthwhile, would it not, to see the Christian Church claim as her own this greatest moral issue of our time, to see her lift once more, as in our fathers' days, a clear standard against the pagan-ism of this present world and, refusing to hold her conscience at the beck and call of belligerent states, put the Kingdom of God above nationalism and call the world to peace? That would not be the denial of patriotism but its apotheosis.

Here today, as an American, under this high and hospitable roof, I cannot speak for my government, but both as an American, and as a Christian I do speak for millions of my fellow citizens in wishing your great work, in which we believe, for which we pray, our absence from which we painfully regret, the eminent success which it desires. We work in many ways for the same end—a world organized for peace. Never was an end better worth working for. The alternative is the most appalling catastrophe mankind has ever faced. Like gravitation in the physical realm, the law of the Lord in the moral realm bends for no man and no nation: "All they that take the sword shall perish with the sword."—
HARRY EMERSON FOSDICK, *A Christian Conscience about War*, September 13, 1925.

(*e*)   A steadfast concert for peace can never be maintained except by a partnership of democratic nations. No autocratic government could be trusted to keep faith within it or observe its covenants. It must be a league of honor, a partnership of opinion. Intrigue would eat its vitals away; the plottings of inner circles who could plan what they would and render account to no one would be a corruption seated at its very heart. Only free peoples can hold their purpose and their honor steady to a common end and prefer the interests of mankind to any narrow interest of their own.—Woodrow Wilson, *For a Declaration of War against Germany,* April 2, 1917.

(f)   We need not abandon hope or patience. Many favorable processes are on foot. Under the impact of Communism all the free nations are being welded together as they never have been before and never could be, but for the harsh external pressure to which they are being subjected. We have no hostility to the Russian people and no desire to deny them their legitimate rights and security. I hoped that Russia, after the war, would have access, through unfrozen waters, into every ocean, guaranteed by the world organization of which she would be a leading member; I hoped that she would have the freest access, which indeed she has at the present time, to raw materials of every kind; and that the Russians everywhere would be received as brothers in the human family. That still remains our aim and our ideal. We seek nothing from Russia but goodwill and fair play. If, however, there is to be a war of nerves let us make sure that our nerves are strong and are fortified by the deepest convictions of our hearts. If we persevere steadfastly together, and allow no appeasement of tyranny and wrongdoing in any form, it may not be our nerve or the structure of our civilization which will break; something else will break and peace may yet be preserved.

This is a hard experience in the life of the world. After our great victory, which we believed would decide the struggle for freedom for our time at least, we thought we had deserved better of fortune. But unities and associations are being established by many nations throughout the free world with a speed and reality which would not have been achieved perhaps for generations. Of all these unities the one most precious to me is, to use an expression I first used at Harvard six years ago, the one most precious to me is the fraternal association between the British Commonwealth of Nations and the United States. Do not, my friends, I beg of you, underrate the enduring strength of Britain. As I said at Fulton, "Do not suppose that half a century from now you will not see seventy or eighty millions of Britons spread about the world and united in defense of our traditions, our way of life, and the world causes which you and we espouse." United we stand secure.

Let us then move forward together in discharge of our mission and our duty, fearing God and nothing else.—Winston Churchill, Address at Boston, Massachusetts, March 31, 1949.

(g)   O Lord our Lord, how excellent is thy name in all the earth: who hast set thy glory above the heavens!

Out of the mouths of babes and sucklings hast thou ordained strength because of thine enemies: that thou mightest still the enemy and the avenger.

When I consider thy heavens, the work of thy fingers: the moon and the stars, which thou hast ordained;

What is man, that thou art mindful of him: and the son of man, that thou visitest him?

For thou hast made him a little lower than the angels: and hast crowned him with glory and honour.

Thou madest him to have dominion over the works of thy hands: thou hast put all things under his feet;

All sheep and oxen: yea, and the beasts of the field;

The fowl of the air, and the fish of the sea: and whatsoever passeth through the paths of the seas.

O Lord our Lord: How excellent is thy name in all the earth!

—*Psalm 8.*

(h)   What is education? Above all things, what is our ideal of a thoroughly liberal education?—of that education which, if we could begin life again, we would give ourselves?—of that education which, if we could mold the fates to our own will, we would give our children? Well, I know not what may be your conceptions upon this matter but I will tell you mine, and I hope I shall find that our views are not very discrepant.

Suppose it were perfectly certain that the life and fortune of every one of us would, one day or other, depend upon his winning or losing a game at chess. Don't you think we should all consider it to be a primary duty to learn at least the names and the moves of the pieces; to have a notion of a gambit, and a keen eye for all the means of giving and getting out of check? Do you not think that we should look with a disapprobation amounting to scorn upon the father who allowed his son, or the state which allowed its members, to grow up without knowing a pawn from a knight? . . .

Well, what I mean by education is learning the rules of this mighty game. In other words, education is the instruction of the intellect in the laws of nature, under which name I include not merely things and their forces, but men and their ways; and the fashioning of the affections and of the will into an earnest and loving desire to move in harmony with those laws. For me education means neither more nor less than this.—THOMAS HENRY HUXLEY, "What Is Education?" from *A Liberal Education and Where to Find It,* 1868.

(i)   They tell us, sir, that we are weak; unable to cope with so formidable an adversary. But when shall we be stronger? Will it be the next week, or the next year? Will it be when we are totally disarmed, and when a British guard shall be stationed in every house? Shall we gather strength by ir-resolution and inaction? Shall we acquire the means of effectual resistance by lying supinely on our backs, and hugging the delusive phantom of hope, until our enemies shall have bound us hand and foot? Sir, we are not weak, if we make a proper use of the means which the God of nature hath placed in our power. Three millions of people, armed in the holy cause of liberty, and in such a country as that which we possess, are invincible by any force which our enemy can send against us. Besides, sir, we shall not fight our battles alone. There is a just God who presides over the destinies of nations; and who will raise friends to fight our battles for us. The battle, sir, is not to the strong alone; it is to the vigilant, the active, the brave. Besides. sir, we have no election. If we were base enough to desire it, it is now too late to retire from the contest. There is no retreat but in submission and slavery! Our chains are forged! Their clanking may be heard on the plains of Boston! The war is inevitable—and let it come! I repeat it, sir, let it come! —Patrick Henry, *Liberty or Death*, March 23, 1775.

(*j*)   I am closing my fifty-two years of military service. When I joined the army. even before the turn of the century, it was the fulfillment of all of my boyish hopes and dreams. The world has turned over many times since I took the oath at West Point, and the hopes and dreams have all since vanished, but I still remember the refrain of one of the most popular barracks ballads of that day which proclaimed most proudly that old soldiers never die; they just fade away. And like the old soldier of that ballad, I now close my military career and just fade away, an old soldier who tried to do his duty as God gave him the light to see that duty. Good-by.—Douglas MacArthur, Address before Congress, April 19, 1951.

(*k*)   All the world's a stage,
And all the men and women merely players:
They have their exits and their entrances;
And one man in his time plays many parts,
His acts being seven ages. At first the infant,
Mewling and puking in the nurse's arms.
Then the whining school-boy, with his satchel,
And shining morning face, creeping like snail
Unwillingly to school. And then the lover,
Sighing like furnace, with a woeful ballad
Made to his mistress' eyebrow. Then a soldier,
Full of strange oaths and bearded like the pard,
Jealous in honor, sudden and quick in quarrel,
Seeking the bubble reputation
Even in the cannon's mouth. And then the justice,
In fair round belly with good capon lin'd,
With eyes severe, and beard of formal cut,
Full of wise saws and modern instances;
And so he plays his part. The sixth age shifts
Into the lean and slipper'd pantaloon,
With spectacles on nose and pouch on side,
His youthful hose well sav'd, a world too wide
For his shrunk shank; and his big manly voice,
Turning again toward childish treble, pipes
And whistles in his sound. Last scene of all,

That ends this strange eventful history,
Is second childishness and mere oblivion,
Sans teeth, sans eyes, sans taste, sans everything.
—WILLIAM SHAKESPEARE, Soliloquy of Jacques from *As You
Like It*, II, vii.

(*l*)   My Friends: No one, not in my situation, can appreciate my feeling of
sadness at this parting. To this place, and the kindness of these people, I
owe everything. Here I have lived a quarter of a century, and have
passed from a young to an old man. Here my children have been born,
and one is buried. I now leave, not knowing when or whether ever I may
return, with a task before me greater than that which rested upon Washington. Without the assistance of that Divine Being who ever attended
him, I cannot succeed. With that assistance, I cannot fail. Trusting in
Him who can go with me, and remain with you, and be everywhere for
good, let us confidently hope that all will yet be well. To His care com-
mending you, as I hope in your prayers you will commend me, I bid you
an affectionate farewell.—ABRAHAM LINCOLN, Farewell Address at Springfield, Illinois, February 11, 1861.

(*m*)   . . . You owe a duty to the public, as well as to the prisoner at the bar.
You cannot presume to be wiser than the law. Your duty is a plain,
straight-forward one. Doubtless we would all judge him in mercy. Towards
him, as an individual, the law inculcates no hostility; but towards him, if
proved to be a murderer, the law, and the oaths you have taken, and
public justice, demand that you do your duty.

With consciences satisfied with the discharge of duty, no consequences
can harm you. There is no evil that we cannot either face or fly from, but
the consciousness of duty disregarded. A sense of duty pursues us ever. It
is omnipresent, like the Deity. If we take to ourselves the wings of the
morning, and dwell in the uttermost parts of the sea, duty performed, or
duty violated, is still with us, for our happiness or our misery. If we say
the darkness shall cover us, in the darkness as in the light our obligations
are yet with us. We cannot escape their power, nor fly from their presence.
They are with us in this life, will be with us at its close; and in that scene
of inconceivable solemnity, which lies yet farther onward, we shall still
find ourselves surrounded by the consciousness of duty, to pain us
wherever it has been violated, and to console us so far as God may have
given us grace to perform it.—DANIEL WEBSTER, *Address to the Jury*,
Knapp-White Murder Case, August 8–20, 1830.

(*n*)   Speak gently, Spring, and make no sudden sound;
For in my windy valley yesterday I found
New-born foxes squirming on the ground—
                    Speak gently.

Walk softly, March, forbear the bitter blow;
Her feet within a trap, her blood upon the snow,
The four little foxes saw their mother go—
                    Walk softly.

Go lightly, Spring—oh, give them no alarm;
When I covered them with boughs to shelter them from harm,
The thin blue foxes suckled at my arm—
　　　　Go lightly.

Step softly, March, with your rampant hurricane;
Nuzzling one another, and whimpering with pain,
The new little foxes are shivering in the rain—
　　　　Step softly.
　　　　　　　　　—LEW SARETT, "Four Little Foxes."

(*o*)　A vision of the future rises:

I see our country filled with happy homes, with firesides of content,—the foremost land of all the earth.

I see a world where thrones have crumbled and where kings are dust. The aristocracy of idleness have perished from the earth.

I see a world without a slave. Man at last is free. Nature's forces have by Science been enslaved. Lightning and light, wind and wave, frost and flame, and all the secret, subtle powers of earth and air are the tireless toilers for the human race.

I see a world at peace, adorned with every form of art, with music's myriad voices thrilled, while lips are rich with words of love and truth; a world in which no exile sighs; no prisoner mourns; a world on which the gibbet's shadow does not fall; a world where labor reaps its full reward, where work and worth go hand in hand, where the poor girl trying to win bread with the needle—the needle that has been called "the asp for the breast of the poor"—is not driven to the desperate choice of crime or death, of suicide or shame.

I see a world without the beggar's outstretched palm, the miser's heartless, stony stare, the piteous wail of want, the livid lips of lies, the cruel eyes of scorn.

I see a race without disease of flesh or brain—shapely and fair—the married harmony of form and function—and as I look, life lengthens, joy deepens, love canopies the earth; and over all, in the great dome, shines the eternal star of human hope.—ROBERT G. INGERSOLL, *Decoration Day Address*, May 30, 1888.

(*p*)　While American labor will continue to foster and maintain a frankly critical spirit and constructive attitude towards our own political, social, and economic weaknesses and shortcomings, and we have them, and we intend to fight against them, we will at the same time intensify our activities to help strengthen the ranks of free labor and of other democratic forces abroad. We not only welcome the recent setbacks to Communism in Italy, India, Germany, and in other countries, but will continue every possible effort to still further advance this process of disintegration now taking place there and elsewhere.

It is our firm conviction that only America is strong enough to discourage, to defeat, and to destroy the aggressors and enemies of world peace. It is our definite belief that this is the historical mission of America to the human race. It is our determination to hold ourselves in readiness at all times to make available American know-how in health, industry, and self-government on a world scale to the economically underdeveloped countries and regions of the world, and to render every service possible to humankind.

In the field of ideology, the A. F. of L. and the American labor movement will redouble its efforts to advance the ideals of democracy and peace as against dictatorship and war, of freedom of enterprise as against state control, of freedom of expression and worship as against fear of persecution and intolerance.

Our enemy is strong, shrewd, and ruthless. Our enemy has a global approach. We will meet and defeat this enemy, not only by military force, but by all other economic, social, cultural, and political measures and weapons at our command and thus hold secure and advance human freedom and human well-being.

American labor has full confidence in the ability of our country and its people to provide dynamic and inspiring leadership in this world struggle for human freedom. In that struggle, the trade and labor organizations of our land will contribute more than their share to help our nation to perform its historical mission, and rally world labor for the triumph of freedom, of democracy, and of peace over tyranny, despotism, and war.

One final observation, and that is this: No matter what avocation we may follow, no matter what trade or occupation we may be engaged in, as Americans let us be happy that we are here, whether as native or foreign-born, for no other nation the world has ever known has offered the great heritage that is yours and mine—the heritage of freedom, the heritage to express ourselves as we please, the heritage of working out our problems as God intended they should be worked out, by the exchange of opinions, by understanding, by mutual cooperation. May that ever be so! God bless America, and may its blessings extend all over the world in the not far distant future!

Thank you, indeed, for this opportunity of presenting these few observations to you.—Philip Murray, *Labor's Role in Higher Education.*

(q)   . . . Science seems ready to confer upon us, as its final gift, the power to erase human life from the earth.

At such a time in history, we who are free must proclaim anew our faith.

This faith is the abiding creed of our fathers. It is our faith in the deathless dignity of man, governed by eternal moral and natural laws. This faith defines our full view of life. It establishes, beyond debate, those gifts of the Creator that are man's inalienable rights, and that make all men equal in His sight.

In the light of this equality, we know that the virtues most cherished by free people—love of truth, pride of work, devotion to country—all are treasures equally precious in the lives of the most humble and of the most exalted. The men who mine coal and fire furnaces and balance ledgers and turn lathes and pick cotton and heal the sick and plant corn, all serve as proudly, and as profitably, for America as the statesmen who draft treaties or the legislators who enact laws.

This faith rules our whole way of life. It decrees that we, the people, elect leaders not to rule but to serve. It asserts that we have the right to choice of our own work and to the reward of our own toil. It inspires the initiative that makes our productivity the wonder of the world. And it warns that any man who seeks to deny equality in all his brothers betrays the spirit of the free and invites the mockery of the tyrant.—DWIGHT D. EISENHOWER, *Inaugural Address,* January 20, 1953.

(*r*)   Let us remember also that the first of the seven deadly sins is spiritual pride: the sin which assures me that I know and you don't, so that I give myself permission to use any dubious or dishonest means to discredit your opinion. Because we have always thought of government as friendly, not as brutal, character assassins and slanderers in the Congress of the United States have a free hand in the methods they use. We never foresaw that the cult of thought-control and of the big lie would come to America. So if their conscience permits, they can say almost anything. And if my opponent's conscience permits, he can try to help all of them get re-elected. But will he have strengthened or weakened the American idea?

For this is no small thing, this remorseless attack upon freedom of conscience, freedom of thought. A few peddlers of hate and fear would be of little consequence if they had not been welcomed as satellites by Senator Taft and included in the leadership of this strange crusade. And none of them would be significant if the General—who was implored to come home by Republican leaders so that they might be quit of Senator Taft—had not yielded to the demands of his beaten foe. But because of that surrender, because of those strange allies in his queer crusade, our role in world history, our faithfulness to the men who made the United States, is challenged in this election.

Finally, then, let us recall that our basic faith in liberty of conscience has an ancient ancestry. We can trace it back through Christian Europe, and through pagan Rome, back to the Old Testament prophets. It is by no means exclusive with us. It is in fact our bond of unity with all free men. But we are its ordained guardians today.

Let us lift up our hearts, therefore—glad of our strength, proud of the task it imposes. So far from being half-defeated, half-divided, half-bankrupt—while we are true to ourselves we can never be defeated; while we accept the honorable burden of leadership, we can never be divided. And in the name of that burden we shall find the means and the determination to spend in money and in labor and in hard thought whatever is needed to save ourselves and our world.—ADLAI E. STEVENSON, *America's Role,* Address at Salt Lake City, October 14, 1952.

(*s*)   To-morrow, and to-morrow, and to-morrow,
Creeps in this petty pace from day to day,
To the last syllable of recorded time;
And all our yesterdays have lighted fools
The way to dusty death. Out, out, brief candle!

Life's but a walking shadow; a poor player
That struts and frets his hour upon the stage
And then is heard no more: it is a tale
Told by an idiot, full of sound and fury,
Signifying nothing.

—SHAKESPEARE, *Macbeth*, V, v.

(t)   This message, Mr. President, comes to you from consecrated ground. Every foot of the soil about the city in which I live is sacred as a battleground of the Republic. Every hill that invests it is hallowed to you by the blood of your brothers, who died for your victory, and doubly hallowed to us by the blood of those who died hopeless, but undaunted, in defeat—sacred soil to all of us, rich with memories that make us purer and stronger and better, silent but staunch witnesses in its red desolation of the matchless valor of American hearts and the deathless glory of American arms—speaking an eloquent witness in its white peace and prosperity to the indissoluble union of American states and the imperishable brotherhood of the American people.—HENRY GRADY, *The New South*, December 22, 1886.

References

Aggertt, Otis J., and Elbert R. Brown: *Communicative Reading*, The Macmillan Company, New York, 1956.

Cobin, Martin: *Theory and Technique of Interpretation*, Prentice-Hall, Inc., Englewood Cliffs, N.J., 1959.

Crocker, Lionel, and Louis M. Eich: *Oral Reading*, Prentice-Hall, Inc., Englewood Cliffs, N.J., 1955.

Cummingham, C. C.: *Literature as a Fine Art*, Thomas Nelson & Sons, New York, 1941.

Dolman, John, Jr.: *The Art of Reading Aloud*, Harper & Brothers, New York, 1956.

Lee, Charlotte: *Oral Interpretation*, Houghton Mifflin Company, Boston, 1952.

Lowrey, Sarah, and Gertrude Johnson: *Interpretative Speech*, Appleton-Century-Crofts, Inc., New York, 1942.

Parrish, W. M.: *Reading Aloud*, 3d ed., The Ronald Press Company, New York, 1953.

Robb, Mary M.: *Oral Interpretation of Literature*, The H. W. Wilson Company, New York, 1941.

Thonssen, Lester T., and Howard Gilkinson: *Basic Training in Speech*, D. C. Heath and Company, Boston, 1953, chap. 22.

Tressider, Argus: *Reading to Others*, Scott, Foresman and Company, Chicago, 1940.

Woolbert, C. H., and Severina Nelson: *The Art of Interpretative Speech*, 4th ed., Appleton-Century-Crofts, Inc., New York, 1956.

PART FOUR

SPECIAL SPEECH

TYPES

TWENTY-ONE

Radio and Television

Speaking

The Television Age

INVENTIONS IN the field of electronics have projected the human voice and human image over tremendous distances. Patrick Henry in his "Call to Arms" and his debates against ratification of the Federal Constitution probably never spoke to groups of more than a few hundred. Even President Lincoln, in his First Inaugural Address, could be heard by only a fraction of the excited crowd of some fifty thousand which thronged Washington. By contrast President John F. Kennedy, on January 20, 1960, communicated by radio and television with millions upon millions of persons both in the United States and overseas.

With the coming of radio after World War I and the expansion of television after World War II, the audience for a single act of speech making has expanded tremendously. According to the Radio Advertising Bureau some 56 million radio receivers were in working order in this country in 1960, and the number is steadily increasing. In 1960, more than 52 million television sets were operating in American homes. There were some 5,000 amplitude modulation (AM) and frequency modulation (FM) radio stations. In addition, 600 TV stations were operating commercially. According to the American Research Bureau, some 38

339

million persons listened to and saw much of the Democratic and Republican National Conventions of July, 1960.

In the presidential campaign the two major candidates, Vice President Richard Nixon and Senator John F. Kennedy, engaged in four debates at prime evening listening hours. Major television networks and radio stations carried these discussions to unnumbered Americans. More than 80 million persons tuned in to hear the election night returns and speech making of November 8.

Commercial television today offers many programs classified as "educational." There are short persuasive speeches that support a product or idea (e.g., American Red Cross), news reports and commentaries, interviews, weather programs, discussions of current problems, serial programs giving formal instruction on a particular subject, documentary or controversial talks, demonstration programs, religious talks, travel talks, comments on plays and books, political campaign speeches, and speeches by local, state, or national government leaders.

By 1961 about sixty stations were operating under educational licenses. Various colleges and universities have their own radio or television outlets (for example, WOI–TV at Iowa State University, Ames, Iowa; and WSUI–Radio at the State University of Iowa, Iowa City, since 1924). Many universities offer student training in radio-television and make use of these media in classroom instruction. Discussional programs may include student speakers. Such programs include "What Do You Think?" "Youth Faces the Nation," "Books on Trial," "The Whole Town's Talking." In 1959, the Federal Communications Commission approved an experiment in which school programs in six Midwestern states are transmitted over eight ultra-high-frequency TV channels, with airplanes being used as relay stations. These and later similar programs suggest the ever-widening methods of televising both educational and other programs.

Adjustment to Radio Speaking

Radio speaking is not unlike speaking before a live audience. The qualities that are important in the speech and in the speaker and the purposes and types of talks are the same for both situations.

What then are the differences? The radio performer has two problems which the ordinary speaker does not have: (1) the mechanical problem of speaking through a microphone and (2) the problem of adjusting to an invisible audience that, indeed, may not even exist. Speakers who perform before a "mike" quickly discover that they must make important adjustments in subject, details, organization, language, and delivery. Even the radio studio may cause the speaker to feel constricted at first. Hand signals advise him to move nearer to the mike, to slow down, to "get on the beam" (in direct line with the microphone), to "bring it up" to greater volume, to respond properly to the various cues, or "to stretch it out." Or he may find it hard to avoid rattling his manuscript or coughing into the microphone.

Since the radio audience is invisible, it is elusive and hard to judge. Your immediate family may be listening to you, but what of the housewives, farmers, businessmen, students, and others within range of your station? Will they listen to you when they have the option of hearing dance music, a news commentary, a baseball game, or a dramatic skit during the same fifteen-minute interval? Even assuming that they do not turn the dial to another program, what assurance have you that they approve of what you say? Your audience is made up of a number of individuals or groups of two or three scattered over a wide territory. How can you weld these individuals together so that they form an audience who share your purpose and react to your appeals?

ADJUST TO YOUR AUDIENCE

Be sure you understand the kind of audience you are to address. Sometimes you may be addressing the entire audience of the station over which you broadcast—when you make a Red Cross appeal, for example. Usually, however, the program in which you participate will be a regular feature and will have a steady following. Sometimes your sponsors may organize in advance a specific group of people who are to be your audience; advance notice to high school debaters that you will argue for or against the national high school question of the year will usually provide you with critical and interested listeners.

In any case, imagine that you are addressing a specific group—high school or college students with whom you are acquainted, your family, and others who have assured you that they will listen. If you direct your remarks to these sample hearers, you will no doubt interest other individuals who discover your talk by chance. Study the audience techniques of President Franklin D. Roosevelt, who became a master at appealing to immense numbers without sacrificing the content that held the attention of more sophisticated Americans.

As in nonradio speaking, your subject and your treatment of it will depend upon the character of your audience and the immediate occasion. Radio, however, is a public utility, and American broadcasters have developed a code to be followed by those who use the air. The best way to protect and promote freedom of speech over the air is to demonstrate good taste and respect for the various groups whose members your talk may reach. Avoid caricaturing, and be respectful of the sincere faith of others.

Display a well-balanced personality. Although audiences like a good show and are occasionally amused by a petulant or bellicose speaker, they do not take him seriously. They will expect you, a college student, to exhibit the traits of an educated person. They object to bitter sarcasm, to artificial humor, and to patronizing aloofness.

ORGANIZE YOUR TALK

Like members of visible audiences, radio audiences respond to clarity and good organization. Do not overdo point-by-point enumeration, but make use of repetition and summaries, since many listeners will hear only a part of your speech. President Roosevelt seldom made the skeleton of his discourse prominent, as President Hoover often did; but Roosevelt amplified and repeated so successfully that the continuity was seldom in doubt.

Make your speech brief. Unless the treatment is compact and the effects quickly obtained, radio audiences are likely to lose interest after fifteen minutes.

Write and rewrite your speech. Radio managers will usually ask for a copy of your speech in order to check its length and content. In writing your speech, however, remember that it is to be delivered orally—that it is not a composition or essay. Read it aloud and study its phrasing. Record it, if possible, and study the playback.

Use an attention-getting beginning, and make your ending quick and simple with a summary or an appeal for endorsement of your position.

Use simple rather than complex sentences. Limit their length to about twenty words, but vary their internal structure. Use periodic sentences and parallel constructions; use questions and exclamations, and occasionally the imperative mood.

Your style should be colorful, clear, and concise. Avoid abstract, hackneyed, and pedantic terms; use figurative and connotative language. Do not use clichés: "each and every," "it may interest you to know," "man in the street," "average American," "give their all," "our boys," and many other such expressions produce only "dead spots" in communication.

Prepare your manuscript for easy reading. See that the copy is typed in capitals and double-spaced, and that almost every sentence is a paragraph. Be sure that it is free from cancellations or other marks that may confuse you. Use only one side of the sheets, and do not clip or fold them. Arrange the sheets in order and number them. Arrange the end of your manuscript so that you will have accomplished your purpose even if you are cut off before you complete the speech. Face the clock as you talk, and watch for the director's cutoff sign—his finger drawn across his throat.

Edward R. Murrow, Director of the U.S. Information Agency, must do much talking about talking in his job. (Columbia Broadcasting System.)

Read the manuscript conversationally, and avoid the effect of reading. Read as though you were talking with friends and entirely free from the pages before you. Edward R. Murrow, when he presented his speech on "Improved Communication for Better Understanding" to the Poor Richard Club talked as informally as if he had no manuscript before him.[1]

Study the effects of intonation on individual words and phrases. Underscore phrases that you wish especially to stress. You need not follow the manuscript word for word. Experienced speakers interpolate phrases and omit or change the phrasing to conform to the mood or requirements of the situation.

CULTIVATE A DESIRABLE RADIO VOICE

NBC, Mutual, CBS, and ABC all specify that the radio speaker should "speak clearly and without affectation." Begin by making the most of

[1] See Appendix C.

your own normal tones and vocal inflections. Do not imitate well-known speakers. Remember that your purpose is to present an idea rather than to exhibit a striking voice. You should, however, increase your skill in voice production constantly.

Radio-station managers state that a baritone voice is more effectively transmitted on the radio than a high tenor voice, since radio transmission tends to emphasize the higher frequencies. However, sopranos and tenors may improve their tonal transmission by retarding their speaking rate, since fast speaking often causes a rise in tone. At the same time, avoid a pitch level that is too low and sounds throaty and "muddy."

How fast should you talk? Your speed should be the rate that is natural for you. If the listeners feel that your speech drags, they may conclude that you are uncertain of what you want to say. A speed of 130 to 150 words per minute is normal, but much depends upon the natural rate of the speaker, the nature of the speech, and the audience. Many news commentators speak at a rate of 170 or more words per minute.

The control man will mechanically regulate intensity so that you can be heard. Nevertheless, you will sometimes be required to speak louder or softer, since mechanical amplification or modification of your intensity may produce distorted tones.

Avoid extremes of vocal stress. Dramatic whispering and convention-hall shouting are equally out of place in a radio speech. Follow the counsel of the studio guide. Talk as though your audience were about 4 feet away. Find out whether your microphone is one-directional, two-directional, or nondirectional, keep an even distance from it, and produce a fairly constant volume. Your tones should keep the indicator oscillating over an even span.

Gesturing and bodily action are necessary. Whether or not there are others at the table with you in the studio, do not inhibit your ideas or voice by restraining your physical actions.

Articulate clearly and pronounce acceptably. Review Chapter Twelve and apply these principles in radio speaking. The fact that your pronunciation is that of the East, the South, or the Middle West should not particularly worry you. Within reasonable limits, however, work for the articulation and pronunciation that is considered typically American.

Careful preparation is the best insurance against "mike fright." Arrive at the station in due season; then relax and talk about irrelevant matters. Assume a casual manner and try to realize that you are merely talking as you have done on hundreds of previous occasions.

Use recordings. Radio stations and many departments of speech are equipped to record your voice. Obtain a recording of your speech and study it critically to determine the areas in which you need drill. Note carefully your pronunciation, articulation, speed, and conversational quality. Good recordings will enable you to be your own critic.

Adjustment to Television

Although many of the principles of radio speaking apply to television, additional limitations are imposed by the television camera. Timing, for example, presents an additional problem. Television performers must reckon with the time required to convey to the viewer the physical movements that accompany the voice (as when a speaker moves to a blackboard and diagrams his explanation). Space creates another limitation. Participants must keep within camera range and be sure that what the director aims at is now close-up, now more distant, "shots." A third factor peculiar to television is lighting. Shadows and bad contrasts can mar the visual effect. Television also involves a sound limitation; if the performers move about, the microphone must pick up sounds that are constantly changing direction.

The following suggestions should help you in preparing and presenting a television talk:

1. *Keep before you your motivative aims and methods.* You are to capture immediate attention and hold it. You will therefore make your ideas clear at every stage; you will impress them so strongly that they will be retained; and you will secure effective response, either the approval of your informational thesis (if that is your goal) or action (if you so point your talk).

2. *Analyze your audience: its relation to you and your topic; its interests and attitudes.*

3. *Develop your subject effectively within your time limits.* The amount of time at your disposal will govern your selection of materials and the order of their presentation. You must apportion your time well if you wish to produce a unified and motivative speech.

4. *Compose a full script.*

5. *Use effective language in your composition.* Your words and combinations of words should be varied, clear, definite in meaning, accurate in grammar and syntax, concise, free from triteness. They should be appropriate to your personality, to your thesis, and to the needs and interests of your listener-observers.

6. *Understand in advance something of the physical factors of the television station and its personnel.* You do not need to familiarize yourself with the jobs of those who operate the unit, but you should know that a director is correlating the program, that perhaps an additional floor director is busy, that a cameraman, a lighting director, and a dolly

(boom, crane) pusher may be at hand, and that other personnel are at work to ensure a smooth broadcast.

7. *Rehearse carefully beforehand.* Several trial performances in the studio will help, if the director offers them. Note that the program is outlined in detail in advance. This outline lists the topics and subtopics that make up your talk; it contains marginal indications of the exact time allowed for each phase of your talk, regardless of its length, and a parallel listing of the visual aids you will use and the physical movements you will make (if you move away from a set camera position).

8. *Learn in advance exactly how you will appear in relation to the camera or cameras.* The production director will decide whether you are to stand or to sit at a desk and whether your full-length image or your full face only will be presented. Will you use visual aids? In any case you must be constantly aware that the camera will magnify your facial expressions and bodily movements instantly and glaringly.

Follow the director's suggestions concerning your appearance, including your dress. For men, brown, blue, and gray suits are preferable to black or white. White shirts create glare. Women should not wear striking colors or jewelry that may wrongly reflect the light or add to the glare.

9. *Look directly into the camera or in the directions that the director suggests.* When on the air, look at the "tally" (red) lights on the front of the camera, but do not stare. When these lights go out, lower your eyes; then focus them directly on the "live" lens.

In such details you will follow the cues of your director.

10. *Speak in a normal voice, as for radio.* The microphone will be directly before and above you. Your unseen audience will be in groups usually of two or three persons, peering into a 14- or 21-inch screen. You will remember the principles and methods of proper breathing, phonation, proper utilization of your resonating chambers, and good articulation. (See again Chapters Eleven and Twelve.)

11. *Handle your manuscript efficiently.* Stevenson, Kennedy, Nixon, and many other political speakers and news and sports reporters may use manuscripts, but often they do not appear to read from them.

Commercials are obviously memorized or read from a teleprompter or from cue cards. Most public service speeches are delivered extemporaneously—or seem to be so. Demonstration talks must be extemporaneous. By memorization and certain other aids, you can produce an entire talk without undue obtrusion of the manuscript. You may extemporize, if you can do so without awkward pauses and hesitations. You may memorize, if you rehearse often enough to ensure conversational delivery. You may use a combination of reading and memorization, provided you become so familiar with your manuscript that you can glance at it only occasionally and without concealing your face from your audience. You may place your entire speech or cue sections of it on large cards beside the camera. Then you can look directly at the audience and at the same time follow the prepared words. In television programs the President, cabinet members, and other important political leaders often use tele-prompters. As the speaker proceeds, the script appears in large letters on a roll of paper which is operated by a single person and which keeps pace with the delivery.

12. *Use visual aids.* Basically, television is a medium for transmitting visual materials in a degree of detail not possible or convenient in other situations, for example, in classroom lectures. Television stations will provide blackboards, pointers, and other equipment. Charts should be dark gray cards with bold lettering and drawings. The speaker should be able to experiment with these aids before the broadcast.

Transparent slides may be used if they are properly prepared and contribute to the television picture. Motion-picture films, silent or with sound, can be used in most cases if they meet standard specifications (16 millimeter exposed at 24 frames per second).

The techniques of performance on television cannot be treated in detail in this book. Here we can only mention a few aspects of television as they apply to the speaker. The references at the end of the chapter offer a thorough treatment of the subject.

Whether you talk over radio and television or not, you will profit as a listener and as an observer by visiting the stations and noting the problems and experiences mentioned above.

Projects and Problems

PROJECT 1

Examine a five-minute speech that you wrote and delivered extemporaneously in the classroom. Indicate as a footnote what changes in content, organization, and language should be made to adapt it satisfactorily for radio or television presentation.

PROJECT 2

Play a tape recording of a radio or television speech. Prepare a brief criticism of the delivery.

PROJECT 3

Present to the instructor your written criticism of a fifteen-minute television talk (newscast or informational or persuasive talk).

PROJECT 4

Secure a copy of a speech recently telecast over a network. Attach to the copy your comment on the content, organization, language, and other features in view of television requirements. Turn in both to your instructor.

PROJECT 5

Give a short oral report on the television techniques of a commentator (for example, Howard K. Smith).

PROJECT 6

Repeat project 5, reporting on a television preacher (for example, Ralph Sockman or Fulton S. Sheen).

PROJECT 7

Evaluate two professional announcers, one from a local station, the other from a network.

PROJECT 8

Give a short classroom report on the speech techniques of a well-known radio or television speaker.

PROJECT 9

With the help of your classmates, a tape recorder, and a stop watch, check the number of words you deliver per minute in ordinary conversation; in reading one of your speech manuscripts; in talking extemporaneously from the outline of your speech not written in full; in the reading of a poem. Draw conclusions concerning your rate.

PROJECT 10

Suggestions for the instructor: Set up projects so that each member of the class may serve as the announcer of a program designed to be broadcast; as an interviewer or interviewee; as director of a program of readings.

PROJECT 11

Visit a television station and study the methods of production and television presentation.

References

Abbot, Waldo, and Richard L. Rider: *Handbook of Broadcasting*, 4th ed., McGraw-Hill Book Company, Inc., New York, 1957.

Barnouw, Erik: *Mass Communication: Television, Radio, Film and Press*, Holt, Rinehart and Winston, Inc., New York, 1956.

Becker, Samuel, and H. Clay Harshbarger: *Television: Techniques for Planning and Performance*, Holt, Rinehart and Winston, Inc., New York, 1958.

Bettinger, Hoyland: *Television Techniques, revised by Sol Cornberg*, Harper & Brothers, New York, 1955.

Bretz, Rudy, and Edward Stasheff: *Television Scripts for Staging and Study*, A. A. Wyn, Inc., New York, 1953.

Chester, Giraud, and Garnet Garrison: *Television and Radio*, 2d ed., Appleton-Century-Crofts, Inc., New York, 1956.

Hyde, Stuart W.: *Television and Radio Announcing*, Houghton Mifflin Company, Boston, 1957.

Lindsley, Charles F.: *Radio and Television Communication*, McGraw-Hill Book Company, Inc., New York, 1952.

Lynch, W. F.: *The Image Industries*, Sheed & Ward, Inc., New York, 1959.

Murrow, Edward R., and Fred W. Friendly (eds.): *See It Now*, Simon and Schuster, Inc., New York, 1955.

Phillips, David C., John M. Grogan, and Earl H. Ryan: *Introduction to Radio and Television*, The Ronald Press Company, New York, 1954.

Seldes, George V.: *The Public Arts*, Simon and Schuster, Inc., New York, 1956.

Stasheff, Edward, and Rudy Bretz: *The Television Program*, Hill and Wang, New York, 1956.

Teaching by Television, Report by the Ford Foundation, The Fund for the Advancement of Adult Education, New York, 1959.

TWENTY-TWO

Speeches for Special

Occasions

THE PRINCIPLES of speech discussed in earlier chapters of this book—especially in Part Two, "Developing Fundamental Processes"—obviously apply to speeches for special occasions, just as they apply, with adaptations, to radio and television speaking. They apply to special occasions with slightly altered emphasis, however. For this reason, we will review in this chapter some of the fundamental principles of speech making as they apply to the following special occasions: announcements, tributes, presentations and acceptances, welcomes and farewells, and introductions.

The purpose of your speech on any one of these occasions is determined by the occasion itself. You will not have the problem of deciding upon your purpose and determining how to achieve it. Thus you will direct your efforts toward getting your listeners' attention and maintaining their interest until you have accomplished the goal established for you by the occasion.

Some Principles for Special-occasion Speeches

Be active. The first principle of the psychology of attention is that people are attracted to movement. The infant in his crib follows a moving

350

toy with his eyes, the hunter in the woods discovers the approach of game because he observes movement among the trees, the sleight-of-hand artist depends on action to keep the audience's attention on one hand while with the other he sets the stage for the trick—all show the power of movement to hold attention. A stage play with fast action is more interesting than a play with little action. On the other hand, action that is too fast becomes meaningless.

Give evidence of making progress in the discussion of the subject. When the speaker merely says the same thing over and over again or follows an argument in circles, listeners lose interest. But a well-structured discussion that suggests the points to be covered and then proceeds to the consideration of one point after another gives a sense of action and progress. To be interesting as a speaker, be alert and keep your ideas moving.

Use contrast and variety. At certain times, lack of activity is more interesting than movement. When activity is the common feature of a situation, inactivity attracts attention. If you are preceded by a speaker who is very active, you may provide relief and contrast by controlled restraint.

As a general rule a monotonous voice is an invitation to inattention. The conversational voice, on the other hand, employs a variety of rates, inflections, qualities, and intensities.

Project your ideas vividly. If your listeners have difficulty hearing, they will become inattentive. If they cannot see what you are trying to show them, they will be attentive to what they can see. Unless you watch your listeners carefully, they are not likely to watch you. Abstract ideas will gain closest attention when you use visual aids or exemplify your idea by means of a story or specific instance with colorful details which appeal to the mind's eye.

Relate your ideas to your listeners. People are ordinarily interested in speakers who show interest in them. One way to show interest in your listeners is to learn as much about them as you can and then to interpret what you have to say in terms of their known experiences and interests. Senator Morse of Oregon is reported to be a subscriber to every county paper in his state. When campaigning for reelection, he discusses the issues in terms of local events and personalities.

Appeal to dominant motives. Interest is a response to motivation, and there are many motives. The speaker who interests his listeners is one who stimulates them; to be stimulated is to be jarred out of indifference— to visualize some goal, to experience some threat. Discover the motives of your listeners and relate your subject to it. (See Chapter Eighteen for a more extensive analysis of this method.)

Arouse curiosity. Man constantly seeks to explain intellectually the chain of events that makes up his experience. New situations arouse his curiosity, and he seeks to anticipate their outcome. To keep your listeners' attention give them the expectation of a satisfying search for answers. Describe situations that call for explanation, and offer the key to the problem. Let the listener think along with you and discover the answers for himself, and he will enjoy the search for the idea.

DEVICES FOR ENTERTAINING

On many occasions audiences ask merely to be entertained. They want relaxation, amusement, forgetfulness. In entertaining them, you are performing a worthwhile social function.

Storytelling. From the time of the troubadours to the age of the television entertainer, storytelling has been the common medium of the professional entertainer. Almost everyone attempts narration in his everyday conversation. Experience and some knowledge of technique will improve your ability; at times, however, you may tell your audience that you are aware that you are not a professional storyteller.

Give an account of a play, motion picture, televised drama, or a story you have recently read. As preparation, review the chief elements of your story—setting, characters, plot, dialogue. Use your voice and use action to express the moods and rhythms of your story. Adapt yourself to your listeners, introduce the narrative properly, and keep it moving to a climax and conclusion.

Anecdote. The anecdote is an abbreviated story. To tell a "funny story" with full effect takes skill. You as a speaker should acquire experience in this type of narrative.

Personal incidents. Review for your audience your experiences as hunter, fisher, job seeker, tourist, householder, cook, mountain climber, salesman, or student. Select the incidents carefully, relate them swiftly, and be responsive to indications of the listener's boredom.

The exhibition. Another form of entertaining talk is the exhibition. Demonstrating an object or process, showing slides, or even doing amateur tricks will keep your audience attentive and interested because it provides a form of activity.

Oral reading. The oral reading of stories, essays, plays, or poetry can be entertaining if you are reasonably skillful at the job. For a general discussion of the principles of good reading, see Chapter Twenty.

Types of Special-occasion Speeches

The announcement. As a common type of short speech, announcements deserve some consideration because they are frequently made so badly. Announcements are of two types: the informative and the persuasive. The informative announcement merely presents the facts; the persuasive announcement presents the facts and appeals for action. The situation dictates the type which is in order.

The essential facts contained in most announcements are the answers to the questions *who, what, where, when,* and sometimes *how much* and *why.* Be sure that these facts are presented so that they cannot be misunderstood and so that they are easy to remember. Get the attention of the audience. Plan your opening sentence with care. Organize the entire announcement carefully, making use of devices that will emphasize the important ideas. But keep the whole short and simple.

The persuasive announcement calls for even greater skill. Let your own enthusiasm be obvious. Appeal to known audience motives, and make it easy for listeners to act. Above all, express your appreciation for the courtesy shown in giving you an opportunity to make the announcement. End with an expression of thanks.

The tribute. All of us have experienced the feeling of appreciation for a great man or woman and have been enriched and inspired by that feeling. The speech of tribute is the oral expression of that feeling and the means of inspiring others to emulation. The most effective tributes arise from genuine motivation; hence the most important requirement is that the tribute come from the heart.

Select as main ideas those characteristics which are most worthy of emulation. Present the speech with dignity and strong conviction.

The presentation speech. The speech of presentation is a tribute in which some token is awarded to the person to whom tribute is paid. Emphasize the man and his deeds rather than the gift or award. Avoid extravagant language or praise. Keep the speech dignified, simple, and sincere. The ultimate goal is to affect the listeners as much as it is to honor the recipient of recognition. Such speeches should, therefore, have no secondary purposes and deal with no other subjects. The act of presentation should come near the end of the speech, when you congratulate the recipient.

The response to tribute: acceptance. When the person to whom tribute is paid or an award is given is present, he may be called upon for a response. With dignity and modesty, thank the donors for their kindness. Give credit to any who have assisted you in your endeavors. Discuss the value of the objectives toward which you have worked. Be brief, but avoid brusqueness and the appearance of indifference.

Welcome and farewell speeches. The purpose of the speech of welcome is to "break the ice" and establish a feeling of fellowship. Extend the courtesies of local organizations and services as well as your appreciation of honor bestowed upon the community. Draw your material from the community, the occasion, and the organizations and persons involved. The speech may anticipate pleasant associations. Make your effort more than mere formality, but avoid exaggerated statement. These principles should also be observed in responses to welcomes.

The farewell speech may look both backward and forward—backward to pleasant memories and common achievements, and forward to best wishes to the departing one in his new surroundings. The farewell speech is centered around and adapted to the person, and it calls for a review of events and deeds worth remembering. Expression of appreciation is in order. The mood should be pleasant but not too gay, friendly but not too sad.

The speech of introduction. The purpose of the speech of introduction is to arouse the audience's interest in the speaker and the subject. If you do not know the speaker, you should make it a point to learn enough about him to perform this friendly service for him. It is appropriate to ask him for any suggestions as to what you should say. Your primary duty is to get the listeners settled and prepare them to hear the speaker.

Tell the audience what it needs to know to appreciate the speaker as a man. Although a word of praise for the speaker is in order, overpraise of his achievements or abilities is embarrassing and in poor taste. Humor is permissible if it fits the man and the situation. The better known the speaker, the less introduction he needs. Better a brief, formal introduction than an extended insincere one. Avoid the intrusion of ideas which distract from the purpose of the occasion. Above all, be brief. You are not the main speaker. Give him the opportunity for which he is present.

Projects and Problems

PROJECT 1: DEVELOPMENT OF INTEREST IN THE SUBJECT

Purposes of this assignment: (*a*) To learn the technique for making a speech interesting; (*b*) to develop skill in using methods of arousing interest.

Procedure: Select a topic, word a central idea for a speech of instruction or persuasion, and outline two or three main points to support the central idea. Develop your main points with material which applies one or more of the principles for making material interesting. Plan to use appropriate methods of delivery for making the speech interesting.

Subject: Your subject should be one which will enable you to do your best as a speaker. Use a subject which requires application of the interest techniques.

PROJECT 2: READING OR TELLING FUNNY STORIES

Purposes of this assignment: (*a*) To develop techniques of using humor to reduce nervousness; (*b*) to acquire skill in voice control for the purpose of telling a funny story; (*c*) to develop your sense of humor.

Subjects: (*a*) A funny story from *The New Yorker.* (*b*) Some anecdotes which illustrate a point. (*c*) A short story by Irvin S. Cobb, Stephen Leacock, Ring Lardner, or Mark Twain. (*d*) Poetry by Don Marquis, Ogden Nash, William Kirk, or Tom Daly. (*e*) Make a speech on types of humor.

Procedure: Decide upon the material you will present. It may be a reading, a story, or a speech using anecdotes or some other type of humor. It should be something which you think is funny and which represents a type of humor you would enjoy sharing with others. Prepare the material carefully and present it to your classmates with the intention of getting the maximum response from them.

PROJECT 3: MAKING AN ANNOUNCEMENT

Prepare and present an announcement of an event of interest to the class. Decide whether it will be an informative or persuasive announcement and prepare accordingly.

PROJECT 4: GIVING A SPEECH OF TRIBUTE

Make a three-minute speech of tribute. Select someone you know, other than a relative. Keep your tribute direct and sincere.

PROJECT 5: GIVING A SPEECH OF WELCOME

Prepare a three-minute speech of welcome to be presented to a conference held in your city. Give the listeners the feeling that you really want them.

PROJECT 6: INTRODUCING A SPEAKER

Take turns introducing the speakers in the class during an assignment. Present the speaker as you would to a group to which you belong.

References

Brigance, W. Norwood: *Speech,* Appleton-Century-Crofts, Inc., New York, 1952, chap. 23.

Crocker, Lionel: *Public Speaking for College Students,* 3d ed., American Book Company, New York, 1956, chaps. 12 and 18.

Gilman, Wilbur E., Bower Aly, and Loren D. Reid: *The Fundamentals of Speaking,* The Macmillan Company, New York, 1951, chaps. 13 and 20.

Gray, Giles W., and Waldo W. Braden: *Public Speaking: Principles and Practice,* Harper & Brothers, New York, 1951, chap. 10.

McBurney, James H., and Ernest J. Wrage: *The Art of Good Speech,* Prentice-Hall, Inc., Englewood Cliffs, N.J., 1953, chap. 26.

Monroe, Alan H.: *Principles and Types of Speech,* 4th ed., Scott, Foresman and Company, Chicago, 1955, chaps. 19, 24–28.

Oliver, Robert T., and Rupert L. Cortright: *Effective Speech,* Holt, Rinehart and Winston, Inc., New York, 1961, chaps. 21–23.

———, Dallas C. Dickey, and Harold P. Zelko: *Communicative Speech*, The Dryden Press, Inc., New York, 1955, chap. 13.

Reid, Loren D.: *First Principles of Public Speaking*, Artcraft Press, Columbia, Mo., 1960, chap. 17.

White, Eugene E., and Clair R. Henderlider: *Practical Public Speaking*, The Macmillan Company, New York, 1954, chap. 15.

Yeager, W. Hayes: *Effective Speaking for Every Occasion*, 2d ed., Prentice-Hall, Inc., Englewood Cliffs, N.J., 1951.

TWENTY-THREE

Parliamentary Procedure

DEBATING IS the characteristic method by which organizations (clubs, courts, legislatures) conduct affairs, and parliamentary procedure provides the rules that govern debates. Group action can be regarded as legal and binding on the organization only if discussion proceeds according to parliamentary regulations.

Principles

Parliamentary rules exist to facilitate orderly procedure rather than to encourage vocal and legal sparring. It is the responsibility of the chairman of the assembly to see that the rules are administered impartially; that the majority vote decides the issue; that minority rights are safeguarded; that every proposition is fully discussed before a decision is registered; that all members have equal rights and responsibilities; that motions are introduced and disposed of in a definite and logical order; and that only one question is considered at a time.

Creating an Organization

How are organizations created? A group comes together under the stimulus of some common purpose. In order to work toward their common goal, the members must delegate responsibility and establish procedures.

357

Electing temporary officers. A member rises and says, "The meeting will come to order. I nominate Mr. X as temporary chairman." Or he may call for nominations for temporary chairman. If more than one nomination is made, he will put the names to a vote by voice or by show of hands. The nominee receiving a majority of the votes cast is declared temporary chairman. This temporary officer then presides over the election of a temporary secretary.

Stating the purpose of the meeting. The chairman then calls upon some member or members to state the purpose of the meeting. Informal discussion follows, presided over by the chairman.

Forming a permanent organization. A member rises upon recognition and presents a resolution which authorizes the formation of a permanent organization: "Mr. Chairman, I move that the meeting form a permanent organization, to be known as the State University of Iowa Forensic Association."

If this motion receives a majority vote, a member then moves that the chairman appoint a committee to draft a constitution and bylaws. If these have already been prepared, the drafting committee is asked to report then and there. If not, a drafting committee is appointed or elected, and the meeting adjourns to reconvene at a time specified by the assembly vote.

The constitution should be brief and clear. The articles usually include (1) the name of the organization, (2) the purposes and scope of the organization, (3) membership qualifications, (4) a list of officers, their duties, and procedure for electing them, (5) the time and place of meetings, (6) the number constituting a quorum, and (7) methods of amending the constitution.

Bylaws. Bylaws usually cover such subjects as (1) details governing membership; (2) a list of committees and their duties; (3) finances, including dues, fines, fees, credits, etc.; (4) the duties and powers of each officer; (5) provisions for meetings; (6) methods of election; (7) order of business; (8) official parliamentary code; (9) methods of voting; (10) quorums; and (11) method of amending the bylaws.

Adoption of the constitution and bylaws. The chairman of the committee on constitution and bylaws moves that the document be adopted. The presiding officer then puts the motion: "It has been moved and recorded that this constitution be adopted."

The secretary records the constitution as a whole if it has already been read to the group; if not, he proceeds section by section. As each section is read, the chairman calls for discussion. Amendments are proposed, discussed, and approved or rejected. After all the sections are thus disposed of, the chairman asks, "Is further discussion on the constitution as a whole or further amendment prepared?" If there is no further discussion, the chairman calls for a vote on the original motion to adopt the document. A majority vote in favor will mean adoption.

The bylaws are discussed and adopted in the same way as the constitution. Then the organization is ready for its permanent business.

Conducting a Meeting

Parliamentary law and most organizational bylaws suggest the following order of business: (1) call to order; (2) reading and disposition of minutes of the previous meeting; (3) statement of agenda; (4) reports of officers and standing committees; (5) reports of special committees; (6) unfinished business; (7) new business; (8) adjournment.

THE PRESIDING OFFICER

It is the responsibility of the presiding officer to see that the meeting moves forward efficiently—that the debate does not bog down in useless filibustering; that parliamentary rules are used only to further the group's discussion and decisions; that the facts being considered are clear to all; and—in general—that the assembly gets results.

The presiding officer should be tactful and impartial; he should never adopt a dictatorial attitude; and he should make the members feel at ease. He should be familiar with the rules of parliamentary procedure and their application; but instead of depending upon memory, he should keep a chart of these rules before him at each meeting. Since members will often veer away from the subject under discussion or introduce other subjects which should not be dealt with at the same time, it is the duty of the presiding officer to keep clearly in mind the business of the meeting and the order in which it is to be presented and to remind the members of this order. The presiding officer will recognize each speaker by name, or ask him to give his name; state each motion clearly and be sure it is properly recorded, having the secretary record it and helping him to repeat it accurately if necessary. He must keep the discussion to the motion and be sure that all who wish to speak have the opportunity to do so. Before a vote is taken, he should state the exact question to be voted on; afterward, he should announce the outcome and explain its consequences.

He must see that the secretary records each step of the meeting and has present a copy of the constitution and bylaws and other material that might serve the purposes of the meeting. In a formal meeting, he must ensure the appointment of a sergeant at arms, whose duties are to attend to the physical arrangements of the meeting and supervise the behavior of the members. In some organizations a parliamentarian should be designated to advise the presiding officer.

VOTING AND QUORUM

Most motions are settled by a majority vote. Usually this term refers to a majority of the qualified votes cast; however, the constitution, by-laws, or rules of the organization should define the term. Voting is done by one of the following methods: *voice* ("Those in favor, say 'aye.' Those opposed say 'no.'"); *rising ballot; show of hands;* and *roll call* (The secretary calls the roll. Those in favor answer "yes" as their names are called; those opposed, "no.").

A quorum is necessary for a legal decision. The quorum, the minimum number of members that must be present in order to make the transactions of the meeting legal, is a majority of the members, unless otherwise stated in the constitution and bylaws.

HANDLING MOTIONS

Business is carried on by motions (resolutions, proposals, propositions, or questions). A member rises and addresses the chairman, and the procedure is as follows:

Member: "Mr. Chairman."
Chairman: "Mr. Blair."
Member: "I move that we vote $50 to provide for a freshman party."
Chairman: "Is there a second?"
Another member: "I second the motion."
Chairman: "You have heard the motion as made and seconded. Is there any discussion?"
                    [Discussion proceeds.]
Chairman: "Are you ready for the vote?" [Hearing no dissent, he continues:] "Those in favor say 'aye.' ["Ayes" are given.] Those opposed say 'no.' The motion is carried." [Or "The motion is lost."]

There are four types of motions: *main, subsidiary, incidental,* and *privileged.* In order of their proposal (priority) these are arranged as follows (incidental motions may be made at any point):

1. Main motions
2. Subsidiary motions
3. Privileged motions

In order of their disposition, these motions rank as follows:

1. Privileged motions
2. Subsidiary motions
3. Main motions

More specifically, the order of disposal of these motions is:

I. Privileged motions

1. Fix time to adjourn
2. Adjourn
3. Recess
4. Question of privilege
5. Call for order of the day

II. Subsidiary motions

6. "Lay on the table"
7. "Previous question" (immediate vote)
8. Limit debate
9. Postpone to a specific time
10. Refer to a committee
11. Amend
12. Postpone indefinitely

III. Main motions

13. Any "general" main motion, and such "specific" main motions as (*a*) reconsider, (*b*) rescind, (*c*) resume consideration (take from the table)

IV. Incidental motions (may be proposed and disposed of at any time)

1. Appeal
2. Point of order
3. Inquiry
4. Suspend rules
5. Withdraw a motion
6. Object to consideration
7. Division of the question

This order of handling motions means that when a motion is before the assembly, any motion of higher rank takes precedence and may be proposed, but not a motion of lower rank. The motion to adjourn takes precedence over all others, and the "main motion" comes last. The last motion proposed should be disposed of first, and so on until the first motion is arrived at and disposed of.[1] In this way, procedure in dealing with motions listed above would be as follows:

I. MAIN MOTION

13. *Original Motion*

PURPOSE: To propose original business.

FORM: "Mr. Chairman, I move that we approve President Eisenhower's proposal for international control of atomic material."

COMMENT: Requires a second, is debatable, can be amended, requires a majority vote; if lost cannot be revived at the same meeting.

13a. *Resume Consideration (Take from the Table)*

FORM: "Mr. Chairman, I move we resume consideration of the motion to approve Mr. Eisenhower's proposal."

COMMENT: Requires a second, is not debatable, is not amendable, requires a majority.

13b. *Reconsider*

FORM: "Mr. Chairman, I move that we reconsider the vote to approve Dwight Eisenhower's proposal."

COMMENT: Requires a second, is not amendable, and requires a majority; is debatable if motion to which it applies is debatable.

13c. *Rescind (Repeal, Annul)*

PURPOSE: To nullify or void a motion previously passed.

FORM: "I move to rescind (or repeal) the motion passed on December 5, which motion approved Mr. Eisenhower's proposal."

COMMENT: Requires a second, is debatable, cannot be amended, requires a majority vote, applies to main motions previously adopted.

II. SUBSIDIARY MOTIONS

12. *Postpone Indefinitely ("Kill" or "Suppress")*

PURPOSE: To suppress a question pending before the meeting.

FORM: "I move that the motion be postponed indefinitely."

COMMENT: Debatable, requires a second, cannot be amended, requires majority vote, applies to main motions only.

11. *Amend*

PURPOSE: To change or modify a motion before the assembly.

---

[1] For the plan outlined above and as a general authority on parliamentary procedure, the authors are indebted to Alice Sturgis, *Learning Parliamentary Procedure,* McGraw-Hill Book Company, Inc., New York, 1953.

FORM: "I move to amend (by adding, striking out, substituting) . . ."

COMMENT: Cannot interrupt a speaker, requires a second, is debatable, can be amended, requires a majority vote, takes precedence over main motion.

10. *Refer to a Committee*

PURPOSE: To transfer a proposal from assembly to a smaller group working under the assembly.

FORM: "I move to refer the motion to a committee."

COMMENT: Requires a second, debatable, can be amended, requires a majority vote.

9. *Postpone to a Specific Time*

PURPOSE: To postpone consideration or decision to a specific time.

FORM: "I move to postpone consideration of the motion until the next regular meeting."

COMMENT: Requires a second, is debatable and amendable; requires a majority vote, applies to main motions only.

8. *Limit Debate*

PURPOSE: To limit amount of time for discussion of a question.

FORM: "I move to limit debate on this question to one hour."

COMMENT: Requires a second, is not debatable, can be amended, requires a two-thirds vote, applies to all debatable questions.

7. *Previous Question (Immediate Vote)*

PURPOSE: To end discussion and bring motion to immediate vote.

FORM: "I move the previous question."

COMMENT: Requires a second, is not debatable, cannot be amended, requires a two-thirds vote, applies to any debatable motion.

6. *"Lay on the Table"*

PURPOSE: To postpone the motion for an undetermined time.

FORM: "I move that the motion be laid on the table."

COMMENT: Requires a second, is not debatable, cannot be amended, requires a majority vote.

III. PRIVILEGED MOTIONS

5. *Call for the Order of the Day*

PURPOSE: To remind the chairman and assembly to take up certain business at a fixed hour, when that business and hour have been previously agreed upon, and when the chairman has overlooked the scheduled event.

FORM: "Mr. Chairman, I call for the order of the day." Chairman: "If there is no objection, we will proceed to the business as scheduled."

COMMENT: No second required, not debatable, not amendable, in order when another has the floor, cannot be reconsidered.

4. *Questions of Privilege*

PURPOSE: To secure action on a motion related to "comfort rights, or privileges of the organization or of its members."

FORM: "Mr. Chairman, I rise to a question of privilege."

COMMENT: Can interrupt a speaker, requires no second, is not debatable, cannot be amended, requires no vote, is decided by the presiding officer.

3. *Take Recess*

PURPOSE: To permit a temporary break in the meeting.

FORM: "I move that we recess for one hour."

COMMENT: Requires a second, is not debatable, requires a majority vote, applies to no other motion.

2. *Adjourn*

PURPOSE: To end a meeting.

FORM: "I move we adjourn."

COMMENT: Requires a second, is not debatable, cannot be amended, requires a majority vote, takes precedence over all other motions, applies to no other motion, can be renewed at the same meeting when a new parliamentary situation develops.

1. *Fix Time to Adjourn*

PURPOSE: To fix time for the next meeting.

FORM: "Mr. Chairman, I move that we adjourn to meet tomorrow at 1 P.M."

COMMENT: Requires a second, not debatable if made when another motion is before the assembly, amendable, majority vote, not in order when another has the floor, can be reconsidered.

IV. INCIDENTAL MOTIONS

1. *Appeal*

PURPOSE: To decide by assembly vote whether the chairman's ruling is to be upheld.

FORM: "Mr. Chairman, I appeal from the decision of the chair."

COMMENT: Can interrupt a speaker, requires a second, is debatable, cannot be amended, requires a majority of the vote to sustain the chairman's position.

2. Point of Order

PURPOSE: To call attention to a violation of the rules.

FORM: "Mr. Chairman, I rise to a point of order."

COMMENT: Can interrupt a speaker, requires no second, is not debatable, cannot be amended, requires no vote.

3. Parliamentary Inquiry

PURPOSE: To enable a member to obtain information from the chairman.

FORM: "I rise to a parliamentary inquiry."

COMMENT: Requires no second, is not debatable, requires no vote.

4. Suspend Rules

PURPOSE: To allow assembly to act in some manner forbidden by parliamentary rules.

FORM: "I move to suspend the rules in order that . . . ."

COMMENT: Cannot interrupt a speaker, requires a second, is not debatable, cannot be amended, requires a two-thirds vote.

5. Withdraw a Motion

PURPOSE: To enable a member to withdraw a motion he has made.

FORM: "I wish to withdraw my motion."

COMMENT: Requires no second, is not debatable, cannot be amended, requires no vote, granted only by unanimous consent.

6. Object to Consideration

PURPOSE: To suppress a motion.

FORM: "Mr. President, I object to consideration of this question."

COMMENT: Can interrupt a speaker, requires no second, is not debatable, cannot be amended, requires a two-thirds negative vote, applies to main motion only.

7. Division of Question

PURPOSE: To divide a motion so that each section can be considered and voted on separately.

FORM: "I request that the motion just stated be divided into two parts . . . ."

COMMENT: Cannot interrupt a speaker, requires no second, is not debatable, cannot be amended, requires no vote.

Table of Parliamentary Motions

Motions	Need of second	Amendable	Debatable	Vote required	May be postponed	May be reconsidered	May be laid on table	May interrupt speaker
I. Privileged Motions								
1. Fix time to adjourn	Yes	Yes	No	Majority	No	No	No	No
2. To adjourn	Yes	No	No	Majority	No	No	No	No
3. To take a recess	Yes	Yes	No (usually)	Majority	No	No	No	No
4. Question of privilege	No	No	No	Chairman	No	No	No	Yes
5. Order of day	No	No	No	Chairman	No	No	No	Yes
II. Subsidiary Motions								
6. To lay on table	Yes	No	No	Majority	No	No	No	No
7. Previous question	Yes	No	No	Two-thirds	No	If lost, no	Yes	No
8. To postpone to a definite time	Yes	Yes	Yes	Majority	No	Yes	Yes	No
9. To commit, refer, recommit	Yes	Yes	Yes	Majority	No	Yes	Yes	No
10. To amend	Yes	Yes	Yes	Majority	Yes	Yes	Yes	No
11. To postpone indefinitely	Yes	No	Yes	Majority	Yes	Yes	Yes	No
12. Limit debate	Yes	Yes	No	Two-thirds	Yes	Yes	Yes	No
III. Main Motions								
13. Any main question	Yes	Yes	Yes	Majority	Yes	Yes	Yes	No
13a. Specific main question								
(13a) Reconsider	Yes	No	Yes	Majority	No	No	Yes	No
(13b) Rescind	Yes	No	Yes	Majority	No	No	Yes	No
(13c) Resume consideration	Yes	No	No	Majority	No	Yes, after change in procedure	Part	No

IV. Incidental Motions

					Debate limited	Majority		
1. To appeal from chair	Yes	No	Yes	No	No	Majority	No	Yes
2. Point of order	No	No	No	No	No	Chairman	No	Yes
3. Parliamentary inquiry	No	No	No	No	No	No vote	No	Yes
4. To suspend a rule	Yes	No	Yes	No	No	Two-thirds	Yes	No
5. To withdraw a motion	No	No	No	No	No		Yes	No
6. To object to consideration	Yes	No	No	No	Yes	Two-thirds frequently	No	No
7. Division of a question	No	No	No	No	No	No vote	No	No

SOURCE: Adapted from A. Craig Baird, *Argumentation, Discussion, and Debate*, McGraw-Hill Book Company, Inc., New York, 1950, Appendix C, pp. 400–402.

Projects and Problems

PROJECT 1

The class will organize a "Forensics Club." A preliminary meeting will be called to establish such a club. A temporary leader will be selected in advance to open the session and conduct the election of temporary officers. Motions will be presented and discussed concerning the purpose and scope of the organization. If the proposed organization is approved, a committee will be elected to draft a constitution and bylaws.

PROJECT 2

The class will hold a preliminary session under the temporary chairman and temporary secretary to read and discuss the proposed constitution (copies of which have been prepared for each member). The document will be read section by section with discussion and possible amendments. The constitution is then read in its complete and amended form for final passage. The same procedure is followed for the bylaws. Permanent officers for the group are then elected and possible agenda for the next meeting suggested.

PROJECT 3

The Forensics Club will meet, following the order of business suggested in this chapter. A resolution, selected in advance by a committee approved at the previous meeting, will be debated and approved or rejected. By agreement, the chairman and secretary may be changed at the middle of the session. Parliamentary procedures will be observed. By agreement, each speech may be limited to two minutes. The instructor will serve as the parliamentarian. Parliamentary complexities and confusion will be discouraged.

PROJECT 4

Each member will be prepared to explain, without notes, each of the following terms: (a) appeal, (b) chair, (c) division of assembly, (d) division of question, (e) floor, (f) incidental motions, (g) lay on the table, (h) main motion, (i) majority vote, (j) object to consideration, (k) order of the day, (l) plurality, (m) point of order, (n) previous question, (o) reconsider, (p) rescind, (q) withdraw.

PROJECT 5

Explain each: (a) What is the precedence of motions? (b) What motions require a second? (c) What motions may be amended? (d) What vote is required for typical motions?

PROJECT 6

A member says, "I move the previous question." What procedures may the chairman follow?

PROJECT 7

As chairman, explain how you will handle the following parliamentary situation: A motion has been made and seconded that this club endorse the Student Council proposal for a higher student-activity fee to include free admission to all campus theatre programs (or some similar campus program).

An amendment to the motion has been proposed to read, "and to all campus operas and student musical shows."

A member moves to lay the entire motion on the table. Another member moves to amend the amendment by striking out all words in the resolution beyond "higher student-activity fee."

PROJECT 8

A member questions the decision of the chairman and says, "I appeal from the decision of the chair." What situations then may confront the chairman, and how does he proceed?

References

Braden, Waldo W., and Earnest Brandenburg: *Oral Decision Making: Principles of Discussion and Debate,* Harper & Brothers, New York, 1955, chap. 25.

Bryant, Donald C., and Karl R. Wallace: *Fundamentals of Public Speaking,* 3d ed., Appleton-Century-Crofts, Inc., New York, 1960, chap. 26.

Eliot, Thomas H.: *Basic Rules of Order,* Harcourt, Brace & World, Inc., New York, 1952.

Gulley, Helbert E.: *Discussion, Conference, and Group Process,* Holt, Rinehart and Winston, Inc., New York, 1960, chap. 16.

O'Brien, Joseph F.: *Parliamentary Law for the Layman,* Harper & Brothers, New York, 1952.

Reid, Loren D.: *First Principles of Public Speaking,* Artcraft Press, Columbia, Mo., 1960, chap. 20.

Robert's Rules of Order, rev. ed., Scott, Foresman and Company, Chicago, 1951.

Sturgis, Alice F.: *Standard Code of Parliamentary Procedure,* McGraw-Hill Book Company, Inc., New York, 1950.

——: *Learning Parliamentary Procedure,* McGraw-Hill Book Company, Inc., New York, 1953.

The Main Symbols

of the Phonetic

Alphabet, for English

THE MAIN SYMBOLS OF THE PHONETIC ALPHABET, FOR ENGLISH

1. (i)	(ē)	be	22. (t)	(t)	lit
2. (ɪ)	(ĭ)	hit	23. (d)	(d)	lid
3. (ɛ)	(ĕ)	bed	24. (k)	(k)	wick
4. (æ)	(ă)	tan	25. (g)	(g)	wig
5. (ə)	(à)	about	26. (r)	(r)	rice
6. (ʌ)	(ŭ)	but	27. (l)	(l)	lice
7. (a)	(ä)	far	28. (f)	(f)	fine
8. (ɔ)	(ô)	law	29. (v)	(v)	vine
9. (ʊ)	(o͝o)	foot	30. (θ)	(th)	both
10. (u)	(o͞o)	fool	31. (ð)	(th)	bathe
11. (ɪʊ)	(ū)	mute	32. (s)	(s)	lace
12. (oʊ)	(ō)	oh	33. (z)	(z)	lazy
13. (aʊ)	(ou)	ouch	34. (ʃ)	(sh)	rush
14. (eɪ)	(ā)	day	35. (ʒ)	(zh)	rouge
15. (aɪ)	(ī)	light	36. (h)	(h)	hit
16. (ɔɪ)	(oi)	oil	37. (ʍ)	(hw)	whine
17. (m)	(m)	men	38. (w)	(w)	wine
18. (n)	(n)	new	39. (j)	(y)	yes
19. (ŋ)	(ng)	sing	40. (tʃ)	(ch)	char
20. (p)	(p)	pin	41. (dʒ)	(j)	jar
21. (b)	(b)	bin			

Speech Performance Scale

Name _____ Date _____ Instructor _____
Project _____ Time _____
Subject _____

Criteria	Rating 1–9*	Comments
1. *General effectiveness:*		
2. *Speech attitudes and adjustments:* Enthusiastic _____ Communicative _____ Poised _____ Forceful _____ Alert _____ Adaptive _____		
3. *Voice:* Easily audible _____ Pleasant quality _____ Not forced _____ Fluent _____ Good rate _____ Varied _____ Good pitch _____ Conversational _____		
4. *Articulation:* Clear _____ Acceptable _____		
5. *Physical activity:* Direct _____ Responsive _____ Well controlled _____ Adaptive _____		
6. *Language:* Acceptable _____ Vigorous _____ Precise _____ Varied _____ Vivid _____ Unified _____		
7. *Ideas:* Acceptable purpose _____ Clear _____ Clear central idea _____ Interesting _____ Well supported _____ Creative _____ Well developed _____ Significant _____ Accurate _____		
8. *Organization:* Well introduced _____ Well arranged _____ Well divided _____ Well concluded _____ Clear transitions _____		
Total		

    * Rate the speaker in each square by using a scale of 1 to 9 for each of the numbered items. Rate him 1, 2, or 3 to indicate various degrees of deficiency in use of the process; rate him 4, 5, or 6 if he is slightly below average to slightly above average in the process; and rate him 7, 8, or 9 to indicate relative degrees of skill in his use of the process. Add ratings to get total score.

Study of Speech Types

SOME OUTSTANDING speeches have become examples that suggest proper methods for the student in his own speech development. This is not to suggest, however, that excellent talks, short or long, are to be closely imitated or copied. But the experiences and methods of successful public communicators give clues and principles that guide the learner in his own effective creativity.

How, then, are we to profit by the illustrative examples in this book, including the speeches in the section below? Some are old; others are of our own time.

Your judgment of a speech and its speaker can well be guided by the principles and methods that make up this book. Review the chapters and also the speech performance scale of Appendix B.

The speech process that you judge is composed of the speaker, the speaking situation, the audience, the speech itself, and the over-all combination of these factors that make up the communication act. (See again Chapters One and Two.)

Pertinent questions that may help the reader to explore a given speech are thus suggested:

1. *Did the speaker compose the speech attributed to him?* We need to question whether a ghost writer produced the document.

2. *Did the text as produced duplicate what the speaker actually said?* If an electrical or other recording of the actual remarks uttered is available, we can compare it with the written text of the speech.

3. *What was the speaking situation?* Was the speaker talking in the midst of a war, economic depression, or another event, large or small, that might have affected what he said? (See Chapters Three and Four.)

4. *What was the nature of the specific audience?* What was its race, education, economic level, or other characteristics? (See Chapters Seven and Fourteen.)

5. *What was the purpose of the speaker?* Was it mainly to inform, persuade, inspire, entertain? (See Chapters Three and Fifteen through Twenty-one.)

6. *What were the chief ideas of the speech?* Were they worthwhile? (See Chapters Three and Four.)

7. *What evidence or other details supported the central ideas?* (See Chapter Six.)

8. *What motivative elements in addition to the logical substance of the speech were apparent, and were they effectively developed?* (See Chapters Seven and Eighteen.)

9. *Was the speech well organized?* (See Chapter Five.)

10. *Was the language effective?* Was it original, interesting, clear, accurate, adapted to the occasion and audience? (See Chapters Nine and Ten.)

11. *Can we determine the effectiveness of the speaker's delivery?* The written speech, to be sure, provides no clues about the speaker's voice, rate, quality, and other vocal features. These can obviously be checked by the testimony of those who heard the speaker. (See Chapters Eight, Eleven through Fourteen, and Appendix A.)

12. *Can we judge the total effectiveness of the speech?* Your judgment here will involve a study of separate details and of the over-all effect. You may judge a speech on the basis of its ideas, its structure, its appeals, or its language—or some synthesis of these factors.

You will need a norm by which to judge these speeches. A review of the principles of this book should help you.[1]

IMPROVED COMMUNICATIONS FOR BETTER UNDERSTANDING

Edward R. Murrow, Director, U.S. Information Agency[2]

Mr. Chairman, honored guests, ladies and gentlemen:

I am, indeed, in your debt. You have done me great honor.

Your club and our Agency have a strong bond in common—the person of Benjamin Franklin. For you, he is a patron saint. For us, he is the man who was probably the first information or propaganda specialist that this country had. When the British brought Hessian mercenaries to help subdue the colonies 185 years ago, Franklin, along with Thomas Jefferson, distributed handbills and leaflets among the troops. The results were startling. Of the 30,000 Hessians, 5,000 of them defected. They settled here to become stalwart citizens of a new country.

Franklin's success—one out of six of his target audience—is a goal for both of us to admire—you as users of advertising, we as purveyors of information.

I read by your citation that I have been singled out for "imaginative thinking, unshakeable courage, fertile ideas and dedicated leadership." I pause here, and the words come softly to mind of a North Carolina minister who responded to the praise of his introduction: "My heavens. I can hardly wait to see what I'm going to say."

As you of course know, I have traded in my private cudgels for a public mace. I am a bureaucrat, and I carry with me the knowledge that a much talking bureaucrat is an ill tuned instrument. Talking bureaucrats sometimes do not get the word. So it was that Captain Pearson of His Majesty's Navy posed the question amid the heat of battle: "Sir, do you give quarter?" John Paul Jones retorted with the now immortal, "I have not yet begun to fight." But I am reliably informed that upon that bloody deck in back of John Paul Jones there lay a crewman who, when he heard the remark, lifted himself on

---

[1] This summary is chiefly based upon A. Craig Baird (ed.), "Introduction," in *Representative American Speeches: 1947–48*, The H. W. Wilson Company, New York; and on Lester Thonssen and A. Craig Baird, *Speech Criticism*, The Ronald Press Company, New York, 1948.

[2] Address presented to the Poor Richard Club, Philadelphia, Pa., Thursday, September 14, 1961. Published with the permission of Edward R. Murrow.

one elbow and cried out in anguish, "Always somebody don't get the word!" I trust that I shall always as a bureaucrat be able to look back to get the word. And I say this in full knowledge that it was Satchel Paige who sagely admonished one and all: "Never look back. Something may be gaining on you." In asking me to speak today you imply that I must ignore that advice and look back on some 25 centuries of history and its lesson that speech-making is basic to man and a free society cannot exist without it. Or to put it in terms of any recent morning's headlines, we can either shoot it out or talk it out.

Communication—and any understanding that comes from it—is basic to humanity. It had its beginnings far back in the early dawn of pre-history when manlike animals first huddled together against the cold and the danger of a primitive world. Language itself came before history. Then followed an alphabet. And somewhere between the starting of language and the inventing of an alphabet came the vital steps of storing information and transmitting knowledge. Some ingenious mind discovered the sounds that could be made by beating a hollow container. Someone else noticed that fires could be seen from distant hill tops. Those first drum beats and smoke signals became the first broadcasts. Stone carved tablets became the first books. And the march of communications was on.

The Romans published a type of wall newspaper. To this day every newspaperman and agency head is in the debt of the first century Chinese who began making paper and ink. During the Middle Ages short documents were printed from wood blocks. On the eastern edge of Asia they began printing with metal type, and 15th Century Europe lay fascinated before that first Gutenberg Bible.

As David Reisman points out, the Western world would not be what it is without the printed word. We could not have fought World War II without the telephone. Gigantic high speed presses mass produce printed matter in almost unlimited volume at infinitesimally low unit cost. Plastic disc, wire, and magnetic tape give new dimension to communicating sound. With film we move into the higher dimension of moving visual imagery—and embellish it with color. We have girdled our globe with cables and wires. With the electromagnetic spectrum we could, if we chose, take this voice to which you now listen and reflect it to any place on the globe where man may desire to hear it. Soon orbiting communication satellites will enable us to beam television in every direction and place save underground. And any and all of these signals can be captured on film or magnetic tape for countless replays. And with simultaneous or delayed translation we even surmount language barriers. There has been literally an explosion in communications. For a race of animals desiring to communicate with his brethren, we have, in the vernacular of my North Carolina forebearers, come a purty far piece.

We sometimes overlook how much communications control our very lives. Walter Lippmann speaks of an island where Englishmen and Germans lived together. The year was 1914, no cables reached the island, and the packet steamer came every 60 days. When last it called news was of an approaching murder trial on the Continent. When next it called the contented island of Englishmen and Germans learned their countries had been at war for six weeks, and that people who had been behaving as friends were in fact enemies. The island was never the same again. Communications, it seems, cannot only tell us whom to hate but, in the name of nationalism and the sanctity of treaties, whom to kill.

Thus did Robespierre tell the French Revolutionaries: "He who can phrase it can lead it." Joseph Conrad said: "If you give me the right word and the right accent in which to speak it, I can move the world." Ralph Waldo Emerson declared: "There is no art more necessary to human kind than the art of putting things." Or as the thing was put by that perspicacious German, Thomas Mann: "Speech IS civilization."

It is in this calling of "phrasing it," of "putting it" that I have spent my own life. It is in many respects a noble calling. Nobility is a virtue with its own reward. All too often communications, which could be an art, is but big business. By its nature it seems destined to be controlled by the few, and herein lies its great danger.

For what they control is our right to know. What man does *not* know, he can neither fear nor act upon. What man *does* know will largely control his behavior. If you tell him the world is flat, he will sail his ships to a point and no further. If you tell him that in a far country men have discovered yellow sand, he will drop his way of life and rush to search for gold. And if you tell him that one people are friends, and another are enemies, he will like and dislike accordingly, and he will even in the surety of his knowledge drop his work and march to do battle. The way the world is imagined will determine what men will do.

So it is that this observer views with sadness what he can only describe as the "attack on truth." Truth and right are under siege. The market place of knowledge has been attacked by the adversary, and he will pervert any and every fact to gain his advantage.

Both our world and the Communist use many of the same words. We both speak of "peace." We both desire "freedom." We both proclaim "democracy." But the same words could never have more different meanings. Their "democracy" is the yoke of communism. Their "freedom" is the dictate of the police state. Their "peace" is the aggressive surge of their greed. As Clausewitz said: "Every aggressor wants peace. He would prefer to march in unopposed."

What better example than Berlin, 1961—a city divided by the wall. We say it makes captive part of a people. They say it is protection against saboteurs and spies. Our U.S. Information Agency in Berlin runs a broadcasting station called RIAS—Radio in the American Sector. Basically it broadcasts news. It reports the truth, it makes commentaries upon that truth, but its dedication to the factual is undeviating. But our truth is their provocation. RIAS is vilified as spies, lies, and packrats. This station was never designed as a provocation to the Soviet. That they find it so is not only a tribute to the power of truth but also a measure of the gulf that divides our two ways of life.

The preservation of our way of life is probably going to require an unprecedented act of self-discipline on the part of this nation. This is not a Berlin crisis. No one spoke of the crisis of 1938 as the Czechoslovakian crisis or the 1939 crisis as the Polish crisis. They were both created by one man.

The so-called Berlin crisis was created by Khrushchev. In this crisis we have no cushion either in terms of time or distance. There is no opportunity for "those who are half asleep to become half ready." Each generation must pay its installment price for freedom. It is never purchased in perpetuity and it is not to be had in the bargain basement. At some point in time we face a rendez-vous with those of our friends and ancestors who paid the earlier installments and I doubt that they paid the price in order that we may have a second out-board motor, color television or cigarettes that light themselves.

We are discovering that the price of leadership is high indeed, that our desire for easy and quick solutions is frequently frustrated, that we confront an adversary both cynical and ruthless, prepared and willing to keep his own people in ignorance while dealing in broken promises and raw terror.

What is at stake is not Berlin but the world and the manner in which its people shall live, whether fear will cause them to flinch or falter when the next payment for freedom falls due.

What is one man's truth is another man's treason. Communicating our truth around the world is what currently occupies my days—and of late, my evenings and week-ends as well. The business of my agency is to make the policy of this country as designed by the President everywhere intelligible and wherever possible, palatable.

Our Agency operates in a difficult, not too well defined area. We embrace a multitude of disciplines and professions. For a quarter century I devoted my career to expression in a single medium of communication. USIA employs not one but seven: radio, television, movies, press, book publishing, exhibits, and the arts. We are involved in an entire range of problems: from a press run in Beirut, an exhibition in Turin, a stage performance in Munich and radio relays in Colombo. From a news telecast in Bogota to a sound tracked film strip in Paris to a book typeset in Manila—upon all the myriad of details we initiate, we create, we facilitate.

But this is only half our problem. We deal not only in communications but in policy. We articulate and distribute not advertising for cigarettes or soap but clarifications of government policy and deeds. And we speak in many lan-guages to many peoples of vastly differing levels of comprehension.

Information is our job. We endeavor to reflect with fidelity to our allies, to the uncommitted nations, as well as to those who are hostile to us, not only our policy but our ideals.

I recognize, as I know you will too, that the role of our Agency has limits. We are but one arm of the U.S. Government. As such, we must respond to the policy of that government. To put it more bluntly, USIA can be no better than the policies it supports and explains. Yet within that limitation there are obviously practices and principles to which we are committed.

It is fundamental that we operate on a basis of truth. Ours is, and must be, a dedication to the factual.

But this itself poses difficulties. We operate abroad; our audience is foreign. And in this world there are no absolute standards of truth. One man's fact is another man's fiction. Our objective is, and must be credibility. It is easy to assume that because we tell the truth as we see it, others will believe us.

But statements that are true are not always believed. It is a measure of our difficulty that in this relentless half-war, truth and credibility are not co-equal.

Candor and openness have their merits—as the successful Alan Shepard flight demonstrated. They also have their demerits—as the abortive Cuban episode demonstrated.

But if truth must be our guide, then dreams must be our goal. To the hunger of those masses yearning to be free, to this sleeping giant now stirring over so much that is our world, we shall say: "We share your dreams."

As a nation we have never been allergic to change. Ours was the first of the great revolutions. It is a birthright we do not intend to let go by default. Our responsibilities of nationhood are predicated on a helping hand to others who would elevate their crushing way of existence by change into a more bountiful society. We offer no panaceas, no final solutions. We offer to join in the search of human betterment. We offer our experience and our energies in partnership in the quest for greater human excellence. This we not only endorse. This we sponsor, and promote and provoke. A tradition of government by the governed, of revolution by consent—all of these are among the greater virtues that we have to demonstrate to a world sorely in need of great virtues.

But to be effective great virtues must first be communicated. We have come a long way since that day in the 1840's when a German named Paul Joseph Reuter decided that he would supplant palace scullery gossip in London with news flown from the continent by carrier pigeon. But there is still a barrier of untold enormity for the world of communicators. That barrier is the state of the world. At the outset I referred to the dawn of early communications. The centuries that have trod the dusty bye-ways of history have not brought us all to the same point in time. There are parts of this minor planet where the best communications are still the signal fire on the hill, the drum beat in the forest, or as in the first days of Reuter's, the pigeon in the air.

The United Nations has inquired into the state of world communications. Their conclusion: nearly 70 per cent of the world's peoples lack even the barest means of being informed about developments at home, let alone in other countries.

But this statistic is optimistic. Standards set up by UNESCO for the inquiry were minimal and rudimentary. Even many countries above the 70 per cent line have communications systems far from adequate. The distribution of facilities is highly unbalanced. What facilities there are concentrate in urban areas. People who live in rural regions—the dominant condition of this globe— have virtually no communication contact at all.

In Africa, for example, with a population of over 236 million peoples, newspapers reach less than 3 million. Not a single country on that continent possesses the UNESCO minimum requirements—rudimentary as they are—for communications and information. Fifteen countries have not a single daily paper.

In the Middle East, over 50 per cent of the newspaper circulation, 40 per cent of the radio receivers, and 42 per cent of the cinema capacity are concentrated in one small country. Of the 13 other countries, 6 of them have no daily press whatsoever.

In the Far East, with one out of every four persons on earth—a population of 767 million—newspapers reach but one and one/third per cent of the people. That leaves about 760 million unaccounted for. Films, commonplace to you in this room, have yet to be seen for the first time by millions of Asians.

These pose communication problems of staggering dimensions. And they resist ease of solution. Literacy is limited. There is no purchasing power to support the advertising or transmission rates which would support communications. There is no capital for communication development. Even with today's limited coverage there is a shortage of trained and technical staffing. There is inadequate electrification. Even present frequencies seriously overlap one another. There are no effective distribution systems. Newsprint and paper are in short supply. Languages abound; the one country of India has over 500 tongues and dialects. World-wide, the problem seems almost insoluble, as some tongues are not alphabetic but ideographic, and some have yet to be reduced to any written form.

It would indeed be good to have "Improved Communication for Better Understanding." But sometimes the dimensions of our difficulties seem to conspire against us.

The corollary of this is, of course, that we must improve communications systems around the world. I agree. So do we all. But may I suggest another difficulty—much overlooked in concern for improving communications?

I testified this summer before the House Science and Astronautics Committee. The subject was space communications satellites, and what it will mean to our country to project instant television around the globe. The difficulty can be stated in these 5 words: What are we to say?

We shall expand our communications, we shall orbit our satellites, we shall transmit our messages to the world. But in the end we shall still deal with the basic elements of human communications: words and pictures. Space satellites and wider world communications will not make it any better. They will simply diffuse it over a wider area—and more quickly.

On a basis of policy, politics, and content, improved communications will not solve the fundamental problem of communications that has haunted man since time immemorial: What is he to say, and how is he to say it?

A communications system is totally neutral. Power sources, transmitters and microphones have no vocabulary. Communication systems have no conscience, only a history. They will transmit both filth and inspiration with equal facility. Distortions and duplicity over new and improved communications will still be propagated by humans.

Television and radio are still television and radio, whether transmitted from a tower 500 yards away or from a satellite 500 miles above. Over much of this globe there are unfed bellies and tired bodies that will turn to progress in communications with but marginal interest. What I am suggesting, gentlemen, is that communications advancement will neither solve our dilemmas nor salve our conscience.

May I continue this subject but change our focus, and talk of "Improved Communication for Better Understanding" not in the world but in this country.

I have spent most of my life in the public arena of private broadcasting. There are aspects of other media that disturb me: I note with concern, for example, that in the last 30 years over a thousand newspapers have perished in the United States, that for the last half century the number of newspapers in this country has been contracting, and that today almost 95 per cent of American communities are one paper towns with no competing news view. It is further a pity that national newspaper criticism is virtually non-existent. I make no pretense of imposing on the sanctity of the free press.

But as broadcasting was my past, let me share with you the thoughts and concerns of a former TV-communicator still concerned with communicating.

In a country of 180 million people, there are now 50 million television sets. There are TV sets in four out of 5 U.S. homes; the reception range of TV covers 97 per cent of America's populated areas.

Exposure to television will increase. More and more people are spending less and less time at work. A century ago the average work week was 70 hours. By 1960, it was below 40 hours. And since the American worker for every hour on the job now has two hours to spend at his discretion, and labor-saving devices make chores and tasks easier, more leisure time will undoubtedly be spent with television.

But this improved tool of communication will not necessarily lead to better understanding. No large segment of the public demands more information or better presentation of it. Public affairs, and better understanding that might come of them, are not recreation. The public wants its fun. By the time most people turn on the television set the work of the day is over. After working hours, most people prefer to be called away from reality, not made to face it. Television by itself does not usher in the democratic millennium, and its inability to do so is not its own peculiar failure. It is due to the unwillingness of men and women, even in as highly developed a democracy as our own, to take more trouble to govern themselves better.

From this arises a problem which I suggest that, as communicators, we might all ponder with some concern. In a totalitarian state the role of television will not be to teach self government. Its main purpose will be to make the governed content not to govern themselves. It will be to distract, and even to entertain. It appears that what we now ask from television is precisely what totalitarian dictators will order when their countries have as much television as we have. For an oppressed people will surely need to be distracted if they are to be ruled by a despot.

Is it not, then, ironic, that we in the United States who ask so much entertainment from television, so much escapism, so much insulation from reality, are not having such programs imposed upon us by force. We adopt the choice freely. But it is a choice made without any awareness of the nature, the intensity, and the inevitability of the contest between the democracies and totalitarianism.

It is the duty of those who control television to use it as a sound mirror to reflect conditions as they are. If what is reflected on the end of that tube is bigotry, poverty, discrimination, or prejudice, that is wholesome so long as the picture is true. Where there is controversy, it must be reflected. We have no alternative so long as we are dedicated to the proposition that the "X" on the ballot is the most important letter in the political alphabet.

The real function of television—indeed, of modern communications—is to operate a market place where ideas may compete on equal footing.

There is no way to guarantee that television will prevent the voter from being as wrong as he has so often been in the past. Television offers no guarantee that demagogues can be kept from political power. It merely provides them with wider and more intimate, more immediate circulation. I doubt that with today's communications a Lincoln or a Jefferson could be either nominated or elected. According to reports, Jefferson had an abrasive voice, and did not suffer fools gladly. While being interviewed on some panel program he might have told an obnoxious questioner what he thought of him, and that would have been fatal. As for Lincoln, he did not move gracefully, he was not a handsome man, but had a wife who was no political asset, and was a solitary man. He would probably at an early age have been sent to a school counselor, received a negative report, told that his attitude of "togetherness" was all wrong, and advised to enter a trade school if he could find one to admit him.

Television must find a little more time to remind us of our inheritance, and it must find more than a little time for the dissenters, the heretics, the minority spokesmen who may be tomorrow's majority.

The camera and all communications must follow politicians in their public guise to the very limits of privacy and decency. When politicians complain that this turns their proceedings into a circus, it should be made clear that the circus was already there and that television merely demonstrated that not all performers are well trained.

Television itself is a limited medium; it can amuse, entertain, and it can sell goods. It can arouse curiosity, and it can stimulate interest. But it cannot reason, and it is no substitute for reading.

Television and all modern communications won't save us, and probably it won't destroy us. It will, however, play an increasingly large role in our lives, and it may come to influence us greatly. The issue, I would suggest, is not so much what television does to us; it is rather what we do with television.

There is dishearteningly small indication that the great mass of the public senses its ability to influence what it is asked to see and hear. It accepts what it is given. It does little to force change or improvement.

Well phrased then was this epigram of advice from George Bernard Shaw: "We must get what we want, or we will come to want what we get."

THE NEW DYNAMICS OF CORPORATE RELATIONS WORK

J. S. Parker, Vice President, Relations Services, General Electric Company[3]

A passage from Lewis Carroll's *Alice in Wonderland* has considerable relevance to the subject of our meeting today:

" 'Let the jury consider their verdict,' the King said . . .

" 'No, No!' said the Queen, 'Sentence first—verdict afterwards . . . Off with her head!' "

[3] Reprinted with the permission of J. S. Parker.

The Queen of Hearts was expressing a viewpoint which is not unlike that of many articulate critics of large-scale business enterprise today. Many citizens are perfectly willing to condemn business with dazzling (or, more precisely, *blinding*) criticism regardless of the facts of the tremendous contributions made to society by private business enterprise.

Constructive criticism of business—as well as any other institution—is, of course, a healthy and indispensable facet of a free society. Businessmen are human, and therefore fallible. That their mistakes and shortcomings be promptly exposed is a natural and desirable consequence of the institutional importance of business enterprise.

But why is it that the relatively *few* examples of business errors are seldom evaluated in the light of the *many* contributions made? Why is it that incredible innovation and peerless performance in production and technology have not brought the degree of public understanding and support which the facts justify?

A partial answer to these crucial questions is that we businessmen have been so preoccupied with this productive efficiency that we too often have paid insufficient attention to the many individual and group relationships which are involved in our work.

This deficiency exists even though we have been amply warned by many thoughtful observers—but notably by Professor J. D. Glover of Harvard University in his book, *The Attack on Big Business*—that mere efficiency in economic performance is not adequate to ward off the devastating and possibly decisive criticism directed at business by those who claim that our basic defect is an inability to make constructive contributions in the area of *human* relationships.

There is, therefore, lasting significance in the fact that there are gathered together in this meeting today a number of business executives who wish to examine thoughtfully the subject of corporate relations work.

Corporate relations work deals with the complex patterns of management relationships with customers, employees, share owners, suppliers, dealers, community neighbors, and the general public.

Each of these groups consists of people who affect, or are affected by, the business operation. These people are individuals who often perform multiple roles—as, for example, the employee who is also a share owner and a customer, as well as a voting citizen. The sum total of the attitudes and actions of these individuals and their institutions, changing day by day, provides the setting in which any company must operate.

In this framework of a corporate relations concept, the enterprise should develop a vigorous program to maintain and improve each major relationship in harmony with the others. The profitable growth of the company depends, to a large degree, on the ability of management to obtain understanding of where common interest lies—and thus permit creative decisions which balance and appropriately serve the interests of each of those associated with the enterprise.

Relations work was spawned voluntarily early in the 20th century. But its broad development came primarily during the crisis of the 1930's, when the early efforts were supplemented by hastily improvised methods which were developed essentially as defense mechanisms against the rapid unionization movement fostered by the New Deal. While refinements have occurred, relations work has undergone few fundamental changes from these early patterns.

This traditional concept of relations work places about 80% of the corporate effort in such areas as wage and salary administration, employee benefits, so-called "personnel work," and the legal and administrative technicalities of implementing union contracts. The evidence is abundant that the scope of this traditional relations effort has been inadequate. Here are some of the more obvious dimensions of our failure:

1. The greater individual output which remains substantially untapped, pending solution by management of complex problems of *human motivation and communication;* there are informed estimates that individual output could be increased as much as 20% if management would both deserve and get employee confidence and cooperation;

2. The steady attrition of power and control to the federal government, and the widening arc of influence wielded by the ever-increasing bureaucracies in Washington;

3. The continuing low-level of general public awareness of the over-all good intentions and solid accomplishments of private business enterprise; public opinion polls often make this fact painfully obvious;

4. The frequent failure of management to win its deserved share of employee loyalty, as indicated by the push-button control in the hands of some top union officials—control which enables them to assert life-or-death power over many business enterprises;

5. The widespread failure to recognize and understand the true role of management, and its social, as well as economic contribution; and

6. The continuing difficulty of gaining mass understanding of such key economic facts as these—(*a*) wages are ultimately paid by customers, not by the owners or managers of a business; (*b*) inflated wages mean inflated prices, which ultimately hurt the wage earner like everybody else; (*c*) employment security depends on the existence of opportunity to continue producing goods and services that customers will buy, at a price they are willing to pay; (*d*) wages should not be determined by "formula"; and (*e*) economic progress depends on the reinvestment of a substantial part of business gains in research, development, and new facilities.

These dimensions of failure of past efforts plead eloquently that some new dynamics—innovations with new force, new thrust—are required if relations work in the second half of the 20th century is to be equal to the needs and opportunities which prevail.

My purpose is not to describe the General Electric approach to relations work—although two of my associates, P. D. Moore and C. J. Dover, will later present a case history of the bargaining strategy and communication which preceded and accompanied the 1960 negotiations and the unfortunate GE-IUE strike.

Rather, my specific purpose will be to discuss broadly certain needed innovations which are changing the traditional patterns of relations activities, and which show great promise of producing new high levels of effective corporate action.

From the mass of observable, post-World War II experience by American companies on the relations front, I have selected five action areas which have already had some degree of success, and which seem to offer great promise for further application in depth:

They are:

1. Purposeful consolidation of relations work
2. Professional, objective management of the relations function
3. Persuasive, forthright communication
4. Firm and fair collective bargaining
5. Effective external relations

PURPOSEFUL CONSOLIDATION OF RELATIONS WORK

In considering the need for purposeful consolidation of relations work, it is important that we understand how the growing interdependence of all groups in society makes unwise the traditional compartmentalization of relations activities.

The still current tendency to diffuse organizationally the responsibilities for so-called public relations and so-called industrial relations is all too likely to detract from total effectiveness. Public relations people have creative skills, and should provide an important awareness of external social, political, and economic trends which vitally affect the enterprise. Industrial relations people have depth understanding of the internal relationships, the neglect of which can bring short-range disaster to any business enterprise.

These great and important strengths are mutually reinforcing and need to be integrated for maximum effectiveness. It should be equally obvious that the needs of relations integration, strategy, tactics, and timing are more difficult if the decision-making authority is divided on an absolute basis among two or more top-level managers. The organizational marriage, therefore, of internal and external relations is one promising new dynamic which can do much to upgrade the total effectiveness of corporate relations work.

PROFESSIONAL, OBJECTIVE MANAGEMENT OF THE RELATIONS FUNCTION

The second of these five innovations, professional, objective management of the relations function, recognizes that there is a spectrum of corporate relationships with society—and that these relationships need to be *managed by objectives*. Thus, relations work needs the same professional skills which have proved so successful in the management of manufacturing, engineering, finance, and marketing—i.e., to plan, to organize, to integrate, and to measure.

We see increasing evidence that the alternative to developing these managerial skills in relations work is the possible loss of advantages gained through effective professional management of the other functions. This should be clear, because all of the advances to date of so-called scientific management have *failed to create* a political and social environment which offers any clear mandate for the continuation of a system most conducive to the further growth and profitability of private enterprise. Thus, professional work in the field of corporate relations is one of the most demanding and potentially productive frontiers in the business world.

We must discard the idea that top management and the managers of the traditional functions can establish a relations organization simply to keep themselves free of relations-type problems—so they can continue to focus all their efforts on making and selling goods and services. Professional relations people can supply guidance and counsel, *but the relations job is and must be part of the daily work of the chief executive officer and managers—line as well as staff.* The role of relations people is to *service* these managers. Except for specific chores such as contract administration, relations people cannot do the relations work of other managers.

PERSUASIVE, FORTHRIGHT COMMUNICATION

The third of these five innovations, persuasive and forthright communication, is one of the most important, and perhaps the least well understood. I would like, therefore, to put some extra stress on this subject, and discuss it in terms of four requirements—(1) the conceptual requirement, (2) the ethical requirement, (3) the professional requirement, and (4) the staffing requirement.

The conceptual requirement calls for understanding of a conceptual framework of simplicity and great usefulness for either internal or external communication by management—the analogy with product marketing experience. Success in marketing today will seldom be achieved (even if the product is good) unless aggressive advertising and merchandising occur. But too many of us still do not understand that relations success by management today will seldom be achieved (even though management acts are generally sound) unless persuasive, forthright communication occurs. In one case, we are marketing a product—in the other, management attitudes, objectives, and needs. Thus, the "silence is golden" concept of relations has long been dead and decayed—and it's time we gave it a decent burial.

Management needs to undergo an agonizing reappraisal of how ineffective its efforts in employee communication, in particular, have been. Effective employee communication does more than merely entertain employees or give them a skeleton outline of a few basic facts. The era of folksy entertainment (gossip columns, how to cook hamburgers, and enchanting photographs of live babies and dead fish) was not equal to the needs of the situation. The era of information (a mixture of news about employee benefits, 2000-word "Messages from the President," and the bland, "free enterprise crusade"), was similarly inadequate. Emerging now, however, is the *era of interpretation and persuasion,* which shows great promise for effective results. Remember, employees are interested—if they understand their personal stakes in the business.

This new trend in employee communication features interpreting the facts in terms of *employee* interest and welfare; it features great emphasis on basic economics which will bring better understanding of business operations and how important many seemingly distant activities become, as related to the long-range welfare of employees.

Fortunately, there has been a growing understanding that our communication cannot be effective unless we reject the traditional "zone of silence," and speak up with courage and conviction on the current issues which affect business, even though they be controversial.

The ethical requirement is full understanding that management has not only the right, but the duty, to speak up persuasively on issues affecting the welfare of the enterprise, even though controversial. We should reject the notion that harmony is an end in itself, and understand instead that often the conflict of ideas is a force for progress and the essence of the democratic process—and if no issue is taken, it is easy to lose by default.

There is nothing sinister about persuasion. We should, of course, condemn distortion, evil intent, and dishonest juggling of the facts in any form.

But we should not condemn persuasion, per se. We should simply insist that our persuasive communication meet proper ethical standards, which means that our purpose must be honest and our message must reflect sound judgment based on a thorough knowledge of the subject. Unless we exercise our freedom, which is the basis of this society, we will not long have it. People can always take more informed action if *both* sides are heard.

The intellectual underpinning, and the very essence of a free society is that conflicting viewpoints are subjected to public scrutiny. Our nation has matured under the principle of free expression. In recent years, however, the notion has grown that *conflict in itself* is immoral or degrading. We tend to frown, for example, on conflict between management and unions at the bargaining table —forgetting temporarily that in this area the worst thing that could happen to the employees, the business, and the general public would be for *honest* differences to cease to exist—either because of excessive power exerted by one party or the other, or because of under-the-table collusion between unions and management, or because one party shied away from standing for what it believed to be right.

It has become fairly fashionable to regard harmony as an end in itself, appearing sometimes more important than any laws or any principles. Such views have spawned, in our generation, the policy of appeasement and the cult of conformity. And experience shows that active detractors inevitably take advantage of the intellectually lazy.

We all have an obligation to avoid needless physical conflict, but in a free society the conflict of ideas is the axis of our intellect and progress. When all conflict ends, when we all conform to one single set of values and ideas, when pure harmony is nowhere disturbed by the voice of the maverick—that era will be the age of faceless humans, and the time when freedom will wither and die.

These philosophical considerations are important to those involved in communication work, because unsound notions about the ethics of persuasion are often responsible for the communication ineptness which we in management so often display. Confusion about the ethics of persuasion has a great deal to do with our all-too-frequent tendency to get foot-in-mouth disease and keep silent on issues of top importance to employees.

The *professional requirement* is that management must become more familiar with the essentials of the communication process. We need to understand and practice the communication principles which have emerged from research in the social sciences and from the experience of many companies in practical communication efforts—the principles of anticipation, of continuity, of repetition, of primacy, of source credibility. Management must also learn how to listen, and how to grasp the fact that good upward communication is made, not born. More managers need to learn specifically how to apply communication skills and principles to employee publication effectiveness, our needed economic education programs, a community or national controversy affecting our business, or any of the other problems which face management and which effective communication can help solve.

The *staffing requirement* is that management makes the necessary investment to train or acquire individuals to fill a new kind of job, still foreign to most management organization charts—the job of (*a*) managing the writers and other creative people needed for the function, (*b*) doing the research which will help managers understand the critical role of communication, (*c*) establishing training courses and otherwise helping to teach the line organization how to discharge its responsibility to attain effective, two-way communication, and (*d*) planning and implementing the strategy which will coordinate the normally diffused communication efforts and make of them an essential internal and external tool of managing the enterprise. *Quality*, not quantity, is the essential manpower need.

Few companies have, as yet, perceived this need, or found the men to manage it. Such men combine a tough-minded knowledge of internal relationships, depth understanding of the role and tactics of union officials in society, a good grasp of social, political and economic forces in the economy, basic creative skills, and—rarest of all—professional competence in the communication process and knowledge of how to apply it to business oriented problems. By generous estimate there are perhaps 100 such men in management jobs today. We could use 10,000 of them, and fast. Remember, however, their effectiveness, growth, and multiplication depends substantially on the attitude of the manager responsible for running the business.

Firm and Fair Collective Bargaining

I have called the fourth of these five innovations we are discussing *firm and fair collective bargaining*. Some of the most promising relations developments have occurred in collective bargaining, and in the wider band of employee-employer relationships as a whole.

The innovation which is attracting the most deserved interest is a shift by many companies away from the traditional "auction" concept of collective bargaining to a firm and fair posture at the bargaining table. The new approach varies, as it should, from company to company, but the procedure features:

Thorough research on economic trends pertinent to collective bargaining; careful listening to and consideration of union demands; careful and thoughtful preparation of a proposal which is fully up to what the facts indicate it should be, and is responsive to demonstrated employee needs or desires; a willingness to change the proposal if warranted by pertinent new facts; an *unwillingness* to change a proposal simply because of union threats or coercion, and the principle of supplying complete information to employees and all others concerned.

Such a procedure makes unnecessary the "horse-trading," the "strike-brink-manship," and the other hallmarks of auction bargaining. If both parties to the collective bargaining process, for example, are really doing their prebargaining homework—the diligent, objective research into the economic issues—and are sincerely seeking the sound solution, they would rarely be far apart on what a proper economic settlement should be.

The growing rejection by managers of the outmoded, auction concept of bargaining is essentially an assertion that they are men of reason, who do their best to treat employees fairly because they *want* to do so.

Remember, anyone can negotiate a settlement starting at zero and working up, while the union starts very high and makes its reluctant concessions and "sacrifices"—but it is very doubtful if this procedure will produce a settlement which is optimum for all those associated with the business. This procedure takes little or no preparation.

It took managers too many years to realize that they lost the respect of the public and their own employees when they offered, at the beginning of collective bargaining, something less than they knew to be right, then permitted themselves to be "forced" by the carefully publicized demands of the union into raising their offer in order to avoid a strike—all done, of course, with the trappings of theatrical exhibition. This wasn't even good theatre, because the audience as well as the players always knew how each act would end. And all concerned knew in advance that the union would become the hero and that management must become the villain!

We can all hope that the bright, new concept of firm and fair collective bargaining, based on full research and consideration of pertinent facts, will bring more constructive results. The outmoded auction approach requires the employer to appear to be anti-employee in order to prove he's *not* anti-union.

Behind sincere, thoughtful collective bargaining are significant changes in how management recognizes the broader fabric of employer-employee relationships. Some of the more important changes are: (*a*) a new emphasis on the importance of the individual; (*b*) a growing understanding by all involved of the mutuality of long-term interests of employer and employee, and the refutation of the Marxian notion of inevitable class conflict; (*c*) realization that the composition of the work force is changing drastically; that unions, though their *political* power is growing dangerously, represent a smaller proportion of the work force than at the end of World War II (now 18 million organized in a total work force of about 73 million); (*d*) a growing recognition that many national union officials are basically politicians with little interest or concern in the success of the business their constituents depend upon, and that compulsory union membership, third-party intervention in collective bargaining, and the continous union demands for "more" are usually not in the best interest of all concerned.

Effective External Relations

The fifth, and last of these new dynamics, is an effective approach to external relations.

More corporate effort and money has been expended on external relationships than in any other area of relations work, but innovation here is still possibly our most urgent need.

Measurements in this area are difficult, but the pragmatic evidence of past, over-all progress is uninspiring, at best. It is a sad commentary that some recent surveys showed that businessmen ranked last, behind union and government officials, when the public was asked who is primarily responsible for preserving freedoms and raising living standards!

Here, briefly, are some of the more promising innovations on the external relations front:

1. There is an encouraging increase in the number of publicly defined corporate objectives which assert that private enterprise, if it is to be successful, must be a force for social good, as well as a purely economic institution—that the sole purpose is not short-range maximization of profit regardless of the best interests of any group except the share owners. Thus, realization is growing in management circles that gaining a widespread understanding of where common interest lies, and then serving the best interests, in balance, of all groups who make the enterprise possible—customers, employees, share owners, dealers, suppliers, and the general public—is indeed the only way in which long-range growth and profitability can be insured.

2. There are more and more corporate programs which are clearly dedicated to the public interest—which try to solve some of society's urgent problems. Two examples which come readily to mind are the efforts by many companies to raise levels of state unemployment compensation, where appropriate, and the many splendid programs of corporate support of educational institutions. Such programs constitute welcome changes from the earlier corporate practices of merely opposing legislative attempts to combat society's business problems, without offering constructive alternative solutions. Such programs also recognize that there are things which can best be done locally, where they are responsive to the needs, and not on a federal basis.

3. There is more recognition of the need and more progress toward improving the relationships between businessmen and the intellectual community. It is encouraging to note that anti-intellectualism has declined to a marked degree in business circles. It is also encouraging to see new, planned efforts by some companies to develop programs aimed at improving their relationships with the clergy, educators, and other thought leaders. This, of course, must be a two-way street.

4. We are witnessing the birth of new techniques and new staff emphasis on investor relations programs. These new approaches will teach us who investors are, why they invest, what they know about the business, and what they want to know. Once these basics are accomplished, management can more effectively enlist the support of share owners as citizens acting in their own behalf, and thus tap a tremendous reservoir of allies for constructive programs and continuing progress.

5. An emerging emphasis on government relations shows great promise. Corporate ground-breakers in this area are doing the research and teaching necessary to encourage (*a*) the development of a working knowledge of the interaction of government and business, (*b*) an understanding of political trends

and issues, and (c) participation in the political party of individual choice. Constructive political action, of course, depends on sound thinking and strength in *both* political parties.

6. Community relations is growing up, too. Once regarded as primarily a process of charitable contributions and participation in civic activities, community relations is increasingly being practiced as a *quid pro quo*, something-for-something, two-way proposition between a job-producing plant and the local community. This is a healthy development, as is the increasing competition between communities for new industry. These events have helped bring about the widespread adoption of another innovation, the "better business climate" concept. Real progress is being made here—progress in spotlighting the *community's* responsibility to provide adequate law enforcement, fair tax treatment of business, educational and recreational opportunities, transportation facilities, etc., as well as the *corporate* responsibility to keep trying to improve its record as a good citizen.

7. There is an encouraging and long-overdue growth of research-mindedness in external relations work. We are witnessing a closer and happier liaison between professionals in external relations work, and those important, but too-often-neglected, scholars of the social sciences. Already this liaison has brought us the promising new tool of corporate image measurement. When fully developed, this measurement may sharpen substantially our ability to measure progress or deterioration in external relations work—and thus give us badly needed bench marks for measuring the return on the substantial investment we make in public relations activities.

In conclusion, it is perhaps appropriate that we take a brief look ahead, and consider some factors which will surely affect the progress of relations work in the future.

First, I would like to say that we at General Electric fully recognize and deeply regret the damage which has resulted from the unfortunate antitrust cases in the electrical industry. Our management accepts its responsibility and is doing all possible to prevent any further such problems.

Mr. Cordiner stated it well at a Management Conference on January 5, 1960:

"We in General Electric believe in and benefit from vigorous competition. The success of the economy of the United States—a success unmatched anywhere, anytime—is based solidly on the concept of a free and competitive market, with the government helping to see that the economy does remain truly competitive. Operating such a competitive economy places great responsibilities on those engaged in business. We must of course observe both the letter and the spirit of the laws that affect business activity. But of equal importance, we must work in an ethical framework that is appropriate to a free, competitive system.

"This system will remain free and competitive only so long as citizens, and particularly those of us with responsibilities in business life, are capable of the self-discipline required. If we are not capable of self-discipline the power of the government will be increasingly invoked as a substitute, until the system is no longer free or competitive. When we speak of business ethics in a free and competitive system, therefore, we are talking primarily about self-discipline."

I believe this situation serves to illustrate so clearly a measure of the total relations problem facing *all* of us in the business community, as indicated by the eagerness and evident satisfaction with which large numbers of people condemn the entire private enterprise system on these rare occasions when a small number of businessmen are guilty of wrong-doing.

Another fact important to relations work in the future will be the impact of last year's presidential elections. We can safely predict that there will be more than lip-service paid to the campaign promises which were apparently made to the top union command—and this development will make all our relations problems even more severe.

More government intervention in union-management disputes, for example, is a demonstrated policy of the new administration in Washington, D.C. If such intervention becomes more extensive, it can virtually destroy the process of free collective bargaining. Those who espouse a major role for the federal government at the bargaining table fail to understand that this will inevitably mean that *fewer*, not more, settlements will be worked out at the bargaining table.

What is the incentive for a top union official to settle with management on *any* terms, if he can seek and get government intervention? Third parties *always* tend to "split the difference." The possibility that the government, or any other third party, would recommend a settlement *less* than any company's offer or position is too remote to warrant serious consideration.

We will be facing up to these and other severe problems in the years ahead, and such developments make the importance of relations work all the more evident.

We must continually remind ourselves that effectiveness for any relations concept is dependent on the good record of the enterprise in trying to treat fairly and equitably the various individuals associated with it. But we must also understand that public and employee favor *does not automatically accrue* to the company which has merely compiled a recognizable record of fair treatment of all groups concerned.

The very absence of deserved public and employee favor is the compelling imperative for new emphasis on relations work. There is much that must be done. It must be done by the many, not the few, because no single individual, no single company, no single industry can bring about alone the environmental changes which may be the conditions for long-range survival of our free economic institutions. Our job is to stimulate people so that they *care*, and are thus willing and eager to *act*.

If managers go on regarding relations work as a distant relative, to be welcomed into our corporate homes only in times of celebration or crisis—if we continue to be overpowered by the inertia inherent in the inadequate concepts of traditional activities—if we can't find the courage and the inclination to gain substantially more widespread adoption of these innovations and trends in relations work—then we face a grim and chilling period of further deterioration of our corporate images and effectiveness.

No pat formula can spell success in relations work for any company. Each must attack its own problems with its own skills and programming.

We need still more attention and creative innovation by all companies—particularly in the five areas we are discussing today.

If we can apply to these important areas the same degree of skill, imagination, and practical accomplishment that has brought such spectacular achievements in technology, we will go far toward solving our pivotal problems of human relationships.

It's an exciting prospect.

THE PSYCHOLOGY OF THE SCIENTIST

Anne Roe, Lecturer, Graduate School of Education, Harvard University[4]

Science is the creation of scientists, and every scientific advance bears somehow the mark of the man who made it. The artist exposes himself in his work; the scientist seems rather to hide in his, but he is there. Surely the historian of science must understand the man if he is fully to understand the progress of science, and he must have some comprehension of the science if he is to understand the men who make it.

The general public image of the scientist has not been and indeed is not now a flattering one, and at best it certainly is not an endearing one. Characterizations of scientists almost always emphasize the objectivity of their work and describe their cold, detached, impassive, unconcerned observation of phenomena which have no emotional meaning for them. This could hardly be further from the truth. The scientist as a person is a nonparticipating observer in only a very limited sense. He does not interact with what he is observing, but he does participate as a person. It is, perhaps, this fact—that the scientist does not expect, indeed does not want, the things that he is concerned with to be equally concerned with him—that has given others this impression of coldness, remoteness, and objectivity. (The social scientist is in a remarkably difficult position since the "objects with which he is concerned" are people, and both they and he may be more than a little ambivalent about this matter of interaction. But this is a special problem which I will by-pass here, noting only that in many ways the social scientist differs from the natural scientist in terms of personality and motivations.)

The truth of the matter is that the creative scientist, whatever his field, is very deeply involved emotionally and personally in his work, and that he himself is his own most essential tool. We must consider both the subjectivity of science and what kinds of people scientists are.

THE PERSONAL FACTOR

But first we must consider the processes of science. Suppose we take the scientist at the time when he has asked a question, or has set up a hypothesis

[4] Reprinted with the permission of *Science* and of the author.

which he wants to test. He must decide what observations to make. It is simply not possible to observe everything that goes on under a given set of conditions; he must choose what to observe, what measurements to make, how fine these measurements are to be, how to record them. These choices are never dictated entirely by the question or hypothesis (and anyway, that too bears his own particular stamp). One has only to consider how differently several of his colleagues would go about testing the same hypothesis to see that personal choice enters in here.

But this is just the beginning. Having decided what is to be observed, and having set up the techniques for observing, the scientist comes to the point of making the actual observations. All the complex apparatus of modern science is only a means of extending the range of man's sensory and perceptual capacities, and all the information derived through such extensions must eventually be reduced to some form in which man, with his biological limitations, can receive it. Here, too, in spite of all precautions and in spite of complete honesty, the personal factor enters in. The records of two observers will not dovetail exactly, even when they read figures from a dial. Errors may creep in, and the direction of the error is more likely than not to be associated with the observer's interest in how the findings come out. Perhaps the clearest evidence on this point comes from research on extrasensory perception. A scientist who is deeply committed to a hypothesis is well advised to have a neutral observer if the import of an observation is immediately apparent. Often, of course, such errors are minor, but they can be important, not only to the immediate problem but to society. I have wondered to what extent the disparity in figures on radioactive fallout may reflect such factors. Very few scientists, including psychologists, who have demonstrated selective perception as a laboratory exercise, take account of the phenomenon in their own work.

Once the observations are recorded, other questions are asked: When is the evidence sufficient to be conclusive, one way or the other? How important are discrepancies? What degree of generalization is permissible? Here, again, we may expect personally slanted answers. Taxonomy offers a very clear illustration of the effect of personality: One biologist may classify a given set of specimens into a few species, and another may classify them into many species. Whether the specimens are seen as representing a few or many groups depends largely on whether one looks for similarities or for differences, on whether one looks at the forest or the trees. A "lumper" may honestly find it impossible to understand how a "splitter" arrives at such an obviously incorrect solution, and vice versa. Such differences cannot be resolved by appeal to the "facts"—there are no facts which cannot be perceived in different ways. This is not to say that the facts are necessarily distorted. The problem of the criterion exists in all science, although some scientists are more aware of it than others.

The matter of personal commitment to a hypothesis is one that deserves more consideration than it usually receives. Any man who has gone through the emotional process of developing a new idea, of constructing a new hypothesis, is to some extent, and usually to a large extent, committed to that hypothesis in a very real sense. It is his baby. It is as much his creation as a painting is the personal creation of the painter. True, in the long run it stands or falls, is accepted or rejected, on its own merits, but its creator has a personal stake in it. The scientist has more at stake than the artist, for data which may support or invalidate his hypothesis are in the public domain in a sense in which art criticism never is. It may even be because of this that scientists customarily check their hypotheses as far as they can before they state them publicly. And, indeed, the experienced scientist continues to check, hoping that if errors are to be found, it will be he who finds them, so that he will have a chance to make revisions, or even to discard the hypothesis, should that prove necessary. He finds it less difficult to discard his hypothesis if, in his efforts at checking, he has been able to come up with another one.

The extent of personal commitment to a hypothesis is a prominent factor in the historical interplay between scientists. The degree of this commitment varies in an individual with different hypotheses, and varies between individuals. One very important factor here is the scientist's productivity. If he has many new ideas he will be less disturbed (and less defensive) if one fails to pan out. If he has very few ideas, an error is much harder to take, and there are many historical instances of errors which the author of the idea has never been able to see himself. I think many scientists are genuinely unaware of the extent, or even of the fact, of this personal involvement, and themselves accept the myth of impersonal objectivity. This is really very unfortunate. It is true that only a man who is passionately involved in his work is likely to make important contributions, but the committed man who knows he is committed and can come to terms with this fact has a good chance of getting beyond his commitment and of learning how to disassociate himself from his idea when this is necessary. There is little in the traditional education of scientists to prepare them for this necessity, and there are many who are still unaware of it. The extent of a scientist's personal involvement in a theory can now be a matter of grave public concern. Scientists who become advisers on political or other policy have an extraordinarily heavy responsibility for achieving some detachment from their own theories. How many of them realize this?

But once one hypothesis is found acceptable, this is not the end of it. One hypothesis inevitably leads to another; answering one question makes it possible to ask other, hopefully more precise ones. And so a new hypothesis or a new theory is offered. How is this new theory arrived at? This is one expression of the creative process, and it is a completely personal process. It is personal regardless of whether one or more individuals is involved, for in every advance made by a group, the person contributing at the moment has had to assimilate the contributions of the others and order them in his own personal way.

THE CREATIVE PROCESS

There have been many millions of words written about the creative process, few of them very illuminating. The reason is not hard to find. The process is intimate and personal and characteristically takes place not at the level of full consciousness but at subconscious or preconscious levels. It has been inaccessible to study largely because we have not yet found any means for controlling it. Many effective scientists and artists have learned a few techniques which may reduce interference with it, but no one to my knowledge has discovered any means by which we can set it in motion at will.

It is probable that the fundamentals of the creative process are the same in all fields, but in those fields in which an advance in knowledge is sought, there is an additional requirement—or rather, one requirement receives particular emphasis. This is the need for a large store of knowledge and experience. The broader the scientist's experience and the more extensive his stock of knowledge, the greater the possibility of a real breakthrough.

The creative process involves a scanning or searching through stocks of stored memories. There seems to be a rather sharp limit to the possibility of very significant advance through voluntary, logical scanning of these stores. For one thing, they vary enormously in their accessibility to conscious recall and in the specificity of their connections, so that reliance upon conscious, orderly, logical thinking is not likely to produce many results at this stage, however essential such procedures become later in verification. This scanning is typically for patterns and complex associations rather than for isolated units. It may be, however, that a small unit acts as a sort of key to a pattern. What seems to happen, in creative efforts in science as well as in every other field, is that the individual enters a state in which logical thinking is submerged and in which thought is prelogical. Such thought is described as random largely because it typically tries seemingly illogical and distantly related materials, and it often makes major advances in just this way. It is not fully random, however, because it is goal-directed and because even in this preconscious work there is appropriate selection and rejection of available connections. This stage of the creative process is accompanied by generally confused or vague states of preoccupation of varying degrees of depth; it is well described as "stewing." It is this stage which apparently cannot be hurried or controlled.

Although termination of this stage (finding a solution, or "getting insight," as it is often called) quite frequently occurs in a moment of dispersed attention, it apparently does not help to induce a state of dispersed attention in the hope of provoking a quicker end to the process. It should be added that, while insights do frequently occur "in a flash," they need not do so, and that the process is the same whether or not the insight turns out to have validity.

To acquire the necessary store of knowledge requires long and difficult application, and as science advances, the amount of information to be assimilated becomes greater and greater, despite increasing generalization in the organizing of the data. Obviously, as more experience is stored and as the interconnections become better established and more numerous, the scanning becomes more effective. Such interconnections develop more and more readily as the process of acquiring experience takes on significance in the light of theory. This process requires not only the basic capacity to assimilate experiences but very strong motivation to persist in the effort. Strong motivation is also required if one is to continue with a search which may for a long time be unproductive. Motivation of this kind and strength derives from the needs and structure of the personality. Its sources are rarely obvious, although they can sometimes be traced. They do not necessarily derive from "neurotic problems," although they frequently do. It is no cause for dismay when they do. The ability of the human being to find in a personal problem motivation for a search for truth is one of the major accomplishments of the species.

If past experiences have brought about a compartmentalization of the storage areas, so that some portions are partially or wholly inaccessible, obviously the scientist is limited in his search. Compartmentalization of particular areas may result from personal experiences of a sort that lead to neurotic structures generally, or it may result from specific cultural restrictions, such as political or religious indoctrination. The extent to which such indoctrination will inhibit creative effort, however, depends upon how close the inaccessible areas are in content to the problems at issue. We have fairly conclusive evidence that political indoctrination need not interfere with inquiry into mathematical and physical science. Religious indoctrination can interfere strongly at any point, as history has documented very fully for us. The conclusion is no different from the basic principle of therapy; the more areas of experience there are accessible to conscious and preconscious thought, the better are the prospects for creativity.

Once an apparent answer to the scientist's question has been found, there is still a long process of pursuing and checking to be gone through. Not every man who can produce new ideas is also good at the business of checking them, and of course the reverse is also true. It is in the utilization of such personal differences as these that a "team approach" can make sense.

THE CREATIVE SCIENTIST

This, then, is a brief review of what little we know of the process of creation. What do we know of the characteristics of scientists who can use this process effectively? Many lines of inquiry have demonstrated that the range of characteristics that are associated with creative productivity in a human being is very wide. These characteristics fall into almost all categories into which personal traits have been divided for purposes of study—abilities, interests, drives, temperament, and so on.

To limit our discussion to scientific productivity, it is clear to start with that there are great variations in the amount of curiosity possessed by different people. Curiosity appears to be a basic drive. I suspect it may vary consistently with sex, on either a biological or a cultural basis, but we have as yet no idea how to measure such drives. No one becomes a scientist without a better-than-average amount of curiosity, regardless of whether he was born with it, was brought up in a stimulating environment, or just did not have it severely inhibited.

Intelligence and creativity are not identical, but intelligence does play a role in scientific creativity—rather more than it may play in some other forms of creativity. In general, one may summarize by saying that the minimum intelligence required for creative production in science is considerably better than average, but that, given this, other variables contribute more to variance in performance. It must also be noted that special abilities (numerical, spatial, verbal, and so on) play somewhat different roles in different scientific fields, but that ability must in no case be below average. A cultural anthropologist, for example, has little need for great facility with numbers. An experimental physicist, on the other hand, does require facility with numbers although he need not have great facility with words.

PERSONALITY PATTERNS

A number of studies have contributed to the picture of the personality patterns of productive scientists, and it is rather striking that quite different kinds of investigations have produced closely similar results. These can be briefly summarized in six different groups, as follows:

1. Truly creative scientists seek experience and action and are independent and self-sufficient with regard to perception, cognition, and behavior. These findings have been expressed in various studies in such terms as the following: they are more observant than others and value this quality; they are more independent with respect to cognition and value judgments; they have high dominance; they have high autonomy; they are Bohemian or radical; they are not subject to group standards and control; they are highly egocentric.

2. They have a preference for apparent but resolvable disorder and for an esthetic ordering of forms of experience. They have high tolerance for ambiguity, but they also like to put an end to it in their own way—and in their own time.

3. They have strong egos (whether this derives from or is responsible for their independence and their tolerance for ambiguity is a moot question). This ego strength permits them to regress to preconscious states with certainty that they will return from these states. They have less compulsive superegos than others. They are capable of disciplined management of means leading to significant experience. They have no feeling of guilt about the independence of thought and action mentioned above. They have strong control of their impulses.

4. Their interpersonal relations are generally of low intensity. They are reported to be ungregarious, not talkative (this does not apply to social scientists), and rather asocial. There is an apparent tendency to femininity in highly original men, and to masculinity in highly original women, but this may be a cultural interpretation of the generally increased sensitivity of the men and the intellectual capacity and interests of the women. They dislike interpersonal controversy in any form and are especially sensitive to interpersonal aggression.

5. They show much stronger preoccupation with things and ideas than with people. They dislike introversive and affect-associated preoccupations, except in connection with their own research.

6. They like to take the calculated risk, but it must involve nature, not people, and must not depend on simple luck.

CONCLUSIONS

How do these personality characteristics relate to the creative process in science as I have discussed it? An open attitude toward experience makes possible accumulation of experience with relatively little compartmentalization; independence of perception, cognition, and behavior permit greater than average reordering of this accumulated experience (the behavioral eccentricities so often noted are consistent with this). The strong liking for turning disorder into order carries such individuals through the searching period which their tolerance for ambiguity permits them to enter. The strong egos, as noted, permit regression to prelogical forms of thought without serious fear of failure to get back to logical ones. Preoccupation with things and ideas rather than with people is obviously characteristic of natural scientists, and even of some social scientists. This characteristic is not directly related to creativity, I think, but rather to the content of it.

I need not add that such statements as these are generalizations and that any individual case may be an exception. We may go farther, however, and generalize differences among men who follow different branches of science. That a man chooses to become a scientist and succeeds means that he has the temperament and personality as well as the ability and opportunity to do so. The branch of science he chooses, even the specific problems he chooses and the way he works on them, are intimately related to what he is and to his deepest needs. The more deeply engaged he is, the more profoundly is this true. To understand what he does, one must try to know what his work means to him. The chances are that he does not know or care to know. Indeed, he does not need to know. We do.

INAUGURAL ADDRESS

John F. Kennedy[5]

President John F. Kennedy (1917–   ), the youngest man ever elected Chief Executive of the United States, delivered this Inaugural Address, at Washington, D.C., January 20, 1961. The ceremonies took place on the east side of the Capitol before an immediate audience of 20,000 and before a national and world-wide radio and television audience of many millions.

The address, in contrast to other inaugural addresses, was directed almost exclusively to peoples abroad. In original language of high eloquence the speaker appealed to the allies, Latin American states, emerging new nations, the United Nations, and especially to the "adversaries" (the Soviet world was not specifically named) to "begin anew" in the quest of survival, peace, and world-wide progress. "Together," he said, "let us explore the stars, conquer the deserts, eradicate disease, tap the ocean depths and encourage the arts and commerce." In phrasing, structural movement, political, economic, and humanitarian concepts, the speech ranks high as an oral state document. Said Senator A. S. Mike Monroney, of Oklahoma, "the best inaugural address I have ever heard." He added that he had heard twelve, beginning in 1917 with Woodrow Wilson's second inaugural. High praise came from national leaders of all parties, many representatives of allied and neutral countries, and favorable comment from behind the Iron Curtain (though no official approval came out of Moscow).

Vice President Johnson, Mr. Speaker, Mr. Chief Justice, President Eisenhower, Vice President Nixon, President Truman, Reverend Clergy, fellow citizens: We observe today not a victory of party but a celebration of freedom

[5] Text supplied by the White House.

—symbolizing an end as well as a beginning—signifying renewal as well as change. For I have sworn before you and Almighty God the same solemn oath our forebears prescribed nearly a century and three-quarters ago.

The world is very different now. For man holds in his mortal hands the power to abolish all forms of human poverty and all forms of human life. And yet the same revolutionary beliefs for which our forebears fought are still at issue around the globe—the belief that the rights of man come not from the generosity of the state but from the hand of God.

We dare not forget today that we are the heirs of that first revolution. Let the word go forth from this time and place, to friend and foe alike, that the torch has been passed to a new generation of Americans—born in this century, tempered by war, disciplined by a hard and bitter peace, proud of our ancient heritage—and unwilling to witness or permit the slow undoing of those human rights to which this nation has always been committed, and to which we are committed today at home and around the world.

Let every nation know, whether it wishes us well or ill, that we shall pay any price, bear any burden, meet any hardship, support any friend, oppose any foe to assure the survival and the success of liberty.

This much we pledge—and more.

To those old allies whose cultural and spiritual origins we share, we pledge the loyalty of faithful friends. United, there is little we cannot do in a host of new cooperative ventures. Divided, there is little we can do—for we dare not meet a powerful challenge at odds and split asunder.

To those new states whom we welcome to the ranks of the free, we pledge our word that one form of colonial control shall not have passed away merely to be replaced by a far more iron tyranny. We shall not always expect to find them supporting our view. But we shall always hope to find them strongly supporting their own freedom—and to remember that, in the past, those who foolishly sought power by riding the back of the tiger ended up inside.

To those peoples in the huts and villages of half the globe struggling to break the bonds of mass misery, we pledge our best efforts to help them help themselves, for whatever period is required—not because the Communists may be doing it, not because we seek their votes, but because it is right. If a free society cannot help the many who are poor, it cannot save the few who are rich.

To our sister republics south of our border, we offer a special pledge—to convert our good words into good deeds—in a new alliance for progress—to assist free men and free governments in casting off the chains of poverty. But this peaceful revolution of hope cannot become the prey of hostile powers. Let all our neighbors know that we shall join with them to oppose aggression or subversion anywhere in the Americas. And let every other power know that this hemisphere intends to remain the master of its own house.

To that world assembly of sovereign states, the United Nations, our last best hope in an age where the instruments of war have far outpaced the instruments of peace, we renew our pledge of support—to prevent it from becoming merely a forum for invective—to strengthen its shield of the new and the weak—and to enlarge the area in which its writ may run.

Finally, to those nations who would make themselves our adversary, we offer not a pledge but a request: that both sides begin anew the quest for peace, before the dark powers of destruction unleashed by science engulf all humanity in planned or accidental self-destruction.

We dare not tempt them with weakness. For only when our arms are sufficient beyond doubt can we be certain beyond doubt that they will never be employed.

But neither can two great and powerful groups of nations take comfort from our present course—both sides overburdened by the cost of modern weapons, both rightly alarmed by the steady spread of the deadly atom, yet both racing to alter that uncertain balance of terror that stays the hand of mankind's final war.

So let us begin anew—remembering on both sides that civility is not a sign of weakness, and sincerity is always subject to proof. Let us never negotiate out of fear. But let us never fear to negotiate.

Let both sides explore what problems unite us instead of belaboring those problems which divide us.

Let both sides, for the first time, formulate serious and precise proposals for the inspection and control of arms—and bring the absolute power to destroy other nations under the absolute control of all nations.

Let both sides seek to invoke the wonders of science instead of its terrors. Together let us explore the stars, conquer the deserts, eradicate disease, tap the ocean depths and encourage the arts and commerce.

Let both sides unite to heed in all corners of the earth the command of Isaiah —to "undo the heavy burdens . . . [and] let the oppressed go free."

And if a beach-head of co-operation may push back the jungles of suspicion, let both sides join in creating a new endeavor not a new balance of power, but a new world of law, where the strong are just and the weak secure and the peace preserved.

All this will not be finished in the first 100 days. Nor will it be finished in the first 1,000 days, nor in the life of this Administration, nor even perhaps in our lifetime on this planet. But let us begin.

In your hands, my fellow citizens, more than mine, will rest the final success or failure of our course. Since this country was founded, each generation of Americans has been summoned to give testimony to its national loyalty. The graves of young Americans who answered the call to service surround the globe.

Now the trumpet summons us again—not as a call to bear arms, though arms we need—not as a call to battle, though embattled we are—but a call to bear the burden of a long twilight struggle year in and year out, "rejoicing in hope, patient in tribulation"—a struggle against the common enemies of man: tyranny, poverty, disease and war itself.

Can we forge against these enemies a grand and global alliance, north and south, east and west, that can assure a more fruitful life for all mankind? Will you join in that historic effort?

In the long history of the world, only a few generations have been granted the role of defending freedom in its hour of maximum danger. I do not shrink from this responsibility—I welcome it. I do not believe that any of us would exchange places with any other people or any other generation. The energy, the faith, the devotion which we bring to this endeavor will light our country and all who serve it—and the glow from that fire can truly light the world.

And so, my fellow Americans: ask not what your country can do for you— ask what you can do for your country.

My fellow citizens of the world: ask not what America will do for you, but what together we can do for the freedom of man.

Finally, whether you are citizens of America or citizens of the world, ask of us here the same high standards of strength and sacrifice which we ask of you. With a good conscience our only sure reward, with history the final judge of our deeds, let us go forth to lead the land we love, asking His blessing and His help, but knowing that here on earth God's work must truly be our own.

THE ART OF CONTEMPLATION

Virgil M. Hancher[6]

President Virgil Hancher (1896–   ) gave this charge to the candidates at the commencement exercises at the State University of Iowa, Iowa City, on June 5, 1948.

In its brevity and its identification of educational purposes with wisdom, perspective, and motives, this address is typical of many of President Hancher's addresses to graduates.

The structural completeness of the speech is based on a problem-solution pattern. Note the effectiveness of the vocabulary in its oral quality, repetition of key words, figurative phrases, analogies, epigrams, direct address, Biblical allusions, restrained humor, sentence variety, and rhythm.

President Hancher has sometimes used a manuscript in delivery but usually he has been an extempore speaker. His voice has been excellent, his manner conciliatory yet forceful.

How do his ideas here compare with those of Emerson in "The American Scholar"?

The staccato tempo of modern life has made difficult the art of contemplation. The days pass, they gather into weeks and months, arteries grow old and reactions slow down without the acquisition of that wisdom which comes only from the distillation of experience. Cynicism may also be the distillation of experience; but it is a bitter brew. The wise man, no less than the cynic, will not be taken in by life; but neither will he let the weaknesses and frailties of men blind him to their aspirations. Wisdom knows that men's eyes can be, and are, sometimes turned toward the stars, even though at other times they may be turned toward the gutter.

"Instinct, Intelligence, Wisdom" are the categories named by Whitehead, and

[6] Text furnished through the courtesy of President Hancher. The talk was printed in A. Craig Baird (ed.), *Representative American Speeches: 1948–49*, pp. 174–178, and in *Vital Speeches of the Day*, 14:590–591, July 15, 1948. It was later distributed as a brochure by the City News Publishing Company of New York City.

they arrange themselves in an order of progression. If life is to have meaning, if the things we do are not illusion, if there is reality in our efforts and our undertakings, the freedom of choice and of action, which we appear to possess, is more than appearance. It is real freedom, and the choices which we make are real choices.

To come to such a decision is in itself an act of faith. It assumes that the universe is not driven by blind, mechanistic forces which we can neither resist nor understand—and, indeed, of which we are a part without our knowledge. Our ultimate view of the universe is always an act of faith, rather than of reason, because our ultimate view of the universe rests upon a first postulate which cannot be proved.

The ancients said that there could be no dispute in matters of taste. "De gustibus non disputandum." Men differ in matters of taste, but there are no absolutes. Perhaps the same might be said of postulates, although this will be disputed and disputed vigorously. For with one postulate you will become a religious orthodox and with another you will become a dialectical materialist.

I do not mean to imply that it is a matter of indifference that you become one or the other, or that you arrive at any one of the infinite number of destinations between the two. Neither do I mean to imply that all postulates are equally valid. What I do mean to imply is that with the infinite variety of men, there will be diversity of outlook, and now, and for a long time to come, one man's meat will be another man's poison.

What I would desire for you is an apprehension of the postulate upon which your faith is founded. Because you do have a faith, or at least a working hypothesis of your relation to the entire scheme of things, on which your life is founded. Whether this hypothesis is formulated or unformulated in your consciousness, it still exists—and your actions, if not your declarations of faith, are witness to it. Indeed your actions may be the true witness.

Your hypothesis may range all the way from a belief that life has purpose to a belief that it is utterly without purpose—that nothing can be done to give it sense or meaning. But your hypothesis exists. Do you know what it is?

The staccato tempo of modern life makes difficult the contemplation necessary for self-knowledge. I make no plea for the good old days. Most of us would not be here if the good old days had not been changed for the better. Disease or famine would have cut off us or our ancestors, and of those who survived only a fortunate few would have achieved the luxury of an education. The triumphs of science and of scientific method are not to be overlooked. Nevertheless the balance sheet has its debit side.

Somewhere along the pathway of progress, the art of contemplation has been lost. The Society of Friends, certain Roman Catholics, an occasional mystic or band of mystics have preserved the art. They retain an anchorage in a sea of ceaseless motion, of disquiet, of drifting. They possess an integrity, a calm and assurance, a wholeness of mind and body that is a kind of holiness. This wholeness, this holiness, I crave for you.

It will be difficult to achieve. All the forces of modern life conspire against it. The church which once exercised such great dominion over the bodies and souls of men now competes with a thousand secular rivals. Competition, activity for its own sake, the lust for success and power make difficult the art of self-mastery. We are slaves and not masters. "Things are in the saddle and they ride mankind." The newspaper, the radio, and now television interrupt our days and disturb our nights. Everyone is a little tired, a little distraught, a little below par, a bit inaccurate in judgment.

Yet this need not be so. It is so, because others have willed that it be so, and we have let them have their way. Mark Twain has been quoted as saying that he once stopped reading the newspapers for seven years and they were the seven happiest years of his life! This remedy for our modern distemper seems a bit drastic, but perhaps nothing less than a radical remedy will now halt the disease. Until the radio and the newspapers have learned that men cannot survive in perpetual crisis, they are in danger of reprisal. A populace made schizophrenic by perpetual crisis and inaccuracy may well construe "the freedom of the press" and the radio to mean freedom to publish the truth—and nothing less.

But nothing compels you to give up your sanity, even though the world conspire to drive you mad. You can make it a rule of your life to withdraw each day into quiet and contemplation—religious quiet and contemplation, if you will, but quiet and contemplation, in any event—so that you may put aside the pressing and temporal things, and look upon those which come out of the deep places of human experience. "The heavens declare the glory of God," said the psalmist, "and the firmament showeth his handiwork." Modern man cannot afford to lose the sense of wonder. Perhaps it has been recaptured by some in the fission of the atom; but, for most of us, this must remain as great a mystery as the origin of life or the nature and destiny of man. Yet against this mystery we pit our intellect and our wills, however feeble they may be, confident that the unexamined life is not for us, but that out of our struggle we shall apprehend the postulates of our faith, and achieve that distillation of experience which is wisdom.

History records the ebb and flow of civilizations, the aspirations and failures of men and nations. Whether it possesses a rhythm or pattern is still a matter for dispute—yet, as one surveys the record, the trend has been upward. There is little evidence that modern man has a better brain than the prophets of Israel or the sages of Greece or Rome, but modern man is the inheritor of ideas and instrumentalities without which our modern civilization could not exist.

These ideas and instrumentalities have come to us because men have believed that they were free to make choices, and that the choices were real. They have believed that what they did, as individuals and collectively, made a difference in the long history of mankind, even in human destiny itself. They counted it the better part of wisdom to be on the side of the angels.

You, too, have a choice, and the choice is real. It should be made, not in response to the staccato drum-beat of temporality but in the quiet and contemplation of eternity. You have but one life, and a short one, at your disposal. There is not time to squander it hastily. Only in leisure can you savor it to the full. "Be still and know that I am God," said the voice to the psalmist long ago. "Be still and know the good" is as modern as tomorrow's television set.

Wise choices are the distinguishing mark of an educated man. You, too, can be on the side of the angels. Can you afford to be anywhere else? With what greater wisdom can you be wise?

FUNERAL ORATION FOR THE ATHENIAN SOLDIERS

Pericles[7]

Pericles (500–429 B.C.), brilliant general, Athenian orator and statesman, leader of the Assembly of all citizens for thirty years, delivered this oration in 430 B.C., in honor of those recently fallen in the battle against the Spartans. Athens, at this time at the pinnacle of its cultural and political power, had entered on a life-and-death struggle with the Spartans. Popular government, life, liberty, property, and all else depended on free public address by the populace. In this oration, which Thucydides perhaps heard, Pericles summed up the glory of his city-nation-state and its democratic ideals in language that might well apply to any nation and its people. How far are his sentiments applicable to America and to your city and state?

Most of my predecessors in this place have commended him who made this speech part of the law, telling us that it is well that it should be delivered at the burial of those who fall in battle. For myself, I should have thought that the worth which had displayed itself in deeds, would be sufficiently rewarded by honours also shown by deeds; such as you now see in this funeral prepared at the people's cost. And I could have wished that the reputations of many brave men were not to be imperilled in the mouth of a single individual, to stand or fall according as he spoke well or ill. For it is hard to speak properly upon a subject where it is even difficult to convince your hearers that you are speaking the truth. On the one hand, the friend who is familiar with every fact of the story may think that some point has not been set forth with that fulness which he wishes and knows it to deserve; on the other, he who is a stranger to the matter may be led by envy to suspect exaggeration if he hears anything above his own nature. For men can endure to hear others praised only so long as they can severally persuade themselves of their own ability to equal the actions recounted: when this point is passed, envy comes in and with it incredulity. However, since our ancestors have stamped this custom with their approval, it becomes my duty to obey the law and to try to satisfy your several wishes and opinions as best I may.

I shall begin with our ancestors: it is both just and proper that they should have the honour of the first mention on an occasion like the present. They dwelt in the country without break in the succession from generation to generation, and handed it down free to the present time by their valour. And if our more remote ancestors deserve praise, much more do our own fathers, who added to their inheritance the empire which we now possess, and spared no pains to be able to leave their acquisitions to us of the present generation. Lastly, there are few parts of our dominions that have not been augmented by those of us here, who are still more or less in the vigour of life; while the mother country has been furnished by us with everything that can enable

[7] This translation by Richard Crowley, 1876, is from Thucydides' *History of the Peloponnesian War*. The text of this oration is available in many reprintings, including the Everyman and Modern Library editions.

her to depend on her own resources whether for war or for peace. That part of our history which tells of the military achievements which gave us our several possessions, or of the ready valour with which either we or our fathers stemmed the tide of Hellenic or foreign aggression, is a theme too familiar to my hearers for me to dilate on, and I shall therefore pass it by. But what was the road by which we reached our position, what the form of government under which our greatness grew, what the national habits out of which it sprang; these are questions which I may try to solve before I proceed to my panegyric upon these men; since I think this to be a subject upon which on the present occasion a speaker may properly dwell, and to which the whole assemblage, whether citizens or foreigners, may listen with advantage.

Our constitution does not copy the laws of neighbouring states; we are rather a pattern to others than imitators ourselves. Its administration favours the many instead of the few; this is why it is called a democracy. If we look to the laws, they afford equal justice to all in their private differences; if to social standing, advancement in public life falls to reputation for capacity, class considerations not being allowed to interfere with merit; nor again does poverty bar the way, if a man is able to serve the state, he is not hindered by the obscurity of his condition. The freedom which we enjoy in our government extends also to our ordinary life. There, far from exercising a jealous surveillance over each other, we do not feel called upon to be angry with our neighbour for doing what he likes, or even to indulge in those injurious looks which cannot fail to be offensive, although they inflict no positive penalty. But all this ease in our private relations does not make us lawless as citizens. Against this, fear is our chief safeguard, teaching us to obey the magistrates and the laws, particularly such as regard the protection of the injured, whether they are actually on the statute book, or belong to that code which, although unwritten, yet cannot be broken without acknowledged disgrace.

Further, we provide plenty of means for the mind to refresh itself from business. We celebrate games and sacrifices all the year round, and the elegance of our private establishments forms a daily source of pleasure and helps to banish the spleen; while the magnitude of our city draws the produce of the world into our harbour, so that to the Athenian the fruits of other countries are as familiar a luxury as those of his own.

If we turn to our military policy, there also we differ from our antagonists. We throw open our city to the world, and never by alien acts exclude foreigners from any opportunity of learning or observing, although the eyes of an enemy may occasionally profit by our liberality; trusting less in system and policy than to the native spirit of our citizens; while in education, where our rivals from their very cradles by a painful discipline seek after manliness, at Athens we live exactly as we please, and yet are just as ready to encounter every legitimate danger. In proof of this it may be noticed that the Lacedaemonians do not invade our country alone, but bring with them all their confederates; while we Athenians advance unsupported into the territory of a neighbour, and fighting upon a foreign soil usually vanquish with ease men who are defending their homes. Our united force was never yet encountered by any enemy, because we have at once to attend to our marine and to despatch our citizens by land upon a hundred different services; so that, wherever they engage with some such fraction of our strength, a success against a detachment is magnified into a victory over the nation, and a defeat into a reverse suffered at the hands of our entire people. And yet if with habits not of labour but of ease, and courage not of art but of nature, we are still willing to encounter danger, we have the double advantage of escaping the experience of hardships in anticipation and of facing them in the hour of need as fearlessly as those who are never free from them.

Nor are these the only points in which our city is worthy of admiration. We cultivate refinement without extravagance and knowledge without effeminancy; wealth we employ more for use than for show, and place the real disgrace of poverty not in owning to the fact but in declining the struggle against it. Our public men have, besides politics, their private affairs to attend to, and our ordinary citizens, though occupied with the pursuits of industry, are still fair judges of public matters; for, unlike any other nation, regarding him who takes no part in these duties not as unambitious but as useless, we Athenians are able to judge at all events if we cannot originate, and instead of looking on discussion as a stumbling-block in the way of action, we think it an indispensable preliminary to any wise action at all. Again, in our enterprises we present the singular spectacle of daring and deliberation, each carried to its highest point, and both united in the same persons; although usually decision is the fruit of ignorance, hesitation of reflexion. But the palm of courage will surely be adjudged most justly to those, who best know the difference between hardship and pleasure and yet are never tempted to shrink from danger. In generosity we are equally singular, acquiring our friends by conferring not by receiving favours. Yet, of course, the doer of the favour is the firmer friend of the two, in order by continued kindness to keep the recipient in his debt; while the debtor feels less keenly from the very consciousness that the return he makes will be a payment, not a free gift. And it is only the Athenians who, fearless of consequences, confer their benefits not from calculations of expediency, but in the confidence of liberality.

In short, I say that as a city we are the school of Hellas; while I doubt if the world can produce a man, who where he has only himself to depend upon, is equal to so many emergencies, and graced by so happy a versatility as the Athenian. And that this is no mere boast thrown out for the occasion, but plain matter of fact, the power of the state acquired by these habits proves. For Athens alone of her contemporaries is found when tested to be greater than her reputation, and alone gives no occasion to her assailants to blush at the antagonist by whom they have been worsted, or to her subjects to question her title by merit to rule. Rather, the admiration of the present and succeeding ages will be ours, since we have not left our power without witness, but have shown it by mighty proofs; and far from needing a Homer for our panegyrist, or other of his craft whose verses might charm for the moment only for the impression which they gave to melt at the touch of fact, we have forced every sea and land to be the highway of our daring, and everywhere, whether for evil or for good, have left imperishable monuments behind us. Such is the Athens for which these men, in the assertion of their resolve not to lose her, nobly fought and died; and well may every one of their survivors be ready to suffer in her cause.

Indeed if I have dwelt at some length upon the character of our country, it has been to show that our stake in the struggle is not the same as theirs who have no such blessings to lose, and also that the panegyric of the men over whom I am now speaking might be by definite proofs established. That panegyric is now in a great measure complete; for the Athens that I have celebrated is only what the heroism of these and their like have made her, men whose fame, unlike that of most Hellenes, will be found to be only commensurate with their deserts. And if a test of worth be wanted, it is to be found in their closing scene, and this not only in the cases in which it set the final seal upon their merit, but also in those in which it gave the first intimation of their having any. For there is justice in the claim that steadfastness in his country's battles should be as a cloak to cover a man's other imperfections; since the good action has blotted out the bad, and his merit as a citizen more than outweighed his demerits as an individual. But none of these allowed either wealth with its prospect of future enjoyment to unnerve his spirit, or poverty with its hope of a day of freedom and riches to tempt him to shrink from danger. No, holding that vengeance upon their enemies was more to be desired than any personal blessings, and reckoning this to be the most glorious of hazards, they joyfully determined to accept the risk, to make sure of their vengeance and to let their wishes wait; and while committing to hope the uncertainty of final success, in the business before them they thought fit to act boldly and trust in themselves. Thus choosing to die resisting, rather than to live submitting, they fled only from dishonour, but met danger face to face, and after one brief moment, while at the summit of their fortune, escaped, not from their fear, but from their glory.

So died these men as became Athenians. You, their survivors, must determine to have as unfaltering a resolution in the field, though you may pray that it may have a happier issue. And not contented with ideas derived only from words of the advantages which are bound up with the defence of your country, though these would furnish a valuable text to a speaker even before an audience so alive to them as the present, you must yourselves realize the power of Athens, and feed your eyes upon her from day to day, till love of her fills your hearts; and then when all her greatness shall break upon you, you must reflect that it was by courage, sense of duty, and a keen feeling of honour in action that men were enabled to win all this, and that no personal failure in an enterprise could make them consent to deprive their country of their valour, but they laid it at her feet as the most glorious contribution that they could offer. For this offering of their lives made in common by them all they each of them individually received that renown which never grows old, and for a sepulchre, not so much that in which their bones have been deposited, but that noblest of shrines wherein their glory is laid up to be eternally remembered upon every occasion on which deed or story shall call for its commemoration. For heroes have the whole earth for their tomb; and in lands far from their own, where the column with its epitaph declares it, there is enshrined in every breast a record unwritten with no tablet to preserve it, except that of the heart. These take as your model, and judging happiness to be the fruit of freedom and freedom of valour, never decline the dangers of war. For it is not the miserable that would most justly be unsparing of their lives; these have nothing to hope for: it is rather they to whom continued life may bring reverses as yet unknown, and to whom a fall, if it came, would be most tremendous in its consequences. And surely, to a man of spirit, the degradation of cowardice must be immeasurably more grievous than unfelt death which strikes him in the midst of his strength and patriotism!

Comfort, therefore, not condolence, is what I have to offer to the parents of the dead who may be here. Numberless are the chances to which, as they know, the life of man is subject; but fortunate indeed are they who draw for their lot a death so glorious as that which has caused your mourning, and to whom life has been so exactly measured as to terminate in the happiness in which it has been passed. Still I know that this is a hard saying, especially when those are in question of whom you will constantly be reminded by seeing in the homes of others blessings of which once you also boasted: for grief is felt not so much for the want of what we have never known, as for the loss of that to which we have been long accustomed. Yet you who are still of an age to beget children must bear up on the hope of having others in their stead; not only will they help you to forget those whom you have lost, but will be to the state at once a reinforcement and a security; for never can a fair or just policy be expected of the citizen who does not, like his fellows, bring to the decision the interests and apprehensions of a father. While those of you who have passed your prime must congratulate yourselves with the thought that the best part of your life was fortunate, and that the brief span that remains will be cheered by the fame of the departed. For it is only the love of honour that never grows old; and honour it is, not gain, as some would have it, that rejoices the heart of age and helplessness.

Turning to the sons or brothers of the dead, I see an arduous struggle before you. When a man is gone, all are wont to praise him, and should your merit be ever so transcendent, you will still find it difficult not merely to overtake, but even to approach their renown. The living have envy to contend with, while those who are no longer in our path are honoured with a goodwill into which rivalry does not enter. On the other hand, if I must say anything on the subject of female excellence to those of you who will now be in widowhood, it will be all comprised in this brief exhortation. Great will be your glory in not falling short of your natural character; and greatest will be hers who is least talked of among the men whether for good or for bad.

My task is now finished. I have performed it to the best of my ability, and in word, at least, the requirements of the law are now satisfied. If deeds be in question, those who are here interred have received part of their honours already, and for the rest, their children will be brought up till manhood at the public expense: the state thus offers a valuable prize, as the garland of victory in this race of valour, for the reward both of those who have fallen and their survivors. And where the rewards for merit are greatest, there are found the best citizens.

And now that you have brought to a close your lamentations for your relatives, you may depart.

SECOND INAUGURAL ADDRESS

Abraham Lincoln[8]

President Abraham Lincoln (1809–1865) gave his Second Inaugural Address on a temporary platform on the east front of the Capitol in Washington, D.C., on March 4, 1865 (see account by Noah Brooks, *Washington in Lincoln's Time*, Century Company, 1895, p. 237ff.).

Thousands listened in the great plaza before the President. Readers of the speech included practically the entire American public and many persons in other lands. The speaker read from a single page of large paper on which the speech was printed in two broad columns. He expressed his political philosophy and program of magnanimity, contrary to the Congressional "invincibles" who would treat the Southern States as conquered territories. Said the London *Spectator*: It was "the noblest political document known in history, and should have for the nation and the statesmen he left behind him something of sacred and almost prophetic authority." Students will analyze the sources of strength in this short address and trace the later history of national policies concerning race and states' rights in relation to those of the Southern states.

Fellow-countrymen: At this second appearing to take the oath of the presidential office there is less occasion for an extended address than there was at the first. Then a statement somewhat in detail of a course to be pursued seemed fitting and proper. Now, at the expiration of four years, during which public declarations have been constantly called forth on every point and phase of the great contest which still absorbs the attention and engrosses the energies of the nation, little that is new could be presented. The progress of our arms, upon which all else chiefly depends, is as well known to the public as to myself, and it is, I trust, reasonably satisfactory and encouraging to all. With high hope for the future, no prediction in regard to it is ventured.

On the occasion corresponding to this four years ago all thoughts were anxiously directed to an impending civil war. All dreaded it, all sought to avert it. While the inaugural address was being delivered from this place, devoted altogether to *saving* the Union without war, insurgent agents were in the city seeking to *destroy* it without war—seeking to dissolve the Union and divide effects by negotiation. Both parties deprecated war, but one of them would *make* war rather than let the nation survive, and the other would *accept* war rather than let it perish, and the war came.

One eighth of the whole population was colored slaves, not distributed

---

[8] The text is from John G. Nicolay, and John Hay, *Complete Works of Abraham Lincoln*, vol. 11, pp. 44–47; reprinted in A. Craig Baird (ed.), *American Public Addresses: 1740–1952*, McGraw-Hill Book Company, Inc., New York, 1956, pp. 116–117.

generally over the Union, but localized in the southern part of it. These slaves constituted a peculiar and powerful interest. All knew that this interest was somehow the cause of the war. To strengthen, perpetuate, and extend this interest was the object for which the insurgents would rend the Union even by war, while the Government claimed no right to do more than to restrict the territorial enlargement of it. Neither party expected for the war the magnitude or the duration which it has already attained. Neither anticipated that the *cause* of the conflict might cease with or even before the conflict itself should cease. Each looked for an easier triumph, and a result less fundamental and astounding. Both read the same Bible and pray to the same God, and each invokes His aid against the other. It may seem strange that any men should dare to ask a just God's assistance in wringing their bread from the sweat of other men's faces, but let us judge not, that we be not judged. The prayers of both could not be answered. That of neither has been answered fully. The Almighty has His own purposes. "Woe unto the world because of offenses; for it must needs be that offenses come, but woe to that man by whom the offense cometh." If we shall suppose that American slavery is one of those offenses which, in the providence of God, must needs come, but which, having continued through His appointed time, He now wills to remove, and that He gives to both North and South this terrible war as the woe due to those by whom the offense came, shall we discern therein any departure from those divine attributes which the believers in a living God always ascribe to Him? Fondly do we hope, fervently do we pray, that this mighty scourge of war may speedily pass away. Yet, if God wills that it continue until all the wealth piled by the bondsman's two hundred and fifty years of unrequited toil shall be sunk, and until every drop of blood drawn with the last shall be paid by another drawn with the sword, as was said three thousand years ago, so still it must be said, "The judgments of the Lord are true and righteous altogether."

With malice toward none, with charity for all, with firmness in the right as God gives us to see the right, let us strive on to finish the work we are in, to bind up the nation's wounds, to care for him who shall have borne the battle and for his widow and his orphan, to do all which may achieve and cherish a just and lasting peace among ourselves and with all nations.

THE AMERICAN SCHOLAR

Ralph Waldo Emerson[9]

Ralph Waldo Emerson (1803–1882), philosopher, essayist, poet, and public lecturer for more than forty years, gave this Phi Beta Kappa address to some

[9] The text of this speech is from the second edition, 1838, and was later printed in Ralph Waldo Emerson, *Nature, Addresses, and Lectures,* Houghton Mifflin Company, Boston, 1876, pp. 83–115. See also text in A. Craig Baird (ed.), *American Public Addresses: 1740–1892,* McGraw-Hill Book Company, Inc., New York, 1956, pp. 122–137.

two hundred members of the society and friends in the First Parish Church, on August 31, 1837, at Harvard Yard, Cambridge.

The address was a well-organized criticism of higher education. Emerson's audience was sharply divided concerning his ideas.

What was his point of view? His concept of nature, books, and action as related to education? Is his language too abstract? Dull? Stimulating? How far are his educational aims and methods applicable to your college or university? Give a short talk that reflects your reaction to Emerson's ideas.

Mr. President and Gentlemen: I greet you on the recommencement of our literary year. Our anniversary is one of hope, and, perhaps, not enough of labor. We do not meet for games of strength or skill, for the recitation of histories, tragedies, and odes, like the ancient Greeks; for parliaments of love and poesy, like the Troubadours; nor for the advancement of science, like our contemporaries in the British and European capitals. Thus far, our holiday has been simply a friendly sign of the survival of the love of letters amongst a people too busy to give to letters any more. As such it is precious as the sign of an indestructible instinct. Perhaps the time is already come when it ought to be, and will be, something else; when the sluggard intellect of this continent will look from under its iron lids and fill the postponed expectation of the world with something better than the exertions of mechanical skill. Our day of dependence, our long apprenticeship to the learning of other lands, draws to a close. The millions that around us are rushing into life, cannot always be fed on the sere remains of foreign harvests. Events, actions arise, that must be sung, that will sing themselves. Who can doubt that poetry will revive and lead in a new age, as the star in the constellation Harp, which now flames in our zenith, astronomers announce, shall one day be the pole-star for a thousand years?

In this hope I accept the topic which not only usage but the nature of our association seem to prescribe to this day,—the American Scholar. Year by year we come up hither to read one more chapter of his biography. Let us inquire what light new days and events have thrown on his character and his hopes.

It is one of those fables which out of an unknown antiquity convey an unlooked-for wisdom, that the gods, in the beginning, divided Man into men, that he might be more helpful to himself; just as the hand was divided into fingers, the better to answer its end.

The old fable covers a doctrine ever new and sublime; that there is One Man,—present to all particular men only partially, or through one faculty; and that you must take the whole society to find the whole man. Man is not a farmer, or a professor, or an engineer, but he is all. Man is priest, and scholar, and statesman, and producer, and soldier. In the *divided* or social state these functions are parcelled out to individuals, each of whom aims to do his stint of the joint work, whilst each other performs his. The fable implies that the individual, to possess himself, must sometimes return from his own labor to embrace all the other laborers. But, unfortunately, this original unit, this fountain of power, has been so distributed to multitudes, has been so minutely subdivided and peddled out, that it is spilled into drops, and cannot be gathered. The state of society is one in which the members have suffered amputation from the trunk, and strut about so many walking monsters,—a good finger, a neck, a stomach, an elbow, but never a man.

Man is thus metamorphosed into a thing, into many things. The planter, who is Man sent out into the field to gather food, is seldom cheered by any idea of the true dignity of his ministry. He sees his bushel and his cart, and nothing beyond, and sinks into the farmer, instead of Man on the farm. The tradesman scarcely ever gives an ideal worth to his work, but is ridden by the routine of his craft, and the soul is subject to dollars. The priest becomes a form; the attorney a statute-book; the mechanic a machine; the sailor a rope of the ship.

In this distribution of functions the scholar is the delegated intellect. In the right state he is *Man Thinking*. In the degenerate state, when the victim of society, he tends to become a mere thinker, or still worse, the parrot of other men's thinking.

In this view of him, as Man Thinking, the theory of his office is contained. Him Nature solicits with all her placid, all her monitory pictures; him the past instructs; him the future invites. Is not indeed every man a student, and do not all things exist for the student's behoof? And, finally, is not the true scholar the only true master? But the old oracle said, "All things have two handles: beware of the wrong one." In life, too often, the scholar errs with mankind and forfeits his privilege. Let us see him in his school, and consider him in reference to the main influences he receives.

I. The first in time and the first in importance of the influences upon the mind is that of nature. Every day, the sun; and, after sunset, Night and her stars. Ever the winds blow; ever the grass grows. Every day, men and women, conversing—beholding and beholden. The scholar is he of all men whom this spectacle most engages. He must settle its value in his mind. What is nature to him? There is never a beginning, there is never an end, to the inexplicable continuity of this web of God, but always circular power returning into itself. Therein it resembles his own spirit, whose beginning, whose ending, he never can find,—so entire, so boundless. Far too as her splendors shine, system on system shooting like rays, upward, downward, without centre, without circumference,—in the mass and in the particle, Nature hastens to render account of herself to the mind. Classification begins. To the young mind every thing is individual, stands by itself. By and by, it finds how to join two things and see in them one nature; then three, then three thousand; and so, tyrannized over by its own unifying instinct, it goes on tying things together, diminishing anomalies, discovering roots running under ground whereby contrary and remote things cohere and flower out from one stem. It presently learns that since the dawn of history there has been a constant accumulation and classifying of facts. But what is classification but the perceiving that these objects are not chaotic, and are not foreign, but have a law which is also a law of the human mind? The astronomer discovers that geometry, a pure abstraction of the human mind, is the measure of planetary motion. The chemist finds proportions and intelligible method throughout matter; and science is nothing but the finding of analogy, identity, in the most remote parts. The ambitious soul sits down before each refractory fact; one after another reduces all strange constitutions, all new powers, to their class and their law, and goes on forever to animate the last fibre of organization, the outskirts of nature, by insight.

Thus to him, to his schoolboy under the bending dome of day, is suggested that he and it proceed from one root; one is leaf and one is flower; relation, sympathy, stirring in every vein. And what is that root? Is not that the soul of his soul? A thought too bold; a dream too wild. Yet when this spiritual light shall have revealed the law of more earthly natures,—when he has learned to worship the soul, and to see that the natural philosophy that now is, is only the first gropings of its gigantic hand, he shall look forward to an ever expanding knowledge as to a becoming creator. He shall see that nature is the opposite of the soul, answering to it part for part. One is seal and one is print. Its beauty is the beauty of his own mind. Its laws are the laws of his own mind. Nature then becomes to him the measure of his attainments. So much of nature as he is ignorant of, so much of his own mind does he not yet possess. And, in fine, the ancient precept, "Know thyself," and the modern precept, "Study nature," become at last one maxim.

II. The next great influence into the spirit of the scholar is the mind of the Past,—in whatever form, whether of literature, of art, of institutions, that mind is inscribed. Books are the best type of the influence of the past, and perhaps we shall get at the truth,—learn the amount of this influence more conveniently,—by considering their value alone.

The theory of books is noble. The scholar of the first age received into him the world around; brooded thereon; gave it the new arrangement of his own mind, and uttered it again. It came into him life; it went out from him truth. It came to him short-lived actions; it went out from him immortal thoughts. It came to him business; it went from him poetry. It was dead fact; now, it is quick thought. It can stand, and it can go. It now endures, it now flies, it now inspires. Precisely in proportion to the depth of mind from which it issued, so high does it soar, so long does it sing.

Or, I might say, it depends on how far the process had gone, of transmuting life into truth. In proportion to the completeness of the distillation, so will the purity and imperishableness of the product be. But none is quite perfect. As no air-pump can by any means make a perfect vacuum, so neither can any artist entirely exclude the conventional, the local, the perishable from his book, or write a book of pure thought, that shall be as efficient, in all respects, to a remote posterity, as to contemporaries, or rather to the second age. Each age, it is found, must write its own books; or rather, each generation for the next succeeding. The books of an older period will not fit this.

Yet hence arises a grave mischief. The sacredness which attaches to the act of creation, the act of thought, is transferred to the record. The poet chanting was felt to be a divine man: henceforth the chant is divine also. The writer was a just and wise spirit; henceforward it is settled the book is perfect; as love of the hero corrupts into worship of his statue. Instantly the book becomes noxious: the guide is a tyrant. The sluggish and perverted mind of the multitude, slow to open to the incursions of Reason, having once so opened, having once received this book, stands upon it, and makes an outcry if it is disparaged. Colleges are built on it. Books are written on it by thinkers, not by Man Thinking; by men of talent, that is, who start wrong, who set out from accepted dogmas, not from their own sight of principles. Meek young men grow up in libraries, believing it their duty to accept the views which Cicero, which Locke, which Bacon, have given; forgetful that Cicero, Locke, and Bacon were only young men in libraries when they wrote these books.

Hence, instead of Man Thinking, we have the bookworm. Hence the book-learned class, who value books, as such; not as related to nature and the human constitution, but as making a sort of Third Estate with the world and the soul. Hence the restorers of readings, the emendators, the bibliomaniacs of all degrees.

Books are the best of things, well used; abused, among the worst. What is the right use? What is the one end which all means go to effect? They are for nothing but to inspire. I had better never see a book than to be warped by its attraction clean out of my own orbit, and made a satellite instead of a system. The one thing in the world, of value, is the active soul. This every man is entitled to; this every man contains within him, although in almost all men obstructed and as yet unborn. The soul active sees absolute truth and utters truth, or creates. In this action it is genius; not the privilege of here and there a favorite, but the sound estate of every man. In its essence it is progressive. The book, the college, the school of art, the institution of any kind, stop with some past utterance of genius. This is good, say they,—let us hold by this. They pin me down. They look backward and not forward. But genius looks forward: the eyes of man are set in his forehead, not in his hindhead: man hopes: genius creates. Whatever talents may be, if the man create not, the pure efflux of the Deity is not his;—cinders and smoke there may be, but not yet flame. There are creative manners, there are creative actions, and creative words; manners, actions, words, that is, indicative of no custom or authority, but springing spontaneous from the mind's own sense of good and fair.

On the other part, instead of being its own seer, let it receive from another mind its truth, though it were in torrents of light, without periods of solitude, inquest, and self-recovery, and a fatal disservice is done. Genius is always sufficiently the enemy of genius by over-influence. The literature of every nation bears me witness. The English dramatic poets have Shakespearized now for two hundred years.

Undoubtedly there is a right way of reading, so it be sternly subordinated. Man Thinking must not be subdued by his instruments. Books are for the scholar's idle times. When he can read God directly, the hour is too precious to be wasted in other men's transcripts of their readings. But when the intervals of darkness come, as come they must,—when the sun is hid and the stars withdraw their shining,—we repair to the lamps which were kindled by their ray, to guide our steps to the East again, where the dawn is. We hear, that we may speak. The Arabian proverb says, "A fig tree, looking on a fig tree, becometh fruitful."

It is remarkable, the character of the pleasure we derive from the best books. They impress us with the conviction that one nature wrote and the same reads. We read the verses of one of the great English poets, of Chaucer, of Marvell, of Dryden, with the most modern joy,—with a pleasure, I mean, which is in great part caused by the abstraction of all *time* from their verses. There is some awe mixed with the joy of our surprise, when this poet, who lived in some past world, two or three hundred years ago, says that which lies close to my own soul, that which I also had well-nigh thought and said. But for the evidence thence afforded to the philosophical doctrine of the identity of all minds, we should suppose some preestablished harmony, some foresight of souls that were to be, and some preparation of stores for their future wants, like the fact observed in insects, who lay up food before death for the young grub they shall never see.

I would not be hurried by any love of system, by any exaggeration of instincts, to underrate the Book. We all know, that as the human body can be nourished on any food, though it were boiled grass and the broth of shoes, so the human mind can be fed by any knowledge. And great and heroic men have existed who had almost no other information than by the printed page. I only would say that it needs a strong head to bear that diet. One must be an inventor to read well. As the proverb says, "He that would bring home the wealth of the Indies, must carry out the wealth of the Indies." There is then creative reading as well as creative writing. When the mind is braced by labor and invention, the page of whatever book we read becomes luminous with manifold allusion. Every sentence is doubly significant, and the sense of our author is as broad as the world. We then see, what is always true, that as the seer's hour of vision is short and rare among heavy days and months, so is its record, perchance, the least part of his volume. The discerning will read, in his Plato or Shakespeare, only that least part,—only the authentic utterances of the oracle;—all the rest he rejects, were it never so many times Plato's and Shakespeare's.

Of course there is a portion of reading quite indispensable to a wise man. History and exact science he must learn by laborious reading. Colleges, in like manner, have their indispensable office,—to teach elements. But they can only highly serve us when they aim not to drill, but to create; when they gather from far every ray of various genius to their hospitable halls, and by the concentrated fires, set the hearts of their youth on flame. Thought and knowledge are natures in which apparatus and pretension avail nothing. Gowns and pecuniary foundations, though of towns of gold, can never countervail the least sentence or syllable of wit. Forget this, and our American colleges will recede in their public importance, whilst they grow richer every year.

III. There goes in the world a notion that the scholar should be a recluse, a valetudinarian,—as unfit for any handiwork or public labor as a penknife for an axe. The so-called "practical men" sneer at speculative men, as if, because they speculate or *see*, they could do nothing. I have heard it say that the clergy,— who are always, more universally than any other class, the scholars of their day, —are addressed as women; that the rough, spontaneous conversation of men they do not hear, but only a mincing and diluted speech. They are often virtually disfranchised; and indeed there are advocates for their celibacy. As far as this is true of the studious classes, it is not just and wise. Action is with the scholar subordinate, but it is essential. Without it he is not yet man. Without it thought can never ripen into truth. Whilst the world hangs before the eye as a cloud of beauty, we cannot even see its beauty. Inaction is cowardice, but there can be no scholar without the heroic mind. The preamble of thought, the transition through which it passes from the unconscious to the conscious, is action. Only so much do I know, as I have lived. Instantly we know whose words are loaded with life, and whose not.

The world,—this shadow of the soul, or *other me,*—lies wide around. Its attractions are the keys which unlock my thoughts and make me acquainted with myself. I run eagerly into this resounding tumult. I grasp the hands of those next me, and take my place in the ring to suffer and to work, taught by an instinct that so shall the dumb abyss be vocal with speech. I pierce its order; I dissipate its fear; I dispose of it within the circuit of my expanding life. So much only of life as I know by experience, so much of the wilderness have I vanquished and planted, or so far have I extended my being, my dominion. I do not see how any man can afford, for the sake of his nerves and his nap, to spare any action in which he can partake. It is pearls and rubies to his discourse. Drudgery, calamity, exasperation, want, are instructors in eloquence and wisdom. The true scholar grudges every opportunity of action past by, as a loss of power. It is the raw material out of which the intellect moulds her splendid products. A strange process, too, this by which experience is converted into thought, as a mulberry leaf is converted into satin. The manufacture goes forward at all hours.

The actions and events of our childhood and youth are now matters of calmest observation. They lie like fair pictures in the air. Not so with our recent actions, —with the business which we now have in hand. On this we are quite unable to speculate. Our affections as yet circulate through it. We no more feel or know it than we feel the feet, or the hand, or the brain of our body. The new deed is yet a part of life,—remains for a time immersed in our unconscious life. In some contemplative hour it detaches itself from the life like a ripe fruit, to become a thought of the mind. Instantly it is raised, transfigured; the corruptible has put on incorruption. Henceforth it is an object of beauty, however base its origin and neighborhood. Observe too the impossibility of antedating this act. In its grub state, it cannot fly, it cannot shine, it is a dull grub. But suddenly, without observation, the selfsame thing unfurls beautiful wings, and is an angel of wisdom. So is there no fact, no event, in our private history, which shall not, sooner or later, lose its adhesive, inert form, and astonish us by soaring from our body into the empyrean. Cradle and infancy, school and playground, the fear of boys, and dogs, and ferules, the love of little maids and berries, and many another fact that once filled the whole sky, are gone already; friend and relative, profession and party, town and country, nation and world, must also soar and sing.

Of course, he who has put forth his total strength in fit actions has the richest return of his wisdom. I will not shut myself out of this globe of action, and transplant an oak into a flowerpot, there to hunger and pine; nor trust the revenue of some single faculty, and exhaust one vein of thought, much like those Savoyards, who, getting their livelihood by carving shepherds, shepherdesses, and smoking Dutchmen, for all Europe, went out one day to the mountain to find stock, and discovered that they had whittled up the last of their pine trees. Authors we have, in numbers, who have written out their vein, and who, moved by a commendable prudence, sail for Greece or Palestine, follow the trapper into the prairie, or ramble round Algiers, to replenish their merchantable stock.

If it were only for a vocabulary, the scholar would be covetous of action. Life is our dictionary. Years are well spent in country labors; in town; in the insight into trades and manufactures; in frank intercourse with many men and women; in science; in art; to the one end of mastering in all their facts a language by which to illustrate and embody our perceptions. I learn immediately from any speaker how much he has already lived, through the poverty or the splendor of his speech. Life lies behind us as the quarry from whence we get tiles and copestones for the masonry of to-day. This is the way to learn grammar. Colleges and books only copy the language which the field and the work-yard made.

But the final value of action, like that of books, and better than books, is that it is a resource. That great principle of Undulation in nature, that shows itself in the inspiring and expiring of the breath; in desire and satiety; in the ebb and flow of the sea; in day and night; in heat and cold; and, as yet more deeply ingrained in every atom and every fluid, is known to us under the name of Polarity,—these "fits of easy transmission and reflection," as Newton called them, are the law of nature because they are the law of spirit.

The mind now thinks, now acts, and each fit reproduces the other. When the artist has exhausted his materials, when the fancy no longer paints, when thoughts are no longer apprehended and books are a weariness,—he has always the resource *to live*. Character is higher than intellect. Thinking is the function. Living is the functionary. The stream retreats to its source. A great soul will be strong to live, as well as strong to drink. Does he lack organ or medium to impart his truths? He can still fall back on this elemental force of living them. This is a total act. Thinking is a partial act. Let the grandeur of justice shine in his affairs. Let the beauty of affection cheer his lowly roof. Those "far from fame," who dwell and act with him, will feel the force of his constitution in the doings and passages of the day better than it can be measured by any public and designed display. Time shall teach him that the scholar loses no hour which the man lives. Herein he unfolds the sacred germ of his instinct, screened from influence. What is lost in seemliness is gained in strength. Not out of those on whom systems of education have exhausted their culture, comes the helpful giant to destroy the old or to build the new, but out of unhandselled savage nature; out of terrible Druids and Berserkers come at last Alfred and Shakespeare.

I hear therefore with joy whatever is beginning to be said of the dignity and necessity of labor to every citizen. There is virtue yet in the hoe and the spade, for learned as well as for unlearned hands. And labor is everywhere welcome; always we are invited to work; only be this limitation observed, that a man shall not for the sake of wider activity sacrifice any opinion to the popular judgments and modes of action.

I have now spoken of the education of the scholar by nature, by books, and by action. It remains to say somewhat of his duties.

They are such as become Man Thinking. They may all be comprised in self-trust. The office of the scholar is to cheer, to raise, and to guide men by showing them facts amidst appearances. He plies the slow, unhonored, and unpaid task of observation. Flamsteed and Herschel, in their glazed observatories, may catalogue the stars with the praise of all men, and the results being splendid and useful, honor is sure. But he, in his private observatory, cataloguing obscure and nebulous stars of the human mind, which as yet no man has thought of as such,—watching days and months sometimes for a few facts; correcting still his old records;—must relinquish display and immediate fame. In the long period of his preparation he must betray often an ignorance and shiftlessness in popular arts, incurring the disdain of the able who shoulder him aside. Long he must stammer in his speech; often forego the living for the dead. Worse yet, he must accept—how often!—poverty and solitude. For the ease and pleasure of treading the old road, accepting the fashions, the education, the religion of society, he takes the cross of making his own, and, of course, the self-accusation, the faint heart, the frequent uncertainty and loss of time, which are the nettles and tangling vines in the way of the self-relying and self-directed; and the state of virtual hostility in which he seems to stand to society, and especially to educated society. For all this loss and scorn, what offset? He is to find consolation in exercising the highest functions of human nature. He is one who raises himself from private considerations and breathes and lives on public and illustrious thoughts. He is the world's eye. He is the world's heart. He is to resist the vulgar prosperity that retrogrades ever to barbarism, by preserving and communicating heroic sentiments, noble biographies, melodious verse, and the conclusions of history. Whatsoever oracles the human heart, in all emergencies, in all solemn hours, has uttered as its commentary on the world of actions,—these he shall receive and impart. And whatsoever new verdict Reason from her inviolable seat pronounces on the passing men and events of to-day,—this he shall hear and promulgate.

These being his functions, it becomes him to feel all confidence in himself, and to defer never to the popular cry. He and he only knows the world. The world of any moment is the merest appearance. Some great decorum, some fetish of a government, some ephemeral trade, or war, or man, is cried up by half mankind and cried down by the other half, as if all depended on this particular up or down. The odds are that the whole question is not worth the poorest thought which the scholar has lost in listening to the controversy. Let him not quit his belief that a popgun is a popgun, though the ancient and honorable of the earth affirm it to be the crack of doom. In silence, in steadiness, in severe abstraction, let him hold by himself; add observation to observation, patient of neglect, patient of reproach, and bide his own time—happy enough if he can satisfy himself alone that this day he has seen something truly. Success treads on every right step. For the instinct is sure, that prompts him to tell his brother what he thinks. He then learns that in going down into the secrets of his own mind he has descended into the secrets of all minds. He learns that he who has mastered any law in his private thoughts, is master to that extent of all men whose language he speaks, and of all into whose language his own can be translated. The poet, in utter solitude remembering his spontaneous thoughts and recording them, is found to have recorded that which men in crowded cities find true for them also. The orator distrusts at first the fitness of his frank confessions, his want of knowledge of the persons he addresses, until he finds that he is the complement of his hearers;—that they drink his words because he fulfills for them their own nature; the deeper he dives into his privatest, secretest presentiment, to his wonder he finds this is the most acceptable, most public, and universally true. The people delight in it; the better part of every man feels, This is my music; this is myself.

In self-trust all the virtues are comprehended. Free should the scholar be,—free and brave. Free even to the definition of freedom, "without any hindrance that does not arise out of his own constitution." Brave; for fear is a thing which a scholar by his very function puts behind him. Fear always springs from ignorance. It is a shame to him if his tranquility, amid dangerous times, arise from the presumption that like children and women his is a protected class; or if he seeks a temporary peace by the diversion of his thoughts from politics or vexed questions, hiding his head like an ostrich in the flowering bushes, peeping into microscopes, and turning rhymes, as a boy whistles to keep his courage up. So is the danger a danger still; so is the fear worse. Manlike let him turn and face it. Let him look into its eye and search its nature, inspect its origin,—see the whelping of this lion—which lies no great way back; he will then find in himself a perfect comprehension of its nature and extent; he will have made his hands meet on the other side, and can henceforth defy it and pass on superior. The world is his who can see through its pretension. What deafness, what stone-blind custom, what overgrown error you behold is there only by sufferance,—by your sufferance. See it to be a lie, and you have already dealt it its mortal blow.

Yes, we are the cowed,—we the trustless. It is a mischievous notion that we are come late into nature; that the world was finished a long time ago. As the world was plastic and fluid in the hands of God, so it is ever to so much of his attributes as we bring to it. To ignorance and sin, it is flint. They adapt themselves to it as they may; but in proportion as a man has any thing in him divine, the firmament flows before him and takes his signet and form. Not he is great who can alter matter, but he who can alter my state of mind. They are the kings of the world who give the color of their present thought to all nature and all art, and persuade men by the cheerful serenity of their carrying the matter, that this thing which they do is the apple which the ages have desired to pluck, now at last ripe, and inviting nations to the harvest. The great man makes the great thing. Wherever Macdonald sits, there is the head of the table. Linnaeus makes botany the most alluring of studies, and wins it from the farmer and the herb-woman; Davy, chemistry; and Cuvier, fossils. The day is always his who works in it with serenity and great aims. The unstable estimates of men crowd to him whose mind is filled with a truth, as the heaped waves of the Atlantic follow the moon.

For this self-trust, the reason is deeper than can be fathomed,—darker than can be enlightened. I might not carry with me the feeling of my audience in stating my own belief. But I have already shown the ground of my hope, in adverting to the doctrine that man is one. I believe man has been wronged; he has wronged himself. He has almost lost the light that can lead him back to his prerogatives. Men are become of no account. Men in history, men in the world of to-day, are bugs, are spawn, and are called "the mass" and "the herd." In a century, in a millennium, one or two men; that is to say, one or two approxima- tions to the right state of every man. All the rest behold in the hero or the poet their own green and crude being,—ripened; yes, and are content to be less, so *that* may attain to its full stature. What a testimony, full of grandeur, full of pity, is borne to the demands of his own nature, by the poor clansman, the poor partisan, who rejoices in the glory of his chief. The poor and the low find some amends to their immense moral capacity, for their acquiescence in a political and social inferiority. They are content to be brushed like flies from the path of a great person, so that justice shall be done by him to that common nature which it is dearest desire of all to see enlarged and glorified. They sun themselves in the great man's light, and feel it to be their own element. They cast the dignity of man from their downtrod selves upon the shoulders of a hero, and will perish to add one drop of blood to make that great heart beat, those giant sinews combat and conquer. He lives for us, and we live in him.

Men, such as they are, very naturally seek money or power; and power be- cause it is as good as money,—the "spoils," so called, "of office." And why not? for they aspire to the highest, and this, in their sleep-walking, they dream is highest. Wake them and they shall quit the false good and leap to the true, and leave governments to clerks and desks. This revolution is to be wrought by the gradual domestication of the idea of Culture. The main enterprise of the world for splendor, for extent, is the upbuilding of a man. Here are the materials strewn along the ground. The private life of one man shall be a more illustrious monarchy, more formidable to its enemy, more sweet and serene in its influence to its friend, than any kingdom in history. For a man, rightly viewed, com- prehendeth the particular natures of all men. Each philosopher, each bard, each actor has only done for me, as by a delegate, what one day I can do for myself. The books which once we valued more than the apple of the eye, we have quite exhausted. What is that but saying that we have come up with the point of view which the universal mind took through the eyes of one scribe; we have been that man, and have passed on. First, one, then another, we drain all cisterns, and waxing greater by all these supplies, we crave a better and more abundant food. The man has never lived that can feed us ever. The human mind cannot be enshrined in a person who shall set a barrier on any one side to this un- bounded, unboundable empire. It is one central fire, which, flaming now out of the lips of Etna, lightens the capes of Sicily, and now out of the throat of Vesuvius, illuminates the towers and vineyards of Naples. It is one light which beams out of a thousand stars. It is one soul which animates all men.

But I have dwelt perhaps tediously upon this abstraction of the Scholar. I ought not to delay longer to add what I have to say of nearer reference to the time and to this country.

Historically, there is thought to be a difference in the ideas which pre- dominate over successive epochs, and there are data for marking the genius of the Classic, of the Romantic, and now of the Reflective or Philosophical age.

With the views I have intimated of the oneness or the identity of the mind through all individuals, I do not much dwell on these differences. In fact, I believe each individual passes through all three. The boy is a Greek; the youth, romantic; the adult, reflective. I deny not, however, that a revolution in the leading idea may be distinctly enough traced.

Our age is bewailed as the age of Introversion. Must that needs be evil? We, it seems, are critical; we are embarrassed with second thoughts; we cannot enjoy any thing for hankering to know whereof the pleasure consists; we are lined with eyes; we see with our feet; the time is infected with Hamlet's unhappiness,—

> Sicklied o'er with the pale cast of thought

It is so bad then? Sight is the last thing to be pitied. Would we be blind? Do we fear lest we should outsee nature and God, and drink truth dry? I look upon the discontent of the literary class as a mere announcement of the fact that they find themselves not in the state of mind of their fathers, and regret the coming state as untried; as a boy dreads the water before he has learned that he can swim. If there is any period one would desire to be born in, is it not the age of Revolution; when the old and the new stand side by side and admit of being compared; when the energies of all men are searched by fear and by hope; when the historic glories of the old can be compensated by the rich possibilities of the new era? This time, like all times, is a very good one, if we but know what to do with it.

I read with some joy of the auspicious signs of the coming days, as they glimmer already through poetry and art, through philosophy and science, through church and state.

One of these signs is the fact that the same movement which effected the elevation of what was called the lowest class in the state, assumed in literature a very marked and as benign an aspect. Instead of the sublime and beautiful, the near, the low, the common, was explored and poetized. That which had been negligently trodden under foot by those who were harnessing and provisioning themselves for long journeys into far countries, is suddenly found to be richer than all foreign parts. The literature of the poor, the feelings of the child, the philosophy of the street, the meaning of household life, are the topics of the time. It is a great stride. It is a sign—is it not?—of new vigor when the extremities are made active, when currents of warm life run into the hands and the feet. I ask not for the great, the remote, the romantic; what is doing in Italy or Arabia; what is Greek art, or Provençal minstrelsy; I embrace the common, I explore and sit at the feet of the familiar, the low. Give me insight into to-day, and you may have the antique and future worlds. What would we really know the meaning of? The meal in the firkin; the milk in the pan; the ballad in the street; the news of the boat; the glance of the eye; the form and the gait of the body;—show me the ultimate reason of these matters; show me the sublime presence of the highest spiritual cause lurking, as always it does lurk, in these suburbs and extremities of nature; let me see every trifle bristling with the polarity that ranges it instantly on an eternal law; and the shop, the plough, and the ledger referred to the like cause by which light undulates and poets sing;—and the world lies no longer a dull miscellany and lumber-room, but has form and order; there is no trifle, there is no puzzle, but one design unites and animates the farthest pinnacle and the lowest trench.

This idea has inspired the genius of Goldsmith, Burns, Cowper, and, in a newer time, of Goethe, Wordsworth, and Carlyle. This idea they have differently followed and with various success. In contrast with their writing, the style of Pope, of Johnson, of Gibbon, looks cold and pedantic. This writing is blood-warm. Man is surprised to find that things near are not less beautiful and wondrous than things remote. The near explains the far. The drop is a small ocean. A man is related to all nature. This perception of the worth of the vulgar is fruitful in discoveries. Goethe, in this very thing the most modern of the moderns, has shown us, as none ever did, the genius of the ancients.

There is one man of genius who has done much for this philosophy of life, whose literary value has never yet been rightly estimated;—I mean Emanuel Swedenborg. The most imaginative of men, yet writing with the precision of a mathematician, he endeavored to engraft a purely philosophical Ethics on the popular Christianity of his time. Such an attempt of course must have difficulty which no genius could surmount. But he saw and showed the connection between nature and the affections of the soul. He pierced the emblematic or spiritual character of the visible, audible, tangible world. Especially did his shade-loving muse hover over and interpret the lower parts of nature; he showed the mysterious bond that allies moral evil to the foul material forms, and has given in epical parables a theory of insanity, of beasts, of unclean and fearful things.

Another sign of our times, also marked by an analogous political movement, is the new importance given to the single person. Every thing that tends to insulate the individual,—to surround him with barriers of natural respect, so that each man shall feel the world is his, and man shall treat with man as a sovereign state with a sovereign state,—tends to true union as well as greatness. "I learned," said the melancholy Pestalozzi, "that no man in God's wide earth is either willing or able to help any other man." Help must come from the bosom alone. The scholar is that man who must take up into himself all the ability of the time, all the contributions of the past, all the hopes of the future. He must be an university of knowledges. If there be one lesson more than another which should pierce his ear, it is, The world is nothing, the man is all; in yourself is the law of all nature, and you know not yet how a globule of sap ascends; in yourself slumbers the whole of Reason; it is for you to know all; it is for you to dare all. Mr. President and Gentlemen, this confidence in the unsearched might of man belongs, by all motives, by all prophecy, by all preparation, to the American Scholar. We have listened too long to the courtly muses of Europe. The spirit of the American freeman is already suspected to be timid, imitative, tame. Public and private avarice make the air we breathe thick and fat. The scholar is decent, indolent, complaisant. See already the tragic consequence. The mind of this country, taught to aim at low objects, eats upon itself. There is no work for any but the decorous and the complaisant. Young men of the fairest promise, who begin life upon our shores, inflated by the mountain winds, shined upon by all the stars of God, find the earth below not in unison with these, but are hindered from action by the disgust which the principles on which business is managed inspire, and turn drudges, or die of disgust, some of them suicides. What is the remedy? They did not yet see, and thousands of young men as hopeful now crowding to the barriers for the career do not yet see, that if the single man plant himself indomitably on his instincts, and there abide, the huge world will come round to him. Patience,—patience; with the shades of all the good and great for company; and for solace the perspective of your own infinite life; and for work the study and the communication of principles, the making those instincts prevalent, the conversion of the world. Is it not the chief disgrace in the world, not to be an unit;—not to be reckoned one character;—not to yield that peculiar fruit which each man was created to bear, but to be reckoned in the gross, in the hundred, or the thousand, of the party, the section, to which we belong; and our opinion predicted geographically, as the north, or the south? Not so, brothers and friends—please God, ours shall not be so. We will walk on our own feet; we will work with our hands; we will speak our own minds. The study of letters shall be no longer a name for pity, for doubt, and for sensual indulgence. The dread of man and the love of man shall be a wall of defence and a wreath of joy around all. A nation of men will for the first time exist, because each believes himself inspired by the Divine Soul which also inspires all men.

THE MORAL UN-NEUTRALITY OF SCIENCE

C. P. Snow[10]

Sir Charles Percy Snow (1905–   ), contemporary leader in scientific thinking, in literature, and in education, delivered this address before the American Association for the Advancement of Science, New York City, December 27, 1960. The speech deals with the basic issue of whether nuclear armaments are to be controlled or whether the general destruction of the planet is in store. Science, according to Snow, has the responsibility to explain this either-or decision. This notable address raises the old questions: What is science? What are the moral components of science? How can laymen better understand modern science and help with the practical control and development of constantly expanding scientific knowledge?

Scientists are the most important occupational group in the world today. At this moment, what they do is of passionate concern to the whole of human society. At this moment, the scientists have little influence on the world effect of what they do. Yet, potentially, they can have great influence. The rest of the world is frightened both of what they do—that is, of the intellectual discoveries of science—and of its effect. The rest of the world, transferring its fears, is

[10] The text was first published in *Science* magazine, 133:256–259, 1961. It is here reprinted by permission of the author and of the American Association for the Advancement of Science. The speech was also included in Lester Thonssen (ed.), *Representative American Speeches: 1960–61,* The H. W. Wilson Company, New York, pp. 41–54.

frightened of the scientists themselves and tends to think of them as radically different from other men.

As an ex-scientist, if I may call myself so, I know that is nonsense. I have even tried to express in fiction some kinds of scientific temperament and scientific experience. I know well enough that scientists are very much like other men. After all, we are all human, even if some of us don't give that appearance. I think I would be prepared to risk a generalization. The scientists I have known (and because of my official life I have known as many as anyone in the world) have been in certain respects just perceptibly more morally admirable than most other groups of intelligent men.

That is a sweeping statement, and I mean it only in a statistical sense. But I think there is just a little in it. The moral qualities I admire in scientists are quite simple ones, but I am very suspicious of attempts to oversubtilize moral qualities. It is nearly always a sign, not of true sophistication, but of a specific kind of triviality. So I admire in scientists very simple virtues—like courage, truth-telling, kindness—in which, judged by the low standards which the rest of us manage to achieve, the scientists are not deficient. I think on the whole the scientists make slightly better husbands and fathers than most of us, and I admire them for it. I don't know the figures, and I should be curious to have them sorted out, but I am prepared to bet that the proportion of divorces among scientists is slightly but significantly less than that among other groups of similar education and income. I do not apologize for considering that a good thing.

A close friend of mine is a very distinguished scientist. He is also one of the few scientists I know who has lived what we used to call a Bohemian life. When we were both younger, he thought he would undertake historical research to see how many great scientists had been as fond of women as he was. I think he would have felt mildly supported if he could have found a precedent. I remember his reporting to me that his researches hadn't had any luck. The really great scientists seemed to vary from a few neutral characters to a large number who were depressingly "normal." The only gleam of comfort was to be found in the life of Jerome Cardan; and Cardan wasn't anything like enough to outweigh all the others.

So scientists are not much different from other men. They are certainly no worse than other men. But they do differ from other men in one thing. That is the point I started with. Whether they like it or not, what they do is of critical importance for the human race. Intellectually, it has transformed the climate of our time. Socially, it will decide whether we live or die, and how we live or die. It holds decisive powers for good and evil. *That* is the situation in which the scientists find themselves. They may not have asked for it, or may only have asked for it in part, but they cannot escape it. They think, many of the more sensitive of them, that they don't deserve to have this weight of responsibility heaved upon them. All they want to do is to get on with their work. I sympathize. But the scientists can't escape the responsibility—any more than they, or the rest of us, can escape the gravity of the moment in which we stand.

There is of course one way to contract out. It has been a favorite way for intellectual persons caught in the midst of water too rough for them.

It consists of the invention of categories—or, if you like, of the division of moral labor. That is, the scientists who want to contract out say, *we* produce the tools. *We* stop there. It is for *you*—the rest of the world, the politicians— to say how the tools are used. The tools may be used for purposes which most of us would regard as bad. If so, we are sorry. But as scientists, that is no concern of ours.

This is the doctrine of the ethical neutrality of science. I can't accept it for an instant. I don't believe any scientist of serious feeling can accept it. It is hard, some think, to find the precise statements which will prove it wrong. Yet we nearly all feel intuitively that the invention of comfortable categories is a moral trap. It is one of the easier methods of letting the conscience rust. It is exactly what the early nineteenth-century economists, such as Ricardo, did in the face of the facts of the first industrial revolution. We wonder now how men, intelligent men, can have been so morally blind. We realize how the exposure of that moral blindness gave Marxism its apocalyptic force. We are now, in the middle of the scientific or second industrial revolution, in something like the same position as Ricardo. Are we going to let our consciences rust? Can we ignore that intimation we nearly all have, that scientists have a unique responsibility? Can we believe it, that science is morally neutral?

To me—it would be dishonest to pretend otherwise—there is only one answer to those questions. Yet I have been brought up in the presence of the same intellectual categories as most Western scientists. It would also be dishonest to pretend that I find it easy to construct a rationale which expresses what I now believe. The best I can hope for is to fire a few sighting shots. Perhaps someone who sees more clearly than I can will come along and make a real job of it.

Let me begin with a remark which seems some way off the point. Anyone who has ever worked in any science knows how much esthetic joy he has obtained. That is, in the actual *activity* of science, in the process of making a discovery, however humble it is, one can't help feeling an awareness of beauty. The subjective experience, the esthetic satisfaction, seems exactly the same as the satisfaction one gets from writing a poem or a novel, or composing a piece of music. I don't think anyone has succeeded in distinguishing between them. The literature of scientific discovery is full of this esthetic joy. The very best communication of it that I know comes in G. H. Hardy's book, *A Mathematician's Apology*. Graham Greene once said he thought that, along with Henry James's prefaces, this was the best account of the artistic experience ever written. But one meets the same thing throughout the history of science. Bolyai's great yell of triumph when he saw he could construct a self-consistent, non-Euclidean geometry; Rutherford's revelation to his colleagues that he knew what the atom was like; Darwin's slow, patient, timorous certainty that at last he had got there: all these are voices, different voices of esthetic ecstasy.

That is not the end of it. The *result* of the activity of science, the actual finished piece of scientific work, has an esthetic value in itself. The judgments passed on it by other scientists will more often than not be expressed in esthetic terms: "That's beautiful!" or "That really is very pretty!" (as the understating English tend to say). The esthetics of scientific constructs, like the esthetics of works of art, are variegated. We think some of the great syntheses, like Newton's, beautiful because of their classical simplicity, but we see a different kind of beauty in the relativistic extension of the wave equation or the interpretation of the structure of deoxyribonucleic acid, perhaps because of the touch of unexpectedness. Scientists know their kinds of beauty when they see them. They are suspicious, and scientific history shows they have always been right to have been so, when a subject is in an "ugly" state. For example, most physicists feel in their bones that the present bizarre assembly of nuclear particles, as grotesque as a stamp collection, can't possibly be, in the long run, the last word.

We should not restrict the esthetic values to what we call "pure" science. Applied science has its beauties, which are, in my view, identical in nature. The magnetron has been a marvelously useful device, but it was a beautiful device, not exactly apart from its utility but because it did, with such supreme economy, precisely what it was designed to do. Right down in the field of development, the esthetic experience is as real to engineers. When they forget it, when they begin to design heavy-power equipment about twice as heavy as it needs to be, engineers are the first to know that they are lacking virtue.

There is no doubt, then, about the esthetic content of science, both in the activity and the result. But esthetics has no connection with morals, say the categorizers. I don't want to waste time on peripheral issues—but are you quite sure of that? Or is it possible that these categories are inventions to make us evade the human and social conditions in which we now exist? But let us move straight on to something else, which is right in the grain of the activity of science and which is at the same time quintessentially moral. I mean, the desire to find the truth.

By *truth*, I don't intend anything complicated, once again. I am using the word as a scientist uses it. We all know that the philosophical examination of the concept of empirical truth gets us into some curious complexities, but most scientists really don't care. They know that the truth, as they use the word and as the rest of us use it in the language of common speech, is what makes science work. That is good enough for them. On it rests the whole great edifice of modern science. They have a sneaking sympathy for Rutherford, who, when asked to examine the philosophical bases of science, was inclined to reply, as he did to the metaphysician Samuel Alexander: "Well, what have you been talking all your life, Alexander? Just hot air! Nothing but hot air!"

Anyway, truth in their own straightforward sense is what the scientists are trying to find. They want to find what is *there*. Without that desire, there is no science. It is the driving force of the whole activity. It compels the scientist to have an overriding respect for truth, every stretch of the way. That is, if you're going to find what is *there*, you mustn't deceive yourself or anyone else. You mustn't lie to yourself. At the crudest level, you mustn't fake your experiments.

Curiously enough, scientists do try to behave like that. A short time ago, I wrote a novel in which the story hinged on a case of scientific fraud. But I made one of my characters, who was himself a very good scientist, say that, considering the opportunities and temptations, it is astonishing how few such cases there are. We have all heard of perhaps half a dozen open and notorious ones, which are on the record for anyone to read—ranging from the "discovery" of the L radiation to the singular episode of the Piltdown man.

We have all, if we have lived any time in the scientific world, heard private talk of something like another dozen cases which for various reasons are not yet public property. In some cases, we know the motives for the cheating—sometimes, but not always, sheer personal advantage, such as getting money or a job. But not always. A special kind of vanity has led more than one man into scientific faking. At a lower level of research, there are presumably some more cases. There must have been occasional Ph.D. students who scraped by with the help of a bit of fraud.

But the total number of all these men is vanishingly small by the side of the total number of scientists. Incidentally, the effect on science of such frauds is also vanishingly small. Science is a self-correcting system. That is, no fraud (or honest mistake) is going to stay undetected for long. There is no need for an extrinsic scientific criticism, because criticism is inherent in the process itself. So that all that a fraud can do is waste the time of the scientists who have to clear it up.

The remarkable thing is not the handful of scientists who deviate from the search for truth but the overwhelming numbers who keep to it. That is a demonstration, absolutely clear for anyone to see, of moral behavior on a very large scale.

We take it for granted. Yet it is very important. It differentiates science in its widest sense (which includes scholarship) from all other intellectual activities. There is a built-in moral component right in the core of the scientific activity itself. The desire to find the truth is itself a moral impulse, or at least contains a moral impulse. The way in which a scientist tries to find the truth imposes on him a constant moral discipline. We say a scientific conclusion—such as the contradiction of parity by Lee and Yang—is "true" in the limited sense of scientific truth, just as we say that it is "beautiful" according to the criteria of scientific esthetics. We also know that to reach this conclusion took a set of actions which would have been useless without the moral nature. That is, all through the marvelous experiments of Wu and her colleagues, there was the constant moral exercise of seeking and telling the truth. To scientists, who are brought up in this climate, this seems as natural as breathing. Yet it is a wonderful thing. Even if the scientific activity contained only this one moral component, that alone would be enough to let us say that it was morally un-neutral.

But is this the only moral component? All scientists would agree about the beauty and the truth. In the Western world, they wouldn't agree on much more. Some will feel with me in what I am going to say. Some will not. That doesn't affect me much, except that I am worried by the growth of an attitude I think very dangerous, a kind of technological conformity disguised as cynicism. I shall say a little more about that later. As for disagreement, G. H. Hardy used to comment that a serious man ought not to waste his time stating a majority opinion—there are plenty of others to do that. That was the voice of classical scientific nonconformity. I wish that we heard it more often.

Let me cite some grounds for hope. Any of us who were working in science before 1933 can remember what the atmosphere was like. It is a terrible bore when aging men in their fifties speak about the charms of their youth. Yet I am going to irritate you—just as Talleyrand irritated his juniors—by saying that unless one was on the scene before 1933, one hasn't known the sweetness of the scientific life. The scientific world of the twenties was as near to being a full-fledged international community as we are likely to get. Don't think I'm saying that the men involved were superhuman or free from the ordinary frailties. That wouldn't come well from me, who have spent a fraction of my writing life pointing out that scientists are, first and foremost, men. But the atmosphere of the twenties in science was filled with an air of benevolence and magnanimity which transcended the people who lived in it.

Anyone who ever spent a week in Cambridge or Göttingen or Copenhagen felt it all around him. Rutherford had very human faults, but he was a great man with abounding human generosity. For him the world of science was a world that lived on a plane above the nation-state, and lived there with joy. That was at least as true of those two other great men, Niels Bohr and Franck, and some of that spirit rubbed off on to the pupils round them. The same was true of the Roman school of physics.

The personal links within this international world were very close. It is worth remembering that Peter Kapitza, who was a loyal Soviet citizen, honored my country by working in Rutherford's laboratory for many years. He became a fellow of the Royal Society, a fellow of Trinity College, Cambridge, and the founder and kingpin of the best physics club Cambridge has known. He never gave up his Soviet citizenship and is now director of the Institute of Physical Problems in Moscow. Through him a generation of English scientists came to have personal knowledge of their Russian colleagues. These exchanges were then, and have remained, more valuable than all the diplomatic exchanges ever invented.

The Kapitza phenomenon couldn't take place now. I hope to live to see the day when a young Kapitza can once more work for sixteen years in Berkeley or Cambridge and then go back to an eminent place in his own country. When that can happen, we are all right. But after the idyllic years of world science, we passed into a tempest of history, and, by an unfortunate coincidence, we passed into a technological tempest too.

The discovery of atomic fission broke up the world of international physics. "This has killed a beautiful subject," said Mark Oliphant, the father figure of Australian physics, in 1945, after the bombs had dropped. In intellectual terms, he has not turned out to be right. In spiritual and moral terms, I sometimes think he has.

A good deal of the international community of science remains in other fields —in great areas of biology, for example. Many biologists are feeling the identical liberation, the identical joy at taking part in a magnanimous enterprise, that physicists felt in the twenties. It is more than likely that the moral and intellectual leadership of science will pass to biologists, and it is among them that we shall find the Rutherfords, Bohrs, and Francks of the next generation.

Physicists have had a bitterer task. With the discovery of fission, and with some technical breakthroughs in electronics, physicists became, almost overnight, the most important military resource a nation-state could call on. A large number of physicists became soldiers not in uniform. So they have remained, in the advanced societies, ever since.

It is very difficult to see what else they could have done. All this began in the

Hitler war. Most scientists thought then that Nazism was as near absolute evil as human society can manage. I myself thought so. I still think so, without qualification. That being so, Nazism had to be fought, and since the Nazis might make fission bombs—which we thought possible until 1944, and which was a continual nightmare if one was remotely in the know—well, then, we had to make them too. Unless one was an unlimited pacifist, there was nothing else to do. And unlimited pacificism is a position which most of us cannot sustain.

Therefore I respect, and to a large extent share, the moral attitudes of those scientists who devoted themselves to making the bomb. But the trouble is, when you get onto any kind of moral escalator, to know whether you're ever going to be able to get off. When scientists became soldiers they gave up something, so imperceptibly that they didn't realize it, of the full scientific life. Not intellectually. I see no evidence that scientific work on weapons of maximum destruction has been in any intellectual respect different from other scientific work. But there is a moral difference.

It may be—scientists who are better men than I am often take this attitude, and I have tried to represent it faithfully in one of my books—that this is a moral price which, in certain circumstances, has to be paid. Nevertheless, it is no good pretending that there is not a moral price. Soldiers have to obey. That is the foundation of their morality. It is not the foundation of the scientific morality. Scientists have to question and if necessary to rebel. I don't want to be misunderstood. I am no anarchist. I am not suggesting that loyalty is not a prime virtue. I am not saying that all rebellion is good. But I am saying that loyalty can easily turn into conformity, and that conformity can often be a cloak for the timid and self-seeking. So can obedience, carried to the limit. When you think of the long and gloomy history of man, you will find that far more, and far more hideous, crimes have been committed in the name of obedience than have ever been committed in the name of rebellion. If you doubt that, read William Shirer's *Rise and Fall of the Third Reich.* The German officer corps were brought up in the most rigorous code of obedience. To them, no more honorable and God-fearing body of men could conceivably exist. Yet in the name of obedience, they were party to, and assisted in, the most wicked large-scale actions in the history of the world.

Scientists must not go that way. Yet the duty to question is not much of a support when you are living in the middle of an organized society. I speak with feeling here. I was an official for twenty years. I went into official life at the beginning of the war, for the reasons that prompted my scientific friends to begin to make weapons. I stayed in that life until a year ago, for the same reason that made my scientific friends turn into civilian soldiers. The official's life in England is not quite so disciplined as a soldier's, but it is very nearly so. I think I know the virtues, which are very great, of the men who live that disciplined life. I also know what for me was the moral trap. I, too, had got onto an escalator. I can put the result in a sentence: I was coming to hide behind the institution; I was losing the power to say no.

Only a very bold man, when he is a member of an organized society, can keep the power to say no. I tell you that, not being a very bold man, or one who finds it congenial to stand alone, away from his colleagues. We can't expect many scientists to do it. Is there any tougher ground for them to stand on? I suggest to you that there is. I believe that there is a spring of moral action in the scientific activity which is at least as strong as the search for truth. The name of this spring is *knowledge*. Scientists *know* certain things in a fashion more immediate and more certain than those who don't comprehend what science is. Unless we are abnormally weak or abnormally wicked men, this knowledge is bound to shape our actions. Most of us are timid, but to an extent, knowledge gives us guts. Perhaps it can give us guts strong enough for the jobs in hand.

I had better take the most obvious example. All physical scientists *know* that it is relatively easy to make plutonium. We know this, not as a journalistic fact at second hand, but as a fact in our own experience. We can work out the number of scientific and engineering personnel needed for a nation-state to equip itself with fission and fusion bombs. We *know* that, for a dozen or more states, it will only take perhaps six years, perhaps less. Even the best informed of us always exaggerate these periods.

This we know, with the certainty of—what shall I call it?—engineering truth. We also—most of us—are familiar with statistics and the nature of odds. We know, with the certainty of statistical truth, that if enough of these weapons are made, by enough different states, some of them are going to blow up, through accident, or folly, or madness—the motives don't matter. What does matter is the nature of the statistical fact.

All this we *know*. We know it in a more direct sense than any politician because it comes from our direct experience. It is part of our minds. Are we going to let it happen?

All this we *know*. It throws upon scientists a direct and personal responsibility. It is not enough to say that scientists have a responsibility as citizens. They have a much greater one than that, and one different in kind. For scientists have a moral imperative to say what they know. It is going to make them unpopular in their own nation-states. It may do worse than make them unpopular. That doesn't matter. Or at least, it does matter to you and me, but it must not count in the face of the risks.

For we genuinely know the risks. We are faced with an either-or, and we haven't much time. The *either* is acceptance of a restriction of nuclear armaments. This is going to begin, just as a token, with an agreement on the stopping of nuclear tests. The United States is not going to get the 99.9-per cent "security" that it has been asking for. This is unobtainable, though there are other bargains that the United States could probably secure. I am not going to conceal from you that this course involves certain risks. They are quite obvious, and no honest man is going to blink them. That is the *either*. The *or* is not a risk but a certainty. It is this. There is no agreement on tests. The nuclear arms race between the United States and the U.S.S.R. not only continues but accelerates. Other countries join in. Within, at the most, six years, China and several other states have a stock of nuclear bombs. Within, at the most, ten years, some of those bombs are going off. I am saying this as responsibly as I can. *That* is the certainty. On the one side, therefore, we have a finite risk. On the other side we have a certainty of disaster. Between a risk and a certainty, a sane man does not hesitate.

It is the plain duty of scientists to explain this either-or. It is a duty which seems to me to come from the moral nature of the scientific activity itself.

The same duty, though in a much more pleasant form, arises with respect to the benevolent powers of science. For scientists know, and again with the certainty of scientific knowledge, that we possess every scientific fact we need to transform the physical life of half the world. And transform it within the span of people now living. I mean, we have all the resources to help half the world live as long as we do and eat enough. All that is missing is the will. We *know* that. Just as we know that you in the United States, and to a slightly lesser extent we in the United Kingdom, have been almost unimaginably lucky. We are sitting like people in a smart and cozy restaurant and we are eating comfortably, looking out of the window into the streets. Down on the pavement are people who are looking up at us, people who by chance have different colored skins from ours, and are rather hungry. Do you wonder that they don't like us all that much? Do you wonder that we sometimes feel ashamed of ourselves, as we look out through that plate glass?

Well, it is within our power to get started on that problem. We are morally impelled to. We all know that, if the human species does solve that one, there will be consequences which are themselves problems. For instance, the population of the world will become embarrassingly large. But that is another challenge. There are going to be challenges to our intelligence and to our moral nature as long as man remains man. After all, a challenge is not, as the word is coming to be used, an excuse for slinking off and doing nothing. A challenge is something to be picked up.

For all these reasons, I believe the world community of scientists has a final responsibility upon it—a greater responsibility than is pressing on any other body of men. I do not pretend to know how they will bear this responsibility. These may be famous last words, but I have an inextinguishable hope. For, as I have said, there is no doubt that the scientific activity is both beautiful and truthful. I cannot prove it, but I believe that, simply because scientists cannot escape their own knowledge, they also won't be able to avoid showing themselves disposed to good.

THE TRAINING OF THE INTELLECT

Woodrow Wilson[11]

Woodrow Wilson (1856–1924), then President of Princeton University, gave this Phi Beta Kappa address on March 18, 1908, before the Phi Beta Kappa fraternity at Yale University. Although he was later distinguished as President (1913–1921), as leader of the "new freedom," as an inspiring public speaker

[11] The text is from J. M. O'Neill (compiler), *Modern Short Speeches,* Appleton-Century-Crofts, Inc., New York, 1923, pp. 261–267.

throughout World War I, and as a highly persuasive protagonist for America's entry into the League of Nations, he had an impressive career at Princeton as educator and as speaker before university audiences.

Outstanding among his educational addresses was his exposition to the Yale audience of the role of the intellect in university training. His assumptions and propositions and his methods of communication may be compared with those of Emerson in his Phi Beta Kappa address at Harvard seventy years earlier.

Wilson, in his political and other concepts, his originality of phrasing, his vigor and persuasiveness as a speaker, ranks among the first three or four American political speakers of the twentieth century.

Mr. Toastmaster, Mr. President, and Gentlemen: I must confess to you that I came here with very serious thoughts this evening because I have been laboring under the conviction for a long time that the object of a university is to educate, and I have not seen the universities of this country achieving any remarkable or disturbing success in that direction. I have found everywhere the note which I must say I have heard sounded once or twice to-night— that apology for the intellectual side of the university. You hear it at all universities. Learning is on the defensive, is actually on the defensive, among college men, and they are being asked by way of indulgence to bring that also into the circle of their interests. Is it not time we stopped asking indulgence for learning and proclaimed its sovereignty? Is it not time we reminded the college men of this country that they have no right to any distinctive place in any community, unless they can show it by intellectual achievement? That if a university is a place for distinction at all it must be distinguished by the conquests of the mind? I for my part tell you plainly that that is my motto, that I have entered the field to fight for that thesis, and that for that thesis only do I care to fight.

The toastmaster of the evening said, and said truly, that this is the season when, for me, it was most difficult to break away from regular engagements in which I am involved at this time of the year. But when I was invited to the Phi Beta Kappa banquet it had an unusual sound, and I felt that that was the particular kind of invitation which it was my duty and privilege to accept. One of the problems of the American university now is, how, among a great many other competing interests, to give places of distinction to men who want places of distinction in the classroom. Why don't we give you men the Y here and the P at Princeton, because, after all, you have done the particular thing which distinguishes Yale? Not that these other things are not worth doing, but they may be done anywhere. They may be done in athletic clubs where there is no study, but this thing can be done only here. This is the distinctive mark of the place.

A good many years ago, just two weeks before the mid-year examinations, the faculty of Princeton was foolish enough to permit a very unwise evangelist to come to the place and to upset the town. And while an assisting undergraduate was going from room to room one undergraduate secured his door and put this notice out: "I am a Christian and am studying for examinations."

Now I want to say that that is exactly what a Christian undergraduate would be doing at that time of the year. He would not be attending religious meetings no matter how beneficial it would be to him. He would be studying for examinations not merely for the purpose of passing them, but from his sense of duty.

We get a good many men at Princeton from certain secondary schools who say a great deal about their earnest desire to cultivate character among our students, and I hear a great deal about character being the object of education. I take leave to believe that a man who cultivates his character consciously will cultivate nothing except what will make him intolerable to his fellow men. If your object in life is to make a fine fellow of yourself, you will not succeed, and you will not be acceptable to really fine fellows. Character, gentlemen, is a by-product. It comes, whether you will or not, as a consequence of a life devoted to the nearest duty, and the place in which character would be cultivated, if it be a place of study, is a place where study is the object and character the result.

Not long ago a gentleman approached me in great excitement just after the entrance examinations. He said we had made a great mistake in not taking so and so from a certain school which he named. "But," I said, "he did not pass the entrance examination." And he went over the boy's moral excellencies again. "Pardon me," I said, "you do not understand. He did not pass the entrance examinations. Now," I said, "I want you to understand that if the angel Gabriel applied for admission to Princeton University and could not pass the entrance examinations, he would not be admitted. He would be wasting his time." It seemed a new idea to him. This boy had come from a school which cultivated character, and he was a nice, lovable fellow with a presentable character. Therefore, he ought to be admitted to any university. I fail to see it from this point of view, for a university is an institution of purpose. We have in some previous years had pity for young gentlemen who were not sufficiently acquainted with the elements of a preparatory course. They have been dropped at the examinations, and I always felt that we have been guilty of an offense, and have made their parents spend money to no avail and the youngsters spend their time to no avail. And so I think that all university men ought to rouse themselves now and understand what is the object of a university. The object of a university is intellect; as a university its only object is intellect. As a body of young men there ought to be other things, there ought to be diversions to release them from the constant strain of effort, there ought to be things that gladden the heart and moments of leisure, but as a university the object is intellect.

The reason why I chose the subject that I am permitted to speak upon to-night—the functions of scholarship—was that I wanted to point out the function of scholarship not merely in the university, but in the nation. In a country constituted as ours is, the relation in which education stands is a very important one. Our whole theory has been based upon an enlightened citizenship and therefore the function of scholarship must be for the nation as well as for the university itself. I mean the function of such scholarship as undergraduates get. That is not a violent amount in any case. You cannot make a scholar of a man except by some largeness of Providence in his makeup, by the time he is twenty-one or twenty-two years of age. There have been gentlemen who have made a reputation by twenty-one or twenty-two, but it is generally in some little province of knowledge, so small that a small effort can conquer it. You do not make scholars by that time; you do not often make scholars by seventy that are worth boasting of. The process of scholarship, so far as the real scholar is concerned, is an unending process, and knowledge is pushed forward only a very little by his best efforts. And it is evident, of course, that the most you can contribute to a man in his undergraduate years is not equipment in the exact knowledge which is characteristic of the scholar, but an inspiration of the spirit of scholarship. The most that you can give a youngster is the spirit of the scholar.

Now, the spirit of the scholar in a country like ours must be a spirit related to the national life. It cannot, therefore, be a spirit of pedantry. I suppose that this is a sufficient working conception of pedantry to say that it is knowledge divorced from life. It is knowledge so closeted, so desecrated, so stripped of the significances of life itself, that it is a thing apart and not connected with the vital processes in the world about us.

There is a great place in every nation for the spirit of scholarship, and it seems to me that there never was a time when the spirit of scholarship was more needed in affairs than it is in this country at this time.

We are thinking just now with our emotions and not with our minds; we are moved by impulse and not by judgment. We are drawing away from things with blind antipathy. The spirit of knowledge is that you must base your conclusions on adequate grounds. Make sure that you are going to the real sources of knowledge, discovering what the real facts are, before you move forward to the next process, which is the process of clear thinking. By clear thinking I do not mean logical thinking. I do not mean that life is based upon any logical system whatever. Life is essentially illogical. The world is governed now by a tumultuous sea of commonalities made up of passions, and we should pray God that the good passions should outvote the bad passions. But the movement of impulse, of motive, is the stuff of passion, and therefore clear thinking about life is not logical, symmetrical thinking, but it is interpretative thinking, thinking that sees the secret motive of things, thinking that penetrates deepest places where are the pulses of life.

Now scholarship ought to lay these impulses bare just as the physician can lay bare the seat of life in our bodies. That is not scholarship which goes to work upon the mere formal pedantry of logical reasoning, but that *is* scholarship which searches for the heart of a man. The spirit of scholarship gives us catholicity of thinking, the readiness to understand that there will constantly swing into our ken new items not dreamed of in our systems of philosophy, not simply to draw our conclusions from the data that we have had, but that all this is under constant mutation, and that therefore new phases of life will come upon us and a new adjustment of our conclusions will be necessary. Our thinking must be detached and disinterested thinking.

The particular objection that I have to the undergraduate forming his course of study on his future profession is this: that from start to finish, from the time he enters the university until he finishes his career, his thought will be centered upon particular interests. He will be immersed in the things that touch his profit and loss, and a man is not free to think inside that territory. If his bread and butter is going to be affected, if he is always thinking in the terms of his own profession, he is not thinking for the nation. He is thinking for himself, and whether he be conscious of it or not, he can never throw these trammels off. He will only think as a doctor, or a lawyer, or a banker. He will not be free in the world of knowledge and in the circle of interests which make up the great citizenship of the country. It is necessary that the spirit of scholarship should be a detached, disinterested spirit, not immersed in a particular interest. That is the function of scholarship in a country like ours, to supply not heat, but light, to suffuse things with the calm radiance of reason, to see to it that men do not act hastily, but that they act considerately, that they obey the truth whether they know it or not. The fault of our age is the fault of hasty action, of premature judgments, of a preference for ill-considered action over no action at all. Men who insist upon standing still and doing a little thinking before they do any acting are called reactionaries. They want actually to react to a state in which they can be allowed to think. They want for a little while to withdraw from the turmoil of party controversy and see where they stand before they commit themselves and their country to action from which it may not be possible to withdraw.

The whole fault of the modern age is that it applies to everything a false standard of efficiency. Efficiency with us is accomplishment, whether the accomplishment be by just and well-considered means or not; and this standard of achievement it is that is debasing the morals of our age, the intellectual morals of our age. We do not stop to do things thoroughly; we do not stop to know why we do things. We see an error and we hastily correct it by a greater error; and then go on to cry that the age is corrupt.

And so it is, gentlemen, that I try to join the function of the university with the great function of the national life. The life of this country is going to be revolutionized and purified only when the universities of this country wake up to the fact that their only reason for existing is intellect, that the objects that I have set forth, so far as undergraduate life is concerned, are the only legitimate objects. And every man should crave for his university primacy in these things, primacy in other things also if they may be brought in without enmity to it, but the sacrifice of everything that stands in the way of that.

For my part, I do not believe that it is athleticism which stands in the way. Athletics have been associated with the achievements of the mind in many a successful civilization. There is no difficulty in uniting vigor of body with achievement of mind, but there is a good deal of difficulty in uniting the achievement of the mind with a thousand distracting social influences, which take up all our ambitions, which absorb all our thoughts, which lead to all our arrangements of life, and then leave the university authorities the residuum of our attention, after we are through with the things that we are interested in. We absolutely changed the whole course of study at Princeton and revolutionized the methods of instruction without rousing a ripple on the surface of the alumni. They said those things are intellectual, they were our business. But just as soon as we thought to touch the social part of the university, there was not only a ripple, but the whole body was torn to its depths. We had touched the real things. These lay in triumphal competition with the province of the mind, and men's attention was so absolutely absorbed in these things that it was impossible for us to get their interest enlisted on the real undertakings of the university itself.

Now that is true of every university that I know anything about in this country, and if the faculties in this country want to recapture the ground that they have lost, they must begin pretty soon, and they must go into the battle with their bridges burned behind them so that it will be of no avail to retreat. If I had a voice to which the university men of this country might listen, that is the endeavor to which my ambition would lead me to call.

HIGH COST OF BIGOTRY

Eric A. Johnston[12]

Eric Johnston (1896–   ), formerly president of the United States Chamber of Commerce and president of the Motion Picture Association of America, was at the time of this address Administrator of Economic Stabilization. He gave this radio-television address on February 18, 1951 over the facilities of the American Broadcasting Company. He spoke as general chairman of Brotherhood Week.

He had frequently spoken vigorously against propaganda that "condemned foreigners, Jews, Catholics, Negroes, and Unionists."

This speech is notable not only for its plea against bigotry, but for its lively and concrete language.

The style is informal, always oral and attention getting. Note, for example, the direct address ("I'd like to tell you now what I mean by brotherhood."); the semislangy but colorful phrasing ("I don't want to be at the same table in a public place or anywhere else with a fellow who makes a heel out of himself."); the light treatment throughout ("I don't like bores, barflies, moochers."); the short sentences that carry "punch" ("We're in a showdown now. Look at the map."); and the fair-minded approach to the problem.

Mr. Johnston has been widely popular as a speaker. He is extemporaneous, energetic, and rapid in rate.

I'd like to tell you now what I mean by brotherhood—and the best way to say it is to tell you what I don't mean by brotherhood.

My belief in brotherhood doesn't compel me to hold open house in my home around the clock, or go to lunch with somebody I don't like. Or go out of my way to be chummy with someone from a different church or with a different kind of ancestry.

[12] Reprinted from Lester Thonssen (ed.), *Representative American Speeches: 1950–61*, The H. W. Wilson Company, New York, pp. 112–116, through the courtesy of the publishers and of Mr. Eric Johnston.

My right to privacy and my right to select my friends are not amended one bit by feeling strongly on the subject of the brotherhood of man. I don't even have to say I'm tolerant to believe in brotherhood. And I don't have to be tolerant. In fact, I don't want to have to tolerate anybody. It's awfully uncomfortable to be in society of somebody that you think you have to tolerate.

Maybe I could put it this way: I don't want to be at the same table in a public place or anywhere else with a fellow who makes a heel out of himself.

But I don't like the idea of kicking a man out of any door because he doesn't fit the Ku Klux Klan conception of a hundred per cent American.

My point is that I don't like bores, barflies, moochers, the bad mannered or the foul tongued, whether they are white or black; whether they belong to the church of Rome or the Sons and Daughters of I Will Arise. Or the church I go to myself.

Brotherhood, to me, doesn't mean showing off your tolerance. I think that's sappy, and it's insincere. Nobody is fooled for very long.

Brotherhood to me means behaving by the simple rules of decency to every decent person, regardless of how he parts his hair, the color of his skin, or the religious faith he follows.

Brotherhood means appraising the other fellow for what he's worth inside— as an associate in business—or as a social friend. Maybe the Elsie Dinsmores and the Little Lord Fauntleroys of this world can honestly say they love people in the mass. I can't. I've got to love them as people—as individuals.

And when you boil that down, what does it mean—except living by the American code that says the individual counts ahead of everything else? Let's explore that a little farther.

Now it seems to me that the blame for bigotry in this country is very largely heaped on the head of the native-born, white Protestant. If he'd only be nice and tolerant, why, we'd all get along as cozily as so many sleepy kittens in a basket. The way we get the story, that's the way it seems to go.

It just happened that I am native born, white and Protestant. My ancestors were the life of the party on some of the first ships to drop anchor off America; and if you take me somewhat farther back, the Johnstons of Scotland knew a little bit more about clans than those who spell the word with "K" in this country.

The Ku Klux Klanners would never take me in, of course, because I have the old-fashioned idea that bedsheets belong on the bedstead instead of over my head on horseback.

But as a native born, white Protestant, I sometimes think I'm discriminated against—and I am, when native born, white Protestants are singled as the sole perpetrators of intolerance. The fact is that individuals in every race among us, every faith among us, every ancestry among us are guilty of not abiding by the rules of brotherhood.

So it adds up that I take the rap when some other Americans of the same stock and faith as myself run amuck on the idea that America belongs to us and to us alone. I have to take a beating for their foolishness—in precisely the same way that the so-called minorities have to take the rap for the foolish sins of their own people.

Some of our hundred per cent Americans by self election who think they have a monopoly on the country have their precise counterparts in racial and religious blocs of lesser numerical strength. They must think they have a monopoly on the country too, for they organize politically to control it if they can. On that score, we are all sinners alike.

One of the grandest things about America is its human panorama—resulting from the intermingling of so many different peoples from so many different cultures. I hope the day will never come when Holland, Michigan, discards its tulip festival and throws away its title to a little piece of Holland in the heartland of America. I hope the day will never come when we cease to celebrate St. Patrick's day and jig to Irish tunes on the 17th of March. I want to see the rich folklore of other lands live on in America—but only aesthetically —not politically.

One of the saddest things about America is our hyphenated voting. So many times we go to the polls as Methodist-Americans, as Polish-Americans, as Catholic-Americans, as Jewish-Americans—as almost anything but what we ought to be—as all-Americans.

What kind of thinking is it that rallies votes against a candidate because his name ends in "ski," for instance, and rallies votes for a man because his name ends in "stein?"

It's not American thinking. That's for sure. It's not brotherhood. It's not decency. It's not common sense. It's plain damned foolishness—an expensive mistake of history.

The accident of birth gave me no right to think of myself as deserving something special from my country, but neither did the accident of birth give anybody else that right.

Truculence and belligerence and blanket name-calling won't get the so-called majority in this country anywhere in the long run—or the so-called minorities either. But every group of us that thinks of itself as a group has a chance to shame all the rest of us into sportsmanship by the exercise of sportsmanship itself.

The armor of courtesy is almost impossible to dent. But bigotry never built a bank balance, bought a bond, or gave a boost to the national income. Withholding jobs and business opportunities from one group doesn't make more jobs and more business opportunities for others. It simply serves as a drag on the whole economic engine. In ordinary times, you can't sell radios and refrigerators and automobiles to people who are denied decent jobs through bigotry.

We're in a showdown now. Look at the map. The Communist empire of Soviet Russia has scooped about 800 million into its sway. The Western world claims the allegiance of another 800 million. That leaves roughly 800 million— give or take a million either way—who could teeter toward the West—or totter toward the Kremlin.

They are mostly all in Asia. And while they may have large misgivings about communism, I haven't noticed any wild enthusiasms among them for the West —either before America came into the Western leadership—or since.

We talk about building bridges of brotherhood around the world in answer to the Communist pretensions. And communism, as we all know, makes a great deal of phony fuss and feathers about the brotherhood of man.

But where does brotherhood begin? It begins on a man-to-man basis here at home and not on a mass-to-mass basis across the oceans. Without that footing, a bridge of brotherhood is idle talk and empty vision. And ours is just as phony in the eyes of Asia as the Communists'.

Ahead of us all is the job of trying to make our democracy work better than it ever has, for it's got to if it's going to last; ahead of us is the job of proving to ourselves and to the world that the greatest experiment of all time—the American system—works for the good of all Americans: that it has justified the faith and hope of all mankind.

That's the kind of society men have been groping for through all the ages. It is here, if we want it to be here—the great and good beginning of a universal brotherhood of men.

Suggestions for the

Instructor

TOPICS TO BE HANDLED BRIEFLY

(1) Purpose of the course; (2) relation of aims to speech education and to *general* education; (3) meaning of speech and general aims of this course; (4) length of course and size of class; (5) order of presenting the materials of the course; (6) learning methods in the course; (7) principles and projects; (8) adjustment to needs, diagnosis, counseling; (9) criticism of performances; (10) readings and class discussions; (11) grades and ratings in general; (12) number of written assignments and speech outlines; (13) the text and the course.

OUTLINE FOR A STREAMLINED COURSE (thirty meetings—two hours per week)

The organization of the chapters according to basic concepts of speaker, audience, speech, and occasion follows:

Essentials of speech (*One*)

  I. *Speaker*
    His habits (Two)
    Confidence (Eight)
    Voice (Eleven)
    Articulation (Twelve)
    Physical activity (Thirteen)
    Personality (Fourteen)
  II. *Audience*
    Adaptation (Seven)
    Listening (Fifteen)
 III. *Speech*
    A. Ideas
      1. Subject (Three)
      2. Materials (Four)
      3. Supports (Six)
    B. Organization (Five)
    C. Language (Nine and Ten)
 IV. *Occasion*
    A. Adaptation in general (Seven)
    B. General occasions

1. Informational (Sixteen)
2. Argumentative (Seventeen)
3. Discussional (Nineteen)
4. Persuasive (Eighteen)
5. Reading (Twenty)
C. Special types
   1. Radio (Twenty-one)
   2. Other types (Twenty-two)
   3. Parliamentary procedure (Twenty-three)

Topics and chapter readings	*Speaking projects*
1. INTRODUCTORY TO COURSE	
2. ESSENTIALS OF EFFECTIVE SPEECH: Chapter One	I. Speech of four minutes (project 1, page 16).
3. IMPROVING SPEECH HABITS: Chapter Two	
4. DEVELOPING CONFIDENCE: Chapter Eight	II. An extempore speech (for suggestions, see Chapter Two).
5. Projects and Exercises	
6. SUBJECTS AND PURPOSES: Chapter Three	III. Prepare and present a four-minute speech. Outline it, including purpose sentence and other details. Justify your subject.
7. SOURCES OF MATERIALS: Chapter Four	
8. Projects and Exercises	
9. Projects and Exercises	IV. A four-minute speech based on a subject suggested by project 1, Chapter Four.
10. GENERAL REVIEW AND QUIZ	
11. ORGANIZATION: Chapter Five	
12. Projects and Exercises	V. Prepare and submit the outline of an informational speech as suggested by the rules and examples of Chapter Five.
13. VOICE IMPROVEMENT: Chapter Eleven	
14. Projects and Exercises	
15. ARTICULATION: Chapter Twelve	VI. Deliver the speech based on the outline of project V. Principles of effective delivery will be emphasized.
16. Projects or Exercises	
17. PHYSICAL ACTIVITY AND AUDIO-SPEAKING AIDS: Chapter Thirteen	
18. INFORMATIONAL SPEAKING: Chapter Sixteen	VII. An informational speech using visual aids. See project 1, page 247.
19. LISTENING: Chapter Fifteen	
20. REVIEW AND QUIZ: Chapters Five, Ten, Eleven, Fourteen, Fifteen, and Sixteen	VIII. A speech in which you report your observation and reaction to a public speech. See project 1, page 230.
21. Projects and Exercises	
22. AUDIENCE ADAPTATION: Chapter Seven	IX. A speech which demonstrates effective adaptation to the audience. Follow project 2, page 116.

23. Projects and Exercises

24. SPEAKER'S PERSONALITY: Chapter Fourteen
25. Projects and Exercises
26. Projects and Exercises
27. LANGUAGE: Chapters Nine and Ten
28. SUPPORTS: Chapter Six
29. GENERAL REVIEW
30. EXAMINATION

X. A speech which completes the suggestions of project 2, page 291.
XI. An autobiographical speech based on project 2, page 30.

XII. A speech on ethics in communication. See project 3, pages 220–221. Use library research methods and accompany the speech with an outline and written manuscript.

Index

443